6/13/05

Bill – To a great coach, a treasured friend
and a valued coaching colleague.
Your character and integrity are
outstanding.
"We have been on the same page."
Regards,
Tom

THE GREATEST GAME

FOOTBALL AT ST. OLAF COLLEGE 1893–2003

TOM PORTER AND **BOB PHELPS**

Tom Porter

Photography Credits
Unless otherwise indicated, photographs are provided courtesy of the St. Olaf Archives, the St. Olaf Communications-Marketing office, or Tom Porter's personal collection.

TABLE OF CONTENTS

INTRODUCTION/ ACKNOWLEDGEMENTS

Football has been a part of campus life at St. Olaf College for more than a century. Discussions about the sport, formal and informal, among students and in faculty committee, began in 1891. A game with Shattuck School was played Oct. 30, 1893. In 1900, the "Athletic Union" was formed and it included a provision for "Foot Ball." Sanctioned interscholastic competition did not begin for St. Olaf, however, until 1918, and then it was a combined St. Olaf-Carleton team.

From that time on, the sport has had an honored history on Manitou Heights, and it seemed time to record it in easily accessible form. Our method has been to note the major developments on and off the field, to describe a great deal of the action and, in doing so, pay tribute to the thousands of men who have played and coached the sport and to those parents, students, and college staff who have supported them. Some of the athletes were called Vikings, some Lions, some Oles. They wore orange and black and black and gold. But they all have been defined by a certain attitude, an approach to the game, a sportsmanship that have been uniquely St. Olaf and, we believe, a credit to the college.

In terms of game action, we have concentrated on the 50-year period, 1940 to 1990, with less comprehensive accounts of action prior to 1940 and from 1991 to 2003. We have done so for two reasons. The first is that it is the time period about which the authors have most personal, first-hand knowledge. Second, it is the time period about which perspective has had time to develop. We hope it is evident that in our minds, this kind of concentration in no way devalues the contributions of the men who played and coached the game at St. Olaf prior to 1940 and after 1990, contributions which have been every bit as significant as others. Future historians will doubtless continue the story and fill in gaps which may exist.

The authors are grateful for interest and encouragement provided by numerous people and information from a variety of sources.

We wish to give special recognition to the following: To Professor Emeritus and College Historian Joe Shaw for his persistent motivation and "put the pen to the paper" attitude. To Archives Director Gary DeKrey for access and permission to use archival material.

To Associate Archivist Jeff Sauve for his valuable assistance in locating information. To Betsy Busa, Rølvaag Library circulation associate, for her assistance in microfilm research. To Archives student worker Ben Paulson for assistance in locating and scanning photographs. To Bridget Smith, student worker, for thorough and accurate work in compiling material for the Appendix.

To Lisa Graff for her high quality, professional work on the layout and graphic design of the volume, for the jacket design and photography, and for scanning the photographs. To Alan Marks and the staff of Northfield Printing for the production.

To Dr. Wes Pearson for his ongoing support of intercollegiate athletics for years — as faculty representative to the Midwest Conference, as the competent official timer and scoreboard operator, and for his Foreword to this work. To writers, through the years, of the *Manitou Messenger* and the *Viking* yearbook from which much original research came. To coaching colleagues, teammates, and other individuals who provided personal correspondence, conversations, and interviews. And to Gloria and Thora, who will be pleased that this project is complete.

Finally, we should emphasize that errors of fact, interpretation, or short-sightedness are ours and not attributable to the persons noted above.

Tom Porter
Bob Phelps
Northfield, Minn., 2004

FOREWORD

The sun sinks lower in the west on a beautiful autumn day, silhouetting the campus buildings and trees. On a lush, green patch of grass, players dressed in black and gold are locked in combat with an equal number of players in maize and blue. It is a St. Olaf-Carleton football game — the greatest game — played on one of the grandest locations, Manitou Field, part of the Ade Christenson Athletic Complex. It is one of many home football games played during the history of football as an intercollegiate sport at St. Olaf.

The history of St. Olaf football is not a story of unbridled success or the lack of it. It is one of wins and losses, of conference championships and cellar standings, and of unusually talented players and not so talented players and many in between. In short, it is representative of a football program at many Midwestern small colleges. This makes the recording of its history an important part of chronicling the incorporation of sports into the American collegiate scene. Football, perhaps more than any other sport, is identified by many as representative of college athletics when the marriage of higher education and sports is contemplated. The history of football on a college campus, therefore, reflects the history of the relationship between the academic and sports communities on college campuses.

Football is a distinctly American game. It grew out of the rough and tumble of a developing nation and, thereby, incorporated some of that nation's cultural values. Football is a collision sport in which physical mastery of an opponent is an important part. In the Midwestern United States, the growth of the sport coincided with the mastery of a new land, mostly by immigrants who, in their unwavering faith in education, also founded colleges at the same time. Mastery of a new land required prodigious physical exertion; football mirrored this in the sporting world. This was, and is, one of the reasons the sport appeals to players and spectators. For many young men of that time the physical demands of football were simply a continuation of those experienced in life as a whole. This, of course, is no longer true, but the desire to have physical mastery is a very American trait. Spectators as well as players can buy into that, and have throughout the history of the sport.

This aspect of football has, however, spawned one of the leading criticisms of the sport. Many today see football as a violent sport; that feeling largely grew from examples of undue emphasis on winning at all costs. Many big-time intercollegiate football programs have fallen prey to requiring winning to please alumni and other supporters, who then work to provide financial resources for the program. Player abuse and cutting corners as to fair play have resulted, even when vigorous policing is done.

Football, as well as other sports, was not meant to be this way. It was to be a game engaged in by the participants for recreation in which spectators could participate vicariously. Small college intercollegiate football (Division III) has largely kept alive this vision of the sport as part of a student's total educational experience. And while injuries occur, deliberate injurious action is not part of the game. How the football program developed at St. Olaf provides an interesting study of the place of intercollegiate sport in the college's over-all program.

Another quality of football that endears it to participants and spectators is that it involves strategy. Playing within the rules, there are ways in which physical strength may be used to advantage or nullified by the use of speed, teamwork, or deception. More than in almost any other game, a plan is devised and followed almost religiously. The pace of a football game is such that both spectators and participants can divine the plan and decide how to react to it. On the offensive, the quarterback is primarily involved in directing the strategy, and spectators identify with him to the point of trying to guess what his next move will be. From this activity, the term "arm chair quarterback" has become synonymous with the imagined act of directing anything that's not in the area of one's responsibility. As a spectator sport, football has benefited from the ability of each fan to get involved in the game in this fashion.

Alumni, at least in the past, were more likely to return to campus for a football game than for any other sporting event. The combination of a beautiful outdoor setting, a format that allows comments and visiting between plays, and, in their minds, the linkage of football and autumn afternoons during their college days provides a special attraction.

Football is a team game, but talented individuals obviously play a major part in the outcome. Teamwork, discipline, concentration, hard work, practice, strategy, proper regard for teammates and opponents, plus talent, are the necessary ingredients for a successful team. In this sense, team accomplishments are more noteworthy than individual ones, but both are important. In this history, as it should be, proper attention has been paid to both team and individuals.

All parts of a college's program should fit into its mission. Football has played its role by providing a means of developing a healthy body to accompany a student's academic and spiritual growth. But it has done more than this. It has provided a forum in which spiritual and cultural values were taught and practiced, in this way reinforcing the need for balance of mind, body, and spirit in a committed and productive life.

It is fitting that this history should be written by Tom Porter and Bob Phelps. Porter, prior to his retirement in 1991, directed the play of more St. Olaf teams than any other head coach. Opposing teams always knew what to expect from a Tom Porter-coached team — a team that played fair, played hard, played smart, and played to the limits of its ability. Porter, and those men who served as his coaching colleagues over 32 years, in a real sense, shaped the character of football at St. Olaf.

Bob Phelps, in a lengthy tenure as director of the St. Olaf News Service and as sports information director, probably wrote more about St. Olaf football than any other individual. His observations were formed not only from watching and writing about the action, home and away, but from personal relationships with the coaches and many of the players, developed on road trips and in other off-the-field contacts.

It is an honor to have been asked to write a foreword to this book, and I thank Tom Porter for asking me. It was a joy to have been a sideline participant at a large number of the games that comprise this history and to be able to attest to the quality of the program that has flourished at St. Olaf. If you are interested in college football, and especially how it has been played at St. Olaf, I commend this book to you. It is must reading.

Wesley A. Pearson
Paul Hardy Distingished Professor in the Sciences

PART I — HISTORY

Chapter 1: Soccer – Rugby – Football

The Early Game

The year was 1823. The British Empire was at the height of its power and influence as the greatest imperial power the world had seen.[1] Despite its power — or maybe because of it — England was also experiencing the first stirrings of true political democracy,[2] symbolized perhaps by the strengthening abolitionist movement, led by William Wilberforce, a member of Parliament. The death penalty had just been abolished for some 100 crimes. In Rome, Pope Leo XII had succeeded Pius VII, and in Germany, composers Ludwig Von Beethoven, Franz Schubert, and Carl Maria von Weber were at the height of their creative powers.[3]

In the far away American "colonies," President James Monroe had just issued his doctrine prohibiting interference by other nations in the affairs of the western hemisphere.[4]

As historic as these events were destined to be, it is unlikely that William Ellis and his classmates at the school in Rugby, England, knew or cared much about them. They were engaged in the age-old game of soccer. Perhaps it was a boring game or nearing dinnertime. Whatever the circumstance, when young Ellis found himself in position to give the ball a good kick, something prompted him to pick it up instead and run with it toward the opposing goal. Players on both sides were so astonished at this flagrant violation of the rules of the game that all they could do was stare at Ellis crossing the goal line far up the field.

Almost immediately, Ellis's unorthodox behavior was decried as "unfair, improper and unbecoming of a gentleman." Others said it "outraged tradition and decency." It was not long, however, before the feeling grew that the unorthodox behavior of William Ellis had introduced a new and interesting feature to the game — running with the ball. Ellis's reaction was not recorded, but he had unwittingly sown the seeds of a new game, destined to be called, appropriately, rugby, after Ellis's school.

From that point on, there were two games of football in England. In one, the ball was kicked and it was known as association football, or soccer; in the other, rugby, it was permissible to carry the ball. Each came to have a specific set of rules which was agreed upon before each match.

In the United States, students at Princeton and Rutgers were playing a game with similar rules. The close proximity of the two New Jersey colleges and the fact that they were playing a similar game made it logical for them to get together and play each other. They met on Nov. 6, 1869, on the Rutgers College field in New Brunswick. The game was played with Princeton's 1867 rules — 25 players on a side, the ball to be kicked or butted with the head. It is often called the first intercollegiate football game played in this country, but it was soccer. Rutgers won six goals to four, with Princeton victorious eight to nothing in a rematch. A year later — 1870 — Columbia, Cornell, and Yale joined Rutgers and Princeton, forming the nucleus of what came to be called the Ivy League.

"The Boston Game" made its debut in 1871, so-called because it was played at Harvard in Cambridge, Mass., a suburb of Boston. The ball was round and inflated rubber. It was essentially a kicking game, but the rules were that it could be picked up at any time. The person who picked up the ball could run with it if pursued. Several years later, in 1875, a rugby team from McGill University in Canada came to play Harvard using Harvard's rules for "The Boston Game." Who won hasn't been recorded, but

The physical education lineup on the athletic field, 1909

St. Olaf students on the Main lawn, 1910

this contest has been identified by Red Blaik and others as the ancestor of, arguably, America's greatest game — intercollegiate football.

If it hadn't been for that visit of McGill to Harvard and the merging of rugby and "The Boston Game," the American game of running, passing, blocking, and tackling might never have evolved. From the British running game of rugby, there grew the highly skilled contest of sweep, imagination, technique, and strategy we know today. It was a game typifying America in its speed, the physical impact of blocking, low tackling, and the spectacular element of forward passing.

Intercollegiate football is a game that stirred a president (Theodore Roosevelt) to save it from excessive violence, another (Woodrow Wilson) to coach it, and two to play and coach it (Dwight Eisenhower and Gerald Ford). It is the game of Stagg, Warner, Zupke, Yost, Williams, Woodruff, Camp, Heisman, Rockne, Bierman — and, one can add, Anderson and Christenson and countless others — coaches of inventive mind and competitive spirit, who had the vision to guide it through a century of experimentation and progress.

It is clear from the record that the Ivies led the way in the development of the game that has lent so much color and excitement to the fall season in America. Amos Alonzo Stagg, the legendary University of Chicago coach, summarized that progression in the *Football Guide* for 1944:

"Undeniably, credit must be given to Harvard, Princeton, and Yale for the adoption of rugby, which formed the basis of our American game. To Harvard goes the credit for taking up rugby and playing it consistently in 1874, 1875, and 1876. To Princeton belongs the credit for initiating the call of the convention that resulted in the formal adoption of the Rugby Union rules with slight changes. And to Yale belongs the credit for persistently contending that the number of players on a team be fixed at 11 instead of 15 and finally winning her point in 1880."[5] It was this game of football, not foot ball, that was modified from the game of rugby that grew in popularity and spread from eastern colleges to those of the Midwest.

Chapter 2: The Beginnings of Football at St. Olaf

When the Canadian rugby players from McGill arrived in Cambridge to challenge the Harvard "Boston Game" players in 1875, some 50 "kind and unsophisticated" young men and women were toiling through their first year at St. Olaf's School in Northfield, Minnesota.[6] They worked hard at a curriculum which included English, geography, mathematics, penmanship, and music (in English) and English language, religion, history, and Norwegian (in Norwegian).

The well-worn frame building they occupied at the corner of Third and Union streets was close to Carleton College to the north and the Northfield Public School to the east. Recreation for the St. Olaf students consisted of a turning pole and croquet in the schoolyard, baseball, and an occasional unscheduled extracurricular, but very competitive, ungamelike skirmish with the schoolboys across Union Street.[7] Five years later, in 1880, the St. Olaf boys made an attempt at organizing an intercollegiate baseball competition. Basketball, track and field, and gymnastics followed.

Though thoughts of foot ball, or football, doubtless flowed in the more competitive boys, it was not until 1891 that the subject was raised, if only unofficially. And it was the *Manitou Messenger,* the college newspaper, that raised it. An editorial by C.M. Wessing in the October 1891 issue of the *Messenger* made a plea for foot-ball. Wessing lamented the fact that baseball seems to have captured the athletic interests of the men leaving no time for foot ball. When a 'scrub' game is played it takes the form of a 'free fight' due to lack of knowledge, techniques, and equipment. The writer implored the upperclassmen to follow the lead of the freshmen to "make a desperate attempt to introduce the most scientific, the most attractive, and the greatest of college games, football."[8]

Football made its debut at St. Olaf during very turbulent times for the college. In 1889, St. Olaf's School became St. Olaf College and the following year was designated "the" college of the new United Lutheran Church, which grew from a serious schism in the Norwegian Synod. Three years later, however, the support of the new church was withdrawn, forcing the fledgling college to sink or swim on its own.

While these trials and triumphs were doubtless uppermost in the minds of faculty and administration, somewhat less momentous interests probably occupied student attention. The October 1893 issue of the *Messenger* noted that "the foot-ball committee which was elected last spring has been at work since the opening of school and now it seems quite probable that foot ball will be established at St. Olaf."[9] The proposed 11 are listed by position, i.e., left guard, right end, quarterback, etc., so it was clearly American football, not rugby or soccer.

They must have organized themselves quickly, because the next month's *Messenger* (November 1893) reported results of a Monday afternoon, Oct. 30, game against Shattuck — Shattuck 14, St. Olaf 6.[10] Several gains were made via the "wedge" as well as end runs, the paper reported. Officiating surfaced in this first intercollegiate game: "St. Olaf again took the ball, and in a few minutes brought it across the line, but the umpire surprised nearly everyone present by declaring an off side play."[11]

The lineup nearly duplicated the proposed list as published in the previous month's *Messenger.* The late

St. Olaf class team, circa 1910

Class team 1904. Note the grandstand and the original Ytterboe Hall in the background.

October game evidently was played without benefit of other games or practices. A *Messenger* writer lamented that players had little experience in playing football and lacked any instruction. The need for "long and hard" practice to make a football player was a valuable lesson gained.[12] Through the years leading to the turn of the century, at least once a year an article appeared in the *Messenger* either extolling the virtues of football or decrying its excesses or deficiencies.

An editorial in the January 1895 *Messenger*, titled "At the Football Game — the Scene as Witnessed by a Sensitive and Tender-Hearted Man," is a humorous description of a brutal activity. A more positive picture was given in an October 1896 article. The writer applauded the "keen interest taken by the boys in athletics and military drill. Foot ball is especially the center of attraction. This is as it ought to be. As many of the men spent summers on the farm, it would be slackening to allow your harvest and stacking sinews to relax. This can be done without lowering your class standing."[13]

The writer stresses the healthy mind in a healthy body concept. "Rush the foot ball even though your shoulder should be slightly twisted out of place or your shoulder even should feel a bit sore afterward. It is immensely preferable to that sluggish gait, the dull gaze and pale face of the 'worm' who may be seen only at the books."[14] A subsequent issue describes the accepted restriction of foot ball to match games between students and cannot be played with teams from other colleges.[15]

Ytterboe "Gym" Leads to Organization; Student Pressure for Football Intensifies

Athletics were not organized in any way at St. Olaf prior to 1900. But in that year, Ytterboe residence hall was completed, and in it was a gymnasium which evidently prompted an increased student interest in athletics.

"Accordingly, the student body met and formed the St. Olaf Athletic Union."[16] The Union was a student organization and was to be in charge of all athletics. The college *Catalog* for 1898–99 (25th anniversary year), described the union: "The Athletic Association was organized in the fall of 1900 for the purpose of controlling all athletic activities at the college. It consists of the following sections: Field and Track, Base Ball, Foot Ball,

Lawn Tennis." "Football goods" were purchased and a team organized.

With practices that would include scrimmages, the students thought they were ready for outside competition, but the faculty felt otherwise. A comment in the *Viking* indicated that even the early student journalists had a fine sense of sarcasm: "The faculty, however, being conservative and wise with long experience, would not permit us thus foolishly to squander our well-earned prestige. So, thanks to their forethought and obedience, a St. Olaf foot ball team has not yet been defeated."[17]

A writer in the 1904 *Viking* makes the case for intercollegiate athletics as a good thing for students, "making school life as attractive and free from drudgery as possible" and as a vehicle for "spreading our name abroad." Petitions to play "outside" football games had been submitted to the faculty almost annually for some years but none had been successful. Nevertheless, the student press reported, "the interest in this game has not disappeared. Every fall two or three teams are in the field, and these have adequately demonstrated that we have material for a team. But they have also reminded us of the fact that systematic training is necessary. This we have not the means to obtain."[18]

A cartoon accompanying this statement depicts a smiling football player entering the president's office, petition in hand. The next panel shows the same player leaving the office, a grim look on his face and the petition crunched in his hand.

A second student brief for the value of intercollegiate football appeared in the November 1905 *Messenger*. The writer injected a student recruitment element into the argument: "We see many of our friends attending other institutions, and their only inducement is the advantage of playing football." Still, the writer demonstrates his conviction that the benefits of the then current game are outweighed by the "evils it leaves in its wake." He proposed, instead, the organization of class, society, and club teams for the present. "When football is lifted to a better level," he writes, "St. Olaf will feel justified in contesting for gridiron honors. Then look out for us."[19]

Excesses Inhibit the Game

The "evils" the writer noted doubtless was a reference to the fact that football on the national level had fallen on bad times. It had acquired characteristics radically different from its parent, rugby. Despite efforts to legislate mass play out of the game, it continued to dominate and get worse. Strategy and finesse played little or no part in the outcome of games; brute force, physical condition, and endurance were the determining factors.

In 1905, the storm broke and football came close to destroying itself. The season ended in an uproar of protest against the brutality of play. Stagg's compilations for the 1905 season showed 18 players dead and 159 seriously injured. Displaying his characteristic decisiveness, President Theodore Roosevelt called

representatives of the leading eastern universities and told them it was up to them to save the sport by removing objectionable features or it would be abolished. They moved quickly. A conference of college representatives from 13 schools met Dec. 9, 1905, to discuss ways to reform the game.

A larger group of representatives, 62, held a second meeting Dec. 28. A set of rules was formulated and the Intercollegiate Athletic Association of the United States was organized to "assist in the formation of sound requirements for intercollegiate athletics, particularly football." Five years later it changed its name to the National Collegiate Athletic Association (NCAA).[20]

While intercollegiate football nationally was on its way to becoming more respectable, at St. Olaf the march toward interscholastic competition moved slowly, but move it did. A first statement of athletic eligibility appears in the St. Olaf *Catalog* for 1908 listing rules governing students and organizations: "No student who has a condition or a failure shall be

allowed to participate or belong to any first (varsity) athletic team."[21] The enforcement of the rules was in charge of the standing committee on athletics.

The next natural step was coaching. The student body hired a Mr. White to assist athletic teams. Prior to that time, a faculty member acted as manager but probably offered little in the area of technique development. As on any schoolyard, those with the better natural skills played. It wasn't long before the administration accepted the need for professional guidance in the area of the physical.

Professor Irving Noakes was hired as "director and instructor of athletics" in the fall of 1908. His efforts were to be primarily in the area of fitness, including formal gymnastics. The 1910 issue of the *Catalog* (Vol. VI) shows a formation of male students lined up on the athletic field in front of the baseball grandstand. The wooden grandstand, situated slightly southwest of the current speech-theater building, was covered and appears to have seating for 250–300 fans. The right field foul line was approximately in line with the east side of Agnes Mellby Hall.

The 1912 class team

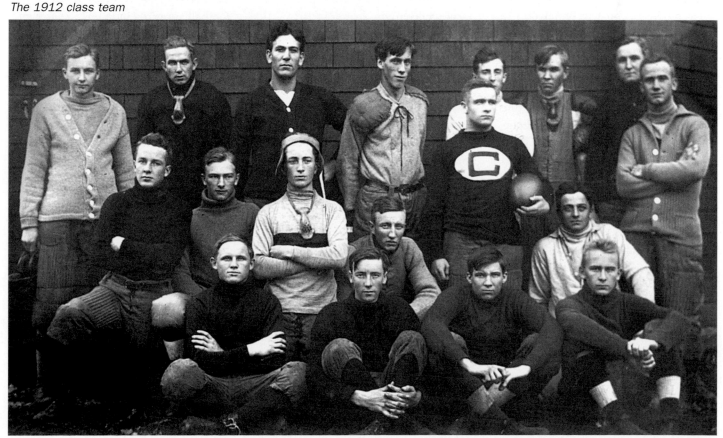

The St. Olaf College football squad, Sept. 30, 1915

An alumnus, Alfred O. Anderson '09, became the first St. Olaf athletic director. After graduate study at the YMCA school in Springfield, Mass., he was called back to Manitou Heights to take charge of the department of physical education and to coach athletics — baseball and basketball.

Intercollegiate football was still in the future. During the first decade and a half of the 20th century, class football teams continued to organize and play "scrub" games. They were not officially sanctioned by the college, but they did attract strong interest and backing from the classes.

Violence in Class Games Hastens Intercollegiate Competition

Football between classes turned out to be a mixed blessing. It served a student need but had some of the same "evils" that had afflicted the pre-NCAA national game. A letter from T.B. Bonhus '14, a prominent member of the baseball team, submitted to the *Messenger* of December 1911: "No one at St. Olaf can deny," Bonhus wrote, "that there are altogether too many football victims at St. Olaf every year as a result of participation in the inter-class games. This is due," he continued, "to unwarranted rivalry between classes and individuals, to improper training, to many weaklings participating and to individual and team 'greenness' as far as knowing the fine points of the game. Intercollegiate football," he said, "is not a panacea for all the evils of inter-class football, but it would tend to minimize them …"[22]

Bonhus was offering a sophisticated verbalization of the age-old feeling known to every gridder who has ever been tired of pre-season practice — "It's always better and more fun to block or tackle somebody from some-

where else than your own guy." Bonhus's tight and persuasive reasoning went on: "In the first place it would be necessary to have a coach. In the second place, weaklings and 'mollycoddlers' would be eliminated. In the third place, unwarranted rivalry between classes and individuals would be abolished."

Bonhus also echoed the student recruitment argument of the *Messenger* writer of 1905: "There are many other reasons why St. Olaf should play intercollegiate football," he said. "We know from statistics and observation that St. Olaf would get better athletes if she allowed intercollegiate football. Many of our best Scandinavian athletes who would like to attend St. Olaf choose some other school where intercollegiate football is allowed."[23]

Some of the same arguments were repeated, with some refinement, in the *Viking* for 1916–18 and also prompted by reactions to the season of 1914. "Intercollegiate football at St. Olaf would undoubtedly be a strong drawing card and advertisement but the greatest advantage would be the fostering of the true St. Olaf spirit." The article also noted the necessity of a coach and the fact that when a gymnasium is built, intercollegiate football must come. "A football team was organized this fall, but no games were played as the boys, excepting for two or three, were inexperienced. The material was excellent and the boys were willing to work — which shows that if a coach would be provided, he would be able to develop a team capable of well representing our school."

"We Want it Bad!"

The drumbeat of student agitation for a program of intercollegiate football continued and intensified. A 1914

Messenger article stated, "Right here is where the system of athletics is far advanced over the system of education through books. St. Olaf College once played intercollegiate football (probably referring to the Shattuck game of 1893 and perhaps others unrecorded), but on account of the roughness which resulted from the old-time rules, it was abolished and interclass football was adopted. And now that we are to have a new gym, we will need other financial sources to keep it going — Now altogether students and alumni, What do we want besides a new gym? Intercollegiate football! And we want it bad!"[24]

With that display of naked emotion, the situation continued to heat up, at least so far as the students were concerned. Editorials stating the potential positive and negative aspects of intercollegiate competition in football appeared in the *Messenger* and the *Viking* and in correspondence to and from the president's office.

"Another year has sustained the telling evidence that more injuries are received at St. Olaf (with interclass competition) than at our neighboring colleges (with intercollegiate competition.) Lack of proper training, inadequate garments of protection, negligence as to physical condition, combined with a 'daggerly' class spirit, are factors … consequently, we nourish the negative qualities of football, while the positive are barred along with intercollegiate football. So, it was an inevitable combustion that occurred in Chapel Thursday, Nov. 4. The entire student body had assembled to talk football. Without a dissenting vote, it was decided to petition the faculty for intercollegiate football."[25]

Chapter 3: Intercollegiate Football Debuts at St. Olaf

Although there still were adherents of inter-class, as opposed to inter-collegiate, football, it appeared that as the "roaring '20s" approached, the weight of opinion, both student and faculty, had shifted in favor of the intercollegiate game. Minutes of a faculty meeting of Oct. 12, 1917, stated that, "Dean Thompson brought up the matter of intercollegiate football, stating that the students are expecting some action by the faculty for or against this kind of sport. The president advised referring this matter to the Board of Education of the Church. A motion by Dr. Dalberg that the faculty recommend to the Board that they permit intercollegiate football at St. Olaf was discussed and passed by a vote of 13 to 7.[26]

President Lauritz A. Vigness was corresponding with presidents of other Minnesota private colleges regarding athletics in general and intercollegiate football specifically. It was clear that Vigness was looking at the question from a number of angles. President Vigness, in response to a letter from Rev. N.E. Boe of St. Paul, Oct. 24, 1917, noted that "our faculty by majority decided to recommend to our Board of Education the introduction of intercollegiate football. ... How long St. Olaf College will be able to exclude the sport and yet maintain its attendance of physically strong and robust boys is a question on which my mind is uncertain."[27]

It didn't take the students long to spring into action following this decision of the faculty. The Oct. 16, 1917, issue of the *Messenger* carried the headline and front page article, "Faculty Favors Football by Large Majority." The article said, "By a large majority, the faculty of St. Olaf College voted last Friday to recommend the introduction of intercollegiate football at St. Olaf. The recommendation will be referred to be acted upon by the Board of Education of the Norwegian Lutheran Church. If the recommendation receives a favorable vote from the Board, intercollegiate football will at last be a reality at the 'College on the Hill.'"

The article continued with the note that "discussion among the men the last few days has centered mainly on the possible choice for captain and the candidates for positions." Carroll Jacobson '18, appeared to be the popular choice for captain. "There are several fast ends and tackles ... the center and guard positions are easily filled."[28] A meeting of men interested in intercollegiate football was held in Hoyme Chapel on Friday, Oct. 19, 1917. Jacobson was elected captain and Albert Tommeraason, manager. "All interclass games will be run off as usual, but the varsity players may not participate in these contests," the paper said. But the students still faced a number of hurdles, the faculty remaining positive on the game but very cautious in implementation.

The student petition had asked permission to play one or two practice games vs. "outside" opponents. The request was considered at the regular

President Lauritz A. Vigness

meeting of the faculty Oct. 25, 1917.[29] The request was referred to the College Committee of the Board of Education [of the Norwegian Lutheran Church]. The permission would have necessitated some revising of the athletic constitution for St. Olaf College. At a Nov. 8, faculty meeting, President Vigness reported that Dr. Granrud (of the committee) had told him the committee felt it was too small a part of the Board of Education to act on the request for permission.

Also in the minutes of the Nov. 8, faculty meeting was a report from Professor Grose of the Committee on Social Affairs that a request from girls for permission to entertain winners of a football game was referred to the faculty.[30]

Meanwhile President Vigness was still discussing the matter with his presidential colleagues. A letter from Vigness to President J.A. Aasgaard of Concordia Jan. 8, 1918, asked Aasgaard's opinion and that of the Concordia faculty on intercollegiate football.[31]

Finally, on June 21, 1918, the decision was announced. At a special meeting of the faculty on that date, President Vigness read from a report by the Board of Education a statement that "the Board had decided to permit intercollegiate football at the colleges of the church."[32]

"Real World" Complications Impact Football Development

The deliberations on the status of intercollegiate football at St. Olaf and other colleges went on as three major disruptive factors were afflicting the country and the church bodies with which St. Olaf was at various times affiliated: (1) the economic depression of the 1890s; (2) church politics which threatened the survival of the college; and, finally, (3) the outbreak of World War I.

President Lars W. Boe

*Endre B. Anderson, the first
St. Olaf football coach*

As the economic depression of the 1890s caused hard times for many people, a split occurred in the Norwegian Lutheran Synod of which St. Olaf was a part. A splinter group formed the United Norwegian Lutheran Church and designated St. Olaf as its college. Two years later, that designation was withdrawn along with the financial support that went with it. The college's survival was threatened as a result.

Fortunes swung again in 1899, and the college once more benefited from the financial support of the United Church. This organization prohibited intercollegiate football at its colleges. In 1917, however, a merger occurred, making the United Church part of a new entity, the Norwegian Lutheran Church in America. With the beginning of the 1917–18 college year St. Olaf became an institution of that body. And the June 1918 approval of the intercollegiate grid sport followed.

On the larger world stage, World War I occupied energies and thoughts and emotions and reduced the number of male students on campus.

Whether or not the difficulties involved with approval of intercollegiate football for St. Olaf were affected pro or con by the changing church affiliation or the other traumas affecting the body politic is hard to know. It is logical to suppose, however, that these events taking place in the country and the churches concurrently with the student drive to obtain approval of intercollegiate football on Manitou Heights did have an impact.

Intercollegiate Football Begins — Almost — Oct. 19, 1918

The Board of Education of the Norwegian Lutheran Church of America had given permission for its colleges to participate in intercollegiate football, but there was a war on with its attendant reduction in male students and training requirements for those who were on campus.

Most colleges had Student Army Training Corps units (SATC) and football seemed a natural activity for these groups. In the case of St. Olaf and Carleton, both of whom had SATC units, the War Department stipulated that for purposes

of athletic competition, the two units would have to be merged. President Lars Boe, who had become the fourth president of St. Olaf on Sept. 26, 1918, asked for and was given authority to make this arrangement.

A team representing the combined units of the two colleges defeated Pillsbury College of Owatonna 40–0 in what could be called the first legally sanctioned (by the church) intercollegiate football game involving St. Olaf students. The *Messenger* for Oct. 22, proclaimed "Intercollegiate football at St. Olaf is a materialized vision … Buck's eleven too much for the opponents (Pillsbury) … Much credit is due Lt. [Ralph] Gruye, who, by his personal interest, has started intercollegiate football on Manitou Heights. Let's keep it up."[33]

Even though the team was a combined one with the Carleton S.A.T.C., the *Messenger* noted that it seemed as though a St. Olaf team was on the gridiron as seven of the 11 were "Oles." It was the first use of the term Oles; previously, St. Olaf teams were called Vikings. Continuing to exult, the Mess noted that "History will say on Oct. 19, 1918, the Oles were let loose …"

Shortly thereafter, the St. Olaf-Carleton 11 was jolted 59–6 by a University of Minnesota team (no mention as to whether it was S.A.T.C., or otherwise) at Lexington Park in St. Paul. But no matter; intercollegiate football was an established fact on Manitou Heights.

In those first two contests, several standouts established themselves. In the Pillsbury contest, the Mess noted that Thune, Grose, and Rowe were St. Olaf mainstays. Against Minnesota, Reiter, Browny, and Glesne were cited for strong play.

Note: Perhaps because of the small student body in the early years of the century, many students were identified in student publications and other publications only by their last names. We have, by necessity, adopted that style here.

Flu Epidemic Prompts First Exclusively St. Olaf Team

Before more games could be played by the combined team, adversity, in the form of the 1918 influenza epidemic, struck the

St. Olaf campus and athletes. Classes were cancelled and the men were confined to a "quarantine zone." The Chapel and barracks were used as hospitals. Four St. Olaf students died. As a result of the epidemic, the combined S.A.T.C. team was disbanded. Players from both colleges wished to continue playing, however, so they organized their own respective teams and played three games against each other. Lt. Ralph Gruye was the coach and Amon Johnson was captain. "The first of these games resulted in a St. Olaf victory, 7–0 …" the Mess said, "but in the two games which followed, we were not so successful."

The First Oles

Men who played on that first exclusively St. Olaf intercollegiate football team included Rowe, Glesne, Jackson, Teslow, Westby, Krogstad, Jacobson, Flaten, Marvick, Johnson, Thune, Strand, Grose, Smith, Nasby, Sharp, Tallackson, Kromer, Leverson, and Berge.[34]

The early days of intercollegiate football on the Hill were spiced by the presence of one of the more colorful characters in Ole athletic history. He was Dr. E.R. ("Doc") Cooke. Although he was not directly involved with the grid program, Doc Cooke nevertheless played an important role. A graduate of the YMCA school in Springfield,

Funeral procession for a student who died from the influenza epidemic, 1918

Mass. Cooke joined the faculty in the fall of 1917. He had obtained his M.D. degree from the University of Vermont in 1893. After a short time at St. Olaf, Doc Cooke moved to Minneapolis, purchased a gymnasium and established a reputation as a "conditioner of men." In not too long a time, he was back in "Y" work as supervisor of athletics in a regiment of the Italian army. He returned to St. Olaf in the fall of 1918 as director, Department of Physical Education.[35]

Soldiers' Return Strengthens Football

With the signing of the Armistice on Nov. 11, 1918, men began returning to civilian life and resuming their educations. Competitive urges, to

some extent influenced by the military conflict, were transferred to the campuses. A surge in sports teams occurred at all levels. Town teams were formed in baseball, football, and basketball and their counterparts developed naturally on the campuses. The era of the professional coach also began and flourished in the 1920s. Previously, men who had been players and had interest in the sport were frequently appointed coaches, but usually they had little knowledge of fundamental techniques. Teams realized the enhanced benefit from coaches who used their playing experience and innovative minds to form unique offensive and defensive strategies.

Endre Anderson First Coach

Recognizing the need for such a man, St. Olaf, in 1919, secured the services of Endre B. Anderson as athletic coach.[36] A native of Cottonwood, Minn., Endre had graduated from St. Olaf in 1914 and had assisted in the physical training department during his senior year. Endre's record in the few years since his graduation made him an excellent candidate. He had been physical director and coach at Yates Center, Kansas, in 1915 and 1916.

Anderson turned out several championship teams in football and basketball and then moved on to Rochester, Minn., high school, where

1918, student military lineup in front of the original Ytterboe Hall

Excerpts From Faculty Meeting Minutes

Nov. 8, 1917
The president reported that he received a communication in regard to the students' petition for permission to play one or two practice games of football with visitor teams this fall, which matter had by the faculty been referred to the College Committee of the Board of Education. The committee had considered the petition, but had decided that it was too small a part of the Board of Education to act in a matter of such importance.

The Committee on Social Affairs had a request from the girls for permission to entertain the winners of a football game. The committee did not wish to decide this matter, because it feared that if the request should be granted, many similar petitions might follow. For this reason, the committee would leave the decision to the faculty.

June 21, 1918
At a special meeting of the faculty, the president read from a report by the Board of Education a statement that the board had decided to permit intercollegiate football at the colleges of the church.

Oct. 8, 1918
At a special faculty meeting, the president stated that by order of the War Department, St. Olaf and Carleton would have to join in athletics. He asked and was given authority to arrange this matter with the Carleton authorities.

Nov. 30, 1918
The faculty met to consider questions arising from the dissolution of the S.A.T.C.

World War I St. Olaf unit parade in Northfield

he produced two championship football teams and a 1917 basketball team that won the state tournament at Carleton. The following year, Endre moved to River Falls, Wis., State Normal, where he produced an outstanding basketball team.

Anderson's position at St. Olaf for 1919–20 was to coach football, basketball, and baseball. "Coach Anderson is well versed in the traditions and spirit of St. Olaf and knows what is desired along athletic lines," the *Messenger* said. "With a coach, an athletic director for men (Dr. Cooke), an athletic director for women, and a new gymnasium, prospects are of the brightest for strong teams and an increased athletic prestige," the paper said. It also announced Dr. Cooke's return from Y.M.C.A. work in Italy and included an artist's sketch of the new gymnasium (labeled St. Olaf College Armory) "to be ready for use next fall; One of the largest in the northwest."[37]

The 1919–20 year opened with a record enrollment of 700 students; "About 25 girls had to be turned away," the Mess said. Work on the gymnasium had been

1904 Viking cartoon: The annual football petition and its fate

delayed during the summer by a shortage of labor and late arrival of materials. A large squad reported to Coach Anderson for St. Olaf's first season of official intercollegiate football. "The warm weather has necessitated practices of a light nature, which have served to get the men hardened into shape," the *Messenger* commented.[38]

The first season had competition from the interclass game, which was dying a lingering death. The *Messenger* reported on the climactic game in the round robin series between freshmen and sophomores. At stake was the red button on top of the freshman beanie. If the first-year players won, the button could be removed as a badge of accomplishment — football superiority over the sophomores.

Such was the importance of the interclass games that some men opted to play that game rather than the intercollegiate variety. Ade Christenson, eventually to become a legendary coach, was an example. Ade did not play varsity football until his junior year. It was clear that the question of whether varsity players could also play with their class teams would have to be revisited and dealt with. It had been

decided once, in 1917, that varsity men could not play the interclass game, but such was the power of the rivalry that the question persisted.

Pillsbury once again supplied the opposition for the opening game of the 1919 season won by St. Olaf 25–0. Strangely enough, student admission appeared to be an issue, despite the clamor for the intercollegiate sport. Students were issued tags to wear to qualify them for free admission. Failure to wear the tag meant an admission fee would have to be paid.[39]

"A heavy wet field slowed play," the Mess said. Nevertheless, Capt. Sam Veldey and Eide were exceptionally good. The most brilliant play of the game, the writer said, was a forward pass to Veldey, followed by a 50-yard run for a score. The Mess writer was disappointed by a small number of supporters and lack of enthusiasm for a first game. The St. Olaf lineup included LE – Thune, LT – Bauman, LG – Lee, RG – Glesne, RT – Halvorson, RE – Flaten, QB – Veldey, RHB – Eide, LHB – Hoidahl, FB – Thompson, C – Hatlestad.

Perhaps in an effort to build enthusasism, a mass meeting "to

learn St. Olaf songs and … yells" was scheduled for Hoyme Chapel the next Friday at 7:30. Apparently the meeting had the desired effect; 300 students and alumni overflowed the grandstand for the next contest. Unfortunately, it wasn't enough as St. Olaf lost to Hamline 19–7. The Oct. 14 *Messenger* noted that the St. Olaf team was "clearly outweighed" but showed unexpected strength.

The squad rebounded the following week and defeated Gustavus 27–7 in a "loose" game. "The battle of the Scandinavians was far from being a football classic," the Mess said. "Much ragged play was done on both sides and lack of polish was evident."[40] Veldey and Eide again were commended for their play. The writer commented that "grilling" practices and possible position changes were in order for the following week in preparation for Macalester.

The Scots used an intercepted pass and a drop kick field goal to come out on top 9–6 in a hard-fought game. Thompson at left tackle and Carl Cole played consistently well, a reporter said. Both student bodies turned out in big numbers, "making for a record attendance at a St. Olaf game."[41]

The first St. Olaf intercollegiate team, 1919

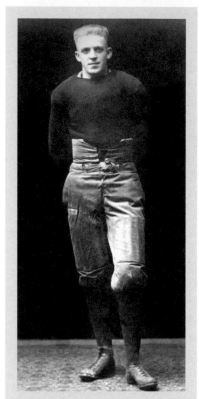

Selmer Velde, 1919 captain

Ted Hoidahl, 1919 squad member

"The most spirited football game ever witnessed in Northfield was played Friday between St. Olaf and Carleton at Laird field, ending with a score of 15–7 in Carleton's favor," the Mess said.[42] With Thune unable to play, Veldey, Thompson, Glesne, and Flaten starred for the Oles. Featured plays included a number of long, successful passes and a 60-yard run by Carleton's Ozzie Cowles, later to be head basketball coach at Minnesota in the 1950s. Coach Buck, who guided the Carls in this contest, had been the mentor of the combined St. Olaf and Carleton S.A.T.C. team in 1918.

The same issue of the *Messenger*, in a page one article, reported on the freshman-sophomore interclass game, won by the sophomores 18–0. "The large red button is essential to the beauty of the freshman caps," the writer said. "The game was the snappiest and most spirited played on the Hill this year. Spurred on by their respective classes, gorgeously arranged *(sic)* in class colors, and supported by their class bands, the two teams clashed."

1919 Termed the "First" St. Olaf Football Season/Team

The 1919 season is generally considered the beginning of intercollegiate football at St. Olaf. A green, inexperienced squad scored against every opponent and ended the season 2–3.

"St. Olaf averaged less than 160 pounds to the man and was outweighed by all of its opponents. However by sheer fight and scrap this advantage was overcome," the *Messenger* commented. Fifteen letters were awarded: Bauman, A. Cole, C. Cole, Eide, Flaten, Glesne, Grose, Halvorson, Hoidahl, Lee, Nelson, Swenson, Thompson, Thune, and Capt. Veldey. "The results indicate that the 'Orange and Black' will have to be considered in the title race in the next few years," a hopeful writer said.[43]

Another step toward establishment status came when P.O. Holland, the college business manager, transferred the sale of athletic goods from the student run Athletic Union to the St. Olaf supply store.

1908 map of the St. Olaf College campus.

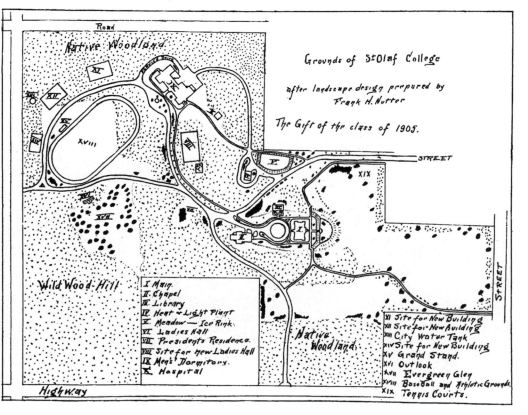

Chapter 4: Conferences Enter the Picture

Just as Columbia, Cornell, Yale, Princeton, and Rutgers found it appropriate to form the nucleus of the Ivy League in 1870, so representatives of the Minnesota private colleges determined that their athletic interests could be served by a similar organization.

At the turn of the century, the organization and control of athletics had been largely student-centered. The formation of conferences to better regulate competition was sporadic and irregular. The first effort in Minnesota was the Southern Minnesota Intercollegiate Baseball League, which lasted from 1892 to 1898. The members were Carleton, St. Olaf, Shattuck, and Pillsbury. In 1898, the "Southern Minny" morphed into the Minnesota School Athletic Conference with more specific regulations along with provision for competition in sports other than baseball. The membership consisted of the same four schools.

St. Olaf, Charter Member of MAC

Three years later, in 1901, the Minnesota Athletic Conference was formed with Carleton, St. Olaf, Macalester, St. Thomas, and some academies.[44] In 1906, the Red River Valley Athletic Association composed of Minnesota and Dakota Colleges, including Concordia of Moorhead, was formed. This was followed in 1911 by the Minnesota-Dakota Intercollegiate Conference, also known as the Tri-State Conference. It included the state colleges of North and South Dakota, several academies, and, at various times, Hamline, Macalester, St. Olaf, St. John's, St. Thomas, and Gustavus Adolphus. There were no round robins or other prescribed scheduling procedures and no provision for awarding championships. Schedules were made by mutual agreements between institutions, and championships were claimed rather than awarded. Mythical all-star teams usually were picked for each state rather than the conference.

Dissatisfaction with the Tri-State conference developed because some felt these methods of determining championships and other regulations were too loose. At a Tri-State Conference meeting in November of 1919, delegates from the Minnesota colleges sponsored rule changes designed to address these shortcomings, but the Dakota representatives outvoted them. After that meeting, the Minnesota minority caucused and decided to consider forming a new conference. Those present were J.T. McCallum, Macalester; E.M. Flynn, St. John's; T. Beyer, Hamline; E.R. Jackson, Carleton; William Lindberg, Gustavus Adolphus (student coach); Endre Anderson, St. Olaf, and a student representative from St. Thomas. McCallum was elected to serve as a committee of one to call a meeting at a later date for the purpose of organizing a Minnesota College Association.[45]

That meeting was held Dec. 22, 1919, with McCallum, Flynn, Jackson and Anderson joined by V.G. Michel (probably from St. John's), J. Dunphy and Lauden of St. Thomas. Hamline and Gustavus were not represented but sent regards and approval of the objective. McCallum was elected chair and Anderson, secretary. That charter meeting of what was called the Minnesota Intercollegiate Athletic Conference (MIAC) was held in Sayles-Hill Gymnasium at Carleton. The MIAC was to be "the lasting conference" for the private colleges of Minnesota.[46]

An aerial depiction of the St. Olaf campus, circa 1920

Messenger Excerpts

April 29, 1919

Having the dimensions of 156 feet by 103 feet and being composed of absolute fire-proof construction, this new gymnasium will be one of the largest and most up-to-date in the northwest. All the standard equipment of a modern gymnasium will be installed. The swimming pool will have terazzo walls and floors and will be 24 feet long and 60 feet wide. Special dressing rooms and showers for the best accommodations of the visiting teams will also be furnished.

One essential feature of the gymnasium will be its special facilities for accommodating college women. They will have a separate section of the basement equipped with individual shower baths. The women will be given full access to the swimming pool and gymnasium floor at certain hours of the day.

Sept. 18, 1919

The new gymnasium is the structure which occupies a central place in the thoughts of old and new students. It was hoped that the erection of the gymnasium would be far enough advanced by the opening of the fall term of school to allow it to be used. But difficulties, such as delay of material and scarcity of labor, have seriously hampered operations.

The gymnasium will have a vestibule reinforced tile floor, with a floor space of 10,000 square feet (length 125 feet, width 80 feet), arrangements being made for three separate basketball floors.

A sketch for the proposed new gymnasium is revealed in 1916

1918, campus administrators review plans for the new gymnasium

A 1924 photo of the new gymnasium, looking quite different from the original sketch

PART II — ACTION

Chapter 5: Consolidation; The '20s, '30s, '40s, and '50s; "Cully to Cleve"; Manitou Field Constructed; The War Years

The War to End Wars was over; college campuses were returning to normal. St. Olaf completed its first official season of intercollegiate football with a two-win, three-loss record. A professional coach, Endre Anderson, was building a program, and a new conference, the MIAC, had been formed. The 1920 season was approached with interest and enthusiasm.

With a squad of 50 candidates, an opening game versus Pillsbury Academy and a schedule of six conference games "assures us of a full schedule for the season," the *Messenger* said. Somehow Phalen-Luther Seminary replaced Pillsbury on the schedule and was promptly outclassed by St. Olaf 54–7. Ade Christenson, frequently referred to

as A. Christensen, emerges as a varsity player for the first time as a junior.[47]

Although he was a varsity participant in basketball and track as freshman and sophomore, Ade had opted to play interclass football those two years. Ade would compile an outstanding record as coach and athletic director at St. Olaf. Other standouts in the early 1920 games were also to be heard from for many years to come. Jake Christiansen, eldest son of choral legend in the making, F. Melius Christiansen, was destined to create his own legend as head football coach at Concordia.

Arne Flaten would become well known as founder of the St. Olaf art department, artist, and teacher. Otto Glesne would become the St. Olaf

College physician. Others mentioned prominently in accounts of the first games of the 1920 season were Ted Hoidahl and "Coon" Swenson, future Athletic Hall of Famers.

The Oles defeated St. Mary's 18–0 in the first conference game. The backfield of Gregor, Ade Christensen, and Cole was outstanding. Jake Christiansen and "Coon" Swenson were also cited by *Messenger* reporters.

A page one headline in the Oct. 12, 1920, *Messenger* trumpeted the fact that the "Champions of Last Year Are Defeated by the Hard Fighting Oles …" The account continued. "The Midway veterans [Hamline] called likely state champions are outplayed by the locals … The St. Olaf backs and ends prove

The 1920 team, Otto Glesne, captain

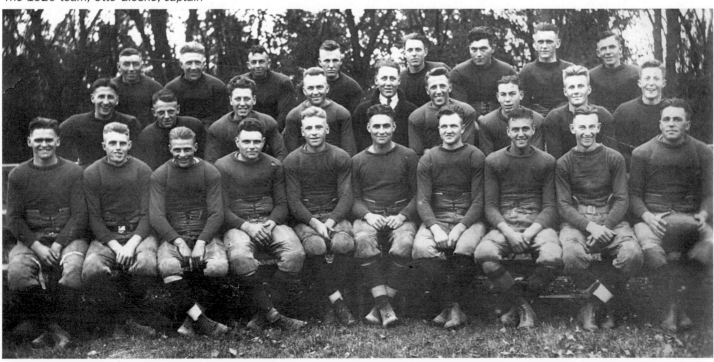

Goal-line play against Carleton in 1921. Note the construction of the goal post.

too fast for the heavy Hamline linemen … Anderson's men, trained almost to perfection, are ably generaled by Christensen (sic) … Swenson and Gregor figure in brilliant passes … Jake Christiansen outpunts Hamline kicker … Cole and Glesne towers of strength in the line."

The 6–0 defeat of Hamline was called the best grade of football ever seen on the local gridiron. A 50-piece band and a thousand cheering spectators inspired the Black and Gold (transformed from Orange and Black) and swarmed onto the field at the end of the game and carried the victors off on their shoulders. A game summary made repeated mention of St. Olaf punting on first down. The defense played well as noted by the shutout. Passes from Jake Christiansen (listed as RE) to "Coon" Swenson (LE) almost resulted in a touchdown before halftime.[48]

In what evidently was a lackluster game ("playing below their usual form"), the Oles defeated Gustavus 14–0. Gregor, Christenson, and Eide were cited for strong play, and Jake Christiansen's long punting was also a feature.

The first four games of the season apparently resulted in a backlog of injuries. Despite the fact that "most of the regulars expected to be back for the upcoming Macalester game," the Scots prevailed 20–14. The *Messenger* reporter attributed the loss to the

absence of key players, particularly regular quarterback Christenson. "The most evident defect in the St. Olaf machine was the lack of smoothness and generalship, which characterized the Hamline game." The bright-eyed scribe also detected a weak spot on the left side of the line, as "a majority of Saturday's gains were made through tackle and guard."[49]

With ideal weather conditions and 800 rooters behind, the famous St. Olaf Band marched down St. Olaf Avenue and across the Cannon River to Carleton's Laird Field. "Augmented by many friends of the school and alumni, St. Olaf's representation approached the 1,500 mark. The Black and Gold was everywhere in evidence" — to no avail, evidently. After a scoreless first half, Coach Hunt's Carleton team "hammered the black and gold" with strong inside running, scoring three touchdowns. Final: 21–0. "The little

general" — Christenson — was still out due to injury.

With Christenson (Ade) and Christiansen (Jake) both shelved by injury, the Oles still managed to outscore St. Thomas 6–0 in the season's final game. Lineup juggling necessitated by the injuries found Gregor at quarterback, Hoidahl at end, and Flaten at halfback. The game, played on Founders Day, Nov. 6, was not as close as the score indicated, the *Mess* said: "The small score does not show the relative merits of the two teams." The game ended with St. Olaf on the St. Thomas one-foot line.

The second season of intercollegiate football had been a success — four wins and three losses, the loss to Macalester having prevented a championship. The Oles gave up only one touchdown in five home games. The verdict from the student press was that, "As can be expected in a team only two years old, the main weakness in the Ole machine lay in a too scanty supply of capable substitutes … A capable assistant coach who could devote time to the development of secondary material would do much toward building a larger squad."

Seventeen lettermen were named. Several deserve special mention: Otto Glesne, the captain, didn't miss a game and was chosen on the all-state team. Ade Christenson, "the little general," weighing in the neighborhood of 135 pounds and standing 5 feet 6 inches, "outgeneraled and outplayed every quarterback that opposed him."[50]

Action against Carleton on the original athletic field, Nov. 5, 1921

A front-page story in the Nov. 30, 1920, Mess noted that Coach Endre Anderson had selected an all-state 11 which included Ingwald "Coon" Swenson at end and Jud Gregor at halfback. Endre, the writer of the article, said he felt justified in selecting a mythical all-state team, because St. Olaf was the only team to play every other conference school.

Maturity

By 1921, the fledgling Ole football program had the feel of a mature enterprise. For the first time, football was listed in the college catalog. Prior to that time, American football had been listed as a class activity, and there was also a listing for rugby football. Attesting to the popularity of the sport and perhaps the fact that more military personnel were returning to civilian pursuits, the Sept. 27, 1921, *Messenger* noted there were 70 (nine lettermen) working out. The same article forecast that the Nov. 5 home game with Carleton would be the biggest game of the season. Maybe the writer or his source was looking back on the 21–0 loss of the previous season. Luther and Concordia are on the schedule for the

first time. The prognosticator figured Concordia would not offer much competition, because it was that school's first year of conference football. Luther, however, was expected to be another story after an "enviable" record the previous season.

Looking forward to new arrivals, a predictor thought highly of "Nelson, Promo, and 'Fat' Hanson" in the line, and in the backfield, "Fevold from Humboldt, Iowa, and Cleve and Swanson, all-city players from Minneapolis South High, are likely prospects." The backfield was expected to have speed with Christenson returning at quarter and Martin Cole at fullback.

The Oles bore out the writer's prediction, overwhelming Concordia 97–0 in the first game. Ade Christenson scored four touchdowns, Cleve and Fevold three each, and Bolstad two. Cleve kicked 13 out of 14 PATs. "Coon" Swenson was noted for his all-state style of play. Jake Christiansen and Captain Arne Flaten missed the game due to injury.

In the next game, Luther lived up to its advance billing, giving the Oles all they wanted before succumbing

10–0. The game was the feature of Luther's 60th anniversary celebration and the first time the two Lutheran schools had met on the gridiron. Ade Christenson's fourth-quarter 35-yard touchdown run with Fevold running interference was the highlight from the Ole point of view. Frank Cleve's field goal and Martin Cole's line play also were cited.

Despite a "subpar" performance the next week, St. Olaf escaped with a 7–6 win over Macalester, breaking a two-year jinx. The coaches' postgame comments give clues to the character of the game, and perhaps reasons for the outcome. Coach Reese of Macalester said, "It was a hard-fought game. That is all I have to say." Coach Anderson of St. Olaf said, "It was a clean game, and now to clear Carleton, that's all,"[51] perhaps indicating he and his charges had been looking past the Scots to the next week's battle with Carleton.

The crosstown rivals were undefeated, and it was St. Olaf's Homecoming. The score, however, was virtually a repeat of 1920 — 20–3 in favor of the Carls. Carleton's strong running game again proved dominant.

The 1921 schedule card, featuring Arnold Flaten, captain

This Schedule is presented with the compliments of The St. Olaf Book Store

1921
ST. OLAF
FOOT BALL
SCHEDULE

ARNOLD FLATEN, *Capt.*

COACHING STAFF
E. B. ANDERSON - - Coach
H. M. THOMPSON
ARTHUR LEE } - Assistants
E. T. TUFTE
Dr. E. R. COOKE - Physical Director
Dr. F. M. BABCOCK - Physician

SCHEDULE

October 8—Concordia		There
St. Olaf 97	Concordia 0	
October 14—Luther		There
St. Olaf 10	Luther 0	
October 22—Macalester		Here
St. Olaf 7	Macalester 6	
November 5—Carleton		Here
St. Olaf 3	Carleton 20	
November 12—St. Thomas		There
St. Olaf 2	St. Thomas 7	
November 19—Gustavus Adolphus		There
St. Olaf 14	Gustavus Ado'phus 0	
TOTAL SCORE		
St. Olaf 133	Opponents 33	

Rules, Eligibility Standards Adjusted

The coming of the 1922 season marked some changes in the rules by which football was played, as well as in eligibility standards for student athletes in all sports.

The point after touchdown (PAT) was to be a scrimmage play from on or beyond the five-yard line. A foul or illegal play by the offense ended the try for PAT. A foul or illegality by the defense resulted in the automatic award-ing of the point to the offense. An offense utilizing a shift had to come to a full stop before continuing with the play.

A concern that students would not spread themselves too thin and/or an effort to see that as many students as wanted to were able to participate in extra-curricular activities resulted in more carefully spelled out eligibility requirements. The new requirements applied to forensics, music, and dramatics as well as athletics.

1. A student had to be regularly enrolled and taking 12 credit hours of work.
2. A "C" average had to be maintained in 12 hours.
3. No unsatisfied failure, condi-tion, incomplete, probation, or disciplinary penalty will be permitted.
4. No student may participate in more than one forensic, musical, athletic, or dramatic activity in one semester or hold a position on the staff of any publication.
5. No student may belong to more than two societies or clubs.
6. Membership on committees, standing or otherwise, designated class officers, or candidates for any other office created shall be limited to such students who are not participants in any of the above mentioned activities.

"Unable to gain consistently through the line, St. Olaf resorted to a dropkick field goal [to score late in the game]. Fevold fell back to kick from the 45-yard line from a difficult angle … in one mighty left-footed boot [Fevold] lifted the ball over the bar in a bit of the most spectacular work ever displayed on a Minnesota college gridiron."[52] Standouts for Carleton were Nordly and Cowles; for St. Olaf, Swanson and Ade Christenson.

In the final game of the season, St. Olaf turned back Gustavus 14–0. Ade Christenson and Frank Cleve were "outstanding stars." "Coon" Swenson and Arne Flaten "played consistently at the wing positions." A reporter noted that a hearty reception tendered the St. Olaf team following the (Gustavus) game "assures the finest type of athletic competition in the future."

Postseason honors went to "Coon" Swenson, who was a unanimous choice for the mythical all-state team for the second year, entitling him to one of the silver

Ade Christenson, 1922

loving cups offered by the Unique Candy Store.[53] Swenson also was elected captain for 1922 during the three-hour third annual football banquet. Bob Lunde, Frank Cleve, and Ade Christenson were second team all-state choices. Sixteen letters were awarded.

Ade Christenson was chosen by the student body as Honor Athlete for 1921–22.[54] Ade had been one of the most noticeable athletic standouts in the Minnesota Conference, competing in basketball and track as well as football. The honor athlete designation was one of the highest honors the student body could award.

1922 — From Rebuilding to Champion

With Captain Arne Flaten, Ade Christenson, Fritz Anderson, and Otto Glesne graduated and "Fat" Hanson, Frank Cleve, and Carl (Cully) Swanson not having returned to school, according to the Mess of Sept. 26, it looked as if 1922 would be a rebuilding season. But as often happens in sport, appearances can deceive. Late in the first week of school, Coach Endre Anderson received a welcome phone call announcing that Cleve and Swanson would arrive in Northfield to register the next morning and report for practice that afternoon.

Frank and Cully, along with a half dozen Minnesota conference athletes, had participated in summer baseball, and, as a result, their eligibility had been questioned. All, however, had been given "absolutely clean eligibility status" by the State Conference of Coaches and School Officials. The Mess echoed the obvious: "Cleve will be a highly valued halfback, while Cully will be a strong candidate for quarter." Captain "Coon" Swenson was back for his senior season and, presumably, his fourth year as a starter. Martin Cole and Promo were ticketed for the tackles with Jake Christiansen at fullback.

With that formidable group in place, 1922 turned abruptly from a rebuilding season to a championship season. The team went undefeated, tying St. Thomas for the title, and scoring St.Olaf's first win over Carleton. Only a 14–14 tie with Macalester marred the record.

Fevold, Cleve, Swanson, Glesne

In the season opener, the hard-hitting, shifty backfield combination of Cleve, Swanson, Fevold, and Glesne started its legendary career with a 35–0 win over Concordia. "Cleve responsible for four touchdowns, four PATs and over 100 yards rushing," the game report said. Swanson, Fevold, Swenson, Cole, and Putzier also were cited for outstanding play.

A penalty-free game with good sportsmanship exhibited by both teams resulted in a 20–10 Ole victory over St. John's. "Quarterback McNally appeared as a pillar of strength for the Collegeville team," the Mess reported. Presumably the McNally referred to was Johnny "Blood" McNally, who would go on to become a National Football League Hall of Famer with the Duluth Eskimos and the Green Bay Packers.

The season highlight occurred the next week as some 3,500 spectators, among them 900 from Manitou Heights, settled into Carleton's Laird Stadium to watch the Oles and the Carls — both undefeated again — settle the issue. Ole backfield ace Frank Cleve was out with a sprained

ankle, and it was widely expected that the Carls would use a weight advantage and a crunching ground game to good effect as they had the previous two seasons. Wrong!

"Maize and Blue Trampled Underfoot by Fighting Ole Machine Last Saturday," the *Messenger* front-page headline blared. Whitey Fevold's 60-yard interception return and Cully Swanson's "bullet" passes and brilliant end running were offensive highlights. Tackles Marty Cole and Otto Jensen played the strongest games of their careers, the game report said.

The victory over Carleton, far from leading to a letdown, evidently made the Oles invincible. They shut out Luther 31–0 and Gustavus 41–0 in the last two contests of the season. Luther fell victim to stellar play by Fevold (a 95-yard interception return), a recuperated Cleve showing his "old time class," and outstanding play by Swenson, Cole, and Glesne.

Seven seniors played their last game against Gustavus and mounted a four-touchdown fourth period to top it off. Captain "Coon" Swenson had started for four years. Bob Lunde also was a standout.

Ingwald "Coon" Swenson, four-year regular, 1922 captain

Coach Endre Anderson again picked his own mythical all-state squad and put Swenson, Swanson, Cole, and Fevold on the first team and Bob Lunde on the second team. One wonders what

The first St. Olaf championship team, 1922

Cheerleaders at the Carleton-St. Olaf game, 1922

1922 Season Notes
Coach Anderson and Fred Putzier were in an accident "returning from the Hamline-Carleton game," the *Messenger* reported. Due to the apt presence of mind of the latter (Putzier), no loss of life was suffered … Anderson had a feature article in the Feb. 13, 1923, issue of the *Messenger* under Faculty Forum … "Jud" Gregor '21, was recognized for his coaching at Redwood Falls High School and as a player on the "powerful gridiron machine" [Redwood Falls town team]. He had been the main scoring cog of the team," the paper said.[56]

Spectators at the Carleton-St. Olaf game, 1922

happened to Cleve. A *Minneapolis Journal* writer, speaking of "Coon" Swenson, noted that, "The captain of the Northfield outfit was again the most feared outpost *(sic)* in the state. He is deadly on defense, while his offensive play this fall was stronger than ever before." Swenson capped a remarkable career by being named Honor Athlete for 1922–23.

"Coon" (so-called, presumably, because some wags thought his eyes resembled the nocturnal animal) missed less than one half of one game over four years. He was three times all-state. "Besides his athletic record," a published report said, "Swenson had the highest scholastic standing of any athlete competing in more than one sport. Eighteen men were awarded letters, and Marty Cole was elected captain for 1923. Coach Anderson received invitations for possible games with the Universities of North and South Dakota. "An early season game with the University of Minnesota is being tentatively arranged."[55]

In its review of the 1922 season, the 1924–25 *Viking* gave tribute to Whitey Fevold, Frank Cleve, Ing Glesne, Cully Swanson, Marty Cole (165 pounds of fighting iron), Otto Jensen, "Coon" Swenson, and Bob Lunde.

1923
Coming off an undefeated season and a conference co-championship, the prospect for the 1923 season looked good. The iron man tackle, Martin Cole, a star for three seasons, was the captain-elect. Otto Jensen and Jake Christiansen were returning linemen, while Fevold, Swanson, Cleve, and Glesne would be playing together in the backfield for the third season.

Coach Anderson urged as many men as possible to come out for practice, "but none is desired who will not take the responsibilities of the squad with a strictly business sense," he said. More than 60 turned out. The coach had assistance for the first few weeks of the season from Sam Veldey '20, a former grid captain who had also been a baseball standout. Veldey would leave to attend the Lutheran Bible Institute in St. Paul.

As the squad readied for the season opener against St. Mary's, the campus was rocked by the destruction by fire of Hoyme Chapel. The new $200,000 power plant was completed at about the same time.

In a typical season opener — penalties, fumbles, and in this case, rain — the Oles downed St. Mary's 31–0, the fourth consecutive shutout, going back to the 1922 season. Both coaches substituted liberally, game reports said. It was unusual practice for that day when a player was usually removed only because of injury. The Oles were jolted to life by the coach moving Frank Cleve from his customary end position to the backfield. It should be noted that at this time, St. Mary's was a two-year school and occasionally used players from its academy to fill out the team.

The Oles continued to struggle against Concordia the following week. St. Olaf fumbles and a strong Concordia punting game kept the Oles at bay early. Injuries also played a role. Fevold didn't play, and Cully Swanson left in the first period. Cleve took over at quarter and Reinertson entered at halfback. Concordia's score came via a fourth-quarter interception return. St. Olaf outlasted the Cobbers 17–7.

An unexpectedly strong Luther 11 nearly handed the Oles their first loss going back to the beginning of the previous season. With seconds left in the game, Luther leading 7–0, and the ball at the Luther 25, Cully Swanson recovered a fumble at the right sideline and threw a high pass diagonally across the field. Cleve caught it at the five and eluded two wouldbe tacklers to score as the final whistle blew. Cleve kicked the PAT to salvage a 7–7 tie.[57]

Unveiling a devastating passing attack the next week, the Oles finally broke the Macalester jinx, downing the Scots 21–0. The Oles completed 14 of 20 pass attempts, the bulk of them from Swanson to Cleve. Simundson and Melby bore the brunt of the running game, and Captain Marty Cole was cited for strong line play.

Endre mandated secret practice sessions the next week, suggesting special strategies for the upcoming Carleton game. The intra-city rivalry stood at 3–1 in favor of Carleton in the four years since the establishment of intercollegiate football for both schools. The starting lineup for St. Olaf had Erickson and Cleve at ends, Captain Cole and Jensen, tackles, Pearson, Vig, or Bolstad, guards, Christiansen or Olson, center, Swanson at quarterback, Fevold and Simundson, halfbacks, and Glesne or Melby, fullback.

The expected aerial battle didn't materialize due to intermittent rain prior to and during the game, but Cully Swanson "directed the team masterfully," and the headline the next week read, "Oles Trounce Maize 6–0 in Hard-fought Battle." The Oles did not use a single substitute in racking up a second consecutive win over the Carls. The victory was costly in one respect, and the bill may have come due the following week. Swanson was lost to injury for the Homecoming contest against St. Thomas.

With Cleve shifted to quarterback, 4,000 spectators witnessed what was called the most sensational conference game of the season. An evenly contested game ended with a 19–14 win for St. Thomas.

Venturing outside the conference the next week, St. Olaf won a spectacular

The Carleton-St. Olaf game, played in a snowstorm, 1923

20–12 victory over Superior, Wis., Normal. The Oles were out-first downed 18–4, but compensated with an aerial game that went 13–21. Cleve was again at quarterback for Swanson, and he carried the offense with yeoman help from Fevold and Enger. Cole and Christiansen were standouts in the line. Otto Jensen, stalwart left tackle, suffered a severe leg injury and was treated at St. Mary's Hospital in Superior and then at the college hospital for an extended period. The Lutheran Athletic Club and the Lutheran Brotherhood of the First Lutheran Church hosted the squad for a banquet following the Saturday

game. Coach Anderson and Captain Cole spoke, after which the squad sang the college song with Alice M. Olson at the piano.[58]

The season ended the following week with a 37–0 thumping of Gustavus at St. Peter. This time the Minnesota Conference championship was undisputed — the second title in two years. With Swanson and Cleve throwing to Enger, Fevold, Simundson, and Christiansen, the Oles bombed the Gusties into submission, completing 19 of 32 passes for 444 yards. The win and the state championship resulted in a half day off from classes (Saturday morning).

The 1923 championship team

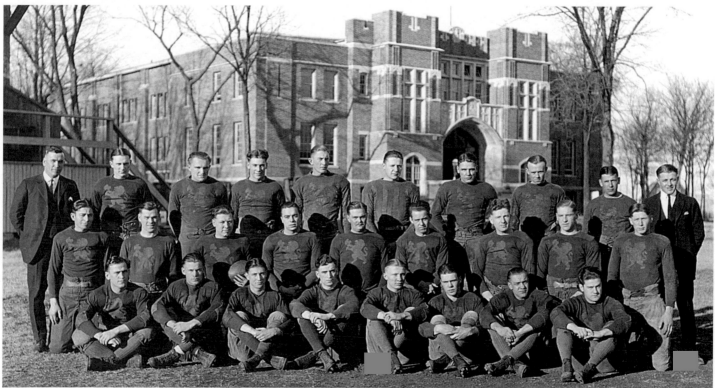

1923, Endre and his pilot: Cully Swanson with Endre Anderson.

1923 Season Notes

During the off-season, several Ole players and Coach Anderson attended a coaching school headed by Knute Rockne.[60] Attending the summer course at Superior Normal were Ade Christenson, Jake Christiansen, Joy Nelson, Irving Vigard, Robert Lunde, and Coach Endre Anderson. It was noted that Rockne had been born in Voss, Norway, 38 years prior. Whether or not it was inspired by Rockne's coaching school, St. Olaf began offering a for-credit course in the Coaching of Major Sports. Coach Anderson was to be the instructor.[61]

All-state selections by Twin Cities' newspapers honored Swanson, Cleve, Fevold, and Captain Marty Cole. Also cited were Christiansen, Simundson, Enger, Glesne, and Bolstad. The latter's selection was curious, given the fact that he was ineligible for conference play all season and had not suited up for a state conference game.[59]

At the banquet concluding the 1923 season, 20 men were awarded letters and Cully Swanson was elected captain for 1924. Gold footballs were awarded to players, coaches, the team manager, and Dr. Remele of Northfield. Ole Christiansen sang a solo, and the college orchestra played.

Captain Marty Cole received the Honor Athlete award; Jacobi (Jake) Christiansen was the other candidate. Cole had earned eight letters — four each in baseball and football. The 1924–25 *Viking* cited the play of Henry Pearson, "Melly" Simundson, Bongsto, Lium, Excog, Tunem, Erickson, Reinertson, Kosmo, Enger, and Gus Mellby. Coach Endre Anderson was the subject of a *Messenger* profile — "Man behind the Guns."

1924

Hopes were high for the 1924 season, even though there were only the three "luminaries" to build the team around — presumably Swanson, Cleve, and Fevold. Other familiar names among the 37 who reported for drills were Howell Skoglund, Harold Mennes, and Merle Olson. Forty freshmen reported to Coach Pete Fossum for the interclass team. That group was to practice with some regularity and serve as a scout team to run opposition plays against the varsity. Their season climaxed with an interclass game against the sophomores.

The opener against St. Mary's was disappointing, as "the Catholics fought the Vikings on even terms."[62] The game ended in a scoreless tie despite the Oles' reputed strength in the aerial game with the likes of Swanson at quarterback, Fevold and Stanley Anderson, backs, and "Tarzan" Syverud and Cleve at the "lookout points" (ends).

Perhaps chastened by their comparative ineffectiveness in the first game, the Oles shut out their next three opponents —

Concordia 16–0, St. John's 23–0, and Gustavus 16–0. Three consecutive conference victories and four consecutive shutouts provided an exciting lead-in to the Carleton encounter the following week.

The Carls appeared to have a strength advantage in the line; the Oles in the backfield. Coach (C.J.) Hunt of Carleton noted that, "In Cleve, Fevold, and Swanson, St. Olaf has a combination that would cause many large universities trouble. Coach Anderson of St. Olaf cited Carleton's one-game advantage in the won-lost column over the five years since St. Olaf had begun intercollegiate football competition.

The following week, a combined *Carletonian-Messenger* issue headlined the outcome: "Maize Defeats Oles, Several Thousand Witness Gridiron Classic."[63] From the same issue: "In the greatest battle ever played on Laird Field, Carleton beat St. Olaf by a score of 16 to 12." Carleton scored 16 first-half points and held off a St. Olaf second-half rally, ending it with an interception late in the game. The Oles' passing game evidently turned around

Martin Cole, 1923 captain, 1924 Honor Athlete

22

to bite them. In addition to the ruinous interception, a Swanson to Cleve pass was muffed, and a Swanson to Enger aerial bounced off the latter's arm.

A *Messenger* article at this time also noted plans to build a new athletic field below the hill, south of the Main, bordering Forest Avenue.[64] The grading was to be done during the coming summer (1925) with no specified time of completion. The site was to include a football gridiron, a running track, a baseball diamond, tennis courts, volleyball court, and dressing/showering facility. A new field was thought to be necessary because of the conflict of the current site (south of the current theater building) with "Greater St. Olaf" building plans, possibly a women's residence quadrangle.

The final two games of the 1924 season were split — a 33–7 win over previously undefeated Luther and a 20–14 loss to St. Thomas — giving St. Olaf a 4–2–1 record and third place in the conference. From the Ole

standpoint, both games featured the potent passing game, principally "Cully to Cleve." "That combination will long be remembered as the most brilliant passing duo the state conference had witnessed."[65] The Oles passed for 211 yards against Luther and 278 against St. Thomas.

1924 Season Notes

Cully to Cleve — The forward pass was a weapon in the St. Olaf offensive arsenal almost from the beginning of intercollegiate play. But it truly arrived in the mid-twenties, the era of some extraordinary athletes, among them Cully Swanson, Frank Cleve, and Harry (Whitey) Fevold.

The end of the 1924 season brought to a close the era of the "Big Three" — Swanson, Cleve, and Fevold. Whitey Fevold had the distinction of being St. Olaf's first and only 16 letter winner. "He holds the record for the longest dropkick field goal in the state (45 yards), was all-state halfback in

football, holds the state high jump record and was captain of the St. Olaf basketball team for two years. He is also an honor student at graduation."[66] Fevold went on to postgraduate work in chemistry at the University of Wisconsin.

Frank Cleve, who completed his college course work in three and a half years, was named Honor Athlete for 1924–25. He went on to teach and coach at Spokane College in Washington, at Concordia in Moorhead, and in the Minneapolis City Conference.

Cully Swanson, the first half of the "Cully to Cleve" combo, was featured in Robert Ripley's *Believe It or Not* for his 1924 passing record of 121 completions in 226 attempts for 1,644 yards, an average of 205-1/2 yards for eight consecutive games, an amazing statistic in the days when football was still largely a running game. Swanson later taught and coached at Kasson, Minn., and in the Minneapolis City Conference, served as a Lieutenant

Cully Swanson, 1925 captain

Frank Cleve, 1925 Honor Athlete

Harry (Whitey) Fevold, St. Olaf's only 16 letter winner, 1924

Commander in the Navy during World War II, and had a distinguished career as dean of men and dean of admissions at St. Olaf.

Swanson, Cleve, and Fevold have all been inducted into the St. Olaf Athletic Hall of Fame.

The Fans — From time to time throughout the history of sport, the importance of the crowd comes up for discussion. Some athletes say it's an inspiration; others, a distraction; still others, an irrelevancy. But the preponderance of opinion is probably with those who count it an asset. One of those discussions arose at St. Olaf in 1924 when a *Messenger* article called the Student Pulse said, "Already we are on our way toward making yelling a more effective and decisive factor; the first step was taken when the student body voted funds for a megaphone for its cheer leaders. Let's move on! — How about some yells that mean something? e.g. Behind you gang; put it over. Hold that line. Fighting all the time. Fight Oles fight. We want a touchdown."

The Opposition — Walt Kiesling, standout tackle for the St. Thomas Tommies, was to follow the path blazed earlier by Johnny (Blood) McNally of St. John's — starring in the NFL with the Duluth Eskimos and the Green Bay Packers.

St. Olaf and Hamline agreed to renew a competitive relationship after a three-year hiatus, the way evidently smoothed by a change in coaching personnel at the St. Paul School.

And Halsey — In another sidelight of the Ole-St. Thomas game in 1924, the head linesman, one Halsey Hall, later found fame in another area — as a sports broadcaster, print journalist, and legendary sports personality throughout Minnesota and beyond.

1925 and Conference Changes

As the 1925 season approached, Ole grid partisans waited with bated breath to see what effect the departure of "the luminaries" — Swanson, Fevold, and

Cleve — would have. In the meantime, the summer conference meeting took several significant actions: It was announced that Carleton would withdraw from the league — changing the character of the Ole-Carl rivalry somewhat. The league also authorized a freshman schedule for conference schools. Each team would be able to play three games against other freshman teams. In another action, the conference allowed St. John's to use high school seniors (from their academy) if they

qualified as to credits and other eligibility criteria. Endre Anderson and Dean J. Jorgen Thompson represented St. Olaf at the meeting. Anderson was re-elected secretary-treasurer.

A week into preseason drills, the outlook for 1925 brightened with the addition of Eli Enger, a fleet halfback, Bongsto at guard, "Fat" Olson, center, "Chick" Hagen and Everson, tackles. Added to Flaten and Fremouw, ends, Bill Johnson, center, and Captain Stan Pearson, guard, this group raised spirits.

The first two games validated the optimism. In the opener, the Oles blew away Phalen-Luther by 51–0. The outstanding play of the game was an 80-yard pass interception return by sophomore Bernie Cole. Against St. John's, Enger's 60-yard touchdown run in the third period keyed a 7–0 victory. Munson dropkicked the PAT. Despite the win, Coach Anderson said the offense "was not up to standard."

After sweeping aside, by 40–0, a Concordia team reputed to be "the best in years," the Oles proved themselves mortal, dropping their next three contests to even the season record at 3–3. A strong Luther 11 downed St. Olaf 16–0 on a perfect Luther Homecoming day.[67] "St. Olaf outplayed from the start," was the reporter's verdict. "Outscored but not oughtfought," the following week, the Oles lost to Carleton 13–0.[68]

In a classic "what if" comment, a reporter noted that had it not been for a blocked punt and a fumble, it could have been a scoreless tie. Gustavus tacked on a 9–6 defeat the following week to even the season record. But not for long. The next time out, a cold northwest wind appeared not to hamper a superior St. Mary's passing attack, as they edged St. Olaf 13–11, to dampen Founders Day activities on Nov. 6. The Oles could take consolation from the fact that St. Mary's had lost only twice in two seasons, both to Marquette University. A late passing offensive, featuring Olson to Flaten, fell short when an interception stopped the threat at the St. Mary's three-yard line.

With the help of strong fan support (a two-coach Dan Patch special), the Oles rebounded against Hamline the next week. A Munson dropkick PAT was the margin of victory in a slim 7–6 win, though the Olson to Flaten pass combination was again potent, leading the Oles to a 16–5 margin in first downs.

In the final game of the season, Macalester gained its first state championship by downing St. Olaf 28–6. Fumbles and a porous pass defense proved the Oles' undoing, a reporter said. Gustavus was runnerup in the conference standings, followed by St. Olaf, Hamline, Concordia, and St. John's in that order.

Twenty-two men won letters. Milo Mielke, a hard-running back, and speedster Elert Enger were named to the mythical all-state squad, and Enger was selected Honor Athlete for 1924–25. J. Jorgen Thompson, dean of men at St. Olaf, was elected president of the conference with Endre Anderson continuing as secretary-treasurer.

1926

Prospects for 1926 were bright — the line strong with good size; the backfield material plentiful. In the line were Bill Johnson, "Fat" Jacobson, "Ade" Lium, Paul Johnson, "Fat" Olson, "Beef" Mennes, and "Ossie" Bongsto. Rudy Flaten and Bernie Cole were at end. Captain Stan Anderson and Joe Rognstad would form the backfield nucleus, while sophomores Hartwich, McKenzie, and Obermeyer are "expected to break into the limelight."

Other preseason *Messenger* reports had Cole and Stageberg showing up well in the backfield with Captain Anderson, Munson, and Rognstad thought to have backfield slots assured. "Chick" Hagen and Aamodt were said to be battling for the right flank, with Rudy Flaten fairly safe at the other end.

With Rognstad, Stageberg, and Cole leading the ground attack, the Oles trounced a light and inexperienced Augsburg squad 26–0. Reserves played most of the second half for the Oles. "In fact, so numerous were the replacements that a dog joined the migration onto the field."[69]

The warning of a *Messenger* editorial writer that "the Vikings and specifically "Burn-Hard-Coal" should not be overconfident because of the comparatively easy Augsburg win was apparently unnecessary as St. Olaf buried Concordia the following week by a four-touchdown margin.[70] Bernie Cole's 90-yard run was a highlight. The

Earle "Binger" Obermeyer, 1928 captain

Cobbers were coached by Frank Cleve, the former Ole star. It was the first time one of Coach Anderson's protégés had coached against him.

An alum attending the Concordia contest in Moorhead was Dr. J. H. Heimark '93. He recalled that 1893 was the year after the fatal accident which put a ban on football at St. Olaf for a quarter century.[71]

After the relatively easy conquest of Concordia, the Oles fell on a two-week stretch of hard times. A thousand Oles, led by a 100-piece pep band, were expected to parade down St. Olaf Avenue and across town to Laird Stadium to watch the Oles challenge Carleton and a superior running attack. Superior it proved to be as the Carls celebrated their homecoming by thumping St. Olaf 42–0, running Carleton's margin in the series to 6–2. The Oles did not cross midfield.

Boe Expands Staff

In the spring of 1927, President Lars Boe took action that resulted in a major step forward for intercollegiate athletic competition at St. Olaf. He appointed two former Ole athletic standouts — Ade Christenson and Carl (Cully) Swanson — to the faculty of the department of physical education and athletics "to assist Coach Endre Anderson with his numerous duties in the coaching of the major sports during the 1927–28 school year."[75]

President Boe's action was doubtless precipitated by a growing program and a somewhat decreased coaching presence. Before that action, Endre Anderson and Doc Cooke constituted the coaching staff. Endre was head coach of football, basketball, and baseball. In addition, he had developed a prosperous business in producing and sexing baby chicks. He had also been re-elected president of the Minnesota Baby Chick Cooperative Association.

The new coaches appeared to be eminently qualified. Both had been stellar athletes in their own rights and had acquired coaching experience after graduation. Prior to the appointments, Christenson, a 1922 graduate, had coached at Story City, Iowa, Coleraine, Minn., and Roosevelt High School in Minneapolis. Swanson, a 1925 graduate, had been in a coaching/teaching position at Kasson, Minn.

Crippled and sore and without the services of Bongsto, Rognstad, Ligrid, and Anderson as a result of the Carleton debacle, the Oles fell to Gustavus 7–0. The "Swedes" used a shift to good advantage, and though they penetrated the Ole 20 only once, it was enough for the one-touchdown victory.

The travail continued as the Oles lost to Luther, Hamline, and Macalester, bringing their losing streak to five and their scoreless skein to four. The acid comment of a Mess writer gave the flavor of the Hamline contest: "The first quarter of the Hamline-St. Olaf tea party was about the seediest exhibition of football given on Manitou Field this year. The Hamline shift was executed with all the speed of a senile turtle; the St. Olaf offense was not much superior. In the second quarter, the Pipers speeded up and never gave the courteous Oles a second look."[72] Hamline intercepted six passes while the St. Olaf backs were "hooked" on fakes by the Piper receivers.

Despite the four shutouts, Bernie Cole was tied for the conference scoring lead at the end of that stretch. But it was undeniably a disappointing season.

A mythical 1926 all-conference team chosen by Arthur Bergo and Thomas Tweito, *Messenger* sports writers, included Saterlie, guard on the first team, and Jacobson, guard on the second team. Hartwich, quarterback, Rognstad and Anderson, halfbacks, Cole and Munson, fullbacks, and Mennes and T.W. Johnson, guards, received honorable mention.[73]

1926 Season Notes

In postseason activity, the conference admitted St. Mary's College of Winona to membership and decided that men who had enrolled as freshmen in the fall would be eligible to compete after Jan. 1. The rule was voted as an amendment to the semester rule, due to colleges terminating their semesters on different dates. An exception to the amendment was that colleges with fewer than 125 men in the three upper classes would not be affected. For those colleges, frosh would be eligible from the beginning of the year. St. John's, St. Mary's, and Concordia benefited from the exception.

A *Messenger* headline noted that several "Senior Athletes [were] Distinguished in College Sports."[74] Two three-sport stars listed were Rudolph (Rudy) Flaten, newest honor athlete, and Stanley (Stan) Anderson. Others noted were Burton (Red) Munson, football fullback and baseball first baseman, and footballers "Fat" Jacobson, Bill Johnson, Merle Olson, Les Mason, Harold Mennes, Ade Lium, "Fat" Holton, Joe Rognstad, and Chick Hagen.

1927

The two additional coaches appointed by President Boe *[see sidebar]* were in place as the 1927 season approached. As a nucleus to build around, the mentors had Captain Elmer Saterlie, tackle; Paul Johnson, guard; Sigurd Flaten, end, and Bernie Cole, quarterback — all lettermen. Listed as candidates for the backfield were Cliff Aamot, Bernie Legrid, Rolf Stageberg, Art Solberg, Huck Olson, and sophomore Mark Almli. Almli was reputed to be a capable kicker and passer.

A green and untested 11 split its first two games — losing to Macalester 18–2 in the opener and edging Augsburg 14–7 the next time out. For the second contest, Coach Anderson switched Bernie Cole from quarterback to end, where he promptly teamed with Almli for a touchdown and a conversion. Almli, the newcomer, also scored on a nifty 32-yard run. "Binger" Obermeyer and Ray Thompson, along with Cole and Almli, were cited for "splendid" games.

Meanwhile, Coach Christenson was making his presence felt. He and Fred Fremouw welcomed "60 husky freshmen for drills. Throwing opening day limbering up exercises to the winds, the coaches sent the yearlings through a stiff program of scrimmage and followed this up on the second day by putting them against the varsity in as stiff a workout as any green squad could wish."[76]

For the season's third contest, former Ole ace Frank Cleve brought his Concordia team to town to challenge his former coach, Endre Anderson, for the second time. The meeting resembled a family reunion with Christenson, Swanson, and Fred Fremouw also involved as coaches.[77] When the dust of battle had cleared, Cleve had evened the score for the previous year's loss with a razor-thin, 13–12 Concordia win over Anderson's charges. Rolf Stageberg's sparkling 94-yard interception return for a touchdown was the big play in an Ole comeback which fell short.

The Oles rebounded with a 12–7 victory over Luther, but then were thumped by Carleton 43–6 and subsequently lost to St. Mary's by 20–6 and Hamline 25–0.

Between the St. Mary's and Hamline contests, the frosh knocked off the sophomores (varsity men who had played in no more than eight quarters) 22–0. "Sophomores Dumped by Green Wave 22 to 0; Tutelage of Christenson Is Factor in Upset of Dope," the *Messenger* said.[78] Captain Kippy Gilbertson led the frosh.

A coaches' mythical all-state team honored tackle Elmer Saterlie on the first team and Paul Johnson, guard, and Mark Almli, fullback, on the second. The *Minneapolis Journal's* Halsey Hall paid tribute to Almli, Saterlie, Johnson, and Obermeyer.

1927 Season Notes

Prior to the 1928 season, two campus news items attracted attention. A front-page headline in the May 8 *Messenger,* premature, as it turned out, said, "St. Olaf Gets New Athletic Field." The article said the field was to be situated on a 15-acre plot below the

hill to the south and east of the Main. There would be space for the three major sports — football, baseball and track. The complex would include a building for dressing, showering, and storage of equipment. The college's future building program also called for erection of other buildings — possibly a women's quadrangle on the field site. The estimated cost of the field and a field house was $65,000 to $75,000. A fund drive was to be launched. A total of only $3,000 was raised during the summer, causing the project to be postponed indefinitely.

The other bit of news was also of special interest to the athletic community. It was the prospective organization of an Athletic Union. It was to be basically a fund raising and management organization for the benefit of St. Olaf athletics and athletes. The major objective of the union was to provide funds for needy athletes of proven ability in both athletics and scholarship." Funds were to be lent to these individuals "at the discretion of an elective board of directors."

Another stipulation was that the prospective loan recipient would have to leave school if financial aid were not forthcoming. The loan contracts were to provide that the funds had to be repaid with a stated rate of interest, which would begin to accrue two years after graduation. "At this time, the

borrower should be in a position to repay the union the funds which he had borrowed."[79] The Athletic Union appeared to be a Class of 1928 initiative with no official sanction by the college administration.

1928

In the fall of 1928, coaches Anderson, Christenson, and Swanson greeted 40 grid candidates, led by Captain "Binger" Obermeyer, Cliff Aamodt, and Mark Almli. "A ray of hope appeared when it was learned that Almli, the Viking Comet, was declared eligible."[80] A protest had been lodged against Mark's eligibility when it was learned he had played baseball with an independent team before the end of the school year. Conference directors allowed the eligibility when it was found the play in question had not occurred until after the St. Olaf season was complete and Almli had completed his final exams.

Another bright spot was the enrollment of Syl Saumer of Montevideo, Glesne of Decorah, Iowa, "Lefty" Swanson of Janesville, and Alvin Droen.

The bloom came off the rose quickly, however, as the Vikings fell to Augsburg's potent aerial attack 13–0 and succumbed to a St. Mary's comeback which resulted in a 21–0 loss. The following week, a punting duel between Almli and McKenzie of Hamline and two apparently stout defenses resulted in a scoreless tie.

The 1928 St. Olaf team, Earle "Binger" Obermeyer, captain

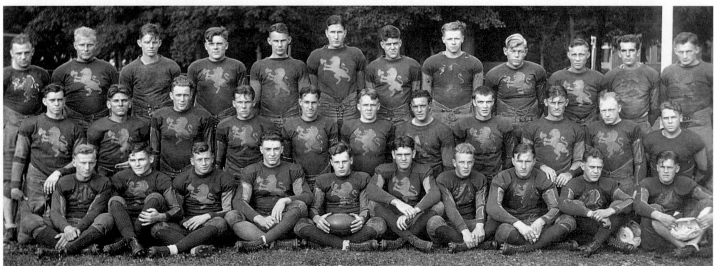

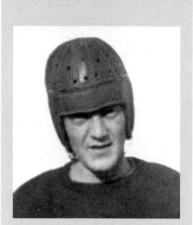

Mark Almli, 1929 captain

Bert Larson, 1930 captain

Syl Saumer, punter, 1930 (photo courtesy of Mary L. Anderson)

Carleton was next and the gloom continued. The Knights amassed 19 first downs to four for the Oles and, according to a writer "clearly evinced" a superior offense. St. Olaf missed its only chance to score when an Almli pass to a "wide open" Johnson was incomplete. Carleton's quarterback and captain, Arnie Simso, was the game's star.

Mess Gets Tough

Three losses and a tie, four scoreless games for the Vikings produced a scathing editorial indictment in the *Messenger* of Oct. 23, 1928: "When St. Olaf football players go into a contest and fight like demons the first half and then throw the game away in the last half, there is only one reason for it. The men have failed to carry out training rules. They are not in physical condition; they have not the endurance to play an entire game … If there is anything despicable, it is a man who gets a position of honor and of responsibility when he doesn't deserve it. And that is our indictment against some of the men on the football squad. They are not particular about their food and they sleep only when they cannot waste their time at something else, despite the orders of the coach. Players who train like that do not deserve to win any game."

That blast had the opposite of its presumably intended effect as St. Olaf was shut out by Concordia 25–0 the following week. Aamodt was lost early in the contest, and Almli and Obermeyer were forced to play though injured. Long trip, poor game, still scoreless — a second consecutive win for Concordia Coach Frank Cleve over his former mentor, Endre Anderson.

Fortunes finally reversed with the next outing as "Oles [a seldom used name at that time] Pass Their Way to Surprise Victory." It was a 26–14 triumph over Gustavus. It was the first score and first (and, as it turned out, last) win of the season. Almli's passes to Gilbertson and Flaten and the smashing running of "Red" Olson and "Doc" McKenzie were strong points.

In the season's final contest, Luther tipped the Vikings 6–0 on the 54th anniversary of St. Olaf's founding.

All that was left of the 1928 season was the freshman-sophomore confrontation.

Cully Swanson's frosh — led by Saumer, Fritz Olson, Glesne, and Droen — downed the sophs 18–0, and the red buttons came off the freshman beanies. Grebstad, Gilbertson, "Red" Olson, and Netland, starters in the last varsity game against Luther, also started for the sophomores.

The *Messenger* chose Grebstad first team all-state center and Obermeyer, end, and Almli, halfback, on the second team.

The 1928 season was barely over when the *Messenger* headline read "Endre Anderson Resigns as Director of St. Olaf Athletics after 10 Years of Coaching." It was Nov. 27. Anderson had submitted his letter of resignation to President Boe the previous week. The president said a successor would not be named until the following spring.

Endre was the guest of honor at the annual football banquet, at which Almli was elected captain for 1929. Maroon slipover sweaters with 1932 numerals were awarded to 20 members of the freshman football squad. Gridders honored by the Mess for their play during the 1928 season were Captain "Binger" Obermeyer, Grebstad, Engleson, Almli, Gilbertson, Stageberg, Stokes, Lundgren, Ted Larson, Aamodt, "Red" Olson, Mikelson, Netland, McKenzie, Flaten, Johnson, Ingvolstad, and Enderson.

Work on Manitou Field Heralds New Era

During the year prior to the 1929 season, discussions were held leading to construction of what was to become Manitou Field. For a decade or more, the need for expanded athletic field facilities had been apparent, and several different sites had been discussed. Now the most often proposed site — below the Main to the south and east, bordering on Forest Avenue — was abandoned, as was an alternative site west of the gymnasium where the second Ytterboe residence hall now stands.

The new site was made possible by the acquisition of two pieces of property east of the power plant and north of the (then) president's residence. Architect's plans for the area provided for a baseball diamond, football playing field, two practice gridirons, a cinder track with a 220-yard straightaway, tennis courts, sufficient space for all track events, and a dressing, showering, and storage building adjacent to the power plant. A sketch of the new facility was published in the *Messenger* of March 12, 1929.

Cost of the development was estimated at $35,000; $6,000 had already been obtained, $1,000 of which was a gift from Endre Anderson "to get the ball rolling." Site preparations included leveling, drainage tile installed, and removal and replacement of black dirt over the clay base. "Grading and sodding problems must be met. Sodding, according to those in charge, will help prevent injuries in football."[81]

Financing was aided by student and alumni organizations. A student campaign, headed by five athletic organizations, raised $10,315 in a one-week drive in April.[82] An enthused Twin Cities alumni group, headed by Newell Nelson '20, along with Ludwig Roe, president of the St. Paul Alumni Association, and E.A. Beito, organized a campaign conducted in May. Among those involved in that campaign were Morris Wee, Frantz Werner, Carl Granrud, Howell Skoglund, Arne Flaten, Randolph Haugen, and Arthur Christenson.

Minor changes from the original layout called for a direct driveway from Lincoln Street to the football field with parking area to the east of Lincoln, on a 10-acre parcel owned by the college, and parking space for baseball games arranged so that fans could sit in their cars and watch the games. Published reports said "work on the athletic field may start early in the summer, water system to be used, light system held probable. It is highly problematic that the field will be ready for use next fall.[83]

As it turned out, work didn't begin on the field complex until August of 1929, and a Sept. 10, *Messenger* noted that six to eight weeks of work remained and that the field definitely would not be ready for the 1929 season. Total pledges, as of the end of August were $21,135 and cash payments were $8,268.

Christenson, Swanson Assume Major Positions

In January of 1929, President Lars Boe announced changes in the athletic department in light of the resignation of Endre Anderson. Boe had appointed Adrian Christenson head football coach, in addition to his present position as head basketball mentor. Carl Swanson would be head baseball coach, freshman football coach, and director of the physical training department. There would be no director of athletics, Boe said.[84] The president's announcement heralded the beginning of a period of almost four decades during which Ade Christenson and Cully Swanson would be major figures on the St. Olaf campus — in terms of athletics and in general.

One of Christenson's first moves was to initiate spring drills. The team picked from these practices would be invited back for early fall practice. Fifty prospective gridders reported for the two-week session.

1929

The outlook was bright in the fall. Mark Almli, Rufus Olson, Bert Larson, Harold Mikelson, Conrad Quam, "Kippy" Gilbertson, and Daryl Lien were among the veterans reporting. Up from the freshman squad were Al Droen, Syl Saumer, Cecil Tellekson, and Melvin Hegdahl. Linford Hildebrandt of Faribault had transferred from Columbus College in Sioux Falls. He was eligible immediately since Columbus had dropped football. Notable freshmen included Harry Newby, Dan Soli, and Irv Christenson of Northfield.

With a new assistant coach — Malcolm Frykman, a former University of Minnesota player under Doc Spears — Ade drilled the squad in preparation for the opener at Hamline Sept. 28. The new head coach's one-word description of the squad during preseason work: "terrible." Good backfield talent, Ade

The 1929 championship team, Mark Almli, captain

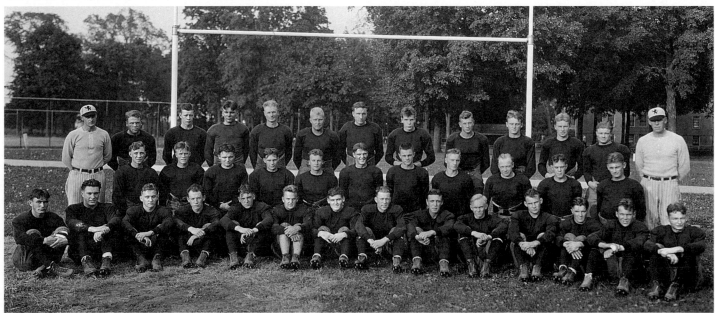

*Mark Almli,
1930 Honor Athlete*

From the 1930 Viking

The passing of Mark Almli from St. Olaf athletics and student life leaves a niche that will indeed be hard to fill.

Winner of 11 letters, three in football and four each in basketball and baseball, Mark was an all-around star. Three all-state selections rewarded his phenomenal basketball ability, and he also received a place on the mythical football eleven. His senior year found him captaining both the football and basketball teams. In baseball, he won the Hulberg Batting Trophy in 1928 and was runner-up the next year, while fielding sensationally throughout.

As a fitting end to his college athletic career, he was elected 1930 Honor Athlete without opposition.

said, but a reliable forward wall would have to be developed.

After a tuneup scrimmage with River Falls Normal, Ade and the team confronted Hamline at Norton Field in St. Paul. *Messenger* headlines of Oct. 1, noted "Vikings Slash Hamline Grid Machine 40–19. Almli, Saumer, Siemers, Hildebrandt, Droen, and Olson made up an overpowering backfield, bringing back memories of Swanson, Cleve, and Fevold. "Slippery" Syl Saumer scored on two beautiful touchdown runs, and Almli ran the team beautifully. "Mark is better than ever," the Mess noted.

The season's first setback came the next week when a stubborn St. Thomas team, coached by Knute Rockne protégé Joe Boland, scored a 6–0 shutout in "one of the hardest fought games ever witnessed in the conference." The Vikings and the Toms had not met since 1925.

Back on a positive track the following week, the Vikings dampened Luther's Homecoming 18–6. Saumer scored three times. The contest was not without cost, however, as Droen sustained a fractured cheekbone and was thought lost for most of the rest of the season. Viking linemen Larson, Hegdahl, and Engebretson were cited for their play.

Coach Christenson's first game against Carleton followed. St. Olaf had not defeated the Carls since 1923. Saumer played a major role (three scores) in putting an end to that streak. Carleton scored two late touchdowns to make it respectable, but the Vikings were clearly dominant — 25–13. Quarterback and captain Almli punted, ran, passed, and directed the squad masterfully. Ade must have devised a new defense using an additional defensive back, as the *Messenger* noted: "Ade's new defense with Ellingson leaving his guard position to protect against a pass attack worked to perfection." So great was the joy on Manitou Heights that by action of the student senate, no classes were held on Monday.[85]

With winning ways firmly established, the Vikings ran over conference foes Gustavus, Concordia, and Augsburg to take runnerup honors in the conference. Gustavus went down 18–6. "Slippery Syl" was a marked man, the *Messenger* said.

"The Swedes chased him as a scotchmen would chase a nickel." Regardless, he had 74 yards in 12 plays. Rufus Olson had 64 yards in eight carries, and Almli had 70 yards in eight trips plus great passing and punting. The defensive gem of the game came with the Vikings shutting off the Gusties at the one after they had first and goal at the four.

Frank Cleve brought his Concordia team to town hoping for a third consecutive win over his alma mater. Not this time. With Hegdahl, Larson, Opperud, Ellingson, and Engebretson controlling the line of scrimmage, the Vikings eked out a 12–7 triumph.

Augsburg was no match for St. Olaf in the season finale. Saumer ran wild, scoring six times in a 51–6 annihilation of the Auggies. Almli ended his college career with a stellar performance. He had 121 yards in 17 plays, four completions in five passing attempts, and one punt for 40 yards. He also played well defensively. Fifty-one points was the highest score in the conference in the '29 season.

Almli and Saumer were on the coaches' all-state team. "Captain Almli, brilliant Ole field general, passer, punter, and ball carrier, and Saumer, the Montevideo Hurricane, who ran up a new conference scoring record with 75 points, were awarded first team berths," the *Messenger* said. The paper raved on about Saumer: "Saumer is without doubt the greatest halfback that has run under Manitou colors."[86]

At the postseason banquet, 19 letter winners were awarded the new official St. Olaf monogram, and Bert Larson, a burly tackle from Benson, was elected captain for the 1930 season.

1930: Stellar Team, New Field

The outlook for 1930 was somewhat guarded. Captain Bert Larson — along with veterans Mel Hegdahl, Al Droen, Lin Hildebrandt, and Maynard Siemers — were returning, but standout halfback Syl Saumer, Swanson, and Opperud were not expected back. Saumer had not been enrolled the previous semester.

However, the hopes for the line went up with the hiring of Leslie "Les" Pulkrabek, a three-year lineman at the University of

Minnesota, as line coach. Cully Swanson was in charge of the freshmen. Fifty-nine men were working out in preparation for the opener against Hamline. Then Saumer showed up unexpectedly and, according to the *Messenger*, "football stock on the Hill soared to new heights."[87]

As the opener approached, the line continued to look very good with Larson and Hegdahl at tackles, Ingvoldstad and Ellingson at guards, and Gilbertson and Mickelson at ends. Norman Nordstrand and Terry Peterson were vying for the center slot. Depth, as well as talent, was plentiful in the backfield with Red Olson, Lin Hildebrandt, Saumer, Dan Soli, Harm Veldey, and a sprinter from Northfield — Harry Newby.

After a final tuneup scrimmage with River Falls Normal, the Vikings — wearing snappy, new white helmets — opened with a convincing 52–6 win over Hamline. Saumer scored twice in the first 10 minutes, Ellingson, Larson, and Gilbertson played well in the line, and newcomer Newby broke a long one. It appears Ade was using a platoon system, substituting whole teams. The accounts carry frequent references to second and third units being able to hold their own. "After Larson, Hegdahl, Ellingson, Gilbertson, and the rest of the boys had finished with the St. Paul lads, we imagine the sight of two new elevens warming up was anything but cheering to the Pipers."[88]

Saumer circles the St. Thomas end, 1930

Proving the opening win was no fluke, Captain Larson — playing a stellar game at tackle — led the Vikings to a brilliant upset win over a much larger South Dakota State team by 20–0. The Oles scored in five plays to open the game, and Newby ran 45 yards in the third quarter, after replacing Saumer, who left with a dislocated jaw.

The Oles appeared off their game in the season's third outing but still managed a 26–7 victory over Macalester. Newby replaced a tiring Saumer and immediately broke loose on a 55-yard scoring run. "Syl's dropkick PAT was good."[89] Rufe Olson intercepted a pass in the flat and scored from the 20.

Next up was a formidable Carleton eleven. Coach Hunt's team had routed Hamline 59–0 and posed a major challenge to the Oles' 2–0 conference record. It was to be the last game on the hilltop field. On this particular day, the Oles were what the *Messenger* called "a perfectly functioning piece of gridiron machinery." Obviously caught up in the euphoria generated by the home team's 19–0 victory, the writer continued, "The faultless head work of Gilbertson, who called the signals, the blocking of Droen and Olson, the all-around play of Saumer and Hildebrandt, the defensive work of Lecy, and the punishing line play of Nordstrand and Larson are all worthy of mention.[90] Newby, the Northfield speedster, had scored in every game so far.

The Inauguration of Manitou Field

The next week, after months of planning and hard work and at a cost of $35,000, the new field at the bottom of the hill below the power plant was ready for use. New goal posts had been erected and the bleachers had been moved from the hilltop field. St. John's was the opponent for the inaugural game on the new field.

On a brilliant autumn day, Ade's three teams romped over a light St. John's eleven for 12 touchdowns and a safety, swamping the Johnnies 82–0. The published verdict on the new field was,

The 1930 undefeated championship team, Bert Larson, captain

Al Droen, 1931 Honor Athlete, member of the 1930 undefeated team.

Lloyd Ellingson, 1931 Honor Athlete, member of the 1930 undefeated team, 1932 U.S. Olympic skier.

"The new field is in surprisingly good shape and should be conducive to better football than the old hill gridiron. The players missed the cement-like consistency of the old field, however."[91]

The band also got into the spirit of the occasion. Led by "Doc" Aamodt as drum major, the band went through some snappy maneuvers at halftime. "Doc" (Dr. Leonard Aamodt '18, a Northfield dentist) apparently was a slicker at the job, having served in that capacity both at St. Olaf and the University of Minnesota.

The fifth conference contest was against Gustavus and yielded a 20–12 victory. The Viking running attack featured Ade's double wing spinner series, which proved superior to the Gusties' usually potent passing game. Saumer, Droen, and Newby each scored.

Stepping outside the conference to renew the rivalry with Luther, the Vikings "flashed" to a 25–7 victory, according to a headline in the Foundation Day issue of the *Messenger*.[92] An 85-yard punt return by Hildebrandt was the standout play. Belgum, a one-time St. Olaf prospect, scored Luther's only touchdown on a fumble recovery.

A banner season concluded the following week as the Oles smothered Augsburg 58–0 to tie St. Thomas for the league crown. When Augsburg standout Kolesar left the game with an injury, the scoring gates opened for the Vikings. Ade again used his shock troops, substituting freely.

With the Oles and the Toms undefeated co-champions of the MIAC, the possibility of a playoff game at Memorial Stadium at the University of Minnesota arose. The proceeds would go to help alleviate the unemployment situation in Minneapolis and St. Paul. The idea died with a letter from President Coffman of the University to President Boe stating his position that "such a contest would be unable to make any substantial contribution to so grave a problem as the stressed situation in the Cities." Coffman further pointed out the danger to college and university athletics posed by commercializing the game to such an extent.[93]

1930 Banner Season: A Coming of Age for St. Olaf Football

If any one season can mark the coming of age of an athletic program, 1930 was probably it for Ole football. The team was truly dominant and obviously held the attention of the campus and beyond. An *Associated Press* report out of New York noted that "only 11 of the nation's hundreds of college football teams can claim records marred by neither defeats nor ties." St. Olaf was one of the 11. Moreover, the Oles were the top-scoring team among the 11 with 302 points in eight games. Among the other colleges listed were Alabama, Washington State, Utah, Notre Dame, Northwestern, and Tulsa.

The *Messenger's* mythical all-state first team had Larson at tackle, Ellingson at guard, Gilbertson at end, Hildebrandt at quarterback, and Saumer at left halfback. On the second team were Hegdahl at tackle, Nordstrand at center, Ingvoldstad at guard, Olson at right halfback, and Droen at fullback.[94]

Other postseason honors abounded. Syl Saumer was honorable mention on the AP All-America team and was selected Ole captain for 1931. Harry Newby was mentioned in *Ripley's Believe It of Not* for having scored on his first play in four consecutive games. The *Viking* proclaimed the squad "… the best football team St. Olaf has ever had." Carl Iverson was selected Honor Athlete. All squad members received gold footballs.

1930 Season Notes

Lloyd Ellingson, standout guard on the championship team, was selected to represent the United States in an international ski jumping competition in Norway on the famous Homenkollen jump. Unfortunately, Ellingson sprained an ankle three days before the meet. He competed anyway, jumping 38 meters on his first run but falling on his second. An estimated 75,000 spectators witnessed the event … End "Kippy" Gilbertson was appointed athletic coach at Waldorf College, Forest City, Iowa, for the coming year … In the off-season following the 1930 campaign, longtime Carleton Coach C.J. Hunt resigned …

Endre Anderson, former Ole mentor, was selected as the commissioner of the Minnesota Conference … 1929 graduate Mark Almli's Ironwood, Mich., high school team was undefeated through four games. Mark was playing some pro football on the side.

1931

In preparation for the season, coaches Christenson and Pulkrabek again held a two-week spring practice for members of last season's freshman team and other aspirants. Veteran team members involved in spring sports were excused.

Hot, humid weather greeted the squad when members reported in September for workouts, for the first time, on the new practice field. Prospects were good coming off the undefeated 1930 season. Many veterans reported, the notable exception being Syl Saumer. The "Montevideo Hurricane" was absent the first week of practice. This appeared to be an annual occurrence by chance or design. Experienced backs returning included Newby, Droen, Ness, Swanson, Soli, Ekegren, and Erickson. Nordstrand, Irv Christenson, Schiotz, Lieg, Peterson, and Glesne were veteran line returnees. Ralph Summers of Northfield was a promising sophomore. Saumer reported for the second week of practice.

The first game of the 1931 season was against North Dakota University, played under the lights at Grand Forks. The heavier, more experienced Sioux scored 20 first-half points, and the "Ademen" never recovered, losing 22–0. Droen, Ellingson, and Schiotz were standouts for the Oles. Saumer punted well and showed flashes of his old brilliance as a runner.

After the loss to UND, the Oles regained form and went on a 6–1 run, defeating Augsburg, Carleton, Gustavus, St. Mary's, Luther, and Concordia while losing to St. John's.

With Saumer at quarterback, Newby running well, and Grove scoring three touchdowns, the Oles sacked Augsburg 58–0. Reserves played a large share of the contest. Ralph Summers was injured in the first half.

On a cool, cloudless autumn day, 3,600 spectators saw St. Olaf spot Carleton a touchdown, then trample the Knights 25–6. A bevy of speedy Ole backs ripped the Carleton line in a "thrilling exhibition of football." Soli, Lecy, Newby, and Grove crossed the double stripe, and Hal Christenson turned in a spectacular interception and 40-yard return.

Enter the Football "Goat"

The Carleton game saw the introduction of the football Goatrophy. The Toggery, a Northfield clothing store situated next to the post office, had funded the design and manufacture of a wooden likeness of a goat to accompany the longtime basketball goat trophy. Unlike the basketball goat, the football trophy was to be up for grabs each fall on the basis of one game.

A sportswriter under the byline of Ernie in the Oct. 20, 1931, *Messenger,* described the introduction of the football goat: "When the abbreviated Carl megaphone manipulator approached the Viking cheering section with what looked like a portable phonograph, fans wondered. A minute later they had been introduced to Goatrophy, a goat as colorful as the classic game. Presumably, the newcomer was a relative of the home-loving creature across the river." At a student body meeting following the Carleton game, Professor Henry Thompson, religion, presented the Goatrophy to the college. Captain Syl Saumer accepted. "It is brightly painted and set in a velvet-lined box," the Mess said. After the Carleton victory, the Oles, perhaps let down, fell to St. John's 13–0. The loss enabled the Johnnies to tie St. Thomas for the league lead

Back on track the following week, the Vikings got 234 yards of offense from Saumer and a 45-yard interception return from center Lund en route to a

The new St. Olaf athletic field in 1930, yet to be named.

Dan Soli and Norman Nordstrand with the Goatrophy and the Philo Cup, 1931

26–0 victory over Gustavus, coached by George Myrum. St. Mary's became another shutout victim, going down 20–0. Saumer was lauded for his field generalship from the quarterback position, as well as for his punting and ball carrying. Droen, Newby, and Soli also stood out.

Stepping outside the conference for the annual clash with Luther, the Oles emerged winners 14–6 in a steady rain on a muddy field. Soli and Saumer tallied touchdowns, and Saumer passed to Tellekson for the second PAT.

In the season closer against Coach Frank Cleve's Concordia team that had already clinched the conference crown, the Oles prevailed 21–6. Soli scored twice. Saumer's kickoffs averaged 55 yards and one punt went for more than 60. Playing their final game for the Oles were Mel Hegdahl, Enoch Glesne, Lloyd Ellingson, Theodore Graber, Eiler Schiotz, Edmund Johnson, Lucius Lund, and Cecil Tellekson.

The *Messenger's* mythical all-state team had Ellingson at guard, Hegdahl at tackle, Droen at fullback, and Saumer at halfback on the first team and Irv Christenson at end, Iverson at guard, and Soli at fullback on the second team.

President Boe awarded the St. Olaf emblem to 25 squad members at the 13th annual banquet. Gracing the podium, in addition to the president, were coaches Christenson, Rufus Olson, and Cully Swanson, Dean J. Jorgen Thompson, captain-elect for 1932 Syl Saumer, and Ray Mohn, president of Mohn Printing Co., son of the college's first president.

In the following spring, Lloyd Ellingson and Al Droen were selected as Honor Athletes.

1931 Season Notes

Halsey Hall, writing in the *Minneapolis Journal,* reported that Ade had turned down an offer to play a home and home series with St. Mary's of California. Lack of a gate guarantee and lost class time were cited as reasons … Mark Almli was playing sensational semi-pro football for the Ironwood Polar Bears. The Ironwood newspaper described the ending of a game that Mark had dominated: "The game ended with Almli burlesquing the game, trying passes from behind his own goal line."[95] The Polar Bears came to Minneapolis to play the Phantom Athletic Club at St. Thomas.

1932

The 1932 season got off to a shaky start. Although Ade held a two-week spring practice session to evaluate candidates, plans for preseason fall drills before classes were to begin had to be abandoned. A few veterans, including Captain Norman Nordstrand and several local frosh, did return early and conducted their own drills. To add to the uncertainty, regular quarterback Eddie Gove had accepted an appointment to the U.S. Military Academy and didn't return.

When practice did begin, it was apparent there would be a solid line of Nordstrand, Summers, Iverson, Glesne, Adams, and two Christensons — Irv and Hal — moving out ahead of a backfield of Newby, Lecy, Soli, Ness, and Dahl. A few prep stars were also expected to contribute. Among them were Ken Kelsey, Don Anderson, and Henry Boldridge from Northfield, Johnson from Milan, Art Sand from Lake Mills, Iowa, Froiland from Viroqua, Wis., and John Kirkeby from Story City, Iowa.

The Vikings opened the season on a positive note, edging St. Thomas 14–12 in a night encounter in St. Paul. A crowd of 6,000 saw Irv Christenson open the scoring by tackling the Tommies' punter, "Wee" Walsh, for a safety. That turned out to be the margin of victory. Later, Newby returned a Walsh punt 55 yards for a touchdown and an 8–0 lead. The teams traded fourth-quarter touchdowns. Adams, Iverson, and Captain Nordstrand turned in stellar line play.

Frank Cleve's Concordia eleven was next on the list, and the Cobbers prevailed 13–7. It was a defensive struggle with Concordia penetrating the Oles' 20 only twice and the Vikings stalled at the four and the one. A 30-yard aerial from Dahl to Adams resulted in the Oles' only score.

Returning to winning ways the next week, St. Olaf shut out Augsburg 26–0, forcing the Auggies to resort to a passing game. Dahl, Soli, and Johnson scored on running plays for the Oles. Mickelson also ran well.

Carleton, having recently returned from a 57–0 defeat by Army, was next, and the Carls broke a three-year victory drought with a 9–0 win. The one touchdown came on a 69-yard drive. Newby was caught for a safety in the last few minutes. Neither Newby of St. Olaf nor Nordly of Carleton, heralded as the stars of the game, performed up to expectations.

Another three-year win streak went by the boards as Luther came to Northfield and went away with a 7–0 win on St. Olaf's Homecoming. The Norsemen's one touchdown came after a fumble recovery at the Ole 26 and a pass to the one. "Christenson was propelled over by the amassed Norsemen for the counter." Hanson of Luther and Eddie Johnson and Dan Soli of the Oles held a punting duel for a good part of the game.

In the last conference game of the season, Gustavus squeezed out a 3–0 triumph on a drop-kicked field goal by Mel Johnson from the 12-yard-line. Soli again gave an outstanding exhibition of punting. The loss left the Oles with a 2–2 conference mark for the season.

The Oles suffered their fourth consecutive shutout, bowing to St. Mary's 12–0 in a non-conference finale at Winona. A blocked punt deep in Ole territory led to St. Mary's first score, while snow, cold, and wind hampered the passing game.

Postseason all-conference honors, bestowed by the *Minneapolis Journal* and the *St. Paul Pioneer Press*, went to

five Oles — Norman Nordstrand, Ervin (crawling on the knees) Iverson, Harry Newby, Dan Lecy, and Hal Christenson. Twenty-one frosh received gold and blue sweaters (class colors) with 1936 across the chest. They included Henry Nicklasson, Arthur Sand, John Kirkeby, and Ovid Smedstad.

At the banquet concluding the 1933 season, President Boe presented letters to 26 of the 35-member squad. Twelve letter winners were expected to return for 1933 with Ralph (Pug) Summers elected captain. Rumor had it that the fabled Syl Saumer might return for his senior season. "The Football Trio" of Al Ness, Harold Christenson, and Dan Soli sang at the banquet. Ness received the Honor Athlete award.

1932 Season Notes

The backfield of Newby, Ness, Lecy, Soli, Dahl, and Santelman was considered "a better all-around group than the famous 1923 quartet of Swanson, Cleve, Fevold, and Christenson."[96] … The Sept. 20, 1932, *Messenger* reported the arrival of a future football candidate by the name of Swanson, who may follow in his "daddy's" footsteps.

The last issue of the 1932–33 *Messenger* speculated about the makeup of the next fall's squad: Syl Saumer had been back in school during the spring and would be eligible. Orv Dahl, who had been selling life insurance, would also return, along with veterans Glenn Adams, Whitey Leirfallom, Roald Glesne, Pug Summers (captain),

Art Sand, Henry Nicklasson, Kermit Anderson, and John Kirkeby.

In preparation for the 1933 season, Ade instituted a new procedure for spring drills. He divided his squad and had one group run plays he anticipated would be used by opponents in the upcoming season. The other group would use the Ole system. A game between the two would conclude the spring practice period. It appears the veterans were split evenly between the two groups.[97] Coaches were "Ozark" Nordstrand and "Big" Jensen for one squad and Irv Christenson and "Dynamite" Dan Soli for the other.

1933 — Rules Evolve

As the 1933 season approached, rules of the game continued to evolve. The penalty for clipping was reduced from 25 yards to 15 yards. Inbounds lines were moved to 10 yards from the sidelines to prevent out-of-bounds plays being used to get the ball into good position. As fall drills began, the tradition (or custom) of former players being hired as coaches continued. Coach Christenson's teammate and classmate, and now St. Olaf art department chair, Arne Flaten became Ade's assistant. Dan Soli, a very recent grad, was coach of the frosh. Saumer was a no-show; Eddie Fox, a Waldorf J.C. grad, was a good addition.

In a preseason tuneup scrimmage with the River Falls Normal 11, the Oles were stymied by a six-man line and could manage only a 6–6 tie.

The 1932 team, Norman Nordstrand, captain

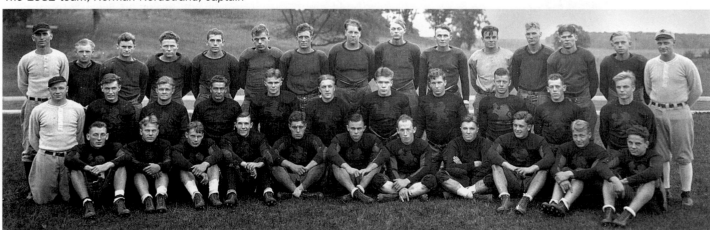

Al Ness, 1933 Honor Athlete,
All-state guard

1933 captain Ralph "Pug"
Summers conditions for the
upcoming season.

Saumer was back in harness. Kermit Anderson and John Kirkeby ran well.

After going down 6–0 to Superior Normal in the season opener, despite dominating for three quarters, St. Olaf roared back to pound Macalester 39–0 and give promise of a fine season to come. The Oles went on to spoil Luther's Homecoming 14–0 and Augsburg's Homecoming 27–7 and downed Concordia 25–12 in the season finale. In between, however, Christenson's men fell to Carleton 6–0 and, in a climactic battle, lost to St. Thomas 20–13.

In the Luther contest, Ade's offense, with a mix of reverse and shovel pass plays, piled up 309 yards from scrimmage and 18 first downs. "Luther scribes gave Bisbee and Halvorson credit for being the most sensational reserves to have played on their field."[98]

Carleton's, and that game's, only score came on a 60-yard punt return by Tag Senior, a nemesis of the Oles for several years. Captain Pug Summers, Glesne, Lund, and C. Johnson shone in the line for St. Olaf.

Heavily favored in their night game with Augsburg at Nicollet Park, the Oles had to dress for the game in the Jefferson Lines bus parked outside. Augsburg's only touchdown came after a blocked punt and just as the final whistle sounded. Glesne and Lund again starred for St. Olaf.

In the St. Thomas contest, the two evenly matched teams traded touchdowns, and the Oles narrowly missed out when a fourth-down, Anderson to Saumer pass was ruled out of bounds at the "one-yard, one-quarter-inch line."

Saumer ended his career with his most spectacular performance in the victory over Concordia. It was the final game also for Captain Summers, Glesne, Lund, and Santelman. Glesne was credited with being the most effective lineman on the field. The Oles finished third in the conference at 3–1, but led in scoring with 102 points. The *Messenger's* all-conference team had Glesne at tackle and Saumer at halfback.

1933 Season Notes

In the off-season following the 1933 campaign, Syl Saumer signed a contract with the Boston Braves of the National Football League and also served as track coach at St. Olaf. The Braves had finished third in the league the previous season and were expected to contend with the champion Chicago Bears the next time around. Saumer subsequently disappeared from the Northfield scene … Harry Newby, the Northfielder who had been the conference 100 and 220 champion in 1932, took over as student coach of track … Cully Swanson, assistant football coach and head baseball coach, resigned to accept a coaching position at Marshall High School in Minneapolis.

1934

A squad of 38, including 11 lettermen, reported for fall practice in '34. Among them was Kenneth "Shine" Brown, a scatback from Waseca, the first African American football player at St. Olaf. Brown earned extra money shining shoes in downtown Northfield, hence the nickname. Orv Dahl had been added to the coaching staff to help Dan Soli with the frosh. Arne Flaten continued to assist Ade with the varsity. Returning veterans included Captain Kermy Anderson, Abe Fox, Harold Vikre, Paul Halvorson, and Mayo Bisbee in the backfield, with Art Sand, 190-pound center, and end Van Johnson in the line.

Forecasters were predicting more scoring for the 1934 season due to a few rule changes, the most significant calling for an incomplete pass in the end zone to be only loss of down rather than a touchback. Because of the previous rule, teams had been reluctant to pass into the end zone, causing the running game to predominate. The rule change encouraged more passing.

In a rough, ragged, but hard-fought Friday night season opener in St. Paul, the Vikings eked out a 2–0 victory over St. Thomas, the margin a safety early in the second quarter. The win was costly as Chuck Nadlehoffer, passer and blocking back, and tackle Whitey Lierfallom were lost to injury. Lierfallom was replaced by Oved Smedstad, who played well. Nadlehoffer played the whole game but became seriously ill after the contest and was hospitalized in St. Paul. He had suffered a concussion. A week later, the *Messenger* reported that Nadlehoffer had suffered a relapse and was in critical condition with "a blood clot on the brain which has partially paralyzed his right side."[99]

Back at home the following week, a crippled Ole team battled Macalester's "trackmen" to a 7–7 deadlock on a beautiful but windy day. The Ole score was set up by a "beautiful off-tackle spinner" that shook "Popeye" Shirley loose for 70 yards. "Art Sand was a mountain of strength at center."

An editorial sports writer for the *Messenger* criticized St. Olaf's "one-man pass attack" as "a problem that must be faced." [An interesting commentary on one of the game's many changes. In the early days, it was common for all the backs and some of the linemen to throw the football. So, the student writer may have felt the coach wasn't taking advantage of all his weapons. In the modern era, when the quarterback, with very rare exceptions, is the only passer, it seems a strange comment.]

Ade viewed the upcoming game with Concordia in Moorhead as a toss up. The Cobbers boasted outstanding fullback Bob Fritz and whatever advantage might have accrued from their coach, former Ole ace Frank Cleve, being familiar with the Ole system. The combination was more than enough, as the Cobbers scored three times in the first half and went on to win 19–7.

The worm turned the following week, as the Oles, back at home, rolled up 26 points in the first quarter and went on to down cellar-dweller Augsburg 44–8. Froiland scored the first touchdown on a blocked punt, and Fox had a 65-yard touchdown run. The victory gave the Oles a second conference win against a loss and a tie, good for second place.

Seeking revenge for losses the previous two seasons, the Oles traveled to Carleton to try to improve the series record, which stood at 5–8 in favor of the Knights. But it was not to be. Tag Senior, Carleton quarterback, returned a Kirkeby punt 80 yards for a score and passed for another as the Carls pulled off a 12–0 shutout. Informed a short time before the game that his mother had died, Art Sand remained and played the entire game.

Homecoming brought better fortunes, as the Oles turned back Luther 13–0 before 4,000 spectators. Kirkeby and Fox scored on a muddy field. Chuck Nadelhoffer, who suffered the serious concussion in the St. Thomas game several weeks before, was on the sidelines — back to school for the first time since his injury. The following March, St. Olaf and St. Thomas played a benefit basketball game, the proceeds going to help defray Nadelhoffer's medical expenses.

The season finale had the Oles facing a heavier, more experienced and powerful South Dakota State team. The Oles hoped to repeat their 1930 upset, but the Jackrabbits eked out a 14–6 win. Fox over right guard was the lone Ole tally.

Looking back on the 1934 season, a *Messenger* writer noted that "even the most critical observer must admit that it was a fairly successful one. No team really beat the Oles decisively."[100]

At the postseason banquet, Art Sand, all-state center, was elected captain for 1935. Twenty-two men were awarded letters and Nadelhoffer, by unanimous vote, was awarded a monogram. President Boe delivered a long dissertation on self-acceptance.

1934 Season Notes

A profile in the Oct. 25, 1934, *Messenger* by "Rock Salt" described Art Sand: "The blushing center enjoys bull sessions, likes banana pie, and coaching a winning football team is an ambition." … A May issue of the *Messenger* following the 1934 season listed names of 50 grads, faculty, and friends who had joined the St. Olaf Lions, an organization that was working to wipe out the debt on the "new" field.

Among the 50 were Newell Nelson, P.O. Holland, Peter Fossum, L.W. Boe, Howell Skoglund, J. Jorgen Thompson, Howard Hong, Ella Hjertaas, Agnes Larson, Gertrude Hillebo, Bessie Gulbrandson, and C.R. Swanson … A first annual football field day was held April 13. More than 14 prep athletes from Minnesota accepted invitations to participate in a day of football drills culminating in one or two games. Medals were awarded and the day ended with a banquet.[101]

The 1935 championship team, Art Sand, captain (front row, fourth from the right)

Van Johnson, 1935 Honor
Athlete, halfback

John Kirkeby, 1937 Honor
Athlete, halfback

1935

Twenty-four men, led by captain and center Art Sand, turned out for drills in September of 1935. Kirkeby, "Shine" Brown, Fortier, Jake Nelson, and converted tackle Sherm Brown were the backfield candidates. Tackles Leirfallom and Smedstad were veteran linemen returning.

Sixty-eight frosh reported to Coach Mayo Bisbee '34. Everett Nyman, 6'1", 190 pounds, from Fergus Falls, was an early standout. As was the usual practice, the freshmen scrimmaged the varsity in their first practice. Ade claimed it made the high school "stars" humble and easier to work with.

"Shine" Brown was an unfortunate casualty of an early scrimmage. He suffered a season-ending knee injury that resulted in a paralysis of the lower leg.

In the opener, Sand, as expected, was a tower of strength at center. Jake Nelson, in his first appearance in a St. Olaf uniform scored in the first quarter and the Oles went on to defeat conference rival St. Mary's 12–0. Nicklasson, who replaced an injured John Kirkeby, scored in the final period.

The first of four non-conference foes, Wisconsin Superior, dealt the Oles a 31–0 setback in the second game. Shorty Thorson's kick returns were one of the few bright spots as the Oles failed to threaten the Superior goal.

On the road for the second week, the Oles challenged the Luther Norsemen and came out on the short end of a 7–0 score. Virtually the only Ole threat stemmed from a blocked punt by Leirfallom on the Luther 23. Kirkeby ran the ball to the three, where the Oles ran out of gas.

Frustration reigned the following week as the Oles went after their first win over Carleton since 1931. Despite moving the ball at will in the middle of the field and holding a 14 to 4 advantage in first downs, the Oles went down 6–0. The lone Carleton counter came on a 60-yard interception return by Carleton's Ken Heacock. [Heacock was to become a longtime teacher and wrestling coach at Northfield High School.]

As the Oles prepped for the Concordia clash the following week, the *Messenger*

remembered the 1921 game in which St. Olaf won 97–0. Ade had scored four times in that game, and the Cobbers' current coach, Frank Cleve, had scored three touchdowns and kicked 13 of 14 points after for the Oles.[102]

With Sherm Brown and Kirkeby running behind Sand, Leirfallom, Smedstad, and Holmstrom, St. Olaf handled the Cobbers 20–6.

The scent of a conference championship fired the Oles to play their best game of the season, downing St. Thomas 18–0 to clinch the crown with an unbeaten conference slate. Fortier passed to Holmstrom for one touchdown; Sand set up a second with a fumble recovery, and Kirkeby ran 88 yards with an intercepted pass for the third.

By conference ruling, the Oles were credited with a win over Augsburg by forfeit after the Auggies withdrew from participation in football as an intercollegiate sport.

The glow from the conference championship was dulled somewhat the following week, as the Oles were trounced 34–0 by the South Dakota State Jackrabbits. State's speed and deception, which had proved the undoing of the University of Wisconsin Badgers earlier in the season, were too much for the Oles.

Postseason honors went to Leirfallom, Sand, Kirkeby, and Nelson (*Messenger* all-conference) and Kirkeby, all-state. Kirkeby succeeded Sand as captain for 1936. The student senate voted to award gold footballs to team members. Everett Nyman, a freshman, was awarded a varsity letter based on his participation in non-conference games. Sports journalist Halsey Hall was the speaker at the first annual press dinner.

1935 Season Notes

Cleve moves on. Frank Cleve, the Ole flash of the early '20s, who had been coaching at Concordia, left to teach and coach at South High School in Minneapolis. During his tenure at Concordia, Cleve's teams had won two football titles and one basketball crown … On Manitou Heights, skiing was installed as a full-time winter sport under the direction of Lloyd Ellingson

… director of facilities John Berntsen was in charge of constructing a ski jump on Pop Hill … It had been a banner year all around for Ole athletics with championships in football, track, tennis, and golf.

From four candidates (Nicklasson, Leirfallom, Holmstrom, and Sand), Henry Nicklasson was named Honor Athlete … The St. Olaf cagers were edged by a point, 32–31, by the Harlem Globetrotters in a benefit game for "Shine" Brown[103] … One of the features of the annual Lettermen's Club program was an exhibition wrestling match between Whitey Leirfallom and Caifson Johnson, the University of Minnesota's Big Ten champion …

As the fall 1936 season approached, the *Messenger* listed nine former Ole athletes who would be coaching in the fall: Art Sand, Rushford; Roy Gilbertson, Minneota; Henry Nicklasson, Milan; Oved Smedstad, Clara City; Evert Holmstrom, North Branch; Vern Anderson, Reder; Norman Hoyme, Osseo, Wis.; Walter Gimmestad, Barrett, and Everette Jarvinen, Humboldt.[104]

1936

With two weeks to prepare for the season opener against St. Mary's, the squad reported on Labor Day. Erling Kloster at end, Nyman at tackle, and Gay Pitts, center, were veterans in the line along with Captain Kirkeby, Shorty Thorson, Bun Fortier, and speedy Jake

Nelson in the backfield. More than 50 frosh reported to coaches Orv Dahl and Lloyd Ellingson

Led by only five returning lettermen, the "Golden" Vikings (new uniforms) displayed midseason form in trouncing St. Mary's 30–6. Kirkeby, the all-state fullback, took up where he left off the previous season, breaking loose early in the game for a 60-yard sprint to the 26-yard line. Fortier passed to Norm Anderson for the score. Two touchdowns by Kirkeby and one each by sophomores Rosenthal and Peterson followed. All 28 squad members saw action.

A recovered fumble by sophomore tackle Ev Nyman resulted in a score and set the tone for a 33–0 victory over Macalester. St. Olaf's speedy backs — Nelson, Rosenthal, Peterson, Heibel, and Kirkeby — took advantage of excellent field conditions and all scored. Kirkeby contributed outstanding punting as well, one quick kick going 75 yards to the Mac two-yard line.

"High Tech" Arrives

Two significant events relating to the football program were noted by *Messenger* sports editor Ruben Gornitzka in an Oct. 6, 1936, column. "Through the efforts of Milford Jensen, manager of WCAL, an amplifying system will be used at all football and basketball games …" It was used for the first time in the Macalester game.

Gornitzka also reported that "Donald Eastman, St. Olaf's movie camera man, …" would film three or four football games.

The first films must have been shot at field level with a hand-held camera. The column goes on to note that if the results are satisfactory, a telephoto lens "may" be added which would make possible filming from a fixed position at a higher level. A film of a portion of the Carleton game of 1936 is the only evidence of this early motion picture venture.

A strong St. John's team knocked the Oles from the unbeaten ranks with a 13–6 win. St. Olaf escaped a shutout in the fourth quarter when a blocked punt followed by a quick pitch to Kirkeby led to the Ole score. Jake Nelson incurred a season-ending shoulder injury. Kirkeby had racked up 250 yards in three games.

The loss to St. John's proved to be the first of three. Carleton downed the Oles 26–7 and then Gustavus prevailed 13–0. In the final game of the season, the Oles and the La Crosse Teachers College squad, champions of the Wisconsin Conference, battled to a scoreless tie. The Oles also played Luther during the 1936 season, winning 6–0, but there is no game summary available.

The lateral pass was big in the Carleton encounter. A double lateral halfback pass was good for Carleton's

The 1936 team, John Kirkeby, captain

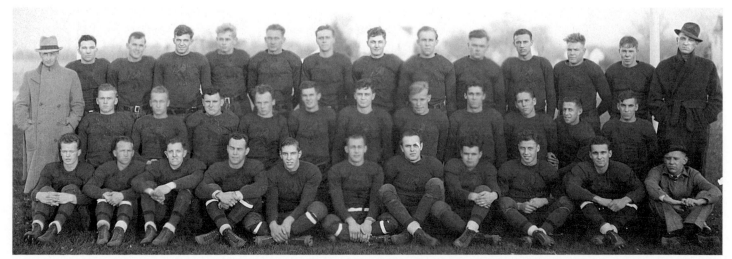

A 1936 PAT attempt with Thorson hill in the background

first score, while a double lateral culminating in a run resulted in the Oles' only touchdown. Forced to leave the contest because of injury, Kirkeby was met with a handshake from Larson of Carleton "amid an ovation from the entire crowd."[105]

Kirkeby sat out the Gustavus game because of the knee injury suffered against Carleton. Nyman, Schwake, and Boe contributed outstanding line play, while Storaasli, Anderson, and Baldwin were targets for passes by Thorson.

The *Messenger* noted that during the 1936 season, the Oles had played five conference champion teams — Gustavus and St. John's of the MIAC, Carleton of the Midwest, Luther of the Iowa Conference, and La Crosse of the Wisconsin Conference. The La Crosse game was the final performance for Kirkeby, Gaylord Pitts, Olaf Storaasli, and Jake Nelson.[106]

First-team all-state selections were Kirkeby, Nyman at tackle, and Pitts at center. Torgerson was named at guard on the second team.

1936 Season Notes

Cully Swanson was named head basketball and baseball coach at Augsburg, while continuing to coach football at Marshall High in Minneapolis … Head football coach Ade Christenson had a semi-emergency appendectomy in December 1936. Coincidentally, Myrtle Spande of the women's athletic department and basketball mentor Carl Iverson were in Fairview Hospital in Minneapolis at the same time for the same ailment. While Ade was in the hospital visiting Carl, he complained of discomfort that had been bothering him for some time and was examined on the spot. It was determined he had appendicitis and underwent surgery the next day …

The student body named John Kirkeby Honor Athlete for 1936–37. Kirkeby had been named athletic coach at Preston, Minn., High School on Jan. 25, 1937. "Having finished his course work, Kirkeby took over the Preston basketball coaching duties the next day."[107] … Kenneth (Shine) Brown had surgery on a damaged nerve in order to regain full use of his right leg. The nerve was injured in a preseason scrimmage in 1935 … Carl Iverson, assistant football coach and head basketball coach, resigned to go into business in La Crosse … Norm Anderson and Erling Koster, both ends, were elected co-captains for 1937 …

At its spring meeting, the Minnesota conference enacted two important changes. Transfers from other four-year schools were to be eligible for intercollegiate athletics after one semester of attendance. Transfers from junior colleges were eligible immediately. A round robin football schedule was adopted. It would consist of five conference games and go into effect with the 1938 season …

At the conclusion of the spring practice intrasquad game between Koster's Bear Cats and Anderson's Pole Cats, *Messenger* sports writer Les Fossil concluded that the Oles had "a collection of outstanding backs, but mediocre new talent in the line." Line returnees Ev Nyman and Schwake presumably were not included in the "new" category … Phi Gamma Rho society sponsored a spring banquet observing Ade Christenson's 10 years as a coach at St. Olaf and a farewell to Coach Carl Iverson. George Myrum of Gustavus was the featured speaker.[108]

1937

Forty gridders reported to coaches Christenson, Kippy Gilbertson, and Endre Anderson for the 1937 season. Gilbertson had replaced Carl Iverson as line coach and head coach of basketball and baseball. Endre, who had coached the Oles to championships in 1923 and 1924, was serving as a volunteer.

Everett Nyman, who had lettered as a freshman because of his play in non-conference games, led a group of linemen that included co-captains Kloster and Anderson, Melvin Schwake, Jack Baldwin, Aurele Torgerson, Rudy Ramseth, Earl Thorpe, and Waldorf

J.C. star tackle Arling Anderson. Shorty Thorson, John Rosendahl, Glen Nelson, Gerhard Peterson, and transfer Wilbur LaBeau were the leading backs reporting.

Thirty frosh reported to Coach Bunny Johnson and got their usual dose of humility by scrimmaging the varsity in their first practice.

The squad started the season on a winning note, downing Wisconsin Stout 27–0. Rosendahl, Nelson, and Wilke scored and all 35 players saw action. Peterson, Nyman and Thorpe were cited for outstanding play. First downs were 13 to 2 and yardage 212 to 19.[109]

That first game proved to be not a predictor of things to come as the "Golden Vikings" went down for the next three weeks — 6–0 to Macalester, 13–7 to Concordia, and 19–6 to Luther.

The Macalester Scots used only 12 men in upsetting St. Olaf. Only Rudy Ramseth's outstanding punting kept the Scots from scoring more. Joe Rognstad, St. Olaf '37, topped his alma mater in his first year as coach at Concordia. Walt Comer scored for the Oles in the fourth period, but two long runs by Concordia in the third made the difference. The return of captains Kloster and Anderson was not enough to salvage the Luther contest. What spark there was for the Oles was furnished by LeBeau and two speedy frosh, Alvan Ose and Milton Nesse.

Ev Nyman incurred a knee injury, which would keep him out of the upcoming Carleton game.

In what the 1938 *Viking* termed "the best game of the year," the Carls prevailed 14–6. Freshman Ose was the offensive star for St. Olaf. Arling Anderson replaced Nyman at tackle.

An open date on the schedule was filled by a game between the Ole frosh and Waldorf J.C. The Oles came out on top 31–12.

Coach Joe Hutton's favored Hamline team supplied the opposition at Homecoming. The Oles scored early and outgained the Pipers 362 yards to 49, but had to settle for a 6–6 tie. Hamline scored in the final two minutes to gain the tie.

A similar scenario played out in the season's final game against St. Thomas. Rosendahl scored in the second quarter and the Oles held a statistical edge, 230 yards to 100, but had to settle for a tie on an unusual play. St. Olaf blocked the conversion kick after the Hamline touchdown, but "members of both teams wandered off" and Jensen, a St. Thomas tackle picked up the ball and crossed the goal for the point.

1937 Season Notes

Four seniors ended their St. Olaf careers: Co-captains Anderson and Kloster, Jack Baldwin, and Shorty

Thorson … Rudy Ramseth, Ev Nyman, and John Rosendahl were selected for the *Messenger* All-State team … The *Associated Press* accorded Nyman honorable mention on its nationwide Little All-America team … Nyman and Ramseth were elected captains for 1938 … Ramseth was also the "ace tenor" in the St. Olaf Choir.

Ade Institutes Grading

In the spring of 1938, Coach Christenson originated and put into practice a new coaching technique, anticipating a procedure that was to become commonplace in later years. He devised a plan to evaluate and grade the abilities of each player in tackling and open field running. "In so doing," Ade said, "I believe we can make the men who are practicing more conscious of their individual faults and … improve them greatly in the matter of football fundamentals."[110] He also conducted a quarterback school each Monday during the spring.

An enthusastic group of footballers looked forward to the spring practice period of four weeks, which culminated in a game with River Falls Normal on April 12. River Falls and St. Olaf had played each other five years before. A freshman, Milt Nesse, was to direct the team at quarterback. Alvan Ose also was slated to be a starter. A headline

Coach Ade Christenson (kneeling) huddles with his football squad, circa 1936.

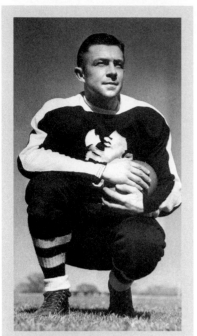

Roy "Shorty" Thorson,
1938 Honor Athlete

Harold Refling,
1941 Honor Athlete

story on the sports page of the April 12, 1938, *Messenger* reported that St. Olaf won the game 20–6. "It was unique as far as a regulation game goes in that both coaches stayed on the field directing their protégés' efforts," the reporter said.[111]

The junior class elected Roy "Shorty" Thorson Honor Athlete. In a *Messenger* sports column, Rambling Around, "Bunny" Johnson questioned Concordia's plan to take a three-game trip to Canada prior to the 1938 season. "No use wasting your energy in Canada," he said.

1938

Fifty varsity candidates reported to head coach Ade and assistant "Kippy" Gilbertson. [Meanwhile, the *Messenger* reported that former coach Endre Anderson was a candidate for political office as a member of the Democratic-Farmer-Labor (DFL) party.]

A good nucleus of veterans was back — Ramseth and Nyman, guard and tackle, respectively; Aurele Torgerson, guard; Rosendahl and LeBeau, running backs; Earl Thorpe, center; Arling Anderson and Paul Wilke, ends, and Gerhard Huggenvik, guard. Thirty frosh reported to Coach Jack Baldwin, among them Vern Zahn, Kermit Wolf, Andrew Droen, and Conrad Thompson.

Following three weeks of practice and with apparent optimism, the Golden Vikings opened against Macalester. The starting lineup had Norm Anderson and Paul Wilke at ends, Ev Nyman and Melvin Schwake at tackles, Rudy Ramseth and "Tiger" Torgerson at guards, Earl Thorpe at center, Wilbert LeBeau at fullback, John Rosendahl and Alvan Ose at halfbacks, and Milton Nesse at quarterback.

Coach Christenson used two complete teams in defeating Macalester 27–12 on Manitou Field before a good opening day crowd. Ose had a 50-yard run for a touchdown. Rosendahl and LeBeau also ran well, making for a formidable attack, though Nesse was sidelined by injury. Ted Bogda was cited for strong play.

Fortunes reversed the following week. In what some called one of the hardest-fought games in many years, St. John's scored late on a 50-yard pass and run play to eke out a 19–14 win. Rosendahl

intercepted three Johnnie passes but it wasn't enough. Receiving recognition for their play, in addition to Rosendahl, were Ramseth, Nyman, Schwake, Torgerson, Bogda, and Arling Anderson — along with sophomore James Trebbin, who replaced the injured LeBeau.

The Oles rebounded the following week, handling St. Mary's 28–9. Arling Anderson set the tone, blocking a punt and recovering for a touchdown — the first of three first-quarter scores. A 71-yard run set up another counter, and a pass from Rosendahl to Ose, who then lateraled to Nesse climaxed a third drive. *[Author's comment: Sounds like the hook and ladder play.]* St. Olaf outgained St. Mary's 307 to 174. Note: "The new black and white outfits of the Oles are sure snappy looking."

Optimism prevailed for a break in the seven-game winless spell versus the Carls as the Oles prepared for the annual Goat game. For the season, the Maize and Blue were in the midst of a three-game losing streak. Pre-game wisemen suggested that "superior Ole line strength could spell the difference since both teams appeared to have speedy, shifty backs."[112] Game day brought decidedly subpar playing conditions: a sloppy, slushy, snow-covered field and a 30-mile gale blowing across Laird Field from the north.

Despite the wretched conditions affecting play (Oles threw three times, Carleton, once), St. Olaf picked up 15 first downs and 282 yards and snapped the Carls' win string with a 6–2 victory. Rosendahl's 27-yard run was the longest of the day in a game that may have been his best. Trebbin was injured and lost for the upcoming Hamline game.

"Noose the Norsemen" was the Piper Homecoming slogan, but it didn't prevent the Oles from gaining their third conference win, 12–7. Jerome Olson, filling in for Trebbin and LeBeau, was the outstanding back on the field. Torgerson at guard also played outstanding football, as did Tom Tucker in his first start at tackle. Ose suffered a broken arm.

Playing their own Homecoming the following week ("Lacquer Luther"), the Oles played perhaps their best game of the season, winning 12–0. LeBeau and Trebbin, back and teaming with Rosendahl, made for a strong running attack during the second-half snowstorm.

Euphoria from the Luther triumph and hopes for sharing second place in the conference went by the board when an underdog St. Thomas team fought its way to a 7–0 victory in the last game of the season. The visiting Oles had a shot at victory late in the game when runs by Rosendahl, LeBeau, and Trebbin brought the ball to the one where the Tommies held.

A host of Oles won postseason honors. Twenty-seven were awarded letters. Everett Nyman, tackle, and Aurele Torgerson, guard, were named to the *Associated Press* All-state first team — Nyman for the second season. Guard Rudy Ramseth and halfback John Rosendahl made the second team, while Arling Anderson and Paul Wilke, ends; Alvan Ose, halfback, and Milt Nesse, quarterback, received honorable mention. Seniors who completed their careers as Ole gridders included

Nyman, Ramseth, Torgerson, Anderson, LeBeau, Rosendahl, Frank Barry, Walter Comer, Fritz Rolvaag, Donald Herfindahl, Gerhard Peterson, Norman Anderson, and Jerule Kise.

The Ole line, which had earned praise throughout the season, was rated strongest of the opponents they had faced by the St. John's squad. In a letter, the Johnnies noted, "The Ole line was the best they had seen in their four years of football at St. John's.[113]

Professor Peter Fossum "was again the principal speaker" at the season-ending banquet. Thorpe was elected captain for 1939 and student body president Ed Sovik was emcee.

1938 Season Notes

Lloyd Ellingson '30, former footballer and Olympic skier, coach and faculty member, was the Dunn County (Wis.) attorney in Menomonie … The Nov. 15, 1938, *Messenger* reported the tragic deaths of Gustavus Coach George Myrum and two of his players when their bus crashed into the back of a

truck near Belle Plaine. They were returning from the season's final game against St. Norbert in DePere, Wis.

Spring drills started in the gymnasium in March. With only one veteran lineman returning — Earl Thorpe, the captain — and his "dream" backfield halved by the graduation of LeBeau and Rosendahl, Ade was looking intently for replacements. Jim Trebbin, Milt Nesse, and Jerome Olson were with the squad, but Al Ose was not in school.

Assistant football coach (line) Clifford (Kippy) Gilbertson resigned effective June 1 after two years on the staff. He had also been head coach of basketball and baseball. Gilbertson cited the "worry and uncertainty that is connected with the life of a college coach." He said he intended to enter private business.

Gilbertson's comments indicate that the pressures felt by college coaches are by no means a recent phenomenon and can be as strong in the "small" college as in the major universities.

Ade Christenson (in hat) "pointedly" gives halftime instructions, 1937.

1939 Season Notes

Milt Nesse was elected captain for 1940 … Ev Nyman, in his first season of coaching at Milan High School, had an undefeated grid team and an 18–1 season in basketball … Bernie Cole '28, finished his third consecutive undefeated season (22–0) as football coach at Marshall High School.

1940 Season Notes

The Sept. 27, 1940, issue of the *Messenger* included a picture of Clyde Hill's bugle brigade — approximately 42 strong — in formation on Manitou Field. "The band is expected to wear, for the first time, gold satin jackets purchased with funds from the student body and administration."

After the close of the 1940 season, Jim Trebbin signed a tryout contract with the Chicago Cardinals of the National Football League. After the tryout camp, Jim played fullback for the Milwaukee Chiefs of the American Professional League.

In the same issue of the *Messenger* that noted Gilbertson's resignation (April 18, 1939), Head Coach Christenson announced that Arthur Grangaard had been hired to replace Gilbertson. Art Grangaard had been a three-sport letterman at Luther and was completing work on a master's degree at the University of Minnesota. His appointment would be effective in the fall.

1939

Forty grid candidates reported on Sept. 11, the opening day of the fall term. With three weeks of one-a-day practices scheduled, Ade had long sessions. The *Messenger* reported "five-hour practice periods," beginning at three in the afternoon and finishing around 7:30 or 8 o'clock under lights strung up behind Agnes Mellby Hall.[114] For a number of years in this era, for some unknown reason, there were no preseason drills, and Ade obviously felt the long sessions were necessary. Preseason drills resumed in 1941.

Captain Earl Thorpe was shifted from center to tackle to take Nyman's spot and to team with Mel Schwake at the other tackle. It was Schwake's third year as a starter; Nolan Dugan took Thorpe's place at center. Wilke and Bogda were at the ends. "Big" Jerome Olson (200 pounds), Jim Trebbin, Milt Nesse, Al Ose, "Pug" Lund, and Walt Comer — all veterans — were the backfield candidates. Forty freshmen were also working out.

In the season opener on the road, the Oles outplayed highly touted St. Thomas but came up short, losing 7–0. The attack misfired three times inside the 10-yard line, while the Tommies capitalized on their only scoring chance. Bogda's left-footed punts kept St. Thomas in poor field position much of the game. Seven Oles played the full 60 minutes with reserves used only at center, right halfback, and the two guard positions.

The home opener was a good outing for the "Ademen," as they whipped Hamline 25–13. Bob Downing, a 130-pound transfer from Itasca J.C., replaced the injured Ose and teamed with the pile-driving fullback Jerome Olson. The pair of them ran behind Milt Nesse, "one of the best blocking backs in the conference," according to a

Messenger writer in the issue of Sept. 10, 1939. Nesse played the entire game.

With Trebbin still out, but Ose back in the lineup, the Oles traveled to Decorah to take on Luther, the defending Iowa Conference champions. In a bitter battle with a spectacular ending, the Vikings edged the Norse 3–0.

A stubborn five-man defensive line anchored by Schwake at tackle and Dugan at center and with Nesse backing up was largely responsible for the shutout.

The Oct.17 *Messenger* described the "storybook" finish: "Nolan Dugan, the Ole center, set up the game-winning play when he intercepted a Luther pass and returned it 25 yards to the Norse 15. Two cracks at the line failed to gain an inch. With the running attack stopped cold, Coach Ade Christenson, in a desperate attempt to score, sent Clarence Olsen in to try a field goal. Calmly, 'Clar' dropped back and [dropkicked] the precious three points from the 27-yard line at a difficult angle from the left side of the field. In the remaining seconds of play, Luther had just enough time to receive the kickoff."

The story of Clarence Olson, the hero, is the stuff of legend. He had been out for football for four years, but had had little playing time. With extensive practice before and after the regular squad drills, he developed into a good dropkicker, but it wouldn't be until this game that his skill would provide the margin of victory.

With a close win following a narrow loss, it appeared the Ole season was on an upswing, but the next week, a fighting Macalester team struck back in the closing minutes to wrest a 7–6 win from Ole clutches. The Scots' score came on a 76-yard, five-first-down drive keyed by an effective passing attack. The Oles had scored late in the first period when Jerome Olson intercepted a pass and then took it in himself on a plunge. A *Messenger* writer wondered editorially whether a price was being paid for consistent lack of substitution. Seven or eight men had been playing entire games.

A well-rested Carleton squad, led by 152-pound halfback Richard Raiter, was the following week's focus. An added incentive was the fact that the goat had "mistakenly" remained on the Carleton campus after the previous season's 6–2 Ole victory.

A strong second-half comeback was not enough for the Oles as Carleton recaptured the goat with an 18–6 win. An 88-yard kickoff return following the Oles' lone score in the third period proved decisive. Bogda, Steffins, and Wilke turned in good games. Schwake and Nesse starred on both offense and defense, playing in their fifth straight 60-minute game.

The 1939 Homecoming game against Joe Rognstad's Concordia squad marked the final home appearance for 13 players. The Oles appeared headed for certain defeat, but a fourth-quarter pass from Bob Downing to Paul Wilke and a Clarence Olson dropkick conversion salvaged a 7–7 tie. It was a moral victory for a lighter, scrappier Cobber team that outplayed the Oles for three quarters.

In the first half of the Gustavus game the next week, St. Olaf looked like the ball club they had hoped to be all season. They led 7–0 at intermission. But then, with Little All-American Russ Buckley leading the charge, the Swedes roared back to win 21–7. Mel Schwake was a standout in the line, finishing the season having played 60 minutes in all seven games.

Schwake and Nesse were placed on the *Messenger* All-Conference team, and Jerome Olson made the *United Press* All-State team.

1940

"St. Olaf will face one of the toughest schedules it has undertaken in the last 10 years," was the preseason assessment as Coach Ade Christenson and his gridders prepared for the 1940 campaign.[115] A dozen lettermen, including Nesse, Trebbin, Downing, Olson, Bogda, Dugan, Grossman, Reding, and Steffins began practice Sept. 9. The "gold dust twins," a Mutt and Jeff combination (Bob Downing at 135 and Jim Trebbin at 195), were counted on to lead the running attack.

A preseason shoulder injury put veteran center Nolan Dugan out for the season; sophomore Andy Droen stepped in to fill the void at the pivot. The backfield had Nesse, Downing, Trebbin, and second semester freshman Martin Nabo. Ade had developed a few new variations in his double wing attack, and Nabo — a good passer — was expected to complement a strong running game.

As it turned out, neither preseason enthusiasm nor the marching band *[see sidebar]* could make up for a plague of injuries and an unusually tough schedule. The Oles went winless in seven games for the first time.

In the opener, a heavier and stronger St. Mary's team scored a 13–6 victory. Droen at center, Nesse, and Bob Viall, a sophomore from Northfield, were cited for good games. A Luther team, out for revenge for the previous

season's last-minute 3–0 loss, uncorked a potent passing attack and took advantage of Ole fumbles to win by a touchdown, 12–6. Trebbin and Downing keyed the Ole running game.

The Concordia Cobbers came to town the following week and handed the Oles a 7–0 Homecoming setback. Downing went down with a knee injury.

A pattern developed that held up throughout the season: The Oles played stubbornly, and at times well, but they were losing by a touchdown.

Carleton posted a 13–6 win in the Goat game. Title-bound St. Thomas won by 26–20. The only teams to manage more than a touchdown margin were St. John's, 19–0, and Gustavus, 20–6.

Against Carleton, the Oles held Dick Raiter in check except for one pass play and scored on a fourth-period drive, which included a pass from Nabo to Bogda, a good run by Trebbin, and a reverse with Earle Green scoring. In the St. John's game, the Oles fumbled four times inside the Johnnies' five-yard line. Sieveke, Trebbin, and Droen were standouts.

Crippled by injury, the Oles nevertheless played St. Thomas to a standstill, leading 13–7 before the Tommies roared back. In the final minutes, passes from Nabo to Sieveke and Bogda brought the ball to the one, and Nesse scored.

It was a tough season for the fans, too. The *Messenger* noted that, "One

The 1939 team, Earl Thorpe, captain

1940 Season Notes

The banquet was Ade's last appearance before leaving for his summer lake home at Northome. Ade had been granted a year's leave of absence to regain his health, and he and his family were to spend the winter and spring of 1941 at their summer home. Ade had incurred an eye injury the previous spring while fishing in Canada. Recovery did not go as expected and when he found it almost impossible to carry on his schedule of teaching and administration, the college, following an eye surgeon's recommendation, granted a leave of absence …

1941 Captain Andy Droen

hundred fifty fans stayed throughout the game (Gustavus) which was played in miserable conditions."[116]

Ray Farness, in a *Messenger* editorial, took issue with the "beefing" about the team and season from "its own student body." He pointed out the close scores and effort put forth by players and coaches during an injury-plagued season.

Ted Bogda, end, and Milt Nesse, quarterback, were selected on the all-conference second team, and Jim Trebbin, halfback, received honorable mention. Nolan Dugan, the center who missed the entire 1940 season because of a shoulder injury, was given honorable mention all-state status by both *Associated Press* and *United Press*.

At the season-ending banquet, 26 men received letters, and Andy Droen and Floyd Knutson were elected co-captains for the 1941 season. Maynard Iverson, the student body president, was emcee at the banquet, and both "Whitey" Leirfallom and Coach Christenson spoke.

1941

During Ade's absence *[see sidebar]*, Art Grangaard served as interim athletic director as well as head coach of basketball and baseball. Earl Thorpe, who recently had been appointed to the physical education department faculty, conducted spring football drills.

Ade's health responded to a daily routine of physical exercise and the absence of teaching and administrative responsibilities, and he and his family returned to Northfield in the fall of 1941.

For the first time in five years, the squad reported for preseason practice prior to the opening of the school year. Thirty varsity candidates reported to Ade and Art Grangaard on Sept. 8, among them Marshall "Mush" Haugen, Elton Lehrke, Mahlan LeBlanc, Martin Nabo, John Dahl, and Stan Tostengard. Forty-five freshman aspirants were greeted later by Coach Earl Thorpe, who had been retained on the staff to coach the yearlings. Their number included Harold Poppitz, a 212-pound fullback, Howie Rose, Wayne Dietz, Lute Mason, Bill Midness, Art Fredrickson, and Royal Peterson.

Christenson vs. Christiansen

A scrimmage with River Falls Teachers ended preseason work, and the squad was ready to take on Concordia in the season opener. This game provided special interest, because J. C. "Jake" Christiansen, former Ole gridder and son of F. Melius Christiansen, the St. Olaf choral master, had taken over as head coach of the Cobbers. He and Coach Ade had been teammates on Ole teams of the early '20s and boyhood friends in Northfield.

A sustained drive by Concordia in the game's closing minutes provided the margin in a 7–0 shutout of the St. Olaf Lions. *[This is the first mention of St. Olaf athletes being called Lions, presumably after the creature on the college seal.]* Andy Droen led a good defense, while sophomore Jim Smith, a triple-threat back, was the outstanding Lion on offense.

The losing streak continued as the Lions were defeated by preseason favorite St. Thomas 19–7 and Luther 20–0. Elton Lehrke was out for the season with a broken ankle suffered in a scrimmage with the freshmen.

Despite the losses, there were good performances, particularly from Earl Green, Jim Smith, Bob Sieveke, and Bobby Vail — a good backfield combination — and from co-captains Droen and Knutson.

The losses ended as the golden-clad Lions played Carleton to a standstill in the Homecoming game — but there was no beginning of a new win streak. The Goat game ended in a 7–7 tie. Kelly Poppitz, the freshman fullback, led St. Olaf on offense, while Droen, Tucker, Dahl, and Knutson shone well in the line. Carleton was not a conference foe, and freshmen were eligible to play.

Finally, in the season's fifth contest, a pent-up, frustrated Ole squad broke out of their losing rut, which included 11 games and extended back to the last contest of the 1939 season. Augsburg was the victim, as St. Olaf scored a 25–0 shutout victory on the Minneapolis South High field. Greene scored twice, Sieveke and Vail, once apiece.

As if to prove it was no fluke, the Lions took it to Hamline in the season's final home game, topping the Pipers 19–7.

Captains Floyd Knutson and Andy Droen hold the Goatrophy, 1941

The tone was set early as Bob Sieveke intercepted a Hamline pass on the first play of the game and returned it 45 yards for a touchdown. A long Jim Smith pass to Floyd Knutson made it 13–7 at halftime, and Smith finished the scoring with a last-quarter touchdown.

A strong St. Mary's team burst the bubble, posting a 24–0 shutout in the season's final game at Winona. The Oles closed the season 2–4–1 for fifth place in the conference.

As a result of his outstanding play and leadership, Andy Droen was chosen as center on the All-State team selected by the *United Press* and *St. Paul Dispatch and Pioneer Press*. St. Paul sports writer Crole Anderson wrote, "Andy Droen had little difficulty in winning the center berth. Good centers were a dime a dozen in the conference this year, and Droen's easy victory was a tribute to his sterling play."[117] LeRoy Quale, tackle; Jim Smith, halfback; Earle Greene, fullback; Floyd Knutson, end, and John Dahl, tackle, received honorable mention All-State.

Twenty-four lettermen, 11 of them seniors, were honored at the annual football banquet. Kelly Poppitz, a

freshman from Chaska, was the first first-year player to receive a letter since 1937 when Nolan Dugan was honored.[118] Dugan himself was the emcee for the banquet, and welcoming remarks were given by Harold Ditmanson, student body president. Bob Sieveke was elected captain for the 1942 season.

1941 Season Notes

Andy Droen and Floyd Knutson would train as platoon leaders in the Marine Corps in the summer of 1942 and be commissioned ... Less than a month

after the end of the season and the banquet, the Japanese attacked Pearl Harbor. The first mention of it was in the Dec. 12, 1941, *Messenger.* It was obvious dramatic changes were about to take place on college campuses and intercollegiate athletics would be affected.

The World War II Years

The initial impact on the college of the massive World War II effort was on male enrollment. Enlistments and draft inductions began and soon decimated the male sector of the student body. Few changes were apparent in the spring of 1942, however. Physical activity was being emphasized, and so intercollegiate athletic programs were continued, albeit with some changes in manpower.

Three football lettermen — Jim Smith, Bob Vail and Lowell Kuntze — were already lost to military service that first spring. Ten lettermen and freshmen candidates reported to Coach Christenson for spring drills on March 8. An evenly divided squad played to a 13–13 tie to finish spring practice. Stan Tostengard's gold team took a two-touchdown lead, one of the scores on a nifty 30-yard run by Howie Rose, a transfer halfback from Drake University. The black and white team came back on passes from Jerry Thompson to Art Fredrickson to tie the score.

Howie Steffens was named Honor Athlete for the 1941–42 year.

The Pipers were snowed under by the Lions, 19–7, at home in 1941.

Interim Athletic Director and Coach Mark Almli, 1942

Almli Returns, Replaces Grangaard

As preparations went forward for 1942, a significant personnel change occurred. Mark Almli, an athletic star and former coach, rejoined the athletic staff replacing Art Grangaard as head coach of basketball and baseball and assistant in football. Grangaard had taken a position as physical training instructor of navy personnel at Wold Chamberlain Field in Minneapolis.

In spite of the unsettled world conditions and the U.S. entry into World War II, changes were minimal at the beginning of the 1942–43 year. Registration was over 1,000, with the junior and senior classes showing the greatest shortage of men.

1942

With freshmen now eligible for conference play, about 40 frosh swelled the ranks of the squad preparing for the opener against Augsburg. A tentative starting lineup listed Paul Embretson and Art Fredrickson at ends, Len Guse and Al Lehrke at tackles, Stan Tostengard and Ken Hagebak at guards, John Dahl at center, Harold Poppitz at quarterback, Jerry Thompson and Captain Bob Sieveke at halfbacks, and Earle Greene at fullback.

Augsburg's secret "XYZ" system failed to stem the St. Olaf attack as the Lions cruised to a 32–0 shutout victory. Bob Sieveke scored early on a 62-yard reverse play.

A muddy field and Jake Christiansen's Concordia squad stopped the Lions, 7–6. Art Fredrickson's punting kept the Cobbers at bay much of the game. Jerry Thompson slashed seven yards for the only Lion touchdown.

With Sieveke and Dahl out of the lineup with injuries, the Lions prepared for the Homecoming game versus Luther. Strong line play by Tostengard and Lehrke forced the Norsemen to a passing game. A contest well played by both teams ended in a 13–13 deadlock.

A last-quarter field goal by Hamline and a 9–7 win sent the Oles into a three-game slide. On successive weekends, St. Thomas shut out the Oles 28–0, and Carleton kept the Goat with a 14–7 decision. The Oles came back, however, to edge Macalester 6–0 in the season finale. A pass interception by Jerry Thompson and later a pass from Poppitz to Thompson for the score were highlights of the game.

A *Messenger* article of November 1942 summarizing the season gives a positive report, "Fine play was prevalent." Seniors having played their last games for St. Olaf included Embretson, Larry Wright, Owen Ellingson, Clint Redstone, Len Guse, Ernie Schlanbush, Earle Greene, and Bob Sieveke. Jake Dahl and Stan Tostengard were elected co-captains for the 1943 season, and 29 letters were awarded.

1942 Season Notes

Gustavus Adolphus was reinstated in the Minnesota Conference following a year's suspension but was not on the Lions' seven-game schedule.

Two happenings that would change the St. Olaf campus significantly occurred in December 1942. One was a direct result of the war; the other was not, but its influence was major nevertheless.

The Navy Arrives

In the first development, the college agreed to accept a Navy pre-flight training unit. Dean J. Jorgen Thompson, acting for ailing President Lars Boe, made the announcement.[119] Naval trainees in groups of 200 would arrive each month beginning in January 1943. Their course of training at St. Olaf would last three months. St. Olaf was one of 20 locations in which these training units would operate.

The announcement and an interview with Lt. Cmdr. E.G. Thorson, commander of the cadet detachment, indicated that no fraternization would be allowed between the Navy cadets and regularly enrolled students on the campus. However, "the cadets will be permitted to get acquainted with St. Olaf students during their liberty hours off campus." Ytterboe Hall was vacated in order to house the cadets.

"Prexy" Boe, Friend of Athletics, Dies

The other significant event was the death on Dec. 27, 1942, of Lars Boe, the fourth president of St. Olaf College. It was Boe's 67th birthday. "Prexy" Boe's 24 years as president (1918–1942) had seen great growth in student enrollment (650–1,150) and the addition of seven major buildings — the Alumni Gymnasium, WCAL building, Agnes Mellby Hall, the art building (later to be named Flaten Hall), Holland Hall, Christiansen Hall of Music, and the power plant. Donald J. Cowling, president of Carleton College and a close friend of President Boe, gave a special memorial address at a service on Jan. 6, 1943.[120]

Boe made a major impact on all phases of the college's life, including athletics, present and perhaps future. Coach Ade Christenson told future coach Tom Porter that on several occasions, usually after a tough loss, he (Christenson) had tried to persuade Boe to offer "incentives," which Ade felt would bring more talented student athletes to the campus and result in continued athletic success.

According to Christenson, President Boe, in no uncertain terms, told him to coach the men to the best of his ability and let God be the judge. One can speculate about the influence this dictum had on Christenson's thinking when several years later he wrote a book, *Verdict of the Scoreboard,* the thesis of which was overemphasis on winning can work to the detriment of the other virtues a football program may produce for its participants and the college.

Granskou Becomes President; Christenson Seriously Injured

Two significant personnel changes occurred in 1943. The April 16, 1943, issue of the *Messenger* reported the election of C.M. Granskou as fifth president of St. Olaf. Granskou, a 1917 graduate of St. Olaf, was president of Augustana College in Sioux Falls, S.D. The other item was the departure for two years of Coach Ade Christenson. Ade was to train to direct a United Service Organization (USO) unit. Following his training in New York, Ade was assigned a unit in Carthage, Mo. Mark Almli took on the added responsibilities of head football coach and athletic director as well as physical education department head.

On the way home from his USO training in New York, Ade was seriously injured in an auto crash. He escaped with his life but was unable to complete his USO assignment, and the effects of the accident appeared to have an impact on his life and activities for several years.

War Curtails Conference Play

With the war making an increasingly significant impact on college life and athletics, athletic directors and coaches of the MIAC met at Macalester on May 15, 1943, to determine the future of the conference during the wartime emergency. Dean of Men Norman Nordstrand and Coach Mark Almli represented St. Olaf.

The outlook was that the colleges, in all likelihood, would discontinue intercollegiate competition in favor of more "intra-college" sports. Instead, the conference representatives compromised. They decided to discontinue football but keep basketball as an intercollegiate sport. Further, it was decided that schools could maintain their own schedules in all sports independent of the conference. In the wake of that decision, the St. Olaf athletic board decided to maintain football on an intercollegiate basis. Coach Almli articulated his and the college's point of view: In the second year of the war, the main concern is for a "well-coordinated military attack that will hasten the day of victory." It would be well to carry on with some form of competitive

1943's largest and smallest — Gordy Peterson and Jerry Thompson.

athletics on the St. Olaf campus. There would not be conference competition in football, but conference basketball would continue.

1943

"Wartime" football began when Coach Almli issued a call for candidates for the 1943 season. Twenty men responded, half of whom had not even played high school football. A three-game schedule was played. The Oles lost twice to River Falls Normal, 20–12 and 19–0. On a snow-covered field, they posted a 31–19 Homecoming win over Luther.

The *Messenger* report of the Luther game mentions a 60-yard pass interception return for one touchdown by Jerry Thompson; the other was scored by Bob Peterson. The account also mentions a PAT by "Midnight" Wilson and the fact that Luther scored the last two touchdowns against Ole "subs." With a squad of 20, there couldn't have been many subs. Adrian Christenson, Jr., "Spud," was a member of that 1943 squad.

1943 Season Notes

During the 1943 three-game schedule, word came that the Navy pre-flight unit at St. Olaf was to be removed as part of a retrenchment. The move was not unexpected as three schools had had their programs terminated the previous spring and seven in the past summer. Two weeks later, however, the *Messenger* headline was, "Recent Orders to 'Weigh Anchor' Rescinded; Naval Unit to Remain on St. Olaf campus.[121]

… Captain Jerry Thompson of the 1943 squad had transferred to the University of Wisconsin where, in 1944, he played as a regular under Coach Harry Stuhldreyer, the quarterback of the legendary Four Horsemen of Notre Dame during the Knute Rockne era.

Cheerleaders in 1944

1944

Little mention is made of preparations for the 1944 season except that there would be an eight-game schedule and the Navy cadets would be eligible to compete. As a consequence of the latter edict, the roster took on a less than exclusively Midwest look as the cadets were from all over the country. Mark Almli continued as head coach, assisted by Coach Hunt.

Thirty-three navy cadets and two civilians — one a veteran player, Dean Linman — comprised the 1944 squad. They were steamrolled 27–0 by St. Thomas in the first game and, though improved, lost to St. Mary's at Winona 20–12. The following week the Lions found their stride and started on a four-game winning streak with a 13–0 shutout of Cornell. They avenged the earlier loss to St. Mary's, turning back the Redmen 21–0, and then downed Cornell in a repeat engagement, 7–0, for their third consecutive shutout victory. In the second St. Mary's game, Jacobsen, the Ole center, went 70 yards with an intercepted pass for the play of the game.

Apparently unleashing some pentup frustration, the Lions gobbled River Falls Teachers 73–6. A first-quarter 82-yard scamper by Bert Young, and, on the first play of the second half, a hook and ladder pass play from Young to right end Byron Behr to tackle Alex Kindling for a 62-yard scoring strike were the big plays. Jack Rudy, a freshman from Marshfield, Wis., a "good ball packer," scored twice.

In the final game of the season, the Lions outplayed a heavily favored Drake University club for a half before falling behind in the second half and losing 26–13. A reporter observed, "All in all, the St. Olaf club looked like a pretty good football outfit."[122] In a summary of the season, coaches Almli and Hunt recognized a greatly improved combined team of Navy-Marines and college men.

At the season-ending banquet, Coach Almli and Dean Nordstrand commended the service men for making a St. Olaf football season possible: "We are proud of the manner in which they represented our school on the gridiron."

1944 Season Notes

An Oct. 27, 1944, *Messenger* article gives Mark Almli a pat on the back: "Not much is said about our director of athletics, Mark Almli, but we think … that he is doing very well with a very tough job. After seeing what Mark can do with a limited supply of men, we are sure that in the post-war days, with plenty of men around, he will develop teams that will be second to none."[123]

The 69th Homecoming weekend, as described in the Oct. 13, 1944, *Messenger*, included the inauguration of President Granskou and the dedication of Rolvaag Memorial Library … The Minnesota Conference had discontinued awarding championships for the duration, but St. Thomas, Gustavus, and St. Mary's, as well as St. Olaf, had fielded teams … Letters for 1944 were awarded to 12 servicemen and one civilian, Linman … Numerals were awarded to seven frosh …

The Jan. 5, 1945, *Messenger* included a long but incomplete list of former St. Olaf athletes serving in the military. A few of the list: Lloyd Ellingson '32, Rudy Ramseth '37, Earl Thorp '39, Cliff Gilbertson '31, Harry Newby '30, Lin Hildebrandt '30, John Kirkeby '37, and Ev Nyman '38.

The Post-War Era Begins

In 1945, the tide of battle had turned and the end was in sight, but World War II continued to have a strong influence on college athletics. The death of President Franklin D. Roosevelt on April 12, struck many as another casualty of the conflict. Service trainees were still a part of the campus and would make up a good share of the 1945 grid squad.

Ade Christenson had returned as director of men's physical education but not to coaching. After recovering from the automobile accident in 1943, he had tried to carry on the USO assignment at Carthage, Mo. — as director of the Servicemen's Club serving Camp Crowder. After several months, however, it was decided his health would not allow him to continue, and he retreated to Northome and managed to regain his health somewhat but not enough to resume the USO assignment. Instead, in late summer, he enrolled at the University of Southern California and spent the 1943–44 year completing a master's degree.

After spending the summer of 1944 at Northome, Ade accepted a teaching-coaching position at Ely High School and produced an undefeated football team. He returned to Northfield in the summer of 1945, but fell seriously ill with pneumonia. A slow recovery into the fall prevented his return to coaching.

1945

Mark Almli served as head coach in '45, assisted by "Pop" Hunt. A squad of 50 men turned out — 40 of them service trainees, one upper classman, Jack Rudy, and a handful of freshmen. The line was good size for that day — averaging 186 pounds — with Tom Stoops, a 200-pounder from the University of Arizona, and Frank Podogil, a 155-pound guard from Kent, Ohio.

The Oles dropped their first two encounters — 8–6 to Gustavus and 18–0 to St. Thomas — before posting a 19–0 win over Bemidji State at the latter's Homecoming.

A *Messenger* headline of Nov. 2, 1945, noted, "Oles Wreck St. John's; Carleton held Scoreless." The Oles did defeat a good St. John's team on Homecoming at Collegeville, but the Carleton half of the headline tells only half (or less) of the story. Carleton had not fielded an intercollegiate squad that fall, but by invitation, a touch football game was played on Laird Field for the Carls' Homecoming. A nine-man team of St. Olaf non-football squad members defeated the Carls 6–0. Such notables as Stan Frear — later to become a longtime faculty member in the English department — Milt Christenson, "Midnight" Wilson, and Phil Eastwood were members of the St. Olaf group.

The University of Minnesota B squad "Bombers" defeated the Oles

The 1945 starting lineup — largely Navy personnel

12–0 for the first Manitou Homecoming loss in 10 years.

Twenty-six letters were awarded — two to civilians Jack Rudy, a sophomore from Marshfield, Wis., and Jim Burtness, a freshman from Oak Park, Ill. Center Tom Stoops and guard Chuck Dawson were named to the all-conference team, Dawson as honorary captain. Looking to the immediate future, Stan Frear, in his *Messenger* column, Sports Highlight, noted, "It will be good to have the Minnesota College Conference back at full strength next year."[124]

1946

The "official" postwar era began in 1946. On Manitou Heights, Ytterboe Hall returned to housing civilian men, while on the eastern crest of the Hill, the new four-story, half-million-dollar Thorson residence hall was under way. Cully Swanson returned from active Navy duty to be dean of men at St. Olaf, and on the sports scene, Ade Christenson was back at the helm as head football coach.

Spring practice resumed with Al Lehrke, Royal Peterson, and Stan Tostengard back in harness. Also showing well in the spring outing were Paul Arvesen, Hal Bergeson, Paul Larsen, and Stan Nelson. Art Sand '36, captain and all-conference center, was added to the coaching staff as the line coach.

The fall season began with a rush, as the Oles posted quick victories over River Falls Teachers 13–6 and Macalester 19–6 in the first postwar conference game. A pair of first-year backs, Don Larsen and Jim Kallas, led the way against River Falls, and Royal Peterson's passing was largely responsible for the Oles' three touchdowns against Mac. Others who were cited for their play early were Ron Henriksen, Lehrke, Tostengard, and Arnie Nelson.

The Oles continued their winning ways, downing a Jake Christiansen-coached Concordia team 20–0, nudging Luther 19–13, and edging Carleton 14–13 to recapture the Goat for the

The 1946 championship team, Stan Tostengard, captain

Stan Tostengard, 1946 captain, all-conference guard

1946 offensive line: Halverson, Lehrke, Tostengard, Swenson, Henricksen, Gordon, Edman; backfield: Morehead, Peterson, Larsen, Kallas

Al Lehrke, 1947 captain, all-conference tackle

Ron Henriksen, 1947 all-conference guard

"Tulsa Toe," John Sibole, 1946

first time since 1938. Peterson's passing again was instrumental in the victory over Concordia. He threw to Kallas for one touchdown and to Art Frederickson for another. John Sibole, the "Tulsa Toe," kicked two extra points. Eddie Morehead, with the help of a two-man block by Lehrke, returned a punt 50 yards for a score against Luther.

Renewing their rivalry for the first time since 1942, Ade and Carleton's Wally Hass and their squads confronted each other before 6,000 fans. The Oles' one-point victory (14–13) came as the result of Henriksen's block of a Carleton conversion attempt and Sibole's PATs.

Gunning for their sixth straight win and third conference victory, the Lions faced Augsburg at Nicollet Park. Thinking to deceive Gustavus scouts in the stands, Ade started reserves, but an all-day rain and resulting slippery field forced the regulars to play most of the game. The Oles squeaked by 7–0 on the strength of a Kallas touchdown and a Sibole PAT.

The stage was set for the title match with Gustavus, and the Gusties deflated the Ole balloon with a 21–6 win. The only bright spot from the Lions' point of view was the play of the reserves, who largely held the Gusties in check and scored themselves in the second quarter with a Thompson to Fredrickson to DeWyze combination.

A 32–6 win by the University of Minnesota B squad in the season finale was an anti-climax.

Postseason honors went to Tostengard, Lehrke, Henriksen, and Peterson — all-conference — and Lehrke, captain for the 1947 season. Graduating seniors included Tostengard, Howie Rose, and Fritz Christofferson.

Arnie Nelson, Jim Kallas, Bob DeWyze, and Royal Peterson, 1946

After the books apparently were closed on the season, a challenge was lodged alleging that a Gustavus player was ineligible to compete. The challenge was upheld, the player declared ineligible, and the Gusties forfeited all conference games. As a result, St. Thomas and St. Olaf were named co-champions.

In the following spring, Stan Tostengard was selected Honor Athlete, and the Athletic Board sanctioned a home-and-home football agreement with Pacific Lutheran University of Parkland, Wash. It would be the first time a St. Olaf football team had traveled to the west coast for an intersectional contest.

With the first game against PLU scheduled for mid-September and the first fall practice scheduled for Sept. 5, leaving only two weeks of preparation, spring drills took on added meaning. Sixty men, including eight regulars from the previous season's co-champions, reported for the spring session. Captain Lehrke, Henriksen, and Royal Peterson — all-conference performers — led the list. Howie Rose served as temporary track coach, while Ade concentrated on football.

Jim Kallas #47 advances the ball against Concordia, 1946.

1947

With the fall came two weeks of preparation and then the train trip to Tacoma. Arriving on Friday, the Oles found themselves installed as favorites. So much for predictions. A good PLC team that would go undefeated during the season and win a postseason bowl contest carved out a 14–0 win. A solid line and the running of Jack Guyat proved the difference. For the Oles, freshman Russ Adamson's punting was

outstanding, as was the play of Kerm Halverson and Kelly Poppitz.

Returning from the coast bruised and disappointed, Ade's men couldn't get themselves up sufficiently for a determined Hamline team. On a muddy field, the Pipers stymied Ade's T formation and prevailed 6–0. Adamson's punting again was a feature. Morehead and "Porky" Bjerken were standouts.

Perhaps inspired by flashy new black, white, and gold uniforms and

A harbor cruise in Tacoma, Wash., on the day following the 1947 game with Pacific Lutheran.

Jim Kallas, the "Galloping Greek," 1946

Ade Christenson — 1948 retirement from coaching?

Paul Arvesen finds a hole, 1947

their first appearance before the homefolks, the Oles exploded out of their scoring drought to post a 26–7 win over Luther. Paul Arvesen's 80-yard touchdown run in the first quarter provided momentum.

It was tough going the following week in Moorhead for the Cobbers' Homecoming. Fighting both Concordia and the weather, the Oles drew first blood on a pass from Royal Peterson to Ellsworth Buskirk. With Sibole's PAT, it stood up for a 7–6 win. Henriksen and DeWyze were stalwarts in the line, while the "Galloping Greek," Kallas, accounted for half the Oles' yardage.

Augsburg supplied the opposition for Homecoming. The Oles built a 19–0 first-half margin with the help of a spectacular pass from Adamson to Fredrickson to set up one score. A lateral play — Don Larsen to Poppitz — was good for 59 yards to the one-yard line. The Auggies came storming back, but Adamson's punting blunted the attack and it fell short, 19–13.

The following week, the Oles picked up another game in the Goatrophy competition, downing Carleton for the second consecutive year, 14–12. Sibole's PATs again proved decisive. Going back to 1920, the Carls led the series 17–6. Carleton took an early lead, sparked by the running of their speedster, Frank Wright. St. Olaf countered on a pass from Peterson to Bjerken. An Arvesen pass, a spectacular leaping catch by Bjerken, and Sibole's conversion closed out the scoring. A 62-yard quick kick by Adamson and the line play of Poppitz, Halverson, Stromner,

DeWyze, and Johnson held the Carls in check in the second half.

The Oles made their fathers happy on Dads' Day, posting a 20–16 victory over St. John's. A fourth-quarter, 64-yard pass play from Royal Peterson to Kallas enabled the homefolks to overcome an early Johnnie lead. Gus Stromner blocked a St. John's punt and Poppitz recovered for a touchdown.

Hopes for a sixth consecutive victory after the two opening losses were dashed. Spearheaded by the running of Earl Bowman, Macalester proved too tough for the Oles. In a close, hard-fought game, the Scots prevailed 14–6. The win enabled Mac to tie St. Thomas for the league championship.

The Oles finished 5–3 overall, 3–2 in the conference. Henriksen was the lone representative on the all-conference first team. Poppitz was selected on the second team, with Kallas and Halverson honorable mention. At the season-ending banquet, Kelly Poppitz and Bob DeWyze were named captains for 1948.

1948

A return game with Pacific Lutheran opened the 1948 campaign and set the tone for an injury-plagued season. Several days of festivities preceded the contest. Student body president Henry Buslee and others greeted the Lutes at the railroad station. Dave Graven, a squad member, was the emcee for a joint pep fest at Finseth Bandstand on Friday evening.

The following day, the Lutes outplayed the Oles and outpointed the hosts 14–6, despite having numerous other scoring opportunities that they failed to convert. The Oles' score came on a Paul Larsen to Jim Kallas 65-yard scoring play. Russ Adamson suffered a season-ending fractured collarbone.

With the conference opener the following week, the Oles were handicapped by the loss to injury of Arnie Nelson, Kelly Poppitz, and Ron Henriksen, in addition to Adamson. Despite the losses, the Oles managed to push Hamline around but were only able to score once in seven opportunities in the so-called red zone. Paul Larsen scored in the fourth quarter to salvage a 7–7 tie.

Having apparently found a makeshift lineup that worked, the Oles "roared to life" the next Saturday, defeating Concordia 30–13. Strong running by Don Larsen and Kallas and Hal Bergeson's passing helped the Oles to a 23–0 halftime lead. The reserves played most of the second half. Stu Barstad and Chet Hausken had good days.

A non-conference game versus Luther provided one of the most dramatic plays in the history of St. Olaf

football. The Oles were pinned on their one-yard line late in the second quarter. While Ade was preparing to send Barstad in to punt, Kallas called his own number and swept left end for 99 yards and the game's only score. Defensive line standouts were Henriksen, Reichel, John Reinertsen, Poppitz, and Norm Bergeson.

Drama also was built into the Carleton game the following week. The Oles had held the goat the last two seasons and it was Homecoming. To add to the buildup, Ade had announced that this was to be his last season as coach, hence his last Carleton game in that capacity and his last on Manitou Field, since the remaining three games were to be on the road.

An opportunistic Carleton squad, again featuring the running of Frank Wright, downed the Oles 13–6 before more than 5,000 fans. Bergeson's passes to Reinertson and Holland led to the lone Ole score. Bob DeWyze was a standout on defense for St. Olaf. [Later, Frank Wright, who was an important factor in the Knights' victory, would serve for many years as the well-respected treasurer of Carleton College.]

Perhaps stung by the loss to the Knights, the Oles rebounded with a 34–6 win over Augsburg at Nicollet Park. Hal Bergeson's passing was a feature. He threw scoring strikes to Kallas, Paul Larsen, and Reinertson. It was one of the few games that season in which the Oles were at full strength.

The following week, the Oles won in nearly every category except the score. An Earl Bowman-sparked Macalester squad cooled Hal Bergeson's hot arm and posted a 21–7 win. The Lions had 18 first downs to Mac's three and 294 offensive yards to 159 for the opposition. St. Olaf's lone score was by Barstad.

With Kallas and Arnie Nelson sidelined by injury, the Oles dropped the season's final game to St. John's. The Oles resorted more than usual to passing, but the Johnnies matched them. A 43-yard pass, Hal Bergeson to Don Larsen playing flanker, set up one score; Don Larsen also scored on a 12-yard run. It was the swan song for Poppitz, DeWyze, Dick Thorp, Sibole, Paul Larsen, Glen Swenson, Arnie Nelson, Bob Zimmerman, and for Ade as coach — temporarily, as it turned out. In a season marked by injury, the

Kelly Poppitz and Bob DeWyze, 1948 captains

Stu Barstad touchdown run against Augsburg, 1948

Helge Pukema, head coach,
1949–50

Don Larsen, 1949 captain

Ron Henriksen, 1949 captain

record was 3–4–1, fifth in the conference, and loss of the Goatrophy.

Henriksen, guard; Holland, end, and Poppitz, tackle, made the all-conference squad with Bergeson, Kallas, and DeWyze receiving honorable mention. Don Larsen and Henriksen were elected co-captains for 1949.

Following the 1948 season, three head coaching vacancies developed. Having previously announced his retirement from coaching, Ade remained as athletic director and chairman of physical education, leaving the football position open. Mark Almli resigned to take a sales position with a sporting goods company. Thus the football, basketball, and baseball coaching slots were open.

1949

The *Messenger* announced on March 11 that Helge Pukema had been named head football coach. Pukema had had an outstanding playing career as an All-American lineman at the University of Minnesota, playing on Bernie Bierman-coached teams that won back-to-back Big 10 and national championships. After World War II service in the Coast Guard, Pukema had coached high school football, basketball, and track. Later in the spring, Joseph Nygaard was appointed head coach of basketball and baseball. Joe had compiled an outstanding baseball career at Wisconsin and had been coaching at Bloomer, Wis., high school.

Helge's first announcement after being named coach was that there would be *five* weeks of spring football practice[125] — inside drills in the gymnasium until weather would permit outside activity. Sixty-seven candidates reported. The offensive plan was to be a "Minnesota" single wing with modifications. The spring practice was spent with both coaches and players getting acquainted with a new style of play.

Preseason practice in the fall brought a dramatic change in the tone of preparation. Helge introduced a strong, autocratic, perhaps "Biermanesque" coaching style, quite different from Ade's more low-key style. Players responded grudgingly but

A Jim Kallas reception against St. Thomas, 1949

well to the system, anticipating a strong season built around returning regulars such as Kerm Halvorson and Ray Holland, ends; Ralph Baily, tackle; Ron Henriksen, guard; Glen Swenson, center, and a backfield of Don Larsen, Hal Bergeson, Russ Adamson, and Jim Kallas.

The Oles dominated River Falls 34–0 in the season opener, almost doubling the yardage on the Falcons — 410 to 230. The big play of the game was a 67-yard interception return for a touchdown by Glen Swenson. Kallas also scored on a 30-yard run.

Labeled the conference darkhorse (Helge's term: workhorse), the Oles traveled to Winona for a night contest with St. Mary's. The visitors made it two straight, winning 29–6 over a stubborn St. Mary's team. Bergeson, Kallas, Larsen, and Holland crossed the doublestripe, while Reinertson accounted for the safety with a tackle in the end zone.

The quick, victorious start to the season, slowed precipitously as Hamline spoiled Ole title hopes for the second year in a row, posting a 13–0 win, and St. Thomas crushed the Lions 51–7.

An opening drive to the Hamline 30 was the Oles' only offensive success in that contest. Ineffective play and a Hamline forward wall that outplayed the Oles spelled defeat. In a third consecutive night game, the heavily favored Tommies toyed with the Oles, scoring at the rate of two touchdowns a quarter.

The tone was set early as St. Thomas recovered a fumble on St. Olaf's first offensive play. The Tommies were paced by the running of Jim "Popcorn" Brandt. A sustained 95-yard drive culminating with a Bergeson to Kallas pass produced St. Olaf's only score. A hand injury ended J.D. Hanson's season.

The following week, the Oles halted the skid at least temporarily and reclaimed the Goat in the bargain as Carleton fell 13–6. A 70-yard quick kick by Adamson gave the Oles good field position, and a Bergeson to Holland pass was good for the first score. The second came on a 76-yard run from scrimmage by Kallas. Jim broke loose on a reverse trap and outsprinted the Carleton secondary. The Knights scored in the closing minutes.

In the season's final four games, the Oles split, posting wins over Augsburg and Luther by identical 14–6 scores, and losing to St. John's 15–6 and Gustavus 20–0.

Two quick touchdown passes in the waning minutes of the first half provided the Oles a lead they never gave up in the triumph over Augsburg. Ed Thompson passed to Reinertsen for the first score. Barstad's interception followed by a Thompson to Hausken pass accounted for the second.

A high-flying St. John's 11 took an early 8–0 lead on a touchdown and a blocked punt resulting in a safety. A Thompson to Kallas pass produced the lone Ole score.

Despite a statistical edge — 18–7 in first downs and 480–284 in yardage — the Lions bowed to Gustavus in a Homecoming/Dads' Day encounter. Two long scoring runs by Gene Payne and Red Malcolm made the difference. The *Messenger* termed the contest the "best game of the year."

The victory over Luther came in the season finale — and the career finale for 17 seniors, the core of the entering class of 1946. The Oles spotted the Norse six first-half points and then came back to score 14 unanswered points after intermission. Several good punt returns by Hausken set up touchdown passes from Thompson to Reinertson and Kallas. It was a winning

season of five wins and four losses, but a conference mark of only 2–4, resulting in a second-division finish.

At the season-ending banquet, the captaincy passed from Don Larsen and Ron Henriksen to Russ Adamson and Tom Porter.

1949 Season Notes

On Feb. 11, 1950, a *Messenger* headline proclaimed "Galloping Greek Signs with Cards." Jim Kallas had signed a tryout contract with the then Chicago Cardinals of the National Football League. Kallas had led St. Olaf scoring in all four of his seasons. He earned 12 letters — four each in football, baseball, and track — and graduated with honors in mathematics.

1950

Fifty candidates, including 13 of the 30 letter winners from 1949, reported for spring drills. Coach Helge Pukema was assisted by Rolf Mellby and "Mush" Haugen. A March issue of the *Messenger* saw the possibilities for improving on the previous sesason's 5–4 record as bleak. The schedule was considered tough with the University of Minnesota-Duluth, new to the MIAC, and South Dakota State on the list.

With only two 200 pounders in the lineup — Bob Wulff and Paul Forsberg — the Oles turned back Concordia 18–12 in the opener. Veterans Hal Bergeson and Chet Hausken hooked up on a touchdown pass play in the last 50 seconds to salvage the win. Bergeson was 10 of 13 passing for the contest.

UMD lived up to its advance billing. The Bulldogs took advantage of a pair of Ole fumbles and a blocked punt to score three times and post a 19–6 triumph. Adamson's score from the three-yard line were the only points for the Oles. The loss of Stu Barstad for the season with a broken collarbone was a serious blow.

"Powerful St. Thomas Favored to Rout Lions on Manitou Field," a *Messenger* headline proclaimed before the second game. Based on the previous season's 51–7 Tommy win, the Mess headline bore some logic. But a spirited Ole 11 nearly turned a major upset — leading in every statistical category except the score, 14–7. The Toms' outstanding runner, Jim Brandt, proved the difference. The Oles' Paul Forsberg was saluted for his play in the first three games, having played all 180 minutes.

The Oles went down for the third time, falling to the undefeated South

Hal Bergeson passing against Carleton, 1950

Captain Russ Adamson, 1950

Hal Bergeson, 1950

Chet Hausken, 1950

Dakota State Jackrabbits on a muddy field in Brookings. The hosts' split-T offense rolled to a 41–14 win. The Ole scores came on passes from Bergeson to Adamson and Adamson to J.D. Hanson.

Homecoming featured the Goat game — Oles versus Knights — with Carleton seeking revenge for the previous season's loss. Carleton led the series 19–9 with the Oles' longest winning string coming in '29, '30, and '31, games featuring the heroics of Mark Almli and Syl Saumer. A special feature of the Homecoming edition of the *Messenger* was an article by Ade Christenson, listing his all-star St. Olaf team. It included legendary names and apt descriptions by Ade. For that reason, it is reproduced on page 59.

It looked as though the Oles were set to repeat the 1949 win over the Knights as they put up 14 unanswered points in the first half. The two scores came in the first quarter, both set up by Carleton fumbles. Perhaps stung by that lackluster performance, the Knights stormed back in the second half to score five times and win, going away 34–21. The passing combination of Marks to Slocum was largely responsible for the Carleton second-half surge. The Oles' first half touchdowns were by Arnie Thowsen and Adamson on a pass from J.D. Hanson. The Goat went back across the river.

The losing string went on the following week as a winless Augsburg team rose to the occasion and upset the Oles 18–6 in a poorly played night contest at old Nicollet Park. The only Ole score came via a Bergeson to Hausken pass in the last three minutes. The only bright spot for St. Olaf was the punting of Duane Hoven — one boomer going for 75 yards.

With avoiding last place in the conference the prize for the winner, the Oles squared off against St. Mary's. The return to the lineup of Forsberg and Adamson helped the Oles rebound to a 27–0 win. Hausken and Hal Bergeson were standouts. Norm Bergeson picked off a pass from his linebacker slot and returned it 45 yards for a score.

Ten seniors in the lineup led the Oles into St. Peter to challenge the Gusties on their Homecoming. Gustavus retained its

Helge Pukema on the sidelines, 1950

undefeated status, running roughshod over the undermanned Oles 53–0. Two plays typified the Oles' day: The Gustavus second-half kickoff was allowed to roll into the Ole end zone where a Gustie fell on it for a touchdown. Hausken returned the ensuing kickoff 98 yards only to fumble on the Gustie two. Gustavus recovered and marched 98 yards the other way for a score; a tough way to end a season, and, for the seniors, a career.

On a promising note for the future, the Ole frosh blasted Carleton 43–0 and downed the varsity reserves 21–6. John Gustafson was selected as the MVP.

1950 Season Notes

Later in the year, Herman (Ham) Muus and Tom Porter, both multi-sport performers, were named Honor Athletes for the year.

Coach Pukema opted out after two seasons and a 7–10 won-lost mark. In his *History of St. Olaf College 1874–1974*, Joseph M. Shaw reports that somewhere along the way, Helge had been heard to remark that St. Olaf boys were not mean enough to play winning football.[126]

1951

With Pukema's departure, Ade stepped back in at the helm. He was greeted by a good nucleus of regulars and the undefeated frosh stepping up. Consequently, hopes were high that 1950's 2–6 record might be reversed. Returning stalwarts

THE MANITOU MESSENGER   October 13, 1950 · Vol. 64, #4

Ade Selects Team of All-time Ole Greats

by Ade Christenson

The task of picking an all-star St. Olaf team is too much of an assignment for any one person. Personally, I am familiar with St. Olaf football only during the era from 1918–1922 and from 1929–1950. I hesitate to pick one team as representing the best in St. Olaf history. In many cases, there are a number of men who would qualify equally well for the starting lineup. My selection is based chiefly on the offensive merits of the individual players.

At left end, I would pick "Kippy" Gilbertson '31. He was fast, aggressive and a fine pass receiver. However, his greatest asset to the team was his ability as a signal caller. He rates as the finest general, in play selection, that I have ever coached. He would direct this team on offense.

At left tackle, I would select Ev Nyman '39. He was big, fast, and a splendid blocker. Because of his speed, he was especially effective as a trap blocker.

At left guard, I would have Lloyd Ellingson '32, the finest blocking guard I have ever coached. He was fast, very shifty, and possessed the desire and enjoyed the thrill of a great block.

Norman Nordstrand '33 draws my vote for the center spot. Nordy was rather small, as centers go, but he made up for it with a tremendous spirit and aggressiveness.

Rudy Ramseth '39 is my right guard. He was big, fast, and a very fine blocker. His high school experience as a fullback made him the ideal guard.

Marty Cole '24 would be my captain and starter at right tackle. Here is the great tackle and great leader for a stalwart Viking team.

Frank Cleve '25 would be my selection at right end. Few receivers in State Conference history could match Frank Cleve in cleverness and ability.

At quarterback would be Cully Swanson '25. The greatest passer in St. Olaf history would find some great receivers in Gilbertson, Cleve, and this great backfield.

The one and only Syl Saumer '33 would be at left half. The greatest running back in St. Olaf history had size, speed, and the finest stiff arm in football. No team could concentrate on pass defense and forget the running game with Syl Saumer in the backfield.

Whitey Fevold '25 would draw the right half assignment. Here was power, speed, and blocking ability. I could hardly visualize the need of a drop kick with such a team, but Whitey could take care of this assignment in case of the need.

John Kirkeby '37 is the fullback. No line could spread out to stop Saumer and Fevold, or Kirkeby would run wild. Speed and drive and a tremendous competitive spirit would make the fullback spot well taken care of by Kirkeby.

This team would scarcely need a spot runner, but I would enjoy having Harry Newby '34 at my side for any emergency that might arise. His record of running for a touchdown the first time he carried the ball in five consecutive games is a record that goes unmatched.

This selection would be in my starting lineup. How could you keep out of the game, for any period of time, such stars as Coon Swenson, Jarle Leirfallom, Aurele Torgerson, Art Sand, Andy Droen, Stan Tostengaard, Mel Schwake, Kermit Halvorson, Lynn Hildebrandt, Mark Almli, Jim Kallas, Don Larsen, Al Droen, Elmer Saterlie, Ron Henrikson, Milt Nesse, O. Bungsto and Ing Glesne, together with a host of other greats. No defensive worries would remain unsolved with this array to choose from.

All-St. Olaf Team

L.E.	Kippy Gilbertson '31
L.T.	Ev Nyman '39
L.G.	Lloyd Ellingson '32
C.	Norman Nordstrand '33
R.G.	Rudy Ramseth '39
R.T.	Marty Cole '24
R.E.	Frank Cleve '25
Q.	Cully Swanson '25
L.H.	Syl Saumer '33
R.H.	Whitey Fevold '25
F.B.	John Kirkeby '37
Spot Runner	Harry Newby '34

Paul Forsberg and Harlan Hogsven, 1951 captains

J.D. Hanson, halfback, 1952 Honor Athlete

Duane Hoven, 1952 captain

included co-captains Harlan Hogsven and Paul Forsberg, Jim Rotramel, John Quam, Russ Mauer, and Dean Ostlie, linemen; and backfield men J.D. Hanson, Duane Hoven, Ray Runkel, Marv Larson, and Don Maland. Assisting Ade with coaching duties were Sherm Brown, a 1937 grad who was fresh from two undefeated seasons coaching at Chatfield; Del Mully, newly appointed basketball and baseball coach, and Major Frank Wrigglesworth, a Wisconsinite, commander of the newly formed Air Force ROTC unit.

The season opener was a 19–13 loss to Wisconsin Stout with all points being scored in the first half. Clint Sathrum's passing and an interception by George Trout set up scores by J.D. Hanson and Dick Werdahl.

A week later, in the first annual "Stone of Scone" game, the Oles overpowered Macalester 42–13 in a battle of Mac's single wing against St. Olaf's T formation. Werdahl's 27-yard touchdown run, a Sathrum to Werdahl aerial, and a 38-yard scoring run by Marv Larson produced a 29–7 halftime lead for the Oles. Sophomore Steve Swanson was credited with checking Mac's good running game.

In the season's third encounter, an untried but burly Hamline eleven ground out a 7–0 win before a capacity Dads' Day crowd. A one-foot quarterback sneak was the only score.

"Game of the Week" was the *Messenger* description of the upcoming St. Thomas tilt. St. Olaf had not won against the Tommies since 1935. The series stood at St. Thomas 13, Oles 4 and one tie. The win-hungry Oles almost pulled it off. Trailing 14–13 with 10 seconds to play and the ball at the Tommy 18, Ade opted for a scrimmage play that came up short. Dick Werdahl and J.D. Hanson were the threats for St. Olaf.

The 29th annual Goat battle was a feature of Carleton's Homecoming. The Carls led the series 19–8, reaching back to 1920. It appeared to be a case of the Oles' speed against Carleton's experience. Carleton Coach Wally Hass termed the Ole eleven the "best he had seen since coming to Carleton in 1936." Led by Ollie Slocum and Ted Smebakken, the Maize and Blue

shut out the Oles 13–0 in a poorly played game. Transfer Paul Johnson saw his first action for St. Olaf.

Iron Men

As the season wore on, the *Messenger* made mention of several Oles as "Iron Men." Co-captains Forsberg and Hogsven turned in several 60-minute performances, as did John Gustafson, Russ Mauer, and Doug Olson.

Describing St. Mary's as "the most improved team in the conference," Ade took his men to Winona and came away with a 25–13 win. The Oles played a strong offensive game sparked by J.D. Hanson, Dick Werdahl, and Ray Runkel, who scored on a 41-yard run.

"Roast the Cobbs" was the slogan for the Homecoming game featuring another coaching matchup of Ole teammates and boyhood friends Ade Christenson and Jake Christiansen. The Concordia backfield included quarterback Rod Grubb, later to be chair of political science at St. Olaf, a longtime Ole assistant coach, and interim head coach in 1996.

New to the Oles were the black and white uniforms they wore for the first time and the electric scoreboard at the west end of Manitou Field. The latter was a gift of the class of 1951. The Oles staved off a last-ditch Concordia rally to post a 33–26 win. J.D. Hanson scored three times, Werdahl, two. Gustafson blocked a punt in the fourth quarter, which led to the Oles' sixth touchdown.

1951 Season Note

A *Messenger* sports page note announced that Don Larsen '50, then coaching at Brooten, had a new, eight-pound, 12-ounce baby boy — who would be Captain Tim Larsen '74.

The Oles, seeking a third-place conference ranking, were scheduled to play St. John's in the season finale. The Nov. 9, 1951, *Messenger* noted that the game was postponed due to weather conditions. Several other conference games scheduled that day were postponed or cancelled.

St. Olaf Joins the Midwest Athletic Conference

A headline in the Dec. 7, 1951, issue of the *Messenger* said, "St. Olaf resigns from MIAC; joins Midwest athletic group." The news had been announced a week earlier at a Chicago meeting of Midwest Conference faculty representatives and athletic directors by the conference commissioner, Dr. Ralph Henry of Carleton.

St. Olaf had been a charter member of the MIAC (Minnesota Intercollegiate Athletic Conference), and a number of valuable traditions and associations had been built as a result, so the decision to switch to the Midwest was not taken lightly. Both athletic and academic factors were in play and when they came together, the result was the change in athletic conferences and the college's affiliation with the conference's academic counterpart, the Associated Colleges of the Midwest.

Over a number of years, there had been a growing concern by St. Olaf athletic personnel, primarily Ade Chistenson, athletic director and football coach, with practices and direction that some MIAC schools were taking. Some of that concern was shared by other conference members, and a fair amount of controversy had been generated. At the same time, the college's long-term

academic objectives were receiving renewed scrutiny by faculty and administration.

Joseph Shaw's *History of St. Olaf College, 1874–1974,* reported that President Lars Boe had noted back in 1941 that "the church has taken the American, New England type of college as an instrumentality for the attainment of its objectives." A part of that attainment had been St. Olaf's endeavor, understood but often not stated, "to take its place among the quality liberal arts colleges of the 'American, New England type.'" It happened that the member colleges of the Midwest Athletic Conference were schools such as Lawrence, Knox, Grinnell, and Carleton, which were thought to conform to that New England model and also to have a great deal in common with St. Olaf in terms of academic program and quality. It was thought that association wth these institutions on several levels would seem to be compatible with St. Olaf's oft-stated long-term goals.

Through conversations among faculty members and presidents, notably President C.M. Granskou of St. Olaf and President Lawrence Gould of Carleton, a mutual interest in having St. Olaf join the Midwest Athletic Conference developed. Albert Finholt, professor of chemistry and faculty

representative, and Athletic Director Christenson were invited to attend, as observers, the fall 1950 meeting of the MAC. Shortly therafter, St. Olaf faculty meeting minutes noted that, "Mr. Christenson reported … [that] St. Olaf has been approached to apply to the Midwest Conference. The faculty voted a 'favorable reaction' toward joining the conference."[127]

The following spring, May 1951, Ade reported on developments regarding possible affiliation with the MAC. At the Oct. 15, faculty meeting, Ade presented a "carefully considered" transfer proposal. Professor William Narum made a motion to apply for membership. O.E. Shefveland seconded, and the motion was passed 50–15. The application was made in November, and on Dec. 17, 1951, Dean Cully Swanson reported that St. Olaf had been accepted for membership in the conference.

Almost as a matter of course, St. Olaf also moved into membership in the MAC's academic counterpart — the Associated Colleges of the Midwest.

Recorded student reaction to the change in conferences was modest. Jerry Nelsen, writing in the March 7, 1952, issue of the *Messenger,* devoted his entire article, "From Where I Stand," to his view of the change. It was a brief statement of his interpretation of

The 1951 team, Paul Forsberg and Harlan Hogsven, captains

Chuck Lunder, assistant coach, 1952–76

Ray Runkel, halfback, 1952 Honor Athlete, co-captain

Clint Sathrum, all-conference quarterback, 1953

Steve Swanson, guard, 1953

St. Olaf's athletic philosophy: "Because our faculty apparently felt the athletic policies of the Midwest Conference more closely approached the plan St. Olaf wished to follow …" Several subsequent *Messenger* issues presented brief sketches of the Midwest Conference members and their recent intercollegiate successes.

Capping a momentous year, the Men's Senate sponsored a first-annual Sports Appreciation Day on March 6, 1952.[128] Captains and coaches of all varsity sports received mention. The main speaker for the evening was Bernie Bierman, the legendary former coach at the University of Minnesota. The Senate's selection of John Hanson (J.D.) as the year's Honor Athlete was a feature of the evening. Duane Hoven and Ray Runkel were elected co-captains for the 1952 season.

Travel, Intersectional Tone Accompanies Change in Conference 1952

1952 ushered in a new era in St. Olaf football, one marked by more extensive travel and an intersectional feel. Fans tuning in to KDHL Radio in Faribault on a Saturday afternoon were soon to hear a new sound: "Hi there, everybody. From the Knox Bowl on the campus of Knox College in Galesburg, Illinois, this is Jim Lundquist, and this is St. Olaf football."

With the change to the Midwest Conference, all away games except Carleton required a five- to eight-hour bus ride and overnight stays in such cities as Galesburg and Monmouth, Ill.; Appleton (Lawrence), Ripon, and Beloit, Wis.; and Cedar Rapids (Coe, Cornell) and Grinnell, Iowa.

1952 also brought a new coach. Charles Lunder was appointed to fill the spot of Del Mully, who had resigned in the spring of 1952. Chuck, a 1937 Carleton graduate, had an outstanding playing career in football, basketball, and baseball. Before coming to St. Olaf, he had coached at Slayton, Clarkfield, and Two Harbors. A three-year stint in the Navy during World War II was largely spent in the South Pacific. Chuck's first coaching assignments at St. Olaf included assistant in football and head coach of wrestling and baseball. It was the start of a long and loyal St. Olaf

coaching career, which also saw him serve as coach of tennis and freshman basketball.

The first Midwest Conference opponent was Knox. The game in Galesburg started off well for the Oles as Ray Runkel took a handoff from Clint Sathrum on the first scrimmage play and raced 67 yards for a touchdown. Knox countered with two second-quarter scores to take a halftime lead. In the waning minutes of the contest, Sathrum threw a 36-yard scoring strike to Jim Varland, but the PAT was blocked, leaving Knox a 14–13 winner. Dr. and Mrs. William Johnson, St. Olaf alumni, entertained the squad at their home for a post-game dinner.

Two non-conference games followed. The Oles romped past Simpson College of Indianola, Iowa, 41–6 and then were shut out by former MIAC rival St. John's 34–0.

Against Simpson, the Oles had an exceptionally good defensive showing, limiting the visitors to 34 yards rushing. The Oles scored three times in the first period. Sathrum passed to Gustafson for one; Werdahl ran 20 yards for another, and Carol Brekken blocked a punt for the third. Three other scores resulted from Runkel's touchdown after a Hoven fumble recovery; Paul (Pug) Johnson's five-yard run, and Varland's pass interception.

The following week, Johnny (Blood) McNally, the former Green Bay Packer and eventual NFL Hall of Famer, filling in as coach at St. John's, led the Johnnies to a lopsided victory. The hosts scored in every quarter and twice in the fourth in what Ade called "the worst afternoon I have spent in 30 years." Injuries picked up in this game would hamper the Lions in the next few contests.

A 20–14 win over Grinnell was the Oles' first Midwest Conference victory. Scores came via Sathrum's passes to Gustafson and runs by Runkel and Johnson. Pug was the game's leading rusher with 109 yards on 22 carries.

The following week, the Oles smashed Carleton 41–12 to reclaim the Goat after a long absence.[129] The game's tone was set by an Ole goal-line stand early and three first-half touchdowns, Werdahl, Noel Olson (pass from Sathrum), and Lowell Mason scoring. Gustafson's 30-yard interception return and another pass from Sathrum were good for 12 more points. Steve Swanson closed out the Ole scoring, recovering a Carleton fumble in the end zone. The victory margin was the greatest in the St. Olaf-Carleton series, which stood at Carleton 12, St. Olaf 6, and one tie.

Unbeaten Lawrence loomed large as the Oles entered the home stretch of the 1952 conference race. Longtime Lawrence Coach Bernie Heselton had another of his good teams and they scored three times in the first 10 minutes before Paul Johnson countered for St. Olaf, capping a 50-yard march. Werdahl made it 13–21 with a 10-yard end run, but Lawrence came back with an 81-yard touchdown drive to post a 28–13 win.

The Oles finished strong with wins over Monmouth and Ripon. Bob Wilkens' talented toe sent Monmouth down to a 21–18 defeat. The Lions spotted Monmouth 14 points. In the third period, Sathrum's pass to Dennis Griffin set up Pug Johnson's score. Sathrum passed 25 yards to Gustafson

for a second touchdown, and Dick Werdahl rambled 58 yards for the clincher. Steve Swanson, Brekken, and Ted Thompson were cited for strong defensive play.[130]

The Ripon Redmen challenged the Oles for fourth place in the league, but the Oles prevailed 25–6. Gustafson scored in the first period on a pass from Sathrum. Pug Johnson followed with a counter in the second quarter as the Oles took a 13–0 halftime lead. Werdahl scored twice in the third quarter, once on a 34-yard pass from Sathrum and again on a seven-yard run. Pass receptions by Noel Olson and Dennis Griffin were also features of the game. The Oles' 5–3 finish was good for fourth place in the league.

Gustafson and Werdahl were the leading scorers for the season with six touchdowns apiece. Sathrum threw for six counters as well. The defensive platoon — led by Brekken, Swanson, Roger Herrlinger, John Pichner, Olson, Quam, and Hoven — had played well all season. The Oles captured six spots on the all-conference squad — Gustafson on offense and defense,

Pichner, Sathrum, Werdahl, and Thompson. All would return for the 1953 season. Ray Runkel was chosen Honor Athlete for the year by the Men's Senate.

1953 — A Banner Season

The Oles had finished with a rush in 1952 and a good group of returning regulars and a talented group of sophomores were back. But Ade had some concerns for several reasons: a new substitution rule precluded platoon football; there had been no spring practice (a Midwest Conference rule), and there were only two weeks of practice before the opener — against Knox for the second consecutive year.

A preseason poll of coaches had selected the Oles third behind Coe and Lawrence. A veteran Knox Siwasher squad scored first in the opener. But in the second quarter, after two Sathrum to Varland passes, Pug Johnson scored to even the count. After intermission, the Oles took over. Willie Mesna, replacing the injured Rog Oie, went 38 yards to score and Werdahl scored twice on runs of 16 and 43 yards. The

Dick Werdahl, Roger Oie, and Paul Quam, 1953 all-conference

Ade and captains Clint Sathrum and John Gustafson, 1953

Roger Oie, halfback, 1953

John Gustafson, end,
Little All-American, 1953

Dick Werdahl,
all-conference halfback, 1953

Dave Bolstorff,
guard/linebacker, 1953

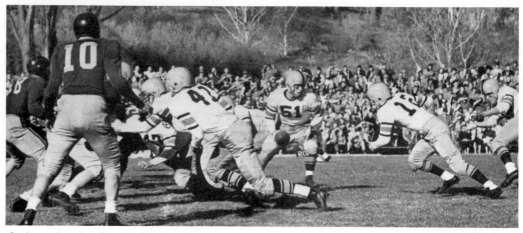

Sathrum hands off to Werdahl, 1953

final score: 28–19. The 28 points would be the lowest Ole production of the season — not a good predictor of the explosive offensive power they were to display. Thirteen sophomores saw considerable second-half action.

Two non-conference victories followed — a 35–14 triumph over Wartburg and a 78–0 destruction of a weak Bethel team. The Oles led 27–0 at the half against Wartburg on scores by Johnson, Oie, and Mesna. Sophomore Paul Quam intercepted a mid-air fumble and rambled toward paydirt but didn't quite make it. Oie broke loose for a spectacular 40-yard touchdown run in the second half. Against Bethel, the high-riding Oles rolled up 33 in the first half, and reserves played the rest of the way. A feature of the game was the play of reserve quarterback Chet Mathison, who completed nine of 12 passes, five for touchdowns.

With the seemingly soft portion of the schedule past, the Oles continued in high

gear, shutting out three of their final five opponents. A Dads' Day game versus Grinnell ended in another scoring outburst, St. Olaf 60, Grinnell 12. Ted Thompson returned a short opening kickoff. On the third play from scrimmage, Oie went 50 yards for the first score and the rout was on. Subsequent touchdowns were by Werdahl, Erv Mikkelson, Varland, and Brekken.

In four games, the Oles had outscored their opponents 201–45. With Carleton next and the Oles cruising, grid expectations and interest were high. The Oct. 23, *Messenger* ran two articles on football history. The first was a profile of the 1930 squad, the only undefeated team in Ole history, featuring legendary players such as Syl Saumer, Lloyd Ellingson, Cliff (Kippy) Gilbertson, and Mark Almli. Members of that team were to be honored at halftime of the Carleton game. The second article described the student pressure for the introduction of intercollegiate football from 1900 to 1919.

Doug Olson, guard, 1953

John Pichner, center, 1953

Ted Thompson,
all-conference tackle, 1953

A second shutout of the season spoiled Carleton's homecoming 34–0. A Werdahl run and a Sathrum to Gustafson pass accounted for the first two scores. A second-half kickoff return featuring a Sathrum to Oie lateral was good for a 91-yard scoring play. Ade gave special credit to his defense. The figures made his case — a 5–0 record, 235–45 margin in scoring, and two shutouts.

"Level Lawrence" was the Homecoming slogan as the undefeated and league-leading Vikings invaded Manitou Field. With five straight wins and a 47-points-per-game scoring average, the Oles were not to be denied this time. They posted a decisive 35–13 victory before a record crowd of 7,000. Oie and Werdahl running outside, Pug Johnson inside, and pinpoint passing by Sathrum to ends Gustafson and Olson combined with great offensive line play to hand Lawrence their only loss of the season.

Coe and St. Olaf, both undefeated, led the conference race with two games to go, and they were not scheduled to play each other.

Rumbling irresistibly toward an undefeated season, the Oles crushed the Monmouth Scots 34–0.[131] After a scoreless first period, the Oles drove for an apparent score, but Oie fumbled on the Monmouth two. Stiff defensive line play forced the Scots to punt out of their end zone, and Sathrum broke

1953 Dads' Day

through to tackle the punter for a safety. Oie returned the subsequent short kickoff for a touchdown, and the Oles were off and running.

Steve Swanson, playing his usual solid defensive end, made the stop on the kickoff, followed it with three defensive plays, driving the Scots back 10 yards, and then came close to blocking the punt.

The Ole grid machine was really irresistible now, at least for this season. The Nov. 6, *Messenger* carried a bit of verse suggesting the fate of the Ripon gridders:

Point happy Oles try for more;
Redmen tremble at Lions' roar.

Twin Cities' scribes were also taking notice. Joe Hendrickson's "Sports View" in the *Minneapolis Tribune* suggested a postseason game between the Lions and the Golden Gusties of Gustavus.[132]

Anxious to add to their nation-leading offensive average, the Oles posted a 58–0 victory over Ripon. Sathrum intercepted a pass to set up a 46-yard score by Johnson. Pichner picked off another Ripon aerial but couldn't outdistance the field. Buzz Helseth's fumble recovery started another Lion drive. It was 33–0 at halftime.

Oie took the second half kickoff back 85 yards for the Oles' sixth touchdown. Reinertson scored on a quarterback sneak. Jack Aamodt went 77 yards to the Ripon 13, and Frank Peterson took it in from there for the final tally. Ripon had crossed midfield only three times, testifying to the Oles' consistent, season-long dominating defense.

With the victory over Ripon, St. Olaf had its first Midwest Conference championship in its second season in the league.

The 1953 team, undefeated conference champions

Buzz Helseth, tackle, 1953

Wayne Brown, 1956 co-captain

Paul Quam, all-conference linebacker, Little All-American, 1956

With one-platoon football the rule, there could be only 11 starters. Some men played both ways, but there were plentiful substitutions — especially with the wealth of talent this season. The starters, however, should be listed: at the ends, co-captain John Gustafson and Bruce Halverson, tackles Buzz Helseth and Ted Thompson, guards Doug Olson and Dave Bolstorff, center John Pichner, quarterback and co-captain Clint Sathrum, halfbacks Dick Werdahl and Roger Oie, fullback Paul Johnson.

St. Olaf placed five men on the All-conference first team, Gustafson, Sathrum, Quam, Thompson, and Oie; three on the second team, Werdahl, Swanson, and Olson; with Pichner honorable mention. Gustafson's selection to the Associated Press Little All-America team was a fitting climax to a spectacular grid career.

There was extensive and well-deserved post-season acclaim and comment and considerable speculation about and pressure for a postseason game. Midwest Conference approval would have been necessary. Ade was outspoken in his praise of the squad: "The 1953 football team is the finest team I have ever coached … Roger Oie is the greatest touchdown runner in St. Olaf history," he said.

Ade was a guest on Jack Horner's Twin Cities television sports program. Horner selected Ade for his Sports Hall of Fame Award on the basis of his impressive 27-year coaching career at St. Olaf. Forty monograms were presented at the annual banquet. The Rev. Cecil Tellekson, a member of the undefeated 1930 squad, was the main speaker. Dave Bolstorff and Dick Werdahl were elected captains for the 1954 season.

The Greatest Team?

Was the 1953 squad the greatest Ole team? There had been stiff competition for that accolade and there would be more, but the 1953 team certainly had staked a powerful claim. The squad scored 362 points — tops in the country — shut out four opponents, and outgained the opposition 3,239 yards to 1,252.

1954

Coming off a perfect 8–0 season, the Oles were picked to repeat as Midwest Conference champions in a preseason poll of league coaches. Co-captains Bolstorff and Werdahl also were optimistic. "We will not have as much depth, but greater experience will help," Werdahl said.[133]

The coaching staff had been reshuffled slightly. Ade continued as head coach and Howie Schultz, a U of M alum, came on as assistant football coach and head wrestling mentor. He replaced Major Frank Wrigglesworth, who was re-assigned from his St. Olaf R.O.T.C. commander slot. Wrigglesworth had served as defensive coach for the gridders the previous three seasons. Schultz was not unfamiliar with St. Olaf, having been a member of the Naval preflight training unit in 1943.

The early season starting lineup for one platoon had Bruce Halverson and Erv Mikkelson, ends; Buzz Helseth and Charles Espe, tackles; Dave Bolstorff and Norm Solie, guards; Paul Quam, center; Mark Reinertson, quarterback; Roger Oie and Dick Werdahl, halfbacks; and Duane "Whitey" Brekken, fullback.

Reality intruded on the euphoria early. On a hot Iowa Saturday, Grinnell shocked the Oles with a 13–13 tie. St. Olaf got away to a quick 13–0 second-quarter lead, but Grinnell countered with a late second-quarter score and another in the third. The deadlock interrupted the string of 10 victories extending back to the end of the 1952 season.

After the tie with Grinnell, the formidable Lawrence Vikings posed a major early season challenge. It would be a battle between the preseason one and two picks. Showing marked improvement from the Grinnell game, the Lions rebounded and dropped the Vikings 13–7 in a close, hard-fought contest. A strong running attack led by Werdahl and sophomore fullback Brekken paced the Lions. Ralph Hagberg blocked a Lawrence field-goal attempt. The ensuing Ole drive was capped by Oie running it in from the five. Another turnover, a fumble recovery by Bill Redmen deep in Lawrence territory, set up the second Lion score. Lawrence tried to get a

Grid ballet, Bolstorff defends, 1954

passing attack going, but the Ole forward wall, led by linebackers Bolstorff and Quam, stymied the attempt.

With confidence somewhat restored, the Oles took on the Ripon Redmen. Leading only 7–6 at halftime, St. Olaf scored three times in the third period to take control and ultimately win 26–6. Ripon scored early, but the Oles quickly retaliated, scoring on Oie's 35-yard run. Werdahl sprinted 55 yards for one of the third-quarter scores. The others came via a Reinertson to Mikkelson pass and a run by Brekken.

The winning string was now at 13, marred only by the tie with Grinnell.

All of that came crashing down the following Saturday, and the Oles lost the Goat to boot. The Knights edged the favored Lions 14–13. The Carls' recovery of an Ole fumble in the end zone and Ted Smebakken's PAT provided the crucial edge. Brekken's 53-yard touchdown run highlighted an Ole-dominated third quarter.

The Oles fought back the next week. Mikkelson's fourth-quarter PAT following Wayne Brown's three-yard touchdown run was the margin over the Cornell Rams.

A spectacular pass reception by Hagberg of a Reinertson pass was the big play leading to the score. Hagberg's

heroics continued late in the game as he foiled a trick play designed to beat the clock.

With their winning ways restored, the Oles tacked on two more conference triumphs, downing Knox 33–13 before a large Homecoming crowd on Manitou Field and smashing Monmouth 33–6 with a strong offensive display.

Against Knox, Brekken, Mikkelson, Reinertson, Oie, and Dick Harapat scored — Harapat on a 35-yard interception return. Bill Lund's head injury ended his season. He was replaced by Chuck Espe. Bill Redman filled in for the injured Norm Solie at guard.

A balanced attack — 232 yards passing, 229 rushing — was too much for the Monmouth Scots. Reinertson did the bulk of the passing, including a late scoring strike to Werdahl. Werdahl also scored on a 62-yard run, and Brekken scored on the familiar fullback pitchout play.

The frosh team, coached by Mark Almli, tied St. John's 6–6. Standouts for the Oles were Cecil Lietch, a 165-pound guard, and George Thronson, a 200-pound tackle.

The Oles' first-ever meeting with the Coe College Kohawks closed out the season. Down but not out, the Oles rallied for two touchdowns in the final seven minutes to tie the Kohawks at 27. Bolstorff blocked a punt to set up a

27-yard touchdown run by Brekken. Reinertson passed to Von Wald to set up a Reinertson quarterback sneak for the counter. Werdahl also scored from the one after a Coe fumble. Mikkelson's three PATs ensured the tie. Brekken's two touchdowns gave him 55 points for the season and the conference scoring title.

Five Oles were selected on the All-Midwest Conference squad. Paul Quam was the lone first-team pick, making it two years in a row. Mikkelson, Helseth, Bolstorff, and Werdahl were second-team selections with Reinertson receiving honorable mention. Fourteen Oles closed out their St. Olaf careers — Bolstorff, Werdahl, Oie, Espe, Simso, C. Brekken, Erickson, Bieberstein, Redman, Mesna, Griffin, Garnett, Olson, and Hemstad.

George Durenberger, athletic director at St. John's University, was the speaker for the annual banquet. Buzz Helseth and Paul Quam were elected co-captains for the 1955 season.

1955

It had been only two years since the storied 1953 powerhouse had been called the best team in the history of St. Olaf football, but the 1955 squad seemed bent on making people forget. It wasn't long before a *Messenger* columnist was asserting flatly that 1955 was the best.

Duane "Whitey" Brekken advances against Knox, 1956

Ralph Hagberg, 1955

Bernie Von Wald, 1956

Carleton, with an 8–0 record in 1954, was the preseason favorite to repeat as league champion with St. Olaf and Coe tagged to challenge. The Oles were considered stronger than the previous year at every position except halfback. Three All-conference picks — Quam, Bolstorff, and Mikkelson — would anchor a strong line that would prove to be a major factor in the squad's success.

The Lions started strong, registering shutouts against Grinnell, 34–0, and non-conference Northland, 51–0. Grinnell was held to minus 10 yards and no first downs in the first half. Only Ole fumbles limited the first half score to 7–0 — a Reinertson to Von Wald pass and a run by Stoike. A feature of the game was Hagberg's interception of an attempted screen pass. Ralph lateraled to Don Johnson, who completed the scoring play. The September temperature in the 90s made playing difficult.

Against Northland, the regulars played only the third quarter, scoring three times. The reserves who started built an 18–0 halftime margin. Dick Norman, the leading rusher for the day with 80 yards, scored the final touchdown on a pitchout play.

Appearing unstoppable, the Oles rocked undefeated Ripon with a six-touchdown assault. A good Ripon passing attack netted two first-quarter scores, but that was all. In a wild first quarter, Von Wald scored three times, including a 53-yard pitchout scamper. The Oles led 20–12 after 15 minutes and shut out the Redmen the rest of the way. Brekken scored twice, and Bob Kalass and Norman also tallied six pointers. Brekken intercepted a pass and Quam registered a fumble recovery. Final: 52–12.

Drama was built into the Goat clash with Carleton — again. The Knights were working on an 11-game winning streak, and the Oles had lost only once in their last 21 games. Carleton Coach Wally Hass termed St. Olaf a "team without a weakness." At the end, the scoreboard read St. Olaf 40, Carleton 13. The *Messenger* account proclaimed it "perhaps the greatest exhibition of football ever displayed by a St. Olaf eleven."[134] Von Wald's running and passing, Quam's interception,

Hagberg's end-around plays, Reinertson's passing, a spectacular reception by Bruce Halverson, Stoike's 52-yard run, and a stout defense all were factors in this "best game." The "Lions' Tale" tagged the squad the greatest and gave due credit to all, even the coaches.

With the Goat safely back on Manitou Heights, the focus jumped ahead to the season-ending clash with Coe, both squads undefeated. En route to that showdown, the Oles disposed of Cornell 20–7 and Knox 32–6.

Von Wald's 30-yard run and Reinertson's 28-yard option were big plays against the Rams. In Galesburg to challenge the Knox Siwashers, the Oles started slow, but picked it up to register a 20–0 halftime lead. Knox scored early in the second half on an 80-yard run by Stanicek, but then Reinertson passed 56 yards to Hagberg for one score and one-yard to Mikkelson for another.

As the Oles and the Kohawks moved toward what appeared to be an inevitable showdown, both had to dispose of "breathers." St. Olaf hosted Monmouth in a Dads' Day encounter — and in the midst of the season's first snowstorm. The sloppy field may have caused a slow start by the Oles. But late in the first period, Brekken ran a patented pitchout play for a 51-yard touchdown. Three scores in the second quarter put the game on ice. A stellar reception by Mikkelsen, Hagberg's tackle for a safety, a 22-yard run by Dick Peterson, and Norman's game-leading rushing total of 101 yards all contributed to the sixth straight conference win and seventh victory of the season. Strong defensive play had resulted in three shutouts and two one-score games.

That brought on the showdown with Coe for the league crown. Coe's Rosenberg and Phillips were 1–2 in scoring. Mikkelson, Brekken, and Von Wald were 4–5–6. Coe ranked fourth nationally in team offense with St. Olaf close behind in sixth place. Adding to the buildup, Ade said, "Our undefeated team of 1953 was a good one, but I believe we are a little stronger this year. We can do more things." Fifteen seniors would conclude their St. Olaf grid careers, including two-time all-conference center Paul Quam, and 10 others who had lettered on the 1953 squad as sophomores. The group included three three-year starters — Helseth, Bolstorff, and Halverson.

A large contingent of students and other fans traveled to Cedar Rapids to support the squad. This group swarmed onto the Kingston Stadium turf, forming a pre-game runway for the Lions as they took the field.

A pair of second-quarter touchdowns gave the Oles a 14–7 halftime lead. One was a sensational 86-yard pass play from Reinertson to Hagberg. The play started with a short pass to Hagberg, but then the "Tracer" outran the conference 220-yard dash champion (Phillips) for the touchdown. The second score was a 26-yard run by Brekken following Reinertson's interception of a Shady Day pass.

But Coe was the better team on this day, and they were not to be denied. The Kohawks shut out the Oles in the second half and rode to a 28–14 victory on the strength of a three-touchdown rally after intermission. A five-play, 79-yard drive broke a tie and an interception return set up the fourth tally.[135]

Helseth, Mikkelson, and Bolstorff were named to the all-conference team. The squad was feted by the St. Paul Alumni Club, with Ade the speaker. Wayne Brown and Bill Lund were selected as co-captains for the 1956 season.

1955 Season Notes

Through much of the first half century of football at St. Olaf, freshmen were not eligible for varsity competition — in the MIAC or in the Midwest Conference. The MIAC barred frosh for the first semester — and later until January 1. The Midwest had a rule which kept frosh out for the first academic year. In either case, first-year men were effectively banned from competition for their first fall season on campus, so there were separate freshman and varsity teams.

Frosh, however, played a key role in the football programs of the various schools even though they could not compete at the varsity level. At St. Olaf, the freshmen assisted the varsity with preparation, serving as a scout unit. Against the varsity, they would run plays used by the upcoming opponent. If something worked against the varsity, the frosh coaches usually kept it in their repertoire throughout the season. The frosh also had a three-game schedule of their own against other freshman teams. Usually, one or two coaches would handle the freshmen, assisted by undergrads who had used up their eligibility or been sidelined by injury.

Two of St. Olaf's all-time great athletes and coaches, Cully Swanson and Mark Almli, served as freshmen football coaches and set an enviable standard, matched later by Bob Gelle and Paul Quam and an array of other varsity assistants.

1956

Coming off a good season and with good and veteran personnel returning, the outlook for 1956 was good.

The Oles got away to a fast start, scoring on their first two possessions and ultimately downing Lawrence 31–13 at Manitou Field. Whitey Brekken's score capped a six-play drive after the opening kickoff. An Al Rice to Dennis Runck pass was a feature of the second possession. Brekken scored again from the Lawrence 30 on a classic open-field run. A Paul Mork to Arnie Nelson pass for 42 yards resulted in the fourth score. Interestingly, three quarterbacks figured prominently in the contest — starter Clyde Olson and reserves Rice and Mork.

In the first road game of the season, the Oles swept aside Ripon 32–13, riding a nearly unstoppable running game which netted 315 yards. George Thronson got a piece of a Ripon punt to set up the first score — an Olson to Brekken pass. It was 19–7 at the half. Sophomore Duane Swenson picked off two passes to set up two second half tallies — a 19-yard jaunt by Bob Kalass and a Rice to Runck pass. Runck also brought back a Ripon aerial for 90 yards, only to have the play nullified by a clipping penalty.

An interesting sidelight of the Ripon contest was the participation of the Thompson brothers — Jerry and Ted. Ted, an all-conference tackle on the Oles' 1953 championship team,

The 1956 championship team, Bill Lund and Wayne Brown, captains

Bill Lund, 1956 co-captain

*Duane "Whitey" Brekken,
Little All-American, 1956*

scouted the Oles for his brother, Jerry, the Ripon mentor. Jerry was an Ole backfield standout in the '40s.

A pair of losses followed the two season-opening wins. A brilliant performance by the Carleton Knights' Bob Scott, who outgained the entire Ole team, keyed an 18–6 Carleton win in the Goat game. The only Ole score came in the first quarter when Dave Robinson jarred the ball loose from Scott's grasp. Brekken picked the ball off in midair and raced down the sidelines behind a solid wall of blocking for a 51-yard touchdown. It was a fall classic played before 5,600 bi-partisan fans on windswept Manitou Field.

A second loss — the first time since 1952 the Oles had dropped consecutive games — came against the Cornell Rams, a preseason conference favorite who had already lost to Knox and Monmouth, but not this time. The Oles jumped away to a quick 12–0 lead after two and a half minutes, but the Rams braced and carved out a 35–18 win. A 97-yard kickoff return and a 46-yard march put Cornell up 14–12. A third Ole score came when Wayne Brown raced 50 yards for a third score, but it was too little too late.

With the season win-loss count at 2–2 and with undefeated Knox coming to town, the Oles mounted an enviable late-season rally. They mowed down Knox, Monmouth, Coe, and Grinnell to nail down a tie for the conference crown (with Carleton and Knox).

The Oles were definite underdogs, a rare role, going into their Homecoming encounter with Knox, but a power attack swamped the Siwashers 40–6. The score was deadlocked 6–6 at halftime, but the Oles exploded for five second-half tallies, resulting in the largest score of the season and keeping title hopes alive. Brekken and Clyde Olson each scored once, Dave Folkestad twice, and Kalass once on a pass from Mork.

Perhaps showing the effects of a combined train and bus trip to Monmouth, Ill., the Oles played the Monmouth Scots to a 0–0 halftime tie but then broke loose for a 34–0 rout in the second half. It was the Brekken show, as Whitey scored three in a row to begin the second half. St. Olaf outgained Monmouth 333 yards to 135 and

16–9 in first downs, but perhaps the key to the win was the Ole defense which allowed Monmouth past midfield only twice. An Al Rice interception on the first scrimmage play of the second half ignited the Oles.

Paced by Dave Folkestad's three touchdowns, the Lions produced a 26-point second half and smothered Coe 33–13. Again a Rice interception sparked the second-half scoring spree. Rog Stoike's five-yard run added to Folkestad's scores of 10, 25, and 17. Ade's post-game accolade: "In the last five years, I don't believe I have seen a better running, harder running quartet of backs than I saw Saturday."[136]

After a fourth consecutive slow start, the Oles broke out of a 6–6 halftime tie to down the Grinnell Pioneers 40–6.

Heroics by Ripon enabled St. Olaf to share the conference crown in a three-way tie with Knox and Carleton. The Redmen powered past Knox 46–0 and Carleton 24–7 to open the door.

Duane "Whitey" Brekken received significant postseason honors. He was the only Ole to be named to the all-conference first team, and he received second-team Little All-America recognition on the Williamson rating system. Dave Folkestad, Bill Lund, Nick Olson, and Dave Robinson were awarded all-conference second-team berths, and Duane Swenson was tabbed for honorable mention. Double letterwinners Waldo Larson and Tom Anderson were elected co-captains for 1957, and Bill Lund was selected by the Men's Senate as Honor Athlete for 1956–57.

1957

As defending conference champions, with Knox and Carleton, and with 22 letter winners returning, the Oles were rated the team to beat in preseason polls.

A solid coaching staff was in place with the addition of Bob Gelle to join the veteran Ade Christenson, Chuck Lunder, and Jim Gabrielson. Gelle, who would be assistant football coach and head basketball coach, was a multi-sport great at the University of Minnesota. A quarterback on one of Bernie Bierman's last teams, Gelle gave up the grid sport to concentrate on basketball and became Coach Ozzie

Cowles' captain. He also performed as a weight man in track. After stints in the Army and as a coach at Edina High School, Gelle came to St. Olaf for what was to be an outstanding coaching/teaching/administrative career spanning 34 years.

In the season opener against Lawrence at Appleton, Wis., the Oles scratched out a hard-fought 19–13 win. After a game-opening 75-yard Lawrence march put them down 6–0, the Oles evened the score with an Al Rice to Roger Stoike pass. Two third-quarter scores put the game away — the first was a five-yard run by Ron Ree set up by Deryl (Skip) Boyum's interception return; the second was a Rice to Nate Schiotz pass. Ree's 74 yards from scrimmage was tops among ground gainers. Rice, Stoike, and Robinson were outstanding on both sides of the line.

A speedy Ripon team, coached by former Ole great Jerry Thompson, blew into town for the home opener and outscored the Oles in a shootout, 31–26. The home team jumped out to a quick lead on Ree's 11-yard run following a midfield pass interception, and his 33-yard reverse ramble after a Rice to Runck pass good for 28. The Redmen retaliated with two touchdowns and a field goal before the Oles scored on a 52-yard Rice to Runck aerial to take a 19–17 halftime lead.

Ripon scored early in the third period and then resorted to a ball control strategy to outlast the Oles for the victory. Cec Leitch suffered a shoulder separation on the opening kickoff and would miss the rest of the season.

The Goat game was next, and the Carls, with a 2–0 season record, were considered a slight favorite. The seers were proved correct, as Carleton eked out a 14–6 victory in a contest marked by fumbles, pass interceptions, and the defensive play of both squads resulting in 25 turnovers in the low-scoring affair. The Oles scored first to take a 6–0 halftime lead on a one-yard Stoike plunge. The Lions tried to give it back via two fumbles, one interception, and a blocked punt, but strong defensive play saved them — until the second half. A fumble gave Carleton the ball on the Ole 14, and the Knights scored and converted to take a slim 7–6 advantage. The Carls scored again with 31 seconds remaining to clinch the win.

St. Olaf bounced back decisively the following week to score a 21–13 Homecoming win over the undefeated Cornell Rams. A capacity crowd witnessed some of the best football of the season. An eight-play opening drive culminated with an Al Rice to Waldo Larson pass for the touchdown. George Thronson's kick was good, and the Oles were not headed from there on. Sophomore Don Jurries, replacing the injured Ron Ree, galloped for 130 yards from scrimmage including a scoring scamper of 66 yards.

Schiotz, Robinson, and Swenson were defensive standouts. All the Oles played well. Carrying the bulk of the load was a strong forward wall of Robinson, Thronson, Tom Anderson, Swenson, Jim Peterson, and Larson. The balanced backfield had Rice, Ree, Schiotz, and Rog Stoike.

Jurries and Jim Ebert, with Schiotz playing primarily on defense, were lineup changes for the Knox contest.

Dennis Runck reaches for one, 1957

Rice hangs on; Larson, Robinson, and Thronson in pursuit, 1957

A dazzling aerial game led by Rice (six for 17 with three touchdowns) smashed the Siwashers 32–6 at Galesburg, Ill. Denny Runck was on the receiving end of two of Rice's scoring passes with Larson catching the other. Ebert scored on a one-yard plunge and Stoike on a 47-yard ramble to account for the other Ole scores. The Lions had a 385 to 145 yardage margin.

As the season wound down, the Oles pushed aside a winless Monmouth team 35–0, and two weeks later were aced out of third place in the conference as the Grinnell Pioneers scored a 6–0 win, their first over an Ole team. The shutout broke a 44-game string — since 1952 — in which the Oles had scored. Ev Sorenson and Dave Robinson were defensive standouts for the Oles, but on offensive punch was lacking. The Oles moved inside the Grinnell 20 five times only to lose the ball four times on fumbles and once on downs. The season count ended even at 4–4 and fourth place in the league.

Six men received conference honors. Tackles Tom Anderson and George Thronson were first-team all-conference with Waldo Larson, end;

Duane Swenson, center; and Al Rice, quarterback, second-team choices. Jim Peterson garnered honorable mention. Robinson and Swenson were elected co-captains for 1958.[137]

1957 Season Note

During the off-season, Beloit was readmitted to the league for the 1959 season. The league had suspended Beloit in 1951 after objecting to some athletic policies.[138]

Christenson Relinquishes Reins; Porter Named Head Coach

In March of 1958, the college announced that Ade Christenson, who had been head football coach for 21 seasons and a member of the athletic department staff for 28 years, would step down to be replaced by Tom Porter, 1951 grad and Honor Athlete. Ade would remain as athletic director.

Christenson compiled a won-lost mark of 100 wins, 60 losses, and nine ties and brought six conference football championships to Manitou Heights. Though he was a highly competitive man, Ade publicly questioned the emphasis on winning. He would not

question the importance of the sport and its influence for good on young men and the college culture. There is no question that he is one of the persons most influential in the growth and development of football at St. Olaf.

Tom Porter, a native of Bayport, Minn., was a standout athlete at Stillwater High School. He majored in biology and physical education at St. Olaf and played baseball, football, and hockey all four of his college years. In addition to being named Honor Athlete in 1951, he captained hockey and football squads and won all-conference honors as a football guard in 1950.

Porter returned to St. Olaf after four years at Neenah, Wis., High School. He started there as an assistant to Ole alum Jerry Thompson. When Thompson moved on to Ripon College, Porter became head coach of football and track at Neenah. His 1956 and 1957 grid teams were undefeated conference champions.

1958

In a classic "welcome to college coaching," Porter's 1958 squad was battered 40–7 by defending conference champion Ripon in the season opener. The Redmen led 28–0 at halftime and coasted to victory. The Vikings' lone tally came late in the game on a 26-yard end sweep by Runck. The Oles were outgained 445 to 127 and were on the wrong end of a 22–4 count in first downs.

More than 6,000 fans turned out for the Goat game the following week to see if there had been some mistake. Carleton overcame a 14–6 halftime deficit to top a determined Ole squad 27–21. The Ole offense functioned well, but the defense had trouble with Carleton's varied attack. Skip Boyum and Nate (Whitey) Aus scored for St. Olaf, and Duane Swenson recovered a fumble in the Knights' end zone for the third counter. The last touchdown was set up by a spectacular 80-yard kickoff return by Ree. The Carleton win left the series at St. Olaf 12, Carleton 24. During Porter's tenure at St. Olaf, the Oles would catch up and go ahead.

The first of what would be 171 career coaching victories for Porter at St. Olaf came the following week. Although outgained by the Cornell Rams, the Oles recovered six fumbles, which helped to squeeze out a 13–8 win. Denny Runck scored first on a two-yard smash after a 35-yard pass from Schiotz. Bob Algoe scored from the eight after a fumble recovery. An oddity occurred on a kickoff when an official picked up the kickoff as it was being played by Schiotz. After a turnover, a tremendous defensive stand stopped the Rams on four downs to seal the victory.

The Oles evened the season count at 2–2 with a 27–21 come-from-behind Homecoming victory over Knox. After probing with a few early running plays, Schiotz lofted a picture pass to the speedy Bill Greenslit for a 70-yard scoring play. After that, the lead changed hands several times before Knox took a 21–14 lead in the fourth quarter. A good kickoff return by Ree and a 62-yard burst by "Bullet Bill" Greenslit set up a short touchdown run by Algoe. Runck's end sweep for a two-point conversion played an important role. A failed Knox gamble on fourth down led to a 33-yard off-tackle slash by Algoe to finish the scoring.

The euphoria occasioned by two straight victories was shortlived as a pair of defeats followed. After a long train ride, presumably the last in Ole football history, and a poorly played game, Monmouth prevailed 20–12. The Oles were victimized by an outstanding passing day on the part of the Scots' quarterback Bill Suffield, who completed 18 of 29 for 173 yards. Fumbles also plagued the Oles, and the Scots converted two of them into first-half scores.

After an open date and two weeks to prepare, the Oles came out strong against league-leading Coe and scored twice early. They then fought gallantly, and unsuccessfully it turned out, to stem the Kohawks' comeback. Two series of plays were important. Late in the second quarter after mounting a tremendous goal-line stand, the Oles fumbled on their own five attempting to run out the first-half clock. In the fourth period, a well-conducted drive led by Mike Simpson was stopped by Coe at the one. The Kohawks went back to Cedar Rapids with a hard-won 16–14 win.

The Oles closed out the 1958 season with a pair of wins to end the campaign 4–4. After trailing 7–0 early, St. Olaf took command and went on to defeat Grinnell 29–7. A 48-yard pass from Simpson to Robinson, Schiotz on an eight-yard dash, Aus on a four-yard burst, and Algoe's seven-yarder constituted the Ole scoring.

With the season count at three wins and four losses and never having finished out of the first division since joining the Midwest Conference, the Oles were anxious to preserve that distinction. The Lawrence Vikings, with only one win to their credit, were the obstacle. A strong defense and the running of Runck led the Lions to a 35–14 victory. Runck scored three times, one on a sparkling 62-yard punt return, another on a fourth-quarter pass from Simpson. Algoe and Aus also scored, capping sustained drives. Pete Obermeyer and Dave Robinson were defensive standouts.

The 4–4 season mark was good for fourth place in the conference.

Completing their St. Olaf careers were Swenson, Robinson, Schiotz, Runck, Aus, Simpson, Arnie Nelson, Harapat, and Howie Morgan. Co-captain Duane Swenson was voted most valuable player. He was the first recipient of that particular distinction in St. Olaf football. Swenson, Robinson, Schroeder, and Schiotz were named to the all-conference squad. Ron Ree and Ron Caple were elected co-captains for 1959.

Schiotz advances against Carleton, 1958

*Duane Swenson,
1958 co-captain*

*Tom Porter '51 takes over the
reins as head coach, 1958*

1958 Season Notes

Experience and perceptiveness will tell. In a pre-1958 season meeting of coaches Porter, Bob Gelle, and Jim Gabrielson, Gelle and Gabrielson predicted: "Just throw the ball out and you should go 4–4." Though not quite that simple, it worked out that way, nevertheless … The frosh were 2–0 after defeating Carleton 27–6. Standouts Ken Hokeness, John Bergstrom, Bill Anderson, Dave Hindermann, and Bill Winter showed promise of good things to come.

1959

There were enough bright spots in the 1958 season to earn the 1959 Oles top contender status along with Cornell, Coe, and Ripon. Beloit was back in the league after a nine-year absence, making it a 10-team loop. A season limited to eight games resulted in an incomplete round robin. Coe was not on the Ole schedule.

The season got off to a resounding start as a Bill Winter-led running attack (75 yards on 13 carries) dominated Beloit 28–0. Bill Greenslit and Don Jurries abetted Winter's heroics. Juries and Greenslit scored once each and Algoe, twice. Wes Moir and Tom Everson combined for four PATs.

Euphoria over the opening-game victory was subdued considerably by the loss, due to a knee injury, of sophomore end Ken Hokeness, who had been a three-sport star at Northfield High School and seemed headed for stardom in college. Hokeness attempted a comeback later in the season, but the injury forced an end to his football career. It didn't, however, keep him from becoming a record-holder in the shot and discus.

Two losses followed the season-opening win, before the Oles put it back together for a 7–6 Homecoming victory over Knox. A senior-dominated Cornell team shut out the Lions 19–0. Fumbles hurt, as did the loss by injury of John Bergstrom, Wes Moir, and John Turnquist. Jim Hembre, Curt Hartzell, and Ron Caple were outstanding in the line. Ree's two interceptions keyed backfield play. Ripon inflicted the second loss, an 18–7

*Ron Caple and Ron Ree, 1959 captains,
with team mascot Eric*

defeat. The Oles' only counter came via a 10-yard run by Winter.

"Put Knox on the Rocks" was the Homecoming slogan. The Siwashers' coach, Al Partin, said he had the strongest defensive line in his six years in Galesburg.[139] Knox's burly fullback Glenn Wehrich bulled over in the second quarter for a 6–0 lead, and the vaunted Knox forwards held off the Ole attack until late in the game when Don Jurries broke loose for a 43-yard touchdown run. The conversion put the Oles up by one, which is how it ended, 7–6. Four interior linemen — Pete Obermeyer, John Turnquist, Harvey Schroeder, and Curt Hartzell — had matched the Knox line. The visitors had 150 yards rushing the first half, only 50 in the second.

Bolstered by the return of Hokeness and Moir to counter the loss of Algoe, the Oles invaded Laird Stadium. A lone tally in the second period and a good defense enabled the Lions to shut out Carleton 7–0. Winter's three-yard run off tackle climaxed a 55-yard drive for the only touchdown. The key play in the drive was a Don Jurries "snake dance" from the Carleton 27 to the 18.

Grinnell was the opponent as the Lions sought win number four, entering the contest at full strength for the first time since the season opener. In addition to Hokeness, others returning from the injury shelf were Ken DeFor, Dave Norman, and Dave Hindermann.

Breaking out of a closely contested first quarter, Jurries romped for two touchdowns and John Turnquist booted a 22-yard field goal, good for a 16–6 victory. Brilliant defensive play held the Pioneers to 51 yards rushing. Tom Everson led the squad in tackles with Jack Rajala, Hembre, and Algoe also cited for outstanding play.

With a head of steam up, the Oles faced the season's final two contests against Monmouth and Lawrence needing a sweep to finish with five consecutive victories.

Trailing 6–0 with less than a minute left in the first half against Monmouth, Jurries scored from the six, Turnquist converted, and the Oles won going away 27–14. In the second half, Jurries scored again, followed by Winter, Greenslit, and Algoe. The latter two set up their own scores with interceptions. The defensive line held Lawrence in check and Jurries, Greenslit, and Winter again ran effectively as the Oles dominated the Lawrence Vikings 28–8. Co-captain Ron Ree confused the Viking defense with his play calling and running as he scored three times. Hartzell, Turnquist, Rajala, Anderson, and Caple were also outstanding.

"They began as also-rans and finished like champions"[140] was the description in the Nov. 13, 1959, *Messenger*. A third-place finish in the league and a number of under-classmen recognized on the all-conference team gave optimism for the season to come.

Curt Hartzell was named MVP in recognition of his iron man play all season. Rajala was the club's only first-team all-conference selection with Jurries, Bergstrom, and Winter

Bill Winter runs against Grinnell, 1959

on the second team, and Obermeyer, Hartzell, Caple, Turnquist, Greenslit, and Ree garnering honorable mention. Greenslit and Rajala were elected co-captains for 1960.

With freshmen not eligible for varsity competition, a frosh coach was

needed, and Ole alum Paul Quam '56, was appointed. Quam was named to all-conference grid teams for three years and was nationally recognized as a member of the Williamson All-America team in 1955.

Don Jurries carries against Knox, 1959

Bill Greenslit runs against Carleton, 1959

Homecoming festivities, 1950s

Chapter 6: The '60s, '70s, and '80s; Conference Changes; Dominance in the Midwest; The Renewed MIAC Challenge

1960

Thirty-five varsity candidates survived two weeks of preseason drills in preparation for the 1960 season. Returning lettermen included an array of strong running backs — Greenslit, Winter, Jurries, Algoe, and Norman. Interior linemen were Everson, DeFor, Oppegard, Hindermann, Moir, Anderson, and Hoven, with Bergstrom, Diedrich, and Einarson working at end.

The Oles opened successfully out of town, downing Beloit 20–6. Winter turned in an outstanding two-way performance with 89 yards rushing and 11 tackles as a linebacker. Everson and Harold Christenson were leading tacklers also.

Cornell came to town for the home opener, and the Lions avenged the previous season's 19–0 loss, controlling the game and winning 21–7. The passing of Denny Davis complemented the strong running of Greenslit and Winter. Hindermann, Everson, and Winter sparked a strong defensive effort.

The Ripon Redmen, featuring several players from Porter-coached Neenah High School teams, came to town for Homecoming. Two dazzling

touchdown runs of 80 and 65 yards by "Bullet Bill" Greenslit, augmented by a Winter score and a scoring pass, Davis to Diedrich, added up to a decisive 26–13 victory. Ends Bergstrom and Diedrich and tackles Hindermann and Anderson keyed a strong defense.

The long trip to Knox was next. The previous two games with the Siwashers had been nailbiters (29–21 and 7–6), and this one was to continue the tradition. Prior to the game, Don Canfield, writing in the *Messenger*, noted that, "it'll be an upset if we lose, but they'll be up for Homecoming."[141]

A strong first half gave the Oles a 21–0 lead. Big plays included a fingertip catch by Bergstrom of a Davis pass, a 42-yard interception return by Algoe, and a quarterback sneak by Davis. But Siwash roared back in the second half to take a 22–21 lead before a sustained drive, culminating in a Greenslit score, pulled out a 28–22 win.

Four in a row for the '60 season, added to the five consecutive wins ending the previous campaign, gave the Oles a nine-game streak heading into the Goat game. A Parents' Day crowd at Manitou Field was disappointed as

the Carleton Knights scored early and hung on to notch a 20–13 win. Two fumbles, two roughing the kicker penalties, and a short punt from the end zone were breakdowns which toppled the Oles in the fourth period.

At the season's midpoint, St. Olaf led the conference with a 4–1 mark; Coe and Monmouth were tied for second with 3–1–1 records. St. Olaf and Coe were not scheduled to play.

The Oles racked up victories five and six (in seven starts) with wins over Grinnell, 21–14, and Monmouth, 36–12. Against Grinnell, Davis' passes on a poor day for passing engineered two touchdowns. A 62-yard punt of a rain-soaked football by Winter kept the Pioneers in poor field position. The win over Monmouth clinched at least a tie for the conference crown. The Oles led 16–6 at the half and continued to play well after intermission. The action included touchdowns by Davis on an 11-yard keeper, Dave Silcox on an 18-yard pass from Davis, Algoe on a 67-yard interception return, and a field goal by Moir.

At Lawrence, Dads' Day is special, and the Vikings didn't disappoint their

The 1960 championship team, Bill Greenslit and Jack Rajala, captains

Bill Winter knifes through the Cornell line, 1960

Stan Oppegard, guard, 1961

faithful as they upset the Oles 20–16. Stellar defensive play by Tom Everson with 15 tackles wasn't enough.

Despite the loss to Lawrence, St. Olaf backed into the undisputed conference championship by virtue of Coe's victory over second-place Carleton.

Co-captain Jack Rajala at center, Dave Hindermann at tackle, and Bill Winter at fullback were rewarded with first-team all-conference slots. Co-captain Bill Greenslit and Tom Everson were named to the second team with John Bergstrom, Bill Diedrich, Bill Anderson, Denny Davis, and Don Jurries garnering honorable mention. The MVP honor went to Greenslit, and Everson and Winter were elected co-captains for 1961.

1960 Season Note

The freshman football squad was referred to as the "Lionettes" in a *Messenger* article.

1961

Coming off two consecutive 6–2 seasons and a conference crown, the Oles were high going into the '61 campaign and promptly reeled off two victories — both in the rain.

The opener was against Coe at Cedar Rapids. It was the first time the Oles and the Kohawks had tangled since 1958. The Kingston Stadium turf was in bad shape, as it often was because of the number of teams that used it, and a driving rain throughout the game turned it into a mudhole. It was a challenging initiation, to say the least, for rookie quarterback Steve Greenfield, but he rose to the occasion and directed the team like a veteran. The Oles scored 19 first-half points and made them stand up for a 19–8 victory. Bill Winter scored all three touchdowns, the first capping an 81-yard drive with the opening kickoff. Winter had 115 rushing yards for the game. Four Coe fumbles helped mightily. The Kohawks' lone score came late in the game.

Sophomores Fred Meyer, Mark Hoven, Ken Throlson, and Chuck Peterson contributed strong defensive line play for the Oles. Dale Liesch and Keith West stood out in the defensive secondary.

Captains Tom Everson and Bill Winter confer with Coach Porter, 1960

Remaining on the road for a second game, the Oles faced similar rainy weather against Beloit. The hosts capitalized on a fumble to open the scoring, but the Oles countered when West went in from the two and Winter slanted off left tackle for the two-point conversion that brought an 8–7 win. Workhorse Winter had 85 tough yards on 21 carries.

The weather and Ole fortunes both changed the next week as Cornell came to town, spotted the home team a touchdown, and then roared back for a 26–7 victory on the strength of a dominating passing game. It was hot and humid, temperature in the high 80s, and a large Luther League crowd in the stands.

It was more of the same the next Saturday, as an aggressive Ripon team invaded Manitou Heights with an aerial game as strong as Cornell's. This time, however, the Oles prevailed, scoring 27 first-half points, and the Redmen were unable to catch up. Winter scored on an 86-yard run and a one-yard plunge. His 201 yards on 26 carries outgained the entire Ripon squad. Greenfield hit Mark Aamot twice with scoring passes of 44 and 51 yards. Harold Christenson was "the Bear" on the field. Sophomores West, Liesch, Meyer, Peterson, Aus, Mostrom, Ruohoniemi, Johnson, Throlson, and Mark McKenzie came through with big games.

The game was costly as eight St. Olaf players had to leave the game due to injuries. Twin Cities' media and national wire services jumped on the game delay due to injuries. An AP story out of New York stated, "At Northfield, Minnesota, the game between St. Olaf and Ripon Colleges was held up for 40 minutes to enable ambulances to carry wounded players from the field."[142] Cause for some of the delay was Jon Mostrom's dislocated shoulder, which compelled Doc Pete [college physician, Dr. Donald Peterson] and a student trainer to transfer Jon to the college hospital. Liesch incurred a possible concussion. No doctor or emergency vehicle was present, so there was a delay until medical personnel could be summoned.[143]

An Ole squad depleted by injury faced the Carls in the Goat game. For the third time in the season, the Oles would attempt to trump a good passing team with a sound rushing offense — and with Mostrom, Liesch, and Ruohoniemi out and Aamot a last-minute scratch (an eye specialist advised against his playing). John Bergstrom hauled in passes of 17 and 44 yards and played his usual bruising game at defensive end. Tom Johnson played an inspired game in Aamot's absence, and the defense held the Carls to 39 yards rushing on 39 tries, but it wasn't quite enough.

Trailing 27–20 with a minute remaining, five yards separated the Oles from the tying or winning score, but a fourth-down play missed a first down by inches. It was one of the most exciting games in the Ole-Carl goat series.[144]

Picking themselves up from the Carleton defeat, the Oles, with Canfield, Everson, and Aamot back in the lineup, mowed down Knox 34–0. "Winter-led Vikings snow hapless Siwashers, 34 to 0," the *Messenger* headline proclaimed. Winter, indeed, ran wild. The fullback carried the ball 25 times for 120 yards, scored 20 points on three touchdowns and a two-point conversion, blocked a punt, punted for a 52-yard average, caught two passes for 45 yards — and backed up the line on defense, as well. Aamot scored twice, and Bergstrom and Everson kicked PATs.

Grinnell brought a 5–1 mark to Manitou Field the next Saturday. The game matched two outstanding fullbacks — Winter of St. Olaf and John Hartung of the Pioneers — each with a strong supporting cast. Leading 15–14 in an even game, Grinnell punched over a third touchdown, but missed the conversion. The Oles, pressed for time, went 70 yards with Winter scoring. With everyone in attendance, including the Grinnell defense, knowing what the next play

would be, Bill vaulted into the end zone for the winning two points and a 22–21 win — a great comeback.

Needing a last-game win over Monmouth and a Grinnell triumph over Cornell, the Oles traveled to Monmouth with high title hopes. Aamot returned the opening kickoff 95 yards for a quick lead and the Oles went on to shell the Scots for a 35–8 victory. A strong defensive line held the Scots to 17 yards rushing, while Winter, Aamot, and Ron Madsen carried the offensive load. Winter scored three times; Aamot added another to his game-opening shocker, and Bergstrom went five for five on PATs. Meanwhile, Grinnell did its part by defeating Cornell, thus insuring a three-way title tie among St. Olaf, Grinnell, and Cornell.

Seniors Harold Christenson, Bill Diedrich, Bergstrom, Bill Anderson, Everson, Winter, Hindermann, Oppegard, Greenfield, Koch, and Bloedel led a group of outstanding student athletes to a three-season record of 18–6 with two conference championships.

"The players were splashing around in Monmouth's fine swimming pool when the news came — Grinnell 30, Cornell 26! Bedlam broke loose as first coaches and then co-captains were tossed into the pool."[145] Three hundred loyal, cheering student fans greeted the

The 1961 championship team, Tom Everson and Bill Winter, captains

Bill Winter, 1961

Captain Mark Aamot, 1962

squad upon its return to the campus at about 1 a.m.

The conference champions placed five men on the first and second all-conference teams, and six others received honorable mention.

Bill Winter was named to the first team on both offense and defense — fullback on offense, linebacker on defense. He was the only athlete so honored. The other Ole first team selections were tackle Hinderman on offense and Aamot, defensive back. Second-team selections included Bergstrom, end on offense and defense, and Hinderman, tackle. Those awarded honorable mention were Bill Anderson, Oppegard, Gene Knutson, Greenfield, Harold Christenson, and Everson. Winter was named most valuable, and Everson won the tackling award for the third consecutive year. Mark Aamot and Don Canfield were elected co-captains for 1962.

1961 Season Notes

Quarterback Steve Greenfield is a grandson of the late Dr. J.A. Aasgaard, an Ole alum of 1916, who would later become president of Concordia College in Moorhead and still later president of the Evangelical Lutheran Church (ELC).

Bill Winter was indeed a remarkable performer on the gridiron, and his prowess was soon to travel beyond Northfield and the Midwest. Winter was signed as a free agent by the New York Giants of the National Football League in the spring of 1962. He passed up his senior season with the Ole baseball team in order to focus on conditioning for his NFL opportunity. In the Giants' preseason training camp that summer, Winter won a slot as a starting linebacker.

It was remarkable enough for an undrafted rookie to make the ball club in any capacity at a time when the NFL included only 14 teams. To crack the starting lineup was unheard of. On track for an outstanding NFL career, Winter's playing days were cut short by a knee injury after four-plus seasons.

His life ended tragically in 1993 as a result of an accident while he was preparing his campground for the season. All who

played with, coached, or watched Bill Winter play were privileged to have had the opportunity to be associated with this man of integrity, character, and outstanding athletic ability.

1962

Back-to-back championship seasons in 1960 and 1961 and the loss by graduation of stellar seniors who had gone 18–6 for their varsity careers posed an intimidating challenge for the 1962 Oles. But it would become apparent that this group, led by co-captains Aamot and Canfield, were up to it.

Aamot's running highlighted an impressive 23–8 victory over the Coe Kohawks in the season and home opener. Coe scored first on a safety, but George Anderson's field goal put the Oles up by one. Aamot's four-yard touchdown run in the third was the only other scoring. In the fourth period, Coe scored only to be trumped by Aamot's 85-yard return of the following kickoff.

Rod Skoge, Aamot, and Fred Russler intercepted Kohawk passes, and Russler returned his for a touchdown with 16 seconds to play.

Linebackers Captain Canfield and McKenzie, along with Fred Meyer at end and Chuck Peterson at tackle, contributed strong games. Anderson chipped in two PATs to go with his early field goal.

St. Olaf mistakes and Beloit's league-leading defense added up to a 19–13 loss the following week, but it was tight. A Beloit pass from the Ole three in the last 1:14 was the difference.

A week later against Cornell at Mt. Vernon, it looked as though the Oles were going down again, but one of those plays that makes the college game thrilling turned defeat to victory in literally the last seconds of the first half. With the Rams leading 9–7, Cornell's Steve Miller intercepted a Dale Liesch aerial and returned it to the Ole 10-yard-line.

Trying to gain a decisive halftime advantage, Cornell passed unsuccessfully twice. On the third attempt the Oles were flagged for interference, and the Rams were in business at the one with 10 seconds left. The Oles blunted two thrusts, and it was fourth down at the one with three seconds left. Cornell's Munson handed off to his halfback Hill who tried to sweep right end. Dave Hirschy crashed through and appeared to have tackled Hill, but while falling, Hill flipped the ball back to Munson. Rushed hard by Canfield, Munson threw into the end zone. Skoge came from the far side of the field, cut in front of the intended receiver, speared the ball, and raced 99 yards to score. Pete Aus rammed in for two and the score was 15–9 and that's how it ended.[146]

Sophomores Warren Tang, Brian Kispert and Hirschy sparkled on defense, while Jim Burner stood out on offense.

With the early season record at 2–1, a Ripon squad, led by quarterback Jack Ankerson, was the next challenge. Memories of the previous season's contest in which seven Oles were lost to injury were not motive for revenge but certainly a reminder that any game with the Redmen in this era would be physical. It was a 14–14 standoff. Both teams had scores nullified by penalties. Both Ole touchdowns came through the air with Leisch throwing to Meyer for 20 and Aamot for 37. Defensively, Bob Heideman, Hirschy, and Ken McKenzie, just back from injury, were standouts.

With Carleton leading the Goat series 26–13–1, the Oles were up for Homecoming to "Snarl the Carls" 27–13. Aamot more or less took things into his own hands, carrying the ball 40 times for 190 yards. On two scoring drives, he carried the ball five times and three times in succession. The Oles also were opportunists. Peterson recovered a fumble at the Carleton 15 to set up one score. Liesch returned an interception to the Carls' 12, and Tom Johnson's late pick stopped the visitors' last effort. Another highlight was Meyer's caused fumble, which Canfield pounced on in the end zone for the Oles' fourth score.

The Oles took two of the last three contests to end the season 5–2–1, only one win fewer than each of the two previous seasons.

After a long bus trip to Galesburg, Ill., the Lions played listlessly but well enough to shut out the Siwashers 10–0. Anderson's second-quarter field goal was the only scoring in the first half. Aamot briefly bobbled the second half kickoff, but regained control, started up the middle and then veered to the sideline and raced 90 yards for the game's only six-pointer.

Harboring visions of a third consecutive conference crown, the Oles were up against undefeated Grinnell. The Pioneers were a complete team, offensively at least, with Bowers, Peterson, and Goldman keying their running attack and a potent Orchard to Peterson passing combination. They dominated the Oles 21–7. Aamot's 47-yard left end sweep was the only Lion scoring.

Alert defensive play — including two interceptions by Jon Mostrom, a third by Tom Johnson and two fumbles recovered by Heideman — kept the Pioneers' scoring total down.

The Lions finished the season in strong fashion with a convincing 27–0 victory over Monmouth on Manitou Field. The Oles amassed a 137 to 78 rushing edge and 104 to 88 passing and didn't allow the Scots past midfield until late in the fourth period. Herm Fogal's bull-like rush from the six opened the scoring. The second touchdown resulted when Kispert blocked a Monmouth punt and Gene Knutson recovered in the end zone. The final two scores came on Aamot's 12th touchdown run of the season and a Liesch to Meyer pass. The alert Ole defense picked off five Scot aerials. Tom Johnson pulled down two, Liesch, Mostrom, and Paul Blom one each.

Aamot on offense and Meyer on defense received first team all-conference honors. Chuck Peterson, Clark Westphal, Bob Heideman, Don Canfield, and Tom Johnson also received recognition. Seniors Knutson, Mohwinkel, Blom, Canfield, Fogal, Madson, Aamot, Johnson, and McKenzie concluded strong careers

The 1962 team, Mark Aamot and Don Canfield, captains

Dale Liesch, 1964

"Mutt and Jeff," 1964 captains Brian Kispert and Clark Westphal

with a three-year record of 17–6–1. Aamot was designated most valuable, and Fred Meyer and Chuck Peterson were elected co-captains for 1963.

Rand Becomes Sixth President

Dr. Sidney A. Rand, a Minnesota native and graduate of Concordia College, became St. Olaf's sixth president at inaugural ceremonies held on Manitou Field Sept. 16, 1963.[147]

President Rand became a good booster of Ole athletes and athletics. He served 17 years in office and was appointed U.S. Ambassador to Norway by President Jimmy Carter in 1979. Rand died in Northfield in 2003.

1963

Whenever a team loses a perpetual offensive threat like Mark Aamot, there has to be concern about the attack. Some of the anxiety was dispelled early as the Oles thumped a favored Lawrence squad 23–8 in the home opener. Dale Liesch and Pete Aus, alternating at quarterback, sparked the offense. Touchdowns were scored by Liesch, Jim Burner, and Captain Fred Meyer. The tempo was set when Liesch's 43-yard punt put the Vikings in the hole on their one. A host of Ole tacklers, led by Tom Mickelson, swarmed the Lawrence quarterback for a safety.

After only one game, the Manitou *Messenger,* overcome by exuberance, picked St. Olaf and Ripon as conference favorites.[148] And the paper looked prophetic as the Oles quickly disposed of Coe 17–12 and squeezed by Beloit 8–7, but an observer might have sensed danger in the slim margins.

In the former contest, Coe led 12–10 late in the game, when linebacker Brian Kispert picked off a Kohawk pass and brought it back to the one. Dave Knudsen pounded over from there for the game-winner. With Ben Danielson and Liesch doubtful, the Oles traveled to Beloit with only 30 players. A defensive battle ensued. The Ole defenders, led by Meyer and Dave Hirschy stopped the Buccaneers three times inside the 10-yard-line. John Schumm's 55-yard touchdown run and Pete Aus's two-point conversion provided the one-point winning margin.

Despite the slim margin of victory in two of the first three contests, the Oles were riding high as Cornell came to town for Homecoming. The game was an occasion for honoring St. Olaf's last undefeated squad — the 1953 team. And as often happens, the celebratory event was to turn to ashes. The score was knotted at 7–7 at intermission, but the Rams returned the second-half kickoff for a touchdown, and minutes later embarked on a 70-yard drive. Coach Bob Gelle observed that "you have a tiger by the tail" — or in this case, a ram. It went downhill from there, and Cornell went home with a 35–7 win.

A week later, Coach Mel Taube's Carleton squad lived up to its slogan, "Spread Ole," and knocked the Oles out of title contention with a 29–20 win. The game broke open late in the first period when the Carls scored nine points in less than a minute on a fumble recovery in the end zone and a touchdown on the ensuing kickoff. The Knights were up 23–0 in the second quarter before Mark Kjeldgaard returned a punt 55 yards for a score and Liesch raced 98 yards with an intercepted pass for another. Halfback Tom Nibbe scored in the fourth period, but it was, as they say, too little too late.

Fighting back gamely, the Oles turned in their best game of the season the following week against the powerful Ripon Redmen. But they couldn't quite contain Jack Ankerson and his mates and went down for the third week, 27–19. For the second game in a row, an opponent returned the second-half kickoff for a score. A John Schumm to Fred Meyer pass narrowed the count to 20–13, and each team added a counter in the final period — Liesch for the Oles after an inspiring pass reception/run by Howie Felber. Tom Heiberg, Meyer and Felber were cited for outstanding play.

Determined to end the three-game string of losses, an inspired Lion squad crunched the Knox Siwashers 52–8. Four hundred twenty-four offensive yards provided a "bench-clearing" game. Burner, Skoge, Meyer (two), Kjeldgaard, and Ylvisaker crossed the double stripe for the Oles — some in spectacular fashion. Meyer picked off a flat pass and went 40 yards; Kjeldgaard, behind great downfield blocking, went 65 yards with a punt return.

Inconsistency returned the next week, and the result was a 26–7 loss to the Grinnell Pioneers. A wobbly, deflected pass, a clipping penalty, and a fourth down fumble were key. The 4–4 season spelled a second-division finish, while Ripon went 8–0 to take it all.

Captain Fred Meyer climaxed an outstanding career by being the Oles' only first-team all-conference pick at defensive end. He also won AP Little All-America honorable mention and was elected MVP. Dale Liesch, Clark Westphal, and Brian Kispert were named second-team all-conference, and Tom Heiberg and Mark Kjeldgaard garnered honorable mention. Westphal and Kispert were elected co-captains for 1964.

1964

Co-captains Brian Kispert, 5'8" and 175 pounds, and Clark Westphal, 6'4" and 210, were the "Mutt and Jeff" combination that led the '64 Oles. Early season starters on offense were Ben Danielson and Howard Felber, ends; Westphal and Tom Heiberg, tackles; Kispert and Tom Michelson, guards; Larry Cohrt, center; John Schumm, quarterback; Rod Skoge and Don Mersch, halfbacks, and

Len Ackermann, Bob Heidemann, Dave Hirschy, and Tom Heiberg, 1964

Jim Berner, fullback. Defensemen who moved in included Dave Hirschy, Roger Stensvad, Paul Skibsrud, Bill West, and Dave Knudsen.

The squad split in their first two contests, posting a convincing 20–0 win over Lawrence, and succumbing to Coe 16–6, at least partially as a result of too many mistakes.

A strong defensive unit shut out Lawrence in the opener, limiting the Vikings to 90 yards rushing and intercepting four passes. Skoge scored twice, capping sustained marches, one on a 25-yard pass from Schumm. Against Coe, the Oles gave up the ball six times — four fumbles and two interceptions —

too much of a handicap to overcome an offensive statistical advantage. Knudsen scored the only Ole touchdown.

"Tuc the Bucs Away" was the Homecoming slogan with Beloit supplying the opposition in game three. The teams were evenly matched, the lead see-sawed, and some younger men contributed heroics when veterans went down with injury. The Oles eventually wound up on top, 15–13. The Ole defense shone again, holding Beloit to 44 yards on 37 rushes.

The Oles were up 7–6 at halftime, but the Bucs scored shortly after intermission to take a 13–7 lead. With quarterback Schumm and halfback

The 1963 team, Chuck Peterson and Fred Meyer, captains

Brian Kispert, 1965

*Dr. Axel C. Bundgaard,
athletic director, 1965–72*

Skoge injured, sophomore signal caller Gary Soderberg moved his squad downfield in eight plays to score. The key play was a 37-yard pass to sophomore end Steve Refsell. With four minutes remaining, fullback Knudsen scored his second touchdown of the day and then carried for the two-point conversion and the 15–13 victory margin. Bill West, Mersch, and Larry Bugni also were cited for their play.

The following week, supplying the opposition for the Cornell Rams' Homecoming, the Oles gave up 14 fourth-quarter points to lose 28–13, evening the season count at 2–2. Soderberg threw scoring strikes to Rod Olson and Felber, but costly fumbles plagued the Oles.

With Schumm and Skoge still sidelined by injury, Mersch took over and racked up 126 yards on 14 carries to lead his team to a 21–7 Goatrophy win over Carleton at Manitou Field. Bill West's interception set up Mersch's 39-yard left end sweep and the Lions' first score. With Soderberg shaken up and on the sidelines, Bob Hjany came on to score the go-ahead touchdown for the margin of victory. Al Wall's interception set the stage for Mersch to pound in from two yards out with his second touchdown and valuable insurance points. The rugged Ole defense limited the Carls to eight yards rushing and contributed to an overall yardage margin of 295 to 140.

In what was considered their best showing of the season, the Oles matched their rugged defense against Ripon's conference-leading offense. The Redmen turned a first-quarter break into a touchdown and then held off the stubborn Oles to post a 7–0 victory. Five Ole drives penetrated inside the Ripon 20 only to be turned back by the Redmen's defense.

Taking their strong defense to Galesburg in search of their first road win of the season, the Oles started slowly, but then came on strong to defeat the Knox Siwashers 27–6. A Paul Skibsrud interception and the first of two blocked punts by Kispert led to a pair of field goals by Schumm and a 6–0 halftime lead.

The Lions erupted for three touchdowns after intermission to win going away. Mersch, Olson and John Anderson provided the

scoring, while the defense that had been playing strongly all season was led, in this instance, by Heidemann, Westphal, Kispert, Hirschy, Heiberg, and Danielson.

This defense met its match in the final game of the season when Grinnell's powerful ground game gouged them for 262 yards and three second-quarter touchdowns. Hirschy blocked a Pioneer punt for a safety in the first quarter, but that was it, offensively, for St. Olaf until Skibsrud recovered a fumble in the the third period. Soderberg's cross-country pass to Burner brought the ball to the 20. Mersch ran it in from the one, and Knudsen ran for the two-point conversion, but the 21-point second quarter was too much to overcome against a good Grinnell team.

The squad was disappointed with the 4–4 season and a fifth-place tie in the conference. It had displayed good football throughout, and at times, outstanding — especially the defensive group. Reflective of the season was the squad's decision not to select an MVP. All-conference selections Tom Heiberg and Tom Michelson were elected captains for 1965.

Christenson Ends St. Olaf Career

Two significant changes in the St. Olaf athletic scene occurred during 1964–65. Prior to the start of the college year, Ade Christenson had announced his retirement effective at the end of the school year. Six years before, Ade had turned over the football coaching chores to Tom Porter. Now he had decided to end his career. Ade had coached at St. Olaf for 37 years, from 1927 through 1958, with the exception of a few years during World War II. His teams had won six conference football championships and others in track and basketball. His intramural program attracted 80 percent of the male students and was nationally recognized as a model for colleges and universities.

When Ade retired, editors of the college alumni magazine wrote, "We shall omit his won-lost record, which is impressive, and his championship teams, which are numerous. Instead, we shall hand him a pen and ask him to write about the principles that guided his coaching and the men he coached, for his athletic record is a story of men and principles rather than wins and losses."

Ade's stamp shall remain forever on St. Olaf athletics. He participated as a student-athlete in the early years and then returned to build and lead the program that is his legacy.

Bundgaard Becomes Athletic Director

In January 1965, Dr. Axel C. Bundgaard was selected to succeed Ade as athletic director, his appointment to be effective with the beginning of the 1965–66 academic year. Ax was a graduate of Midland College in Nebraska and earned graduate degrees from the University of Michigan and the University of Iowa. He came to St. Olaf from South Dakota State University where he was director of athletics. Prior to that service, he had been basketball and track coach at Wartburg College.

1965

The *Messenger* for Sept. 17, 1965, carried a gloomy projection, "Injury, Desertion Knock St. Olaf Football Hopes." The headline would appear to have been an overstatement. Dave Knudsen's leukemia diagnosis and John Schumm's lingering recovery from a knee injury were real blows fueling the pessimistic outlook. Two other veterans chose not to play the grid sport.

Still, the squad had high aspirations for improving on the 4–4 record of 1964. Al Wall, Lee Mesna, Rod Olson, John Anderson, Doug Blanchard, Gary Soderberg, Mark Kjeldgaard, Don Liesch, and Paul Anderson were proven men back in the backfield. Captains Tom Heiberg and Tom Michelson, along with Steve Refsell, Mike Solhaug, Howie Felber, Ranier Lobitz, and Mike Gorton promised to be solid up front.

An eight-game schedule and a 10-team league prevented a complete round robin, so the Oles entertained the Monmouth Scots in the opener without having played them in the previous two seasons. Sophomore quarterback Anderson directed an 80-yard drive late in the third period and scored himself on a sneak, but the Oles fell short. The Scots walked off with a 7–6 squeaker.

The Oles traveled to Appleton, Wis., the following Saturday to challenge the Lawrence Vikings in the dedication of their fine new stadium, the Lawrence Bowl. It was a good ball game on a beautiful day, but again the visitors fell a few points short. Three Ole fumbles in the first half led to a pair of Viking touchdowns. An Anderson to Refsell 44-yard pass play, a 38-yard aerial, Anderson to Ward Haugen, and an Anderson sneak for a touchdown were the Ole tallies. The Lions were stopped at the one on an attempt to tie the

score, and the Lawrence Vikings packed it away 26–21.

The season's third game, Homecoming against Coe, was notable for two features — a strong defensive unit began to come together, and junior halfback Dave Krahn, "a heretofore unknown," gave promise of future greatness with a 120-yard rushing performance. The defense — Lobitz, Nelson, Heiberg, Bohdan Melnychenko, Mueller, Refsell, Solhaug, Anderson, Wall, and Don Webber — limited the Kohawks to 51 yards rushing. It all added up to a convincing 34–14 win. Krahn and Doug Blanchard each scored twice and Anderson once. Schumm booted four PATs. A Wall fumble recovery and a blocked punt by Nelson and Lobitz set up touchdowns.

The following week, the defense proved it was no fluke as they held a highly touted Beloit aerial game to 78 yards. The Anderson-led offense piled up 244 yards, with Krahn contributing 144 of them, including a 61-yard breakaway, and the Buccaneers went down 24–7. Refsell gathered in four Anderson passes, and Blanchard complemented Krahn's outside game with 69 tough yards, largely on inside plays.

The 43rd St. Olaf-Carleton game — with the Knights leading the series 27–15–1 — provided the season's third victory. The defense again played a major role in a 28–20 triumph. The

The 1965 team, Tom Heiberg and Tom Michelson, captains

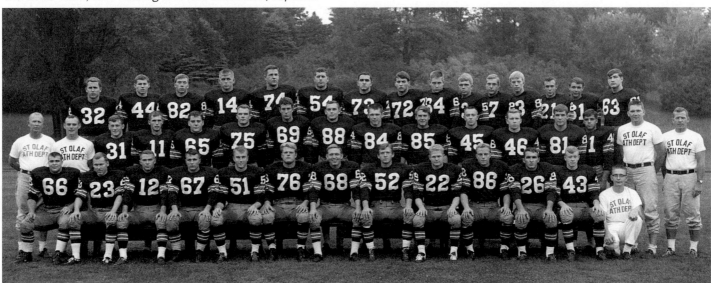

Dave Knudsen, 1965

*Mike Solhaug and
Steve Refsell, 1966 captains*

*Brothers Harry and Dave
Mueller, starting tackles, 1966*

defenders came up with two goal-line stands, a fourth and one stop and an intercepted pass and 30-yard return by Bryce Heumoeller for the final Ole tally. Singled out for special plaudits was Mike Solhaug, linebacker and defensive signal caller. Carleton's final score came via an end zone recovery following an Ole miscue after the Knights had been stopped at the Ole half-yard line

Cornell evened the season count at 3–3 the next week with a 21–15 win. The Rams' three long scoring plays — 68, 35, and 18 yards — were countered by Anderson's sneak for a score and his pass to Haugen.

Krahn rolled up 190 yards rushing and Schumm booted three field goals to lead St. Olaf over league-leading Ripon, 22–7. The high-powered Ole offense, in this game at least, rolled up 467 yards against the league's leading defensive unit. Anderson's play calling had the Redmen on their heels all afternoon. A 29-yard halfback pass, Lee Mesna to Krahn, set up one score and a 66-yard Krahn "dive" play was good for another. Again outstanding, the defense allowed the Redmen only 18 yards rushing and contributed a goal line stand from the six in the fourth period.

Coach Porter called it "the finest team effort in recent years."[149]

Momentum from that excellent effort carried over to the next Saturday when the Oles amassed 554 offensive yards in trouncing Knox 53–0 in the season finale on Manitou Field. Anderson tossed touchdown passes to Krahn and Haugen, while Soderberg fired scoring strikes to Rod Olson and Mike Wittkamper. Wall also tallied twice. The vaunted shovel pass play resulted in touchdown jaunts by Krahn and Olson. Krahn also had a 94-yard touchdown scamper to round out a fine offensive display. Needless to say, the shutout spoke for excellent defense also.

Krahn's 210-yard day gave him 942 for the season and a gaudy 7.2 yards per carry. The 5–3 season was good for third place in the conference, the best finish since 1961. The offense wound up leading the league with 2,739 yards, while the defense was third. John Schumm provided the strongest kicking game in years. The Toms — Heiberg and Michelson — were an

outstanding blocking combination as well as fine leaders.

First-team all-conference honors went to Heiberg, tackle; Gorton, center; Lobitz, tackle; Refsell, end, and Solhaug, linebacker. Michelson and Krahn landed second-team berths. Ranier Lobitz credited Coach Chuck Lunder for his all-conference performance. "He taught us how to play defense," Lobitz said. Nine seniors concluded their careers: Heiberg, Michelson, Kjeldgaard, Schumm, Harold Peterson, Rod Olson, Felber, Wayne Mortenson, and Tom Ylvisaker.

Dave Krahn was designated MVP, and Mike Solhaug and Steve Refsell were elected captains for 1966.

Leukemia Claims Dave Knudsen

Late in the 1965 season, on Oct. 29, Dave Knudsen lost his fight against leukemia. The 1966 *Viking* carried the following tribune:

"This fall, St. Olaf lost David Stephen Knudsen to leukemia. After a summer of illness, he was able to be at school for the first few weeks in the fall and hoped to finish his senior year. Although his many friends and classmates prayed his recovery might somehow be a permanent one, Dave died on Oct. 29 at the Northfield Hospital. On the Hill, Dave gained many athletic honors, setting both college and conference records in track and becoming a mainstay of St. Olaf's football team. Those who knew him, though, remember him not as number 34, but rather as a warm person with a sense of humor as well as a sense of conviction. In the words of a friend, 'We are sorry he's gone. But we will never forget.'"

1965 Season Note

The Sept. 16, 1966, Manitou *Messenger* had a front-page article describing the Skoglund Athletic Center, then under construction. Completion was scheduled for September 1967.

1966

A squad of 42 — 20 of them letter winners — prepared for the '66 campaign. Probable starters were Steve Refsell and Ward Haugen, ends; Harold and Dave Mueller, tackles; Mike Solhaug and LeRoy Klemp, guards; Denny Myers, center; Paul

Anderson, quarterback; Dave Krahn and Lee Mesna, halfbacks, and Doug Blanchard, fullback. On defense, it was Refsell and Myers, ends; Erik Nelson and Ranier Lobitz, tackles; Bohdan Melnychenko, middle guard; Solhaug, Kirk Anderson, and Al Wall, linebackers; Haugen and Bryce Huemoeller, halfbacks, and Dan Heartl, safety.

The squad opened with a rush, avenging the previous season's 7–6 loss to the Monmouth Scots with a 55–14 drubbing. The defense set a tone, holding Monmouth to a minus 13 yards rushing, including 56 yards in quarterback sacks. Picking up from the previous season, Anderson was on target with eight of 11 passes and Krahn rushed eight times for 113 yards.

The Lions spotted the Scots a one-yard quarterback sneak for a touchdown early, but were never challenged from that point on. It was 35–7 at the half.

Led by their outstanding quarterback, Chuck McKee, Lawrence put together two fourth-quarter touchdown

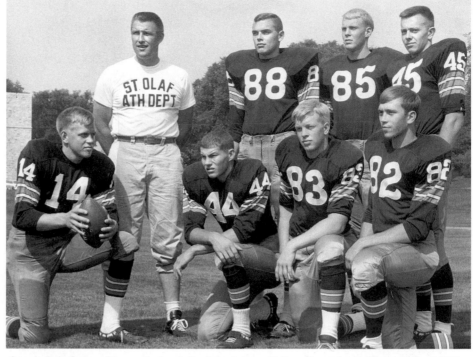

Coach Bob Gelle with quarterback Paul Anderson (14) and receivers Steve Refsell (88), Conrad Braaten (85), Dave Krahn (45), Lee Mesna (44), Jim Kindem (83), and Ward Haugen (82), 1966.

drives to edge the Oles 24–21. It was a seesaw battle of two good football teams. Krahn and Blanchard both had 100-yard plus games rushing.

The next week, Krahn made it nine consecutive games rushing for 100 or more yards as he led the Oles to a 19–9 victory over Coe. The Kohawks

Roll call prior to a trip, 1966

Kirk Anderson, 1967 captain

Dave Krahn, St. Olaf's first 1,000-yard rusher, MVP 1965, 1966

Lee Mesna, 1967 captain

managed a 9–7 lead in the third period, but the fourth belonged to the Oles as Krahn scored twice to ice the game.

Sparked by a defense that yielded only seven yards rushing and contributed two touchdowns of its own, St. Olaf "exploited" Beloit 36–0 in the Homecoming tilt. A first-quarter Paul Anderson to Refsell touchdown got things started, followed by a Kirk Anderson return of an interception for 23 yards. The second score for the defense was a brilliant 63-yard punt return by Heartl. Heartl also took a turn on offense, teaming with fellow sophomore Mike Schmiesing on a scoring pass. Krahn had his 10th consecutive 100-yard rushing game in the bag but lost four yards on his last two carries to fall back to 97. Still, not bad.

Amid cheers of "back to the books" from the Ole cheering section, a stingy Lion defense and the running of Blanchard and Krahn put down the Carls for the third year running. The score was 26–7. Blanchard scored twice in the first quarter and twice in the third. Both Doug and Krahn topped the 100-yards-rushing mark (again). Carleton was held to 168 total yards, including four attempts from the one-yard line. Seniors could boast of defeating Carleton all three of their varsity seasons.

In another convincing triumph, the Oles routed Cornell 49–7. Anderson threw to Refsell and Krahn for two scores and ran for a pair. A three-touchdown third quarter included an 85-yard run by Schmiesing and a Dan Franklin to Conrad Braaten scoring pass. Krahn galloped for 129 yards, bringing his season total to 747.

Undefeated Ripon was the next challenge with Kindem, Klemp, and Harry Mueller questionable. The Redmen's Bob Pellegrino got the contest off to a flying start, returning the opening kickoff 96 yards for a touchdown. The Oles struck back immediately with a 52-yard scoring bomb — Anderson to Refsell. In the second quarter, Anderson and Krahn ran for scores and a Mesna to Anderson throw-back pass went for a third, and the Oles led 28–14 at intermission. The teams traded touchdowns in the third period, but the Oles won going away with a pair of scores in the final quarter — a plunge by Krahn and a 12-yard pass from Anderson to Haugen. St. Olaf had a 499 to 287 statistical edge, and Krahn piled up 193 yards.

The following week's season finale was almost an anti-climax. The Oles led by a slim 7–0 margin at halftime, but they scored four unanswered touchdowns in the second half to shut out Knox 41–0. The scoring included a 15-yard run by Anderson, a fumble recovered in the end zone by Refsell, a 21-yard scamper by Krahn, and a final burst by Mesna. Krahn's game total of 90 yards put him at 1,030 for the season, making him the first Ole gridder to gain over 1,000 yards rushing in a season.

A *Messenger* headline provided a good season summary, "Oles Share Grid Title, Krahn nets over 1,000."[150] The Oles, Knox, and Ripon all had 7–1 seasons. The Oles boasted the league's top stats on offense and defense: 993 yards, 36 points per game, 129 yards and 10.2 points per game allowed by the defense.

Six Oles won all-conference recognition: Mike Gorton, tackle; Doug Blanchard, fullback; Dave Krahn, halfback; Steve Refsell, end; Bohdan Melnychenko; middle guard, and Ward Haugen, defensive back. Some deserving squad members not chosen for all-conference: Paul Anderson, quarterback, Mike Solhaug, linebacker, Kirk Anderson, linebacker, Ranier Lobitz and Erik Nelson, defensive tackles. Krahn was named MVP for the second season. Kirk Anderson and Lee Mesna were elected co-captains for 1967.

1966 Season Note

Good things were on the 1967 horizon as Bob Gelle's freshman team went undefeated.

1967

Eighteen returning lettermen and a good group moving up from an undefeated freshman squad gave a solid basis for optimism for the 1967 season. After a hiatus of two years, the Oles traveled to Grinnell to take on the Pioneers — a relatively unknown quantity because of the gap in competition. With junior Mike Schmiesing rushing for 135 yards in 28 carries, the Lions got out to a 21–0 second-quarter lead. But a rash of turnovers forced them to hold on to salvage a 28–20 win.

Schmiesing scored once, while Paul Anderson ran for two scores and passed to Lee Mesna for the fourth. Six turnovers put pressure on the defense, which responded heroically, holding the Pioneers to 30 yards rushing. They very nearly made up for the rushing drought with 173 yards passing.

In the home opener, the Oles outscored the Monmouth Scots 42–32 in a shootout. Schmiesing, running for 211 yards to go with his 135 the previous week, seemed to be proving himself a worthy successor to Dave Krahn. Paul Anderson scored four times and passed for nearly 200 yards. Kirk Anderson returned an interception for a score.

Monmouth's three scores in the fourth period tightened up an otherwise well-played game. Cited for their play on the Ole side were Haugen, Kindem, Tom Peinovich, Bob Wetterberg, Bohdan Melnychenko, and Anderson.

Hopes for another championship season received a jolt the following week when Lawrence, again led by their stellar quarterback, McKee, bested the Oles 28–7. Three Lawrence scoring drives began in Ole territory, the result of turnovers — a blocked punt, an intercepted pass, and a fumble. An Anderson to Wetterberg pass was the lone St. Olaf tally. Dick Hatle, Tom Stoltenberg, Dave Mueller, Don Krahn, and Dan Heartl were among those playing particularly well.

The Oles returned to the right side of the scoring tally the following week with a 34–0 shutout of Coe. Punter Bryce Willett, strong defensive play, and five solid scoring drives were highlights. Krahn, Hatle, Mueller, and Stoltenberg were defensive standouts, while Peinovich, Kindem, Mesna, Steve Weiner, Denny Myers, and Tim Smith shone on offense. Schmiesing and Wetterberg each hit paydirt twice, and Anderson passed to Mesna for the other score. Stoltenberg suffered a broken leg and hence was lost for the season.

An outstanding defense and a field goal by Schmiesing were enough to turn back Carleton 3–0 in the Goat game.

The 1966 team, Mike Solhaug and Steve Refsell, captains

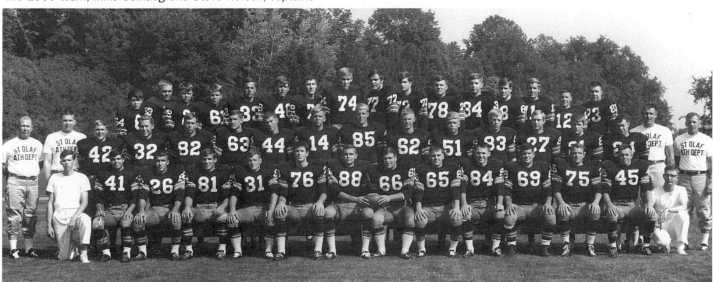

*Mike Schmiesing and
Denny Myers, 1968 captains*

Dan Heartl, 1968

The Carls completed seven passes — three of them to Oles. Dan Franklin picked off two, while the "lion," Ron Hunter, got one.

Tenacious Beloit held off an inconsistent St. Olaf offense for a 14–13 win. A fine punter kept the Oles' "backs to the wall." Wetterberg, on a 32-yard strike from Anderson, and Schmiesing, also on a pass play, accounted for the Ole scoring.

The Cornell Rams, whose 4–2 record matched the Oles,' invaded Manitou Field. Perhaps anxious to atone for the previous week's one-point loss, the Oles missed their third shutout of the season when Cornell scored in the last quarter. The final was Oles 23, Rams 8. Ron Hunter's ball-stealing play was a highlight. Kirk Anderson, Dick Swiggum, and Ward Haugen had interceptions, while Krahn, Mellby, and Franklin also played well on defense. Number one punter Bryce Willett was lost for the remainder of the season via injury.

Perennial power and keen rival Ripon was up in the season finale. Twelve seniors, who had gone 17–6 for their careers, had never lost to the Redmen. They made it three in a row with a 21–18, come-from-behind victory. Trailing three times in the course of the game, including an 18–14 deficit in the fourth period, the Oles mounted a "never say die" rally to win.

Coach Porter concluded that "this game was the highlight of the season." It wrapped up a 6–2 season and the runnerup spot in the conference. Paul Anderson provided great leadership; Schmiesing (15 points) and Wetterberg both ran well, while Haugen, Myers, Peinovich, Krahn, Melnychenko, and Gary Iverson stood out on defense.

Three-year starters were co-captains Kirk Anderson and Lee Mesna, Paul Anderson, Ward Haugen, and Bohdan Melnychenko. Other seniors, part of a strong contingent, were Bryce Huemoeller, Jim Kindem, Lynn Knutson, Conrad Braaten, Gary Erickson, Jon Hersch, and Bruce Stensvad. Kirk Anderson, Lee Mesna, and Paul Anderson, fittingly, were chosen as trio MVPs. All-conference honors went to Melnychenko, Kirk Anderson, Schmiesing, and Paul Anderson. Denny Myers and Mike Schmiesing were named co-captains for 1968.

*1968 coaches Dave Hauck, Chuck Lunder,
Jim Dimick and Bob Gelle*

At the beginning of the 1967–68 college year, Jim Dimick was appointed to the physical education faculty. A graduate of St. Cloud State, Jim had an impressive teaching and coaching career at the high school level in Wisconsin and Minnesota. His coaching assignments at St. Olaf were head baseball coach and assistant in football and basketball. "Dimmer" was to become legendary in the list of loyal and dedicated coaches who have served St. Olaf. In football, he was noted for his "fireside" chats with his defensive "trucks."

On Oct. 5, Bud Wilkinson, legendary former coach at the University of Oklahoma and former special advisor to the president of the United States on physical fitness, gave the address on the occasion of the opening of Skoglund Athletic Center. The center was a gift of Margaret and Howell Skoglund, both '25. Mr. Skoglund, an ex-Ole gridder, was for many years a member and chair of the St. Olaf Board of Regents.

Steve Ashley (future all-conference performer and Hall of Fame selection) was selected MVP of the 1967 freshman team.

1968

With Coach Porter on sabbatical leave at the University of Colorado, defensive secondary coach Dave Hauck took over the head coaching responsibilities, assisted by Jim Dimick and Chuck Lunder. Athletic director Ax Bundgaard returned to coaching to assist Bob Gelle with the freshman football squad.

Conference scoring leader Mike Schmiesing and two-way player Denny Myers led a veteran squad of 53, including 21 lettermen.

The Oles shut out Grinnell 28–0 on rain-soaked Manitou Field in the season opener. With Schmiesing getting special attention from the Pioneer defense, fullback Bob Wetterberg led the offense, prompting Coach Hauck's postgame comment: "the most outstanding back on the field."[151]

Schmiesing, despite the stacked defense, had scored twice by halftime — an 18-yard pass reception from Heartl and a 52-yard run. Wetterberg plunged for a third score. A Denny Nelson to Mike Holmquist pass in the fourth period completed the scoring. Steve Ashley, Arne Melby, and Steve Wiener intercepted Grinnell aerials, while Tim Onncn, Wiener, Iverson, Saxhaug, and Leon Lunder also contributed outstanding defensive play.

Rebounding from a 14–0 halftime deficit, the Oles fought back to gain a 21–21 tie with a powerful Monmouth squad. On the second play of the second half, Denny Nelson fired a

WESTERN UNION TELEGRAM

Philadelphia Eagles' telegram to Mike Schmiesing (photo courtesy of Mike Schmiesing)

short pass to Ashley. Steve pulled the ball in between two Scot defenders, and sprinted 73 yards to score. A series later, facing fourth and inches, Wetterberg burst up the middle for a 45-yard scoring run. Sometime later, a pass play moved the ball to the Scots' 30, and Nelson bootlegged it in from 14 yards out.

Wetterberg and Schmiesing carried for 250 yards in 55 plays from scrimmage. Myers and Dick Qualset also were cited for their play. On the downside, Dan Heartl and Don Krahn were victims of first-quarter knee injuries.

In another rain-spattered home game, the Oles handed the defending champion Lawrence Vikings their first shutout in four years, 21–0. On an early exchange of punts, Iverson recovered a Lawrence fumble, and Wetterberg subsequently scored from the seven. Near the end of the second

Schmiesing, led by Wiener and Holmquist, 1968 (photo courtesy of Mike Schmiesing)

Ole Gunderson, St. Olaf's all-time leading rusher, 1969

Tim Smith, 1969 captain and MVP (photo courtesy of Mike Schmiesing)

quarter, the "lion," Ron Hunter, snagged a Viking pass and returned it to the Lawrence 17. With the ball on the three-yard-line and 16 seconds left on the clock, the Oles called a strategy timeout. The field-goal unit, with Schmiesing the kicker and Ashley the holder came on the field. On a well-executed fake, Ashley kept the ball and ran it in for a touchdown and a 14–0 halftime lead.

The second half was played almost entirely on the Lawrence side of the midfield stripe. Coach Hauck praised the defensive secondary which held Lawrence to 11 yards passing. Kudos, also, to Coach Gelle for his thorough scouting report. Fullback Wetterberg was added to the injury list.

Upset-minded Coe took full advantage of injuries suffered by Oles in earlier games and walked away with a 19–0 victory. In particular, the injury to Wetterberg the week before enabled the Kohawks to concentrate on Schmiesing. Coe scored all its points in the first half, the last score coming with 25 seconds to play. The Oles were unable to mount a consistent offense.

The following week, however, the offense bounced back with a vengeance to outscore Carleton 38–7 in the Homecoming game. Ashley got the contest off to an explosive start, returning the opening kickoff 95 yards for a touchdown. The clock showed 14:47 to go in the first quarter. Halfback Bob Freed returned a punt to the Carleton 27, and Schmiesing scored from the two a few plays later. A Nelson to Steve Ahlgren pass and a Schmiesing PAT made it 21–0 with 7:19 left in the half.

Pressure on the Carl quarterback resulted in a lofted pass. A Dan Franklin interception and a 36-yard pass play, Nelson to Holmquist, put the ball near the Carls' goal. Wiener punched it in to make the halftime count 28–0.

Carleton avoided a shutout by pushing across a third-quarter touchdown, but an ensuing onside kick backfired, and the Oles drove for another tally. The deep three — Swiggum, Franklin, and Ashley — earned praise. Franklin and Ashley had two and three interceptions, respectively. A pair of Northfield sophomores, Leon Lunder and Doug Munson, also earned plaudits.

With both the offensive and defensive units at the top of their games, the Oles scored their third shutout of the season, victimizing Beloit 44–0. Five interceptions, good linebacking by Lunder and Munson, Melby back in the lineup after three weeks, and smart defensive signal calling by Franklin all contributed to shutting down Beloit. An 83-yard march was climaxed by a Nelson to Kent Johnson pass.

Schmiesing scored on a 14-yard pitchout play for a 14–0 first-quarter lead. In the second period, following a Rich Omland fumble recovery, Schmiesing took a shovel pass from Nelson and scored to increase the lead to 27–0 at the half. After intermission, Freed showed his heels to Beloit defenders when he raced 80 yards around right end, making it 37–0. After appearing trapped, Doug Johnson found Lynn Nickerson open in the end zone for a 33-yard pass play to close out the scoring.

Perhaps still savoring the high of their third shutout of the season, the Oles were brought up short at Cornell the following week. The Rams and their talented receiver Joe Campanelli, perhaps aided by Ashley's absence from the lineup, overwhelmed the Oles by a 51–27 score. After an evenly played first quarter, the roof fell in as the Rams scored on every possession to take a 35 to 7 halftime lead.

Two fumbles led to another pair of Cornell touchdowns early in the third period before the Oles mounted a comeback. Schmiesing and Wiener ran well, but a 51–14 deficit was too much to make up. There were bright spots, although it didn't seem like it at the time. Denny Myers was a stalwart; Freed ran well. Dave Mueller, Franklin, and Dick Swiggum also were cited for outstanding play.

Ripon had already wrapped up the conference crown when St. Olaf arrived for the season finale. The Oles kept the Redmen from an undefeated season with a 14–10 upset. Both St. Olaf touchdowns came in the first half, though the offense was hampered frequently by penalty flags. The Oles were flagged for 100 yards in penalties and had two touchdowns called back. Coach Hauck commented, "We were never penalized until we got into scoring position."

Schmiesing concluded a brilliant career with a 224-yard effort on 40 carries, putting him over the 1,000-yard mark for the season. The defense was outstanding also, limiting Ripon to minus six yards rushing. Dave Mueller returned a pass interception 60 yards to set up the second St. Olaf score. "This game was the best of the season," Coach Hauck said.

Five Oles won all-conference recognition: Tim Smith, guard; Mike Schmiesing, halfback; Dave Mueller, end; Dan Franklin, defensive back, and Steve Ashley, safety. Schmiesing was named MVP; Smith and Don Krahn were selected to captain the 1969 Oles.

1969

The graduation of quality players such as Schmiesing, Myers, and Franklin, among others, could have caused pessimism for the 1969 season. However, 25 lettermen returning, many of them regulars, a number of authentic standouts, and a strong contingent from the previous year's first-year squad were real reasons for Coach Porter, fresh from sabbatical, and his crew to look forward to the fall with enthusiasm.

A nine-game schedule resulting in a complete round robin was established — means to establish a true champion.

As the bus pulled out of the parking lot en route to Mt. Vernon, Iowa, and the opener with the Cornell Rams, Coach Hauck stood in the well of the bus and loudly stated, "We are not going down there to get beat 51–27 again." In fact, the game was a near turnabout from the previous year, as Bob Freed, Ole Gunderson, and Bob Wetterberg each rushed for over 100 yards in a 42–27 Ole win.

Freed and Gunderson had touchdown runs of 89 and 49 yards, respectively, and Wetterberg, the busiest ball carrier with 26 carries, was nearly unstoppable on short yardage plays. Denny Nelson passed for 162 yards and two touchdowns. Greg Carlson started a streak as he kicked six PATs.

Gunderson's 49-yard touchdown scamper around left end came on his first varsity carry, a portent of things to come.

The following week, the Oles were plagued by a slow start, but an outstanding third quarter carried them to a 29–13 win over Ripon. Leading 7–6 at intermission, the Oles moved

quickly after the break. Nelson passed to Steve Ahlgren to cap a seven-play drive. Steve Ashley's interception set up a Wetterberg touchdown, and Steve Schwarten punched in after an 80-yard march. Cited for outstanding play were Gunderson, Mike Holmquist, Wetterberg, Ahlgren, Al Hinderaker, Tim Smith, and Tom Peinovich on offense; Tim Onnen, Ralph Wasik, Bob Gustafson, and Mike Peterson on defense.

With a high-powered offense moving at 519 yards per game (granted, it was after only two games), the Oles took their 2–0 record to Knox. Down 19–14 at halftime, the visitors again put together a strong third quarter accented by four interceptions. Four touchdowns in seven minutes turned the halftime deficit into a 49–19 victory. Gunderson and Wetterberg scored on the ground, and Ahlgren scored on a 15-yard pass set up by a Ron Hunter fumble recovery. Linebacker Leon Lunder rambled 38 yards with an interception for the fourth touchdown. Carlson extended his PAT string to 16.

The Homecoming game — between two high-powered offensive

Ole Gunderson "126" off tackle play, led by Steve Schwarten, 1969

The 1919 team celebrating the 50th anniversary of St. Olaf's first intercollegiate team, Oct. 11, 1969.
Left to right: Elmer Holter, Oscar Eide, Arnold Flaten, Newell Nelson, G. Harvey Thompson, Frederick Grose, Harold Havig,
R. Otis Marvik, Alfred Cole, Nels Quam, Ted Hoidahl, Arthur Lee, and Otto Glesne.

clubs — was one to be long remembered by anyone who saw it. The Oles amassed nearly 600 yards in offense and held off a second-half rally by the Monmouth Scots to triumph 38–31. The game featured a spectacular performance by Gunderson, who gained 356 yards from scrimmage on 33 carries. Ole's heroics brought national attention. NCAA statistics revealed that the legendary Jim Thorpe was the only major college player to exceed that rushing total. Only four men topped Ole's effort in all-time NCAA college division records.[152]

The Oles got away to an early lead with Gunderson scoring after an 82-yard march, but they were under pressure throughout from the Scots who had a decided advantage in size and strength. Monmouth retaliated soon after Gunderson's opening score, but Holmquist returned the ensuing kickoff 87 yards for a touchdown with 1:19 left in the first quarter. Early in the second quarter (14:42 left), Gunderson broke loose for an 80-yard touchdown, and the Oles led 28–14 at halftime.

The Scots kept pounding away and closed the gap to 31–24 and tied it at 31 following a 75-yard march. After several punt exchanges, the Oles took possession on the 46. A short drive ended with a scoring pass, Nelson to Freed, with 4:06 remaining. The Scots drove for the tying score, but Dick Swiggum's theft of a Monmouth aerial at the Ole 14 blunted that thrust. The Oles planned to run a series, gain a first down and "burn" the clock, but Gunderson cut between tackle and guard and outmaneuvered the entire Monmouth defense for 79 sensational yards. He was finally tackled at the Scot 14 as the game ended. Many observers contended that every Scot defender had at least one shot at Gunderson; some had two.

Ole's brilliant performance and the overall superlative play of the entire squad ranks this game as one of the great contests in Ole football history.

The game marking the 50th anniversary of the St. Olaf-Carleton rivalry was played at Laird Stadium,

with the Oles' ground offense matched against Carleton's aerial attack led by quarterback John Snowberg. It was close in the first half; two rushing touchdowns and a Nelson to Kent Johnson pass gave the Oles a 20–18 halftime lead. But in the second half, the ground troops got the upper hand and produced a six-touchdown explosion. Nelson and Freed scored once each, while Gunderson and Schwarten had two apiece. With the defense focusing on Gunderson, who still managed 143 yards on 25 attempts, Wetterberg had a field day, running for 178 yards on 21 carries.

Though they yielded some passing yards, the Ole defense also picked off four Carleton aerials — two each by Ashley and Hunter. Gunderson's 143 yards rushing brought his season total to 1,067, esclipsing the record of 1,020 set by Dave Krahn in 1966.

The league's top offensive and defensive clubs clashed the following Saturday at Appleton, Wis., and the defense won. The Lawrence Vikings limited the powerful Ole ground attack to one touchdown and racked up a 22–8 victory. The first quarter was a stalemate until the Vikings recovered a fumbled punt at the Ole 49 and scored with 3:57 to play in the period. With the Oles trailing 14–0 in the third quarter, Gunderson scored from the seven, and Ashley ran for the two-point conversion. But on the first scrimmage play after the Ole score, Viking halfback Lance Alwin ran 64 yards to score and sew up the game.

With 19 seniors playing their last game on Manitou Field, the Oles shook off the effects of the Lawrence loss and eliminated the Coe Kohawks from title contention with a convincing 42–8 win. Gunderson scored three times in the first half beginning with a 41-yard scamper less than four minutes into the game. His other scores were set up by a 35-yard punt return by Freed and an Ashley interception. The most spectacular play of the game was Ashley's 83-yard kickoff return following Coe's lone score. Ashley, Swiggum, and Ecklund were cited for defensive backfield play.

Gunderson's 175 yards rushing preserved his position as the top rusher in the NCAA college division.

Winding up the most successful St. Olaf football season since 1953, St. Olaf smothered Beloit 82–7. The

50th Anniversary Reunion Intercollegiate Football

St. Olaf College
October 11, 1969

The Team		
	Fritjof Anderson*	Joseph Johnson
	Jul Baumann	Olaf Langehough*
	Alfred Cole	Arthur O. Lee
	Carl Cole*	R. Otis Marvick
	Oscar Eide	Newell Nelson
	Arnold Flaten	Austin Peterson*
	Otto Glesne	Nels Quam
	Frederick Grose	Ingvald Swenson
	Jacob Halvorson*	Harvey Thompson
	Harold Havig	Elgar Thune*
	Theodore Hoidahl	Selmer Veldey (Captain)
	Elmer Holter	Nels Voldahl*
	Martin Jackson	*Deceased

The 50th anniversary of intercollegiate football at St. Olaf, 1969

Oles found themselves unable to do anything wrong. Gunderson and Kent Johnson each scored four times. Wetterberg, Freed, and Schwarten also scored, and Greg Carlson connected on 10 of 12 PAT attempts. First downs totaled 34 and yards gained, 806. Gunderson's 262 yards rushing brought his season total to 1,591.

Commenting on the one-sided victory, Coach Porter noted that the 33-player traveling squad mandated by the league hampered the coaches'

ability to lessen the potency of the Ole offense. "I'll never ask a player to give less than his best," he said.[153]

The Ole victory combined with a Monmouth loss gave St. Olaf its first outright league championship since 1961.

Five men were named to the all-conference squad: Tim Smith and Gary Iverson, guards; Tom Peinovich, tackle; Gunderson, halfback (the only unanimous pick), and Ashley, safety. Captain Tim Smith, a three-year regular at guard, was named MVP.

The 1969 championship team, Don Krahn and Tim Smith, captains

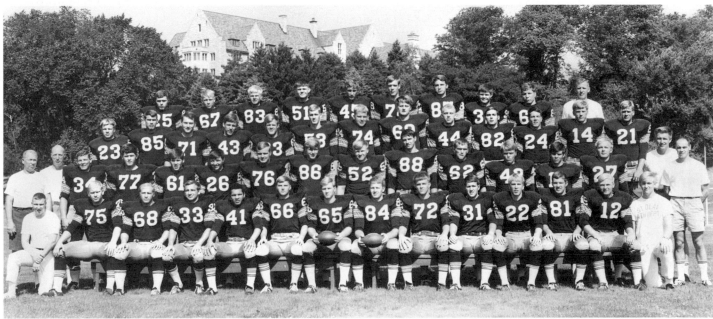

St. Olaf professor Arnold Flaten, an end on the 1919 team, challenges current squad member Tom Peinovich, 1969.

A number of individual and team season records were established: team rushing yardage, 3,321; yards passing, 1,042; total offense, 4,363 yards; scoring, 407 points; individual rushing, Gunderson 1,591 yards; scoring, Gunderson 132; and single-game individual rushing, Gunderson 356 yards. The total rushing offense (3,392), scoring (407), and individual rushing (Gunderson's 1,591) were also tops in the NCAA college division for 1969. Steve Ashley and Bob Matson were chosen captains for 1970.

One runs out of superlatives in trying to describe this exciting season and the sparkling performance of this squad, certainly one of the finest to wear the black and gold.

Milestone

An important milestone marked Parents' Day/Homecoming. It was the 50th-year reunion and halftime introduction of 13 members of St. Olaf's first intercollegiate football team, the 1919 squad. Those attending included Alfred Cole, Oscar Eide, Otto Glesne, Fred Grose, Ted Hoidahl, Art Lee, Elmer Holter, Newell Nelson, Harvey Thompson, Harold Havig, Arnold Flaten, Nels Quam, and Otis Marvick. Thompson had saved his 1919 postseason banquet program, including the line, "bounteous meal and a big black cigar were enjoyed."

Arne Flaten, chair emeritus of the St. Olaf art department, noted that "football began largely because we got a real professional coach, Endre Anderson, and because it seemed a good way to lessen the violence that had become associated with intramural competitions [interclass play]."

1969 Season Note

Freshman coach Gelle identified offensive power as a key after his charges blanked Augsburg 34–0. He cited, in particular, quarterback Mike Veldman, fullback Gary Jacobson, and halfback Al Montgomery.

1970

Trying to live up to the level of play set by the 1969 Oles might have been intimidating to the 1970 edition — until one looked at who they were. On paper, the offense appeared formidable again with backfield regulars Ole Gunderson and Mike Holmquist back, along with two-year veteran, and almost regular, Bob Freed. Reliable end Kent Johnson was the only regular holdover up front. On defense, it was the same story with Captain Steve Ashley, Todd Eklund, Leon Lunder, and Doug Munson in the defensive secondary, along with linemen Captain Bob Matson, Bob Gustafson, and Winslow Stenseng.

By the time Lawrence, the only team to defeat the Oles in '69, came to town to open the season, the lineups were in place, and they were intimidating. On the offensive side of the ball, Al Montgomery, Gary Jacobson, and Doug Johnson joined Gunderson in the backfield. Holmquist was moved to guard to team with veteran Ralph Wasik. Tim Hermann was at center, Gustafson and Bill Koeckeritz were at tackles, and Paul Olson teamed with Kent Johnson at end. On defense, Art Hultgren and Gustafson were at ends, Matson and Marv Schumacher at tackles, Willard Iverson at middle guard, Lunder, Munson, and Stenseng backing up the line, and Ashley, Eklund, and Steve Sviggum, the deep three.

The Lawrence Vikings were determined to repeat their heroics of the previous year, and they were tough, holding Gunderson to 58 yards, but 220-pound sophomore Jacobson picked up 80 in his varsity debut. St. Olaf struck quickly for two first-quarter scores, and that was enough to top the Vikings 14–0. Gunderson slithered through the line on a seven-yard touchdown run with 3:15 gone in the contest. A great goal-line stand stopped Lawrence at the two, and the Oles responded with a 98-yard drive, with quarterback Doug Johnson rolling out and going the last 24 yards. Bob Schumacher converted both times.

Kingston Stadium in Cedar Rapids was rain-soaked and almost ankle deep in mud as the Oles arrived to challenge the Kohawks. Strangely, given the conditions, the Oles exploded for 23 points in the second half to subdue Coe 26–10. Bob Schumacher's 45-yard field goal tied the score 3–3 at halftime. In the third quarter, Doug Johnson and Jacobson scored. Subsequently, Schumacher added his second field goal and defensive tackle Bob Gustafson put the game away when he picked off a Coe aerial and lumbered 48 yards to score.

Jacobson was the Oles' leading rusher with 105 yards in 24 carries. Munson, Montgomery, and Schumacher sustained knee injuries. The players first showered with full uniform and then stripped in layers under the showers to clean off the mud.

A short-handed Beloit team (using freshmen to fill out the ranks) was an easy foe, losing 53–13. Within a six-minute span in the first quarter, the Oles struck for three touchdowns and led 35–7

Gary Jacobson plunges against Beloit, 1970

at the half. Reserves played extensively and well, Dave Schwerin, Rick Skogrand, and Jon Johnson garnering their first college touchdowns. Johnson's came on a pass from Mike Veldman.

The following week, St. Olaf's strong defensive charge thwarted a vaunted Cornell passing game and the Oles beat the Rams 28–14. Cornell scored twice through the air, but their aerial totals for the day were only four of 18 for 48 yards.

Jacobson had 140 net yards and two touchdowns. Gunderson ran for 76 yards and one touchdown, while quarterback Doug Johnson was eight for 14 passing for 155 yards and a touchdown. Ashley sparkled in the defensive

secondary, intercepting one pass and making two touchdown-saving tackles.

In a contest which the Ripon *Commonwealth Press* termed "a dramatic showdown of two unbeaten elevens," St. Olaf topped the Redmen 27–21. A rare Gunderson mistake led to Ripon's first touchdown and a 7–6 lead. On the second play of the game, Ole's halfback pass was intercepted, the return setting up the Ripon score. Ole compensated by having a breakout game — touchdown jaunts of 72, 66, and 72 yards and a rushing total of 285 yards.

Montgomery, replacing the injured Jacobson, had his best game as an Ole ball carrier: 96 yards on 21 carries,

Steve Ashley returns an interception, 1970

Steve Ashley, 1970 captain

Bob Matson, 1970 captain

including a 30-yarder. Freed scored on a pass from Doug Johnson in the second quarter. The Oles put it away with a 21-point third quarter. A strong line rush, led by Brian Harter, on Ripon's passer, Jeff Trickey, resulted in three interceptions, two by Ashley and the other by linebacker Lunder.

Placekicking end Bob Schumacher tallied 10 points as the Oles overcame winless, but stubborn, Carleton 30–13 in the annual Goat battle. The Knights held off the powerful Lion offense for a quarter, but in the second stanza, Schumacher kicked a 23-yard field goal, scored on a 47-yard pass reception from Johnson, and booted the PAT. A Lunder fumble recovery, set up a short Montgomery touchdown run, and 14 points in the fourth quarter outdistanced the Carls. At 6–0, St. Olaf was the only unbeaten four-year college in Minnesota.

With fall break coming up (with a relatively empty campus) and Knox coming to town, the practice field talk was about maintaining focus and avoiding a letdown. Whether or not the preaching had any effect, the Oles came out with their best half of the season and led Knox 35–0 en route to a 56–22 win.

Offensive end Kent Johnson scored twice in the first half — once on a pass from Doug Johnson and again on an end zone fumble recovery. Jacobson and Gunderson also scored before intermission. Gunderson crossed the double stripe twice more in the second half, and his sometime understudy and regular cornerback, Sviggum, notched a six-pointer on a 16-yard run. It was a dominating offensive show by the Oles, who ran 97 plays from scrimmage and only once were forced to give up the ball without scoring.

The following week at Grinnell, St. Olaf spotted the Pioneers an early first-quarter touchdown, but came back to lead 14–7 at halftime. Gunderson accounted for the two touchdowns with tackle-breaking runs of 48 and 35 yards. The Oles shut out the Pioneers the rest of the way while scoring three more times themselves. Second-half scores were a five-yard sneak and a 12-yard run by Doug Johnson and a right end sweep by Montgomery. Gunderson left the game with an injury after accumulating 159 yards.

The stage was set for the season's climactic finale at Monmouth. The squads both stood at 7–0. Both had defeated a strong Ripon team by six points. The contest attracted a great deal of media attention with the Minneapolis and St. Paul newspapers, the Milwaukee *Journal*, and Chicago *Tribune* all speculating on the outcome. It was offense against defense once again — the Oles' "irresistible force" versus the Scots' "immovable object" which had limited opponents to 70 yards per game.

The Monmouth coaching staff and sports information office made friendly phone calls to Oleville, inquiring into the health of Ole Gunderson, who had been removed from the Grinnell game because of a leg injury. Monmouth Sports Information Director Steve Roberts, in a call to his St. Olaf counterpart, Bob Phelps, expressed concern. "Gee, I hope if he plays, he'll be fully recovered," Roberts said. "Our team is physical, and we'd sure hate to see him get hurt." Phelps suggested, "Ole is a tough kid; he can probably take care of himself." The Scots doubtless remembered the previous season when Ole had shredded their defense for 356 yards in a 38–31 win.

With all those word games out of the way, the Oles journeyed to Illinois for the real contest. It was a cold, raw November day. It was also "Al Hracek Day" — a tribute to the Scots' quarterback recovering from an early-season neck injury, giving the home team a psychological boost.

The Oles came roaring back from a 17–13 halftime deficit to blitz Monmouth with four touchdowns in 12 furious second-half minutes and pack away a 41–32 come-from-behind victory, an undefeated season, and the Midwest Conference title.[154]

The Scots were shocked early. On the first play from scrimmage, Doug Johnson faked to Gunderson going off right tackle, pivoted and gave to Jacobson who cut behind an interior trap on the other side and went 70 yards for an apparent first-play score. A clipping penalty nullified the touchdown, but the Scots and the crowd were shocked by that concrete example of the Oles' explosive offense.

Gunderson runs through a gaping hole provided by Holmquist and Olson against Lawrence, 1970.

Refusing to be deflated by the penalty, the Oles marched the ball the same 70 yards, Gunderson scoring on a one-yard run. The teams then exchanged touchdowns (Jacobson scoring for the Oles) and Monmouth also notched a field goal with the help of a questionable timing procedure. Halftime score: 17–13 Monmouth. At the beginning of the third period, St. Olaf put together a 15-play, 67-yard drive. Gunderson scored from the six and then ran for the two-point conversion to give the Oles a 21–17 lead. On the second play of the next series, Art Hultgren covered a Monmouth fumble at the Scots' 35. Johnson promptly faked a run and lofted a perfect pass to Jacobson 10 yards behind the nearest defender. Schumacher converted, making the score 28–17.

Desperate to retaliate, the Scots fired down the middle only to have the aerial picked off by Sviggum. Three plays later, Doug Johnson rolled right and threw back across the field to Kent Johnson alone in the end zone to end the blitz with the score 35–17. A Jacobson score made it 41–17 with 11:31 to play. The Scots scored twice more, but were also thwarted twice, once on an on-side kick recovery by Paul Olson and again on an interception by Doug Munson. The Oles had moved the ball through the vaunted Scot ground defense for 312 yards, 205 of them by Gunderson. Quarterback Doug Johnson had a great day. His poised leadership played a huge role in the victory.

The perfect 8–0 season was the first since 1953 and only the third undefeated season in St. Olaf history.

The Oles were league leaders in points scored and offense and fourth in defense. Gunderson led the league with 86 points scored. Schumacher was fourth with 40 and Jacobson sixth with 36.

In close balloting, the squad chose not to accept the anticipated invitation to play in the postseason Amos Alonzo Stagg Bowl playoff.[155]

Most valuable selections for the season were Doug Johnson, Steve Ashley, and Ole Gunderson. Captains-elect for 1971 were Paul Olson and Win Stenseng.

1970 Season Note

Oliver Towne, *St. Paul Dispatch* columnist, came to the campus to interview Coach Porter, halfback Gunderson and others for a column titled, "What Makes St. Olaf Run?"[156]

1970 team, the third undefeated team in St. Olaf history, Steve Ashley and Bob Matson, captains

Ole Gunderson advances against Beloit, 1971

1971

"Aces and spaces" was the description Sports Information Director Bob Phelps used in his 1971 preseason brochure — outstanding regulars returning but with voids left by departing standouts. Any discussion started with Ole Gunderson, returning for his senior season. Offensively, he was joined by Captain Paul Olson at end, Tim Hermann at center, and Tom Olson at tackle. On the defensive side, a few more aces returned: Brian Harter, nose guard; Marv Schumacher, tackle; Art Hultgren, end; Captain Win Stenseng, linebacker; Steve Sviggum, cornerback, and Al Beal, safety. Filling the spaces was the challenge as the Oles were the conference coaches' unanimous choice to repeat as champions.

With an 11-game win streak on the line, the Oles prepared to open against a solid Coe squad in Cedar Rapids. It was a rainy day, but Kingston Stadium was nothing like the "mud bowl" of 1970. On the second possession, Mike Veldman threw 25 yards to Gunderson to set up a two-yard touchdown dive by Steve Schwarten. Schumacher converted. A 59-yard Veldman punt and a pass interference penalty on Coe set up a second score, and St. Olaf was in front 13–0 at halftime.

Coe started strong in the second half, but the Oles held at the two. With a wet ball and a wet field, play slowed after intermission. Veldman's towering punts with good coverage kept Coe in poor field position. With Coe at their own 15, an aggressive defensive rush caused the passer to fumble. The ball was kicked around, but Todd Eklund eventually made a sliding recovery, which was turned into a touchdown. For the game, Gunderson rushed for 84 yards and Schwarten 83. Final score: St. Olaf 30, Coe 6.

Playing in the rain for the second Saturday, St. Olaf mauled an under-manned Beloit team 54–13 for the 13th consecutive win. Gunderson set a new single-game scoring record with a 36-point performance, one touchdown coming on a 78-yard punt return. Schwarten and Dave Schwerin scored one touchdown each. Yardage was surprisingly close, 387 to 370, the Bucs' aerial game gaining most of the Beloit yardage. Seven turnovers, four interceptions and three fumble recoveries, neutralized the yardage totals.

The opponents' passing game again gave the Oles trouble, as Cornell came back from a 23–0 deficit to push the Oles to the wall before succumbing 37–26. Two Gunderson touchdowns,

one on a 64-yard off-tackle play, a Schumacher field goal, and a quarterback keeper by Veldman were the early St. Olaf scores. Then Cornell quarterback Rob Ash, finding his ground game stymied, went to the air with success. A Rams' threat at the end of the first half was quashed on a great defensive play by Stenseng, who batted away an apparent touchdown pass at the goal line.

Schwarten was the big rusher for the Oles, reeling off 172 yards in 26 carries, one for 35 yards and the clinching score. Marv Schumacher and Tim Larsen stood out on defense, while center Tim Hermann had no zeros on his grading card.

It was all St. Olaf for three quarters against Ripon as the Oles led 23–6. But then the bubble burst, and with it the 14-game win string, as the Redmen exploded for 20 unanswered points in the final period to score a 26–23 upset win. A fumble, three pass interceptions, and a high pass from center leading to a safety gave the Oles a 9–0 halftime lead. The touchdown came on a beautifully executed bootleg pass, Veldman to Schumacher, for 27 yards. One of the interceptions was Brock Nelson's touchdown-saving effort at the goal line.

Two Ripon touchdowns narrowed the score to 23–19. An Ole punt gave the ball to the Redmen at their 37. Quarterback Robinson was about to be dropped deep in his own territory when he found his fullback on an outlet pass resulting in a 38-yard gain. Two plays later, Robinson hit his flanker, Bush, on a spectacular 26-yard scoring play for the game winner with 1:13 remaining. Eklund, Harter, Dale Hinderaker, and Jon Johnson were lions on defense.

The Oles got back on the winning track at Homecoming the following week, but it took a gutsy, come-from-behind effort and some last second heroics to edge Knox 28–26. A short run by Gunderson and a 19-yard pass, Veldman to Schumacher, put the Oles up 14–7 at halftime. Knox dominated the third quarter, scoring twice to go ahead 20–14. The Siwash fumbled the ball back to the Oles, and they put together an 80-yard drive, Gunderson scoring his third touchdown of the game. With the score 28–20 St. Olaf and 19 seconds to play, Knox regained possession. A pass play put the ball at the St. Olaf 20 with three seconds left. A hook and ladder play scored and brought Knox to within two points, 26–28. With little or no time left, Knox passed for the two-point conversion, but the effort was batted away by big Marv Schumacher.

Quarterback Veldman had his best day in a St. Olaf uniform. His passes to Bob Schumacher and Olson were good for over 100 yards. Gunderson and Schwarten ran effectively, and Stenseng, Larsen, and Harter were outstanding on defense.

Journeying across the Cannon River, the Oles swept past Carleton 35–0. It was the seventh consecutive Ole win in the Ole-Carl series. Schwarten's 178 yards and three touchdowns on 25 carries compensated for the loss by injury of Gunderson and Sviggum. A Schwarten blast for four was the first score. A 78-yard pass from Veldman to Schumacher put the Oles up by 14. Schwarten scored twice in the second quarter, on runs of 25 and 16 yards, giving him nearly 100 yards, and putting the Oles ahead by 28–0.

The lion greets a young Ole fan

Sophomore tailback Gary Johnson closed out the scoring in the fourth quarter on a seven-yard run. The play of the day was Art Hultgren's interception of a ball he tipped and then caught at the Carleton eight-yard-line. Dave Nitz and Dave Rommereim showed capable leadership in reserve quarterback roles. On defense, Brian Harter, Brock Nelson, and Win Stenseng had 15,14, and 12 tackles, respectively. Eklund and Hultgren played a whale of a game.

Rolf Mellby's jingle in the *Viking* scorebook depicted the final games of the season:

> *"Knox for the money*
> *Carleton for the Show*
> *Grinnell to get ready and*
> *Monmouth to go."[157]*

The Oles' 51–7 triumph over Grinnell vaulted them over the last obstacle on the way to the season's showdown with Monmouth. Gunderson, recovered from the injury suffered in

the Carleton game, had his best day as a senior — 264 yards and four touchdowns — in leading the Oles to their sixth win of the season.

Starting fast, St. Olaf put up 23 points in the first quarter, slowed in the second and came on strong again in the second half with 28 points. The only Pioneer score came on a 68-yard screen pass play. Al Beal and Brock Nelson hit with authority in the secondary, as did Harter and Stenseng. Hinderaker was a rock up front. A fitting climax to the day was Captain Paul Olson's one-yard scoring smack, running from the full-back position — a first for Paul in a stellar four-year career.

The stage was set for another typical St. Olaf-Monmouth matchup — the Scots' size and strength against the Oles speed and finesse.

On a cold, raw, windy day on Manitou Field, the Oles threw a gritty ground defense into the gears of Monmouth's inside power attack and beat the Scots at their own game, 33–21.[158] A ferocious Ole defense contributed to six Monmouth fumbles and an intercepted pass leading to two defensive touchdowns. The Lion offensive line turned in a stellar performance, allowing Gunderson to have a third brilliant day versus Monmouth — 41 carries, 241 yards, including a 70-yard breakaway touch-down jaunt.

The 1971 team, Paul Olson and Win Stenseng, captains

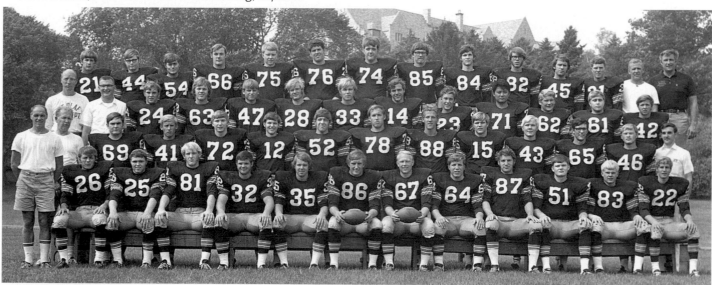

Ole Gunderson being carried off the field following his final game, 1971.

The Oles rocked the Scots back on their heels early. With the visitors running from inside their five-yard line, Schumacher met the Scot quarterback and halfback at the handoff point, the ball landing on top of the offensive blocker. Marv scooped up the ball and charged in for the score. Three minutes later, after the defense had gotten the ball back via a fumble recovery, Rommereim, playing wingback on the right side, took the ball on a reverse running left, and threw a left-handed 32-yard scoring strike to Bob Schumacher. Score: 14–0

After a Monmouth score and six minutes into the third quarter, Gunderson broke over right tackle on a 126 for 70 yards, brushing aside several Scot tacklers along the way.

With Monmouth passing in its own territory, Harter deflected an aerial, and Tim Larsen, playing the tip drill, picked the ball out of the air and ran it in like the fullback he once was. As the game wound down, Bob Schumacher kicked an insurance 33-yard field goal. Al Beal saved a kickoff return threat by running the return man out of bounds at the Ole 48. The defense held Monmouth and on the next series, Veldman's

76-yard punt put the Scots on their one. Hultgren downed the quarterback in the end zone for a safety and the final 33–21 score.

In the season's final contest, Lawrence stood between the Oles and a conference crown. A win meant a share of the title; a loss would give the crown to Monmouth.

At halftime, it was 7–7, the Oles having scored on a 22-yard Veldman to Schumacher pass. Ten minutes into the third period, an interception gave the Oles the ball at the Lawrence 47. Gunderson capped a nine-play drive with a seven-yard run to daylight dash. A 48-yard Schumacher field goal — the turning point of the contest — made it 16–7.

Lawrence quickly went to the air, but the Oles picked off three passes, two by Beal, to set up two final scores, a one-yard sneak by Gunderson and a short pass, Nitz to Olson. Gunderson rushed for 161 yards on a sprained ankle, bringing his three-season total rushing to 4,060.

It had been a remarkable three years for a talented and committed group of seniors — Todd Eklund, Ole Gunderson, Brian Harter, Jon Johnson, Jon McBroom, Paul Olson,

Bob Schumacher, Steve Schwarten, Dave Schwerin, and Win Stenseng. They and their teammates compiled three straight conference titles and a 25–2 won-lost record. All in all, a proud chapter in the tradition of championship St. Olaf football.

Gunderson's performance earned him the most valuable player distinction, and defensive back Al Beal and offensive tackle Tom Olson were selected captains for 1972.

1971 Season Notes

The first athletes to be selected for the newly established St. Olaf Athletic Hall of Fame were recognized at halftime of the Homecoming game against Knox and inducted at a postgame banquet. The ten inductees: Mark Almli, Ade Christenson, Rube Mostrom, Selmer Veldey, Ing Swenson, Stan Tostengard, Harry Fevold, Endre Anderson, Cully Swanson, and Herman (Ham) Muus. Much credit for establishment of the Hall of Fame should go to Rolf Mellby for his tireless efforts in working with the alumni lettermen's club. His contacts, both personal and via the *Viking* scorebook, created interest that led to establishing the Hall.

Tim Hermann — a two-year regular, steady performer at offensive center, and a writer for the *Messenger,* wrote a glowing tribute to Ole Gunderson in the Nov. 19, 1971, issue, "You are searching for superlatives when you talk about Ole … He has the capacity to perform well all the time and especially at the right time. He gives of himself completely to the squad. He played hard for you and you played hard for him. I'm glad I played with him and not against him."

1972

The 1972 season marked several changes in the Midwest Conference and St. Olaf football. The primary change made freshmen eligible for varsity competition. A second change abolished the round robin closed schedule of nine games, which had been in effect for several years, prescribed an eight-game conference schedule, and permitted a non-conference ninth game. As a result of the latter change, St. Olaf entered a two-year home and home schedule with Mayville State College of North Dakota.

Understating the obvious, the fall sports brochure for 1972 noted, "Whenever you lose an Ole Gunderson, the character of your offense is liable to change." The outlook for the 1972 season was for a somewhat less explosive offensive show but a defense that would yield fewer points.

The offense had four regulars returning in the line and two in the backfield. Bill Nelson, guard; and Tim Hermann, center; and tackles Dale Hinderaker and Tom Olson were the returnees in the line. Quarterback Mike Veldman and wingback Bruce Peterson were backfielders returning. The defense was anchored by Little All-America candidate Art Hultgren at end. Other returnees were Marv Schumacher, tackle; Tim Larsen, nose guard; Channing Gove and Brock Nelson, linebackers. Returning in the defensive secondary were Steve Sviggum, Len Whyte, and Tim Bigalke, cornerbacks, and Captain Al Beal, safety.

After 20 years versus Midwest competition, the Oles stepped out of the league to face a non-conference foe. In the opener against Mayville, the Oles got away to a quick start. Sviggum returned the first Comet punt to the Ole 45. Bruce Peterson went 30 yards on the first play from scrimmage. Dave Keller got six and freshman tailback Mark Gelle swept end for 15 to the two-yard line. Veldman's sneak was good for the last two. Keller's kick made it 7–0. Jeff Blaisdell recovered the first of five fumbles to start the second drive. Gelle scored from the nine. Chan Gove recovered another Mayville fumble midway in the second quarter. A 15-play drive keyed by the offensive line ended with reserve quarterback

Dave Rommereim scoring. The third quarter went to the defense with the front five of Hultgren, Schumacher, Larsen, Jim Dimick, and Brad Covert forcing three fumbles. Schumacher capped the defensive display by downing the Comet quarterback for a safety.

A fresh offensive unit started the final quarter. Lefty Rommereim passed 30 yards to freshman flanker Craig Collins, making the final score 30–0. Sixty-five players saw action. Mark Gelle had an impressive first game, running for 111 yards on 24 carries, narrowly missing a touchdown on his first collegiate carry, being run out of bounds at the one-yard line. Gelle was soon to follow in the proud tradition of dominating Ole tailbacks such as Harry Newby, Syl Saumer, John Kirkeby, Mark Aamot, Dave Krahn, Mike Schmiesing, and Ole Gunderson, among others.

Coe College was the first conference opponent. The Kohawks dominated the first half, but St. Olaf came on strong in the later periods for a 17–7 victory, keeping a long home-field victory string alive. At halftime, the score was deadlocked at 7–7, thanks to Steve Sviggum's brilliant interception and 57-yard return to the Coe nine, setting up a Gelle touchdown.

The Oles blunted Coe's momentum in the second half, taking the opening kickoff 57 yards in nine plays. Keller

The 1972 team, Al Beal and Tom Olson, captains

Tom Olson, 1972 captain

Al Beal, 1972 captain

scored from the two. The third period was a punting duel between Veldman and Coe's Harlron. Jerry Berg closed out the scoring in the fourth with a 30-yard field goal. Gelle had his second 100-yard game, 110 yards on 28 carries.

The offense sputtered but a strong defense and a good kicking game shut out Beloit 14–0 on their home field. Punter Veldman kicked nine times for a 37-yard average. The defense gave up only 97 yards rushing and 63 passing and picked off four passes, three by Beal and one by Oison. St. Olaf scored on sweeps of 17 yards by Greg Olson and 14 by Gelle. Between the scores, the Oles lost the ball five times on fumbles and twice on interceptions and saw two drives stopped by infractions, one nullifying an apparent 70-yard touchdown run by Gelle. In reaction, Tim Hermann's *Messenger* account of the game noted that, "it's what's on the scoreboard that counts."[159]

In a well-contested, complete game, a combination of tough defense and inspired offense turned back Ripon 14–6 on Parents' Day. Gelle had his best rushing effort thus far with 194 yards. Freshman fullback Joel Simpson, stepping in for Keller, who was sidelined with a broken thumb, chipped in 81 yards in a strong start.

Following three punt exchanges, the Oles took over at their 38. On the third play, Gelle ran "126" to the right with the double team led by Hultgren and Hinderaker, the extension block by Ferg and kickout block by Simpson. Mark cleared the line of scrimmage, veered to the outside, stiff-armed two defenders and went 49 yards to score.

In the third quarter, the Redmen stole an Ole pass at the 22 and scored six plays later. In what may have been the key play of the game, the "River Falls Gambler," nose man Tim Larsen, broke through, getting to the tee at the same time as the center snap, and blocking the PAT attempt. Oles led 7–6. On the next series, St. Olaf went 71 yards in 10 plays with Veldman scoring on a one-yard sneak. Gelle lugged the leather 61 of the 71 yards. The entire defense played well, in particular Gove and Larsen. Veldman had a 40-yard average on 10 punts, two going dead inside the five.

Leading tacklers: Gove, 14; Beal, 13; Larsen, 11.

Superior quickness by the usually tough Cornell Rams shut down the Ole offensive machine for the first time in a long time, and the Oles lost for the first time in five contests, 19–0. The die may have been cast early when the Rams went 82 yards on the opening possession. Quarterback Rob Ash completed 19 of 42 passes for 256 yards, and running back Frana rushed for over 100 yards, as the Rams scored in each quarter. Cornell's defense held the Oles to 50 yards rushing. St. Olaf's feature of the day was an almost goal-line stand. Cornell was second and two at the Ole three. A fourth-down play made a first down at the one. Another fourth-down conversion yielded the touchdown — seven plays, three yards, three inches.

Rolf Mellby wrote a special tribute in the Oct. 16, 1972, *Viking*, titled "An Almost Postlude." A law of physics states, for every action or force there is an equal and opposite reaction. This could explain the post-game feelings of the two football squads and followers as they departed from the stadium. As high Cornell, as equally low St. Olaf; as fully demonstrating joy Cornell, as equally sad St. Olaf. This is athletics. This writer sincerely believes the joys and sorrows experienced by athletes are a valuable part of college life. I respect every athlete for being willing to put himself on display, if you will, tested in full public view and able to cope with the joys and sorrows that result. They have courage and competitiveness, self-endowed qualities, cultivated in this learning experience."

With 12 townies on the two rosters, the Carls invaded Manitou Field hoping to wrest the Goat from the Oles after eight years. It was a cool, rainy Ole Homecoming. The power running of Mark Gelle (105 yards) and a stingy defense added up to a 27–14 Ole win and continued residence of the Goat on the west side of the river. Jerry Berg put the only points on the board in the first quarter with a field goal from the 13. In the second quarter, Veldman punts of 47 and 57 yards kept the Carls in poor field position. Later in the quarter, Al Beal fielded a Carleton punt at midfield.

He angled to the sidelines, then cut diagonally across the field for a 47-yard return to the five. Gelle scored on the next play to make it 10–0.

As halftime approached, Veldman showed deft handling of a race with the clock, mixing short passes to Hultgren, Collins, and Bob Ferg with hard running by Gelle and Steve Peinovich. With 20 seconds left, Gelle started an apparent sweep, stopped and threw a 40-yard scoring strike to Collins. The Oles held a 220 to 50 edge in rushing yards in wrapping up their ninth consecutive victory over Carleton.

In depressing contrast to the Carleton contest, the Oles took the long trip to Galesburg, Ill., only to lose to Knox 7–6. Fumbles, penalties, and injuries plagued the Oles and a good Knox team took full advantage. Gelle, knee strain; Larsen, hamstring pull, and Sviggum, hip pointer, all left the game. St. Olaf countered an early Siwash score with a 13-play drive with Gary Johnson scoring. The PAT was missed and 7–6 was the final. Midway in the fourth quarter, Veldman lofted a high punt. The receiver fumbled a fair catch attempt, and Bill Nelson recovered for the Oles. But Knox stiffened, and Berg's field goal attempt from the 34 fell short.

The wild swing of fortune continued the next week as senior Mike Veldman, playing his final game on Manitou Field, cranked up his throwing arm and led his mates to a 56–7 win over Grinnell. Mike had a hand in five scoring plays — passes of 20, 28, 10, and eight yards and a roll-out run from the one. Craig Collins and Jim Christensen each tallied two touchdowns in the game which saw eight different Oles score. A 28-point second quarter overwhelmed the Pioneers. Veldman was 10 of 17 passing for 154 yards and four touchdowns. Christensen was the leading rusher with 83 yards. Berg kicked seven straight PATs and Gove got the other. Seventy plus players saw game action in extending the home winning streak to 28 games over six seasons.

Monmouth, mud, and muscle proved too much for the Oles as the conference champion Scots ground out a 27–7 win. Monmouth drove for a touchdown on their first possession and maintained the lead throughout. An intercepted pass and 50-yard return led to the second touchdown and a 13–0 halftime score. The Scots scored twice more before St. Olaf capitalized on a Len Whyte fumble recovery. After four plays from the 11, Veldman sneaked it in for the lone touchdown; Gove converted. Steve Peinovich was the leading runner with 52 tough yards on 15 carries

The 6–3 season record was good for third place in the conference. Five Oles landed all-conference berths: Art Hultgren, defensive end; Bill Nelson, offensive guard; Tim Larsen, defensive middle guard; Al Beal, safety, and Chan Gove, linebacker. Beal was named MVP and was named a first-team defensive back on the 1972 All-Lutheran College

Coach Porter huddles with his team, 1972

football team. Chosen captains for 1973 were Dave Rommereim and Tim Larsen. "Lars" followed in the footsteps of his father, Don, who was captain in 1949.

1972 Season Notes
The 1972 Carleton contest was the 50th anniversary of the first St. Olaf win over Carleton, 19–0, in 1922. That year also saw St. Olaf's first undefeated football team, three years after intercollegiate play officially began … Four former Ole football greats were inducted into the Athletic Hall of Fame at a pre-game banquet. The new honorees were Ted Hoidahl '21, Frank Cleve '25, John Kirkeby '27, and Russ Adamson '51.

St. Olaf Rejoins MIAC
The Jan. 26, 1973, issue of the *Messenger* carried the headline "MIAC Admits St. Olaf." Discussions had been under way for some time about St. Olaf rejoining the Minnesota Intercollegiate

Dave Rommereim,
1973 captain

Tim Larsen, 1973 captain

Athletic Conference. From the point of view of some at St. Olaf, travel costs to Iowa, Wisconsin, and Illinois were becoming prohibitive in both dollars and time. Others felt it was difficult to establish healthy rivalries with colleges situated so far apart. On the other hand, some felt the academic similarities between St. Olaf and other members of the Associated Colleges of the Midwest/Midwest Athletic Conference were a positive benefit outweighing logistical considerations.

1973

Seventy-two men reported for the 1973 season of St. Olaf football — the last season in the Midwest Conference. The switch to the MIAC would be effective with the 1974–75 college year.

A number of position changes were in order to get quality players on the field on a regular basis rather than in backup roles. Joel Simpson went to pulling guard, Greg Olson to wingback, Brad Covert to offensive guard, Jim Christensen to defensive back, and Dave Keller to linebacker. Al Edwards, Steve Hill, Mark Wangsness, Dale Pippin, Dennis Miller, and Tom Bickel moved into starting positions.

Playing their first night game in 18 years, St. Olaf was ambushed by a fired-up Mayville State squad and went down 20–6 in the season opener. The hosts spotted the Oles a six-point lead in the first period when Mark Gelle sliced in from six yards out. But that was all. On the first play of the second quarter, Comet halfback Lewis, on his way to a 140-yard performance, went 57 yards to score. It was 6–6 at halftime, but Mayville drove for a third-quarter score and added a final tally with 31 seconds to play. St. Olaf's offense moved freely between the 20s but was stymied near paydirt by the Mayville defense. An interception and failure to convert on key third down situations were telling.

Staying on the road for a second weekend, the Oles traveled to Cedar Rapids. The opportunistic Coe Kohawks converted two offensive mistakes by the Oles into touchdowns, then used a hard-running offense and a rock ribbed defense to carve out a 30–0 victory. A field goal and a 46-yard touchdown run gave the hosts a 10–0 halftime margin. Five minutes into the

third quarter, the Oles were unable to get a punt away. Coe took over and scored in five plays. A second miscue came a minute and a half later when a Coe cornerback picked off an Ole pass and returned it 57 yards to score, making the count 24–0 going into the final period. A 60-yard, 13-play drive tacked on Coe's final score.

The Ole secondary intercepted three passes for the only bright spot in a dismal day. Gelle was the leading Ole rusher with 51 yards — attesting to the strength of Coe's defense against the run.

With two consecutive road losses, the Oles welcomed the home opener and the opportunity to play with a full roster rather than the 38-man travel squad. The team responded well in routing Beloit 35–7. After blunting the Bucs' first offensive series without a first down, safety Maury Johnson returned the Beloit punt 30 yards, setting up a one-yard touchdown plunge by Bruce Peterson. Gove kicked the first of his five placements and St. Olaf was up 7–0. Though the Oles dominated play the rest of the first period and into the second, it was not until1:40 remained in the half that they could score again — Gelle going in from the one. A 34-yard Rommereim to Olson pass was the big play in the drive.

The Ole offense, featuring Olson, had a big third quarter. Greg swept left end and went 75 yards to score, and eight minutes later took a 30-yard halfback pass from Gelle for his second tally. Maury Johnson scooted 38 yards on a dive play for the final score. Larsen, Gove, Whyte, and Blaisdell were outstanding defensive performers, as were Gelle and Olson on offense. Greg had 82 yards rushing from scrimmage, caught four passes for 107 yards and a touchdown and returned three punts for 47 yards.

The Oles survived a heavy aerial bombardment from Ripon's Robinson to down the Redmen 28–22 in their last Midwest Conference trip to Wisconsin. En route to the victory, St. Olaf had drives of 81, 72, and 78 yards, mostly on the ground. In addition, the defense stopped the Redmen at the one-yard line twice, took over on downs at the 19, and forced an unsuccessful field goal try from the 12.

A Larsen-led defense stopped Ripon's first drive. The Oles then put together a 14-play drive capped by Gelle's four-yard scoring run. On their next drive, Ripon was first and goal at the five. But defensive stops by Dennis Miller, Jim Dimick, and Larsen gave the ball to the Oles at the one. Freshman punter Randy Sanders boomed one out of the end zone putting Ripon back to their 30, but they responded with a 10-play drive to make it 14–7.

On the next series, the Oles appeared stalled at midfield when Rommereim found Olson along the sidelines, and Greg turned a spectacular bobbling catch into a 66-yard scoring play to put the Oles up 21–7 at the half. With a score early in the second half, St. Olaf appeared to be in command at 28–7. But the Redmen roared back to score 12 points in two and a half minutes. Even though both two-point conversion attempts failed, visions of 1971 danced in Ripon heads until Ole cornerback Charlie Mangrum took a Ripon pass from the receiver's outstretched hands to foil the comeback.

It was an expensive victory, as Tom Hendricks, Dale Pippin, Dimick, and Greg Olson all went down with injuries. The game closed out a keen 22-year rivalry with Ripon. St. Olaf held a 15–6–1 advantage, but the games were invariably hard fought and often close.

With a large home crowd for Parents' Day, the Oles spotted the Cornell Rams an early field goal then scored 20 unanswered points before Cornell could push across a six-pointer. At halftime, it was 27–10. St. Olaf scored three touchdowns and a safety in the last two periods before the Rams countered with a safety with 1:53 left to make the final 43–12. Testifying to the aggressiveness and alertness of the Ole defense, the visitors lost the ball three times on fumbles, three times on interceptions, and once on a blocked punt. Four of the miscues led directly to St. Olaf scores.

Fullback Steve Peinovich scored three times on two four-yard runs and a 51-yard breakaway. Rommereim had a nifty 14-yard scamper for a touchdown and Peterson raced 54 yards for another. Keller booted field goals of 33 and 36 yards. Christensen, Blaisdell, and Mangrum picked off Ram passes. Sophomore defensive tackle Dennis Miller had a great game, blocking a punt and harassing Ram runners all afternoon. Sixty players saw action, a major coaching accomplishment.

Back on the plus side of the won-lost column, the Oles headed to Laird Stadium for the 52nd renewal of the goat rivalry with Carleton. The Knights featured a balanced attack and were opportunistic in converting Ole miscues into points as they upset

the visitors 16–14. The loss broke a nine-game Ole victory streak versus the Carls.

As the Knights came up with big plays when apparently stalled, the Oles fell short on short-yardage situations. St. Olaf scored first on a well-excuted halfback pass, Gelle to Collins. Gove's PAT ran his string to 16. A Northfield combination, Mike Barnes to Jon Grossman, hooked up on a 26-yard scoring pass with 48 seconds in the half to put Carleton up 10–7 at intermission. St. Olaf opened the second half with a 63-yard, 14- play march, Peinovich scoring, to retake the lead at 14–10. Carleton scored on a 50-yard drive but the kick failed, giving the Oles life.

The Ole defense against Barnes' passes was a feature of the fourth quarter. Blaisdell intercepted in the end zone to stop one serious threat. Larsen and gang blunted another at the 11. With 2:40 remaining, St. Olaf had first and 10 at their own 11. Six plays netted 55 yards. A Carleton penalty advanced the ball another 15 yards, and a running play put the ball at the 19. Keller's field goal attempt was on target but barely short, and the Carls had a 16–14 upset.

Fall break, with the student body gone, always posed a problem for the squad when they played at home on that weekend. On this occasion, the gloom of the Carleton loss the previous

The 1973 team, Dave Rommereim and Tim Larsen, captains

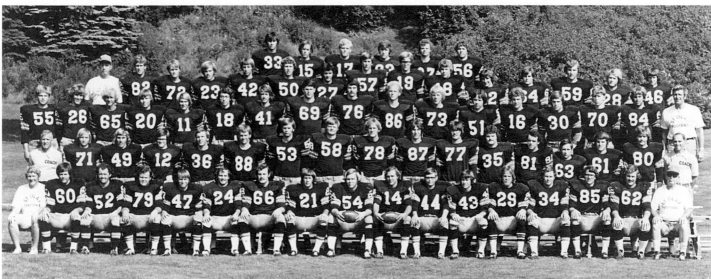

Plaque presented by Coe College prior to the last contest between the two colleges, 1973. Pictured are Ole captain Tim Larsen, Ole coach Tom Porter, Coe coach Wayne Phillips and Coe captain Dave Ostrander.

week made it worse. As it turned out, however, the sparse crowd that did show up to see the Oles play host to the Knox Siwashers saw one of the best games of the '73 season.

St. Olaf opened the scoring with a picture perfect 41-yard pass from Rommereim to flanker Greg Olson. Gove kicked his 17th straight PAT. After a poocher punt (a short punt designed to go dead or be fielded close to the goal line) to the Knox 15, a solid hit caused a fumble which Dennis Miller recovered at the 11. Four plays later, Rommereim sneaked it in. Gove's kick was wide, breaking his string and leaving the score at 13–0. Much of the third quarter was a punting duel, but with three minutes left, Gelle broke off right tackle, veered to the outside and raced 71 yards to score.

With the count 27–0, Knox changed quarterbacks and went to the air. The new quarterback, Paradise, completed 10 of 18 passes for 196 yards and three touchdowns. The Ole defense stiffened in the nick of time to preserve a 27–19 win. Gelle had 198 yards in 24 carries in perhaps his best game as a collegian thus far. Bruce Peterson added 117 yards, also on 24 attempts. Both benefited from crisp line blocking. Defensive standouts were Larsen, Gove, and Whyte.

On the last Midwest Conference foray into Iowa , the Oles swept to a convincing 48–7 triumph over Grinnell. The offense moved relentlessly to seven touchdowns, all on the ground. Defensively, the Oles controlled the line of scrimmage and an alert secondary picked off four passes. Interceptions by Christensen and freshman Tom Bickel led to early scores by Rommereim and Peterson. Gelle rambled for a pair of second-quarter tallies. Mark had 134 yards for the day on only 11 carries. Two PATs by Gove and a two-pointer by Rommereim brought the halftime count to 28–0.

Sophomore quarterbacks Tom Monahan and Steve Hill engineered the second half fireworks — scores by Peinovich and Ferg, effective ball carrying by Gary Johnson, Maury Johnson, and Bill Green. The most interesting play of the game was Monahan's option play stopped by a Grinnell reserve, who couldn't resist the temptation to come off the bench and make the tackle. The ball was placed half the distance to the goal, and Ferg scored on the next play. The Pioneers scored with a minute to play, aided considerably by a high center snap.

A trio of mistakes in the first half was too much for the Oles to overcome as they dropped the season's finale to Monmouth 16–14 in a hard-fought battle. The Oles blunted four Scot offensive thrusts in the first quarter

by good defensive play and a fumble recovery. Early in the second stanza, St. Olaf moved 73 yards in seven plays. Highlights were two Rommereim passes to Olson — one for 36 yards and a spectacular one-handed catch, the other a 14-yarder in the corner of the end zone.

Monmouth dominated in the last half of the quarter, scoring a safety on a high pass from center on an end-zone punt situation. As the clock ran down, the Scots added 11 points on a touchdown, a two-point conversion and a field goal. The Scots were held to a field goal in the second half, but it was enough. Rommereim passed to Rick Hultgren from the seven with 38 seconds remaining to close out the scoring. The strong Monmouth ground attack outdistanced the Oles by 336 to 271.

The 5–4 season mark, 5–3 in the conference, was good for fifth place. For the 22-year Midwest Conference run, the Oles had a league record of 119–45–4 and eight championships. Tim Larsen, Len Whyte, Chan Gove, and Bruce Peterson were named to the all-conference squad. Tim Larsen was designated the Oles' MVP. Jim Dimick and Steve Peinovich were elected co-captains for 1974.

1973 Season Notes

Captain Tim Larsen celebrated his 22nd birthday with another outstanding defensive performance against Ripon. The celebration continued postgame with two birthday cakes provided by some Ole coeds.

Before the kickoff of the Coe contest, Jack Laugen, St. Olaf class of 1950, vice president of Coe College and onetime director of public relations at St. Olaf, presented a plaque to Coach Porter and captains Rommereim and Larsen. "Twenty years of memorable competition with unfailing good sportsmanship," the plaque said. "A fine gesture," said Tom Porter. Laugen passed away in June 2003.

1974

Rod Grubb, St. Olaf chair of political science, who had played quarterback for Jake Christiansen at Concordia in the '50s and later was an assistant coach there, was a welcome addition to the coaching staff beginning with the '74 season. Rod's knowledge of the game, coaching techniques and familiarity with the MIAC were to prove invaluable.

Due to the switch to the MIAC, eight of the nine opponents were new to the schedule in the 1974 season, Carleton being the only holdover. The 1973 offensive line returned intact: Collins and Hultgren at end, Hill and Hinderaker at tackle, Simpson and Covert at guard, Wangsness at center. Gelle, Olson, and Captain Peinovich returned in the backfield. Defensive regulars back included Brian Anderson and Mitch Long at end, Captain Jim Dimick and Al Edwards at tackle, Tom Bickel and Charlie Mangrum in the secondary. Steve Winegarden, Steve Madson, Gary Uecke, Tim Kruger, Jim Wilkens, Jim Kunitz, and Art Skenandore were strong candidates for regular status.

Sporting new gold jerseys with the traditional old gold pants, the Oles opened the season against Macalester. It was a non-conference game, both teams filling in a schedule opening. It took last-minute heroics by Olson,

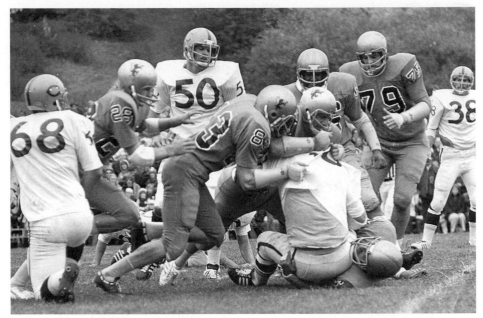

Mitch Long and Jim Dimick put the squeeze on a Concordia runner. Carlson and Al Tindall move in, 1974.

Gelle, and Steve Hill (Little Steve)* to bring home a 15–14 victory. The contest was a defensive standoff for three periods. Mac used up virtually the whole third quarter (except for four plays) on two long drives, but came up empty.

On the first play of the fourth quarter, Tom Bickel picked off a pass and returned it 89 yards for the first score. Macalester retaliated six plays later and then added another touchdown to take a 14–7 lead with 10:43 to play. At the four-minute mark, Skenandore recovered a fumble at the Ole 30. Two first downs and a 32-yard Gelle to Olson halfback pass ate up much of

the distance and Hill then threw 30 yards to Olson, who grabbed it away from a Mac defender in the end zone. An option keeper was good for the two-point conversion.

Gelle was the leading rusher with 140 yards on 24 carries. Olson caught three passes for 70 yards and a touchdown. Captain Jim Dimick led a stout defense that checked a strong Macalester running attack.

The defense that had played well against the Scots had a rude awakening the next week in a 51–21 loss to St. John's at Collegeville. The Johnnies converted a blocked punt into a touchdown with

The 1974 team, Steve Peinovich and Jim Dimick, captains

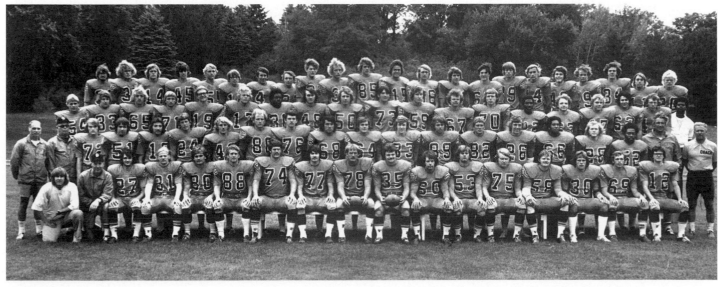

Steve Peinovich, 1974 captain

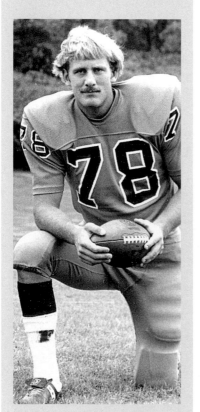

Jim Dimick, 1974 captain

a minute and eight seconds gone in the game. They made it 28–0 at the quarter and 42–7 at halftime, the lone Ole score coming on Gary Uecke's fumble recovery in the end zone.

After intermission, a 41-yard kickoff return by Olson followed by a 47-yard march in 13 plays led to a touchdown by Peinovich. Later, Hill threw 17 yards to John Kroll after a successful on-side kick. Bill Green led Ole rushers with 60 yards.

The renewal of the Concordia rivalry brought out the numerous personal connections between the two schools and the two teams. Assistant coach Rod Grubb had played and coached under legendary Cobber coach Jake Christiansen, who was a teammate of Ade Christenson at St. Olaf in the 1920s. Ade's brother, Irv, was now the athletic director at Concordia, and Al Rice, an Ole footballer in the late '50s, was a Cobber defensive coach. And Frank Cleve, an Ole legend and member of the Hall of Fame, had been a very successful Concordia coach in the '30s.

The Oles played their best football of the young season, but it was not quite enough as the Cobbers eked out a 6–3 win, the margin a last-minute field goal. It was a classic defensive struggle with neither team able to cross the other's goal — all points coming on field goals. The Oles mounted two drives in the second period, the first stopped by an interception at the five, the second leading to Randy Sanders's field goal from the 15.

The Cobbers retaliated with a field goal of their own with 13 seconds left in the first half. The winning field goal came after a punt was downed at the Ole one. The Cobbers had a 49–25 edge in scrimmage plays. The Oles gave up yardage in the middle of the field but repeatedly came up with big plays in four-down territory.

It had been 24 years since St. Olaf and Augsburg had played a night game in Minneapolis, and, for the Oles, it didn't turn out any better this time than it had in 1950. On a cold, rainy evening at Parade Stadium, the Auggies repeated their previous conquest, downing St. Olaf 16–0. Two Sanders punts had kept Augsburg in poor field position early, but then they put

together a 65-yard march culminating with a field goal. The second quarter was a standoff until Roger Olson picked off a Gary Austin pass and snaked his way to the Auggie six only to have the ball pop out when he was tackled, the Auggies recovering to kill the threat; halftime score: 3–0.

Two Ole stalwarts were lost to injury in the first half — noseman Skenandore and linebacker Al Tindall. Greg Olson returned the second half kickoff and two first downs followed, but the Auggies then intercepted to blunt that thrust. Augsburg tallied two insurance touchdowns in the final period. Post-game thoughts: The defense played well, Winegarden, Olson, and Bickel each having an interception.

A Parents' Day crowd of 4,000 watched the Oles play an exciting, though ultimately disappointing, game against Hamline. The feeling at the end was that the Pipers didn't so much win it as the Oles lost it, 21–14.

Sanders' punt pinned the Pipers on their one early, but the subsequent punt from the end zone (nearly blocked) was mishandled at the 30 and fell into the hands of a covering Hamline lineman who trundled 70 yards to score. Two minutes into the fourth quarter, Fletcher, a Piper forward, blocked Sanders' punt and returned it 45 yards for the decisive touchdown.

With 11 seconds left in the first quarter, Greg Olson gathered in a punt at his 40 and outdistanced the Hamline defenders to score. Trailing 14–7 early in the second half, Mitch Long recovered a fumble at the Hamline 26, and quarterback Tom Monahan threw a scoring strike to Olson to tie the score and set the stage for Fletcher's heroics.

The Ole defense again was outstanding, and Olson shone on offense with 211 total yards.

Carleton came to Manitou Field as a non-conference foe, and the host Oles sent the Knights home, minus the Goat, on the short end of a 24–7 score. The bearded animal returned to its rightful home after a year's hiatus. The stout Ole ground defense shut down the Carls' running game, but they scored their lone touchdown early on a 59-yard Barnes to Pepper aerial. The Oles countered with a 77-yard drive, Gelle

Tom Monahan to Roger Olson against Carleton, 1974

Shaking off that failed upset attempt, the Oles headed to St. Peter to challenge Gustavus. And it looked as if fortunes had indeed turned. Leading 20–0 at the half and 20–14 with a minute to play and the Gusties pinned at their one after a Sanders punt, it appeared the Oles had it bagged. But then came the storybook finish (for the Gusties). Quarterback Mark Pfundstein threw over the Ole defense, and the receiver dashed away to complete a 93-yard scoring play. The conversion gave Gustavus a 21–20 win.

The first half was all St. Olaf as the Oles scored three times and shut out the Gusties. Joel Simpson's one-yard plunge capped an 83-yard drive. Monahan passed to Greg Olson for a second touchdown, and Roger Olson's interception set up Monahan's pass to Collins, who made a spectacular one-handed grab. A late second-quarter thrust by Gustavus was stopped by two quarterback sacks — the first by Dimick and Long and the second by Long and Anderson. In the third period, before the unbelievable ending, Pfundstein threw for two touchdowns — to Ryan and Langemo.

going the final yard. Monahan threw to Rick Hultgren for 28 and a score, and Randy Sanders notched a 26-yard three pointer to give the hosts a 17–7 halftime advantage.

The Carls fumbled the second-half kickoff at their 39, the Oles recovering. Gelle ripped off 37 yards on the second play from scrimmage, and Monahan took it in from the three to complete the scoring. Gelle rushed for 181 yards, and Peinovich added 103. The Ole defense limited Carleton to 76 yards rushing, while Charlie Mangrum, Roger Olson, and Mitch Long each intercepted a pass.

Returning to MIAC opponents, the Oles came up short in their bid to upset St. Thomas, dropping a hard-fought game, 14–6. The Tommies drove 70 yards with the opening kickoff to take an early lead, but the Oles fought back with a 60-yard touchdown drive, Gelle going the last five. A St. Thomas interception of an Ole pass led to a second touchdown and the end of scoring for the day. The defensive units took over, and their play was a feature of the game.

A jolting tackle by linebacker Steve Madson knocked the ball loose and Roger Olson recovered to stop a Tommy drive at the six as the first half ended. The Oles had a fine opportunity in the

third period as Bickel intercepted and returned the ball 32 yards to the Tommy 13. A third-down halfback pass fell incomplete, and Sander's 26-yard field goal attempt sailed wide. Randy's punting kept St. Thomas bottled up the remainder of the game, but the Oles could not mount another credible offensive threat. Madson led the stout Ole defense with 22 tackles and assists.

Touchdown celebration against Gustavus, 1974. Greg Olson scoring, Hultgren, Hill, Collins and Gelle celebrate.

Coaches and sons — Jim and Jim Jr. Dimick, Tom and Mark Porter, Bob and Mark Gelle, 1974.

Gelle led Ole rushers with 93, followed by Simpson, running at full-back for the injured Peinovich, with 75.

Winless against MIAC opponents in their first year back in the league, the Oles hosted league-leading University of Minnesota-Duluth in the season finale. On a cold, gray November day (shades of Grant Rice),° the Oles upset the Bulldogs 7–0, knocking them out of the championship.

St. Olaf jumped out to a fast start. Greg Olson returned the opening kickoff to the Duluth 42. A third-down halfback pass, Gelle to Olson, was good for 18 to the 21. Mark carried on three of the next four plays, going nine, six, and four yards — the last run for the game's only tally. Duluth threatened in the second period after recovering an Ole fumble at the host's 35. They drove to the four, where the Ole defense stiffened and turned back Duluth's stellar running back, Terry Eggerdahl three times. Two additional first-half threats by Duluth were thwarted by a Mangrum interception at the 10 and a missed field goal.

After intermission, Tindall recovered a Bulldog fumble at the 26. The Oles drove to the one, and Steve Winegarden appeared to score but the play was nullified by a motion penalty. The last Duluth scoring opportunity was stopped again by Mangrum on an interception at the 10, his second of the day.

Ignoring a driving rain that fell through the last three periods, the defense was a game standout. McKnight was the leading Duluth rusher with 88 yards. Simpson had 62 for St. Olaf.

Six seniors led this premier season in the MIAC: Jim Dimick, Steve Peinovich, Mark Wangsness, Al Edwards, Jim Hanson, and Dale Hinderaker. Defensive back Roger Olson and offensive standout Mark Gelle were designated all-conference, with Dimick, Long, Greg Olson, and Al Hultgren receiving honorable mention. Dimick was named MVP, and Steve Madson and Joel Simpson were designated captains for 1975.

1974 Season Notes

° Steve Hill of Northfield, whose father, Don, was head coach at Northfield High, played for the Oles at the same time as Steve Hill of Viroqua, Wis. Steve from Northfield was a slender 5'11" and 170, while Steve from Viroqua was 6'3" and 245, hence the names Little Steve, Big Steve or Northfield Steve, Wisconsin Steve.

° The late Grantland Rice, a well-known and revered sports writer, is reputed to have coined the term "four horsemen" for the famed Notre Dame backfield of the 1920s — or at least made it famous with his description: "Outlined against a blue-gray October sky, the four horsemen rode again. In dramatic lore they are known as famine, pestilence, destruction, and death. In reality, their names are Stuhldreher, Miller, Crowley, and Layden."[160]

Captain Jim Dimick questions a call, 1974

1975

With 16 seniors among the 28 returning lettermen and more familiarity with MIAC opponents, St. Olaf looked forward to the 1975 season with optimism. The defensive line returned intact with the exception of Jim Dimick — a big exception indeed. The unit had played strongly the entire '74 season. Included were Collins, Hultgren, Steve J. Hill (Big Steve), Langfeldt, Kruger, Thorfinnson, Wilkens, and Wangsness. With Monahan, Steve D. Hill (Little Steve), Gelle, Simpson, and Greg Olson returning in the backfield, the offense was experienced as well.

Macalester was again the opener but would not count in the standings. The evening game at the Mac Stadium on Snelling Avenue was a good one for the Oles, as they shut out the Scots 37–0.

Capitalizing on Macalester miscues, St. Olaf built a 31–0 halftime lead.

Roger Olson's interception led to a 42-yard Sanders field goal. Steve Madson's fumble recovery started a 45-yard march ending with Monahan passing two yards to Collins for the score. Mark Arvesen's interception led to Monahan's six-yard keeper for the second touchdown. A 50-yard Sanders punt and stout defensive play gave the ball to the Oles at the Mac 29. Five plays later, Simpson ran it in from the three. Rocky Ryland's fumble recovery at the 11 set up Monahan's sprint out for the score to close out a 21-point second quarter. The only second-half score was a 20-yard field goal by Sanders.

The Ole defense was aggressive, holding the Scots to nine first downs, only one in the second half. The kicking game was excellent with Sanders averaging 43 yards punting and two out of three in field goal attempts, one from 42 yards.

Featuring a strong second-half defense, St. Olaf played defending champion St. John's to a 14–14 tie, a vast improvement over the previous season's 55–21 loss. With a drizzling rain and wind affecting play, St. John's scored all of its points in the second quarter. After two punt exchanges in the third period, Sanders hung a 45-yard punt into the wind. The surprised Johnnie receiver fumbled the punt and Ryland recovered at the 12. Two plays later, Gelle went nine yards to score. Sanders converted and the score was 14–7. A St. John's quick kick put the Oles back to their 31. But then the Oles put together a 12-play drive featuring three completions from Monahan to Olson with Gelle going the final yard. Sanders' conversion tied the score.

With nine minutes remaining, the Oles had one more scoring opportunity

Former Northfield High School players, 1975. Front row: Mark Porter, Steve D. Hill, Co-captain Steve Madson, Steve Gilbertson. Middle row: Greg Olson, Dale Ness, Mark Gelle, Mike Gass. Back row: Jon Iverson, Jim Wilkins, Tom Bickel, Steve Remes.

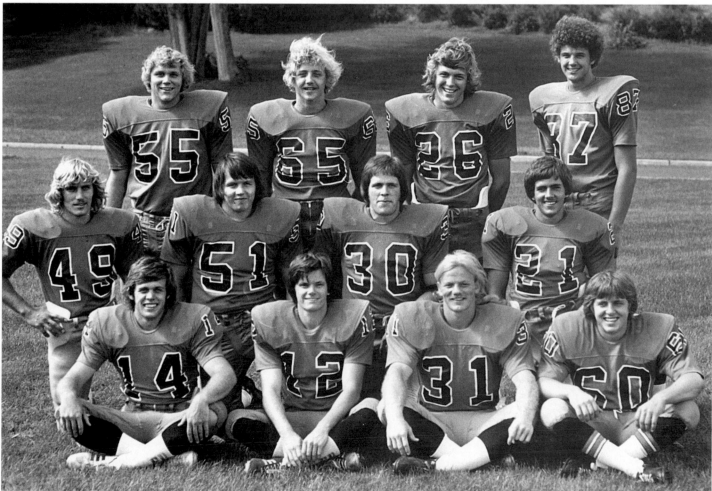

Mark Gelle runs against Carleton, 1975

Greg Olson advances the ball against Carleton, 1975

when Mitch Long recovered a Johnny fumble at the 26. Three plays netted only two yards, and Sanders' 42-yard field goal attempt fell short. The game ended in a heavy downpour. Brian Anderson, along with Uecke and Olson, were outstanding on defense for the Oles. Anderson had three sacks, one interception, five tackles, and four assists. Other leading tacklers were Ryland, 15; Roger Olson, Madson, and Tim Carlson, 12 each, and Dave Mylrea, 11. On offense, Greg Olson, Hultgren, and Monahan stood out.

St. Olaf and Concordia hooked up in another epic defensive struggle, and the Cobbers came out on top 9–6. The Oles' points came via field goals of 35 and 12 yards by Sanders, and the winning margin was a 21-yard three-pointer with 1:18 remaining. Sanders punted eight times for a 51-yard average, prompting Ade Christenson, who was in attendance, to comment, "I have never witnessed such excellent punting which played such a significant part in a game."[161]

Sanders' first field goal followed a 33-yard punt return by Greg Olson. The second came at the end of a 60-yard march. A strong goal line stand by the Cobbers forced the 12-yard kick. Concordia scored the game's only touchdown on a nine-play, 70-yard drive after an interception.

Steve Madson and Dave Mylrea had outstanding games backing up the line. Dave Ryland and Tim Carlson played tough inside, as did Brian Anderson and Mitch Long on the perimeter.

In contrast to the previous season's cold, rainy night against Augsburg at Parade Stadium, the Oles and Auggies played at Manitou Field on a brilliant, 80-degree autumn day. The home folks responded by holding Augsburg to four yards on the ground while rushing for 217 themselves in a 31–6 win. A capacity crowd of nearly 7,000 students, parents, and alumni attended.

There were frequent penalties and mistakes — nine turnovers by the two teams in the first half alone. On the plus side, fine quarterback play by Monahan and strong running by the senior backs — Gelle, Simpson, and Winegarden —

sparked the Oles. Midway in the second quarter, after receiving a short punt, Monahan hit Collins in the end zone for the first score.

St. Olaf struck quickly in the second half. A towering Sanders punt was mishandled and fumbled by the receiver and recovered by Ryland at the Augsburg 15. Gelle scored two plays later. Other Ole scoring included a touchdown by Monahan and a field goal by Sanders. Augsburg's aerial attack, aided by three circus catches, netted their only points. Conversely, the last play of the game summed up Augsburg's day. Auggie flanker Bromwell got behind the Ole secondary and received a perfect bomb from his quarterback, Eckstein. With a clear field ahead, Bromwell fumbled at the Ole five, and Lee Dunfee recovered in the end zone for a touchback. What had appeared to be a perfect 65-yard scoring play became the 13th turnover of the game.

St. Olaf traveled to St. Paul to challenge the Hamline Pipers. The only breakdown of the afternoon was the team bus a mile from the stadium. The football machine functioned well despite curtailed warmup time, disappointing Hamline's Parents' Day crowd with a 34–6 victory.

On the second play of the game, Mylrea blitzed and hit the quarterback, causing a fumble at the Piper 11. Monahan passed to Collins for the score, but Sanders missed his first conversion of the season. A short Hamline punt provided good field position, and Gelle ran for 18 and a score on the patented off-tackle play. Early in the second period, the Oles had a first down at the six-inch line. Gelle was stopped short of the goal, but he didn't have the ball.

Monahan had executed a perfect keeper and was standing in the end zone. Unfortunately, the play confused the officials, as well as the people who tackled Gelle, and they whistled the play dead when Gelle went down and gave the ball to the Pipers at the line of scrimmage.

The defense forced the Pipers to punt out past midfield. Monahan, with great play selection, marched the team 68 yards to score with a minute left in the half. On the first play after the ensuing kickoff, Arvesen intercepted a pass. A piling-on call added 15.

Monahan's pass to Kroll was intercepted. The Hamline defender lateraled to a surprised teammate who fumbled, Jon Iverson recovering at the eight with 15 seconds on the clock. A quick pitch to the outside and a great lead block by Simpson enabled Gelle to score. Sanders' PAT made it 27–0 and closed out the finest half the Oles had played thus far in the season. The Pipers got on the board in the third quarter.

Donnie Watson and Rick Rost filled in capably when Mangrum went down, and Steve Vandenheuvel played most of the game in place of the injured Mitch Long.

In the first of a four-year string of shutouts in the Carleton series, the Oles rolled to a convincing 48–0 victory over the Knights at Laird Stadium. The scoring started when a Sanders punt backed the Carls' receiver into the end zone where he was tackled by Winegarden. Following the safety kickoff, Gelle broke loose for a 32-yard scoring burst, and the Oles were up 9–0. Fumble recoveries by Madson and Ryland set up short scoring drives — a Monahan to Collins pass for one score and a three-yard run by Winegarden for the other.

Roger Olson stepped in front of an intended receiver, picked off the pass and went 34 yards for the final tally of

1975 Captains Joel Simpson and Steve Madson with Coach Tom Porter

the first quarter and a commanding 29–0 lead. Monahan passed to Collins for the only second-quarter score. Second-half scores were by Gelle and freshman Steve Remes on a pass from Hill. Freshman Jeff Stevenson ran well, and Remes made several impossible catches, including the one for a touchdown. Bergstrom with 14 and Winegarden with 12 were the leading tacklers.

The high of the Carleton victory lasted a week, and then St. Thomas spoiled both any remaining hopes of a championship and Homecoming with a 21–7 win. Early in the first quarter, the Tommies were backed up to their three by Arvesen's poocher punt. A 50-yard pass play and a 41-yard run ate up the

distance. On the next two possessions, Olsonoski, St. Thomas linebacker, picked off Monahan passes, each one setting up a short scoring drive, and the Tommies were up 21–0 at halftime. The remainder of the game was a defensive battle/punting duel. The two teams punted 22 times in the game. Gary Uecke returned one St. Thomas punt 68 yards for the Oles' only score.

Monahan threw for two touchdowns, and Gelle and Winegarden scored on the ground as the Oles downed Gustavus 27–14 in 1975's last home contest. The victory evened the overall series with the Gusties at 11 apiece. Gustavus scored first, but St. Olaf quickly countered with a drive which concluded with a beautiful 65-yard scoring pass, Monahan to "Hooks" Collins. The teams traded second-quarter touchdowns to make the count 14–14 at the half.

Two quick third-quarter scores by the Oles put the game away. An 84-yard drive was capped by Winegarden bouncing in from the one. Mylrea's fumble recovery set up the other, a 61-yard Monahan to Greg Olson aerial. Sixteen seniors played well and felt good about their last performance at Manitou Field.

The season concluded with a well-played but disappointing 14–6 loss to the University of Minnesota-Duluth. The Bulldogs used up most of the first quarter in posting their opening score. Fumbles plagued the Oles in the

Mark Gelle runs off tackle against St. John's, 1975 Parents' Day program cover.

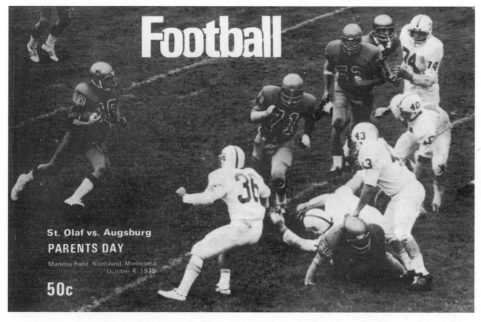

Football

St. Olaf vs. Augsburg
PARENTS DAY
Manitou Field, Northfield, Minnesota
October 4, 1975

50c

1975 Homecoming, St. Thomas runner stopped by Captain Steve Madson

second period, and one of them gave Duluth field position for their second touchdown.

The second half belonged to the Oles, but it turned out to be too little, too late. The Oles' first series drive started at their 21 and was at the Duluth 36, second and one, when Monahan's pass to Sanders hit Randy in the clear, but a following Duluth defender stripped he ball at the four and it rolled out of the end zone for a touchback. The Oles posted their only points with 6:25 remaining when Gelle scored on the end of a 54-yard drive. It was Mark's best rushing day of the season — 132 yards on 27 carries.

Monahan had a fine day as field general and passed for 116 yards. Big Steve Hill and Mark Wangsness were outstanding offensive linemen, and Hultgren played his usual strong game. On defense, Roger Olson, Dave Ryland, and Dave Mylrea gave strong performances.

A 3–3–1 record in the conference (5–3–1 overall) was good for fifth place.

Wangsness, Roger Olson for the second year, and Mark Gelle for the second year were named all-conference. All three also were named to the District 13, NAIA Honor Team. Greg Olson, Collins, Hultgren, Ryland, and Brian Anderson received honorable

mention. Gelle was voted MVP, and Long and Roger Olson were named captains for 1976.

1975 Season Notes

Recent graduates were coaching at area high schools — Mike Schmiesing at St. Paul Alexander Ramsey and Paul Olson at Woodbury.

In the Augsburg game, a St. Olaf coach's protest of what he considered a questionable call by the officials resulted in consecutive 15-yard penalties, giving the Auggies the ball at the five, first and goal. On the second play, a hard hit caused a fumble, which was recovered in the end zone for a touchback. The coach's comment as the defensive unit came off the field; "Thanks, guys; I needed that."

Two stellar performers, Mark Gelle and Big Steve Hill, had professional tryouts prior to the 1976 season, Gelle with the Minnesota Vikings, Hill with the Atlanta Falcons. Both reported interesting and valuable experiences. After his return, Mark volunteered his services as an assistant coach for the 1976 season.

1976

Graduation — happy occasion that it is for all concerned — dealt a major blow to Ole football for the 1976 season. Of

the 16 members of the '75 squad who graduated, eight had been offensive regulars, including the entire starting backfield, two ends who had been four-year regulars, a tackle and center who had been three-year starters.

The defense would have to carry the load early and, luckily, they appeared up to the task. The group was led by co-captains Mitch Long at end and Roger Olson at strong safety. Eric Ristau, tackle, and Dave Ryland, nose guard, were returning regulars. Dave Mylrea, Carl Bergstrom, and Jim Kunitz were all strong linebackers. Forming an experienced secondary along with co-captain Olson, were Gary Uecke, Charlie Mangrum, Mark Arvesen, and Tom Bickel, the latter returning after a year's absence due to injury. Steve VandenHuevel and Jed Downs would team up with Long at defensive end.

Experienced offensive performers back included Joe Langfeldt, Tim Kruger, Tom Thorfinnson, Jim Wilkens, and McKinley Moore. Randy Sanders' return assured a strong kicking game as well as a regular tight end.

The opener with Wartburg, a non-conference opponent, had special significance. Don Canfield, veteran coach of the Wartburg Knights, was an Ole, class of '63, and a former guard and co-captain. The game was billed as a teacher-pupil encounter.

St. Olaf converted two recovered fumbles into nine points in the first seven minutes of play and went on to defeat Wartburg 29–7. The first fumble was forced by freshman tackle Nate Bergeland and recovered by Roger Olson. Sanders' 36-yard field goal followed. On the ensuing Wartburg series, Uecke recovered a Knight fumble, and Andy George, ironically a junior running back transfer from Wartburg, took a quick pitch and went 24 yards to score, aided mightily by a crushing block by freshman tackle Steve Lidke.

A second Ole touchdown came on a 37-yard scoring strike from senior quarterback Steve Lass to Gary Mikkelson, and just before halftime, the Oles went 59 yards in four plays. A Lass to Sanders pass ate up 37 yards, and George went the final nine to score. It was 22–0 at intermission. Wartburg failed to gain a first down in five third-quarter possessions, while Lass piloted the Oles to another touchdown, hooking up with Mikkelson again, this time for 32 yards.

Steve Lass' first start was a fine one — good field generalship, nine completions in 19 attempts for 192 yards and two touchdowns. Sanders' punting enabled the Oles to pick up about 10 yards on each exchange. Leading tacklers were Mylrea, Kunitz, and Bergstrom. Ryland and Bergeland contributed strong interior line play, and the secondary performance of Mangrum, Olson, Arvesen, and Uecke was solid.

Returning to Northfield the next week, St. Olaf blitzed Carleton with 28 points in the first half and went on to down the Knights (the second week facing a team called Knights) 42–0. The victory brought the Goat series count to Carleton 28 wins, St. Olaf 26 wins and one tie.

The experienced Ole defense scored twice and set up two others with a pass interception and a fumble recovery, while the offense moved with a confidence and authority that had been questionable the previous week. The Oles moved 81 yards in 14 plays, Lass sneaking in for the first score. Penalties and a John Nahorniak interception put the Carls in a hole. VandenHeuvel hit Carleton quarterback Franz as he released the ball. The wounded duck was picked off by Mylrea, who jogged 14 yards for the second score.

Minutes later, Arvesen picked off another Franz aerial. George broke loose for 50 yards, and Lass bootlegged into the end zone on the run-pass option. Sanders' kick made it 21–0. A minute before halftime, Arvesen broke Carleton's back when he fielded a punt at his 44 and went 56 yards down the sideline to make the score 28–0 at intermission. After a scoreless third period, a second Arvesen intercept set up a score by halfback John Ederer, and Tim Bates passed to Wally Hustad for the final tally.

Freshman Terry Westermann picked off another Carleton pass as the game ended.

With two non-conference wins packed away, the Oles faced Augsburg in the league opener. St. Olaf scored seven points in the first quarter, another touchdown in the second and two field goals in the third to down the Auggies 19–6. Mylrea's interception of an Augsburg pass put the ball at the Augsburg 26. On the first play from scrimmage, quarterback Bob Ringham optioned to flanker Lee Dunfee who turned the corner and raced 26 yards to score. Starting from their 41 in the second period, the Oles went 59 yards in 10 plays, Andy George scoring.

Coaches Hauck and Dimick at the sideline

Sanders field goals of 27 and 31 yards completed the scoring. Fullback Tom Feibiger led Ole runners with 61 yards.

The victory over Augsburg was bittersweet in several ways. It was a victory, and more than that, it was victory number 100 for Coach Porter as a college mentor. But there was a downside. Steve Lass, who had labored faithfully as a reserve quarterback, appeared to be on his way to an outstanding senior season, his first as a starter, when he suffered a season-ending shoulder separation in the Augsburg encounter. In his first start (against Wartburg), Lass had completed nine of 19 passes for 192 yards and two touchdowns. He also ran for two touchdowns in the first two games. A bad break which was hard to accept.

The Oles used an opportunistic defense, an error-free offense, and a strong kicking game to edge a larger, more physical Hamline squad 3–0 on Parents' Day. The Lions were pushed

The 1976 team, Mitch Long and Roger Olson, captains

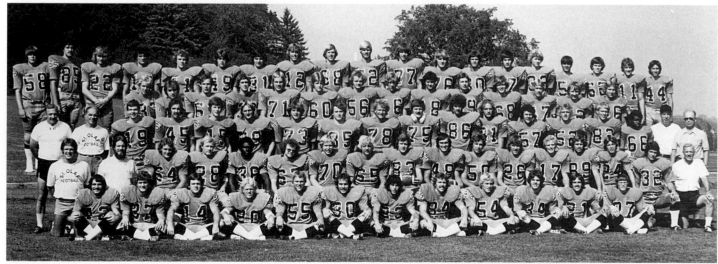

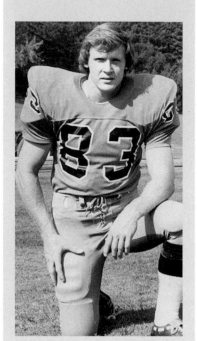

Mitch Long, 1976 captain

Roger Olson, 1976 captain

around most of the first half, and except for a fumble recovery by VandenHeuvel and a good punt return by Arvesen, the score could have been in Hamline's favor instead of 0–0 at halftime.

In the third period, the Oles used a fumble recovery by Dunfee and a 25-yard field goal by Sanders to go up 3–0 and then hold on to win. The Pipers stormed back and had first and goal at the five but were denied on a strong goal line stand. A field goal attempt from the six went wide. Other Hamline thrusts were stopped by two Arvesen interceptions and a fumble forced by Long and recovered by Ristau. In their final five possessions, the Pipers were intercepted twice, fumbled twice, and missed a field goal.

In a battle of unbeatens, Concordia stayed that way with a hard-fought, 17–8 victory in Moorhead. After a scoreless first period, the Cobbers notched a 40-yard field goal after picking off an Ole pass. St. Olaf threatened when Arvesen returned a punt 42 yards and a Mark Porter to Mikkelsen pass brought the ball to the Cobber 23. A failed field goal attempt closed a frustrating first half. The Oles had three passes intercepted, a punt blocked and missed a short field goal attempt, yet trailed a good Concordia club only 10–0.

The fates improved marginally in the second half but not enough to produce a win. The opportunistic Cobbers recovered a fumble and marched 67 yards in 12 plays to take a 17–0 lead, while the Oles had trouble moving the ball. Uecke finally put the Lions on the board when he stepped in front of a Cobber wide receiver, picked off the ball and returned it 15 yards to score. Tim Bates closed out the scoring by running for the two-point conversion off a fake kick.

Despite a cold wind and snow flurries, the Oles shook off the Concordia defeat and delighted Homecoming fans with a 36–0 conquest of Macalester. On Mac's first possession, the Oles moved them backward enabling the hosts to take over at midfield. From there, they moved for the first score in seven plays, culminating with Porter's bootleg pass to Gary Mikkelsen. The aggressive defensive play continued to tell, forcing Mac to punt from their end

zone. Arvesen's punt return, Porter's pitch to Dunfee, and a quarterback sneak brought the score to 15–0.

While interceptions by Olson, Uecke, and Mylrea kept the Scots bottled up, Arvesen fielded a punt in stride at the 40 and went in to score, his second punt-return score of the season. The final Ole touchdown came on a 13-yard pass from quarterback Bob Ringham to end Todd Porter capping a 16-play, 73-yard drive, an errorless march by the reserves. Chuck Benson's PAT was the 36th point.

Traveling to St. Peter, the Oles posted a 22–15 victory and, in so doing, handed Gustavus its first Homecoming loss in 15 years. Steve Remes and Randy Sanders played major offensive roles in the triumph. Steve grabbed two key third-down passes from Mark Porter in the fourth period, while Sanders kicked field goals of 22, 33, and 41 yards. Andy George ran 10 yards for the final score. John Kroll passed 26 yards to Sanders to go with Sanders' first two field goals to make the count 12–7 at halftime. After intermission, the Gusties went ahead 15–12. A roughing-the-kicker penalty allowed the Oles to maintain possession, and they took advantage, moving 69 yards in 13 plays, George scoring his second touchdown, this one from the one, to make it 29–15. Sanders's last field goal tacked on the final three points.

The Ole defense limited Gustavus to 61 yards rushing. Standouts were Mylrea, who stole a pass late in the game to stop a Gustie threat, Ryland, VandenHeuvel, Olson, and Ristau.

Bethel had replaced UMD in the league, but their game with the Oles didn't count as a conference tilt. Nevertheless, the Royals gave notice they were to be reckoned with, downing the Oles 20–0, taking advantage of a subpar performance by St. Olaf. The Royals built a 14–0 halftime lead by dint of a fumble recovery and a pass interception. The Oles came out strong in the third period but stopped themselves with penalties. The Royals drove 55 yards in 13 plays for their final score. St. Olaf was intercepted twice in the fourth period making seven turnovers for the game.

ABC Television Sports was emphasizing Division III football, and they determined that the St. Olaf-St. John's game would be a good example of Division III at its best. So those tuned to ABC affiliates in the region heard the following:

"From Manitou Field on the campus of St. Olaf College in Northfield, Minnesota, this is Bill Frenk, along with Rick Forzano, inviting you to stay tuned for NCAA football, St. John's at St. Olaf."[162] The personable Forzano, former coach of the Naval Academy and later of the Detroit Lions of the NFL, was the color commentator for the telecast. He was to return for another telecast three years later. So charmed was Forzano by the ambience of Manitou Heights that he was heard to remark to Athletic Director Bob Gelle, "If I were you, I'd chain my leg to that desk (Gelle's) and never let anyone pry it loose."

The Ole defense held the nation's leading rushing team (St. John's) at bay early and drew first blood on a Mark Porter to Gary Mikkelsen bootleg pass. A Nate Bergeland-caused fumble recovered by Charlie Mangrum turned the Johnnies back a fourth time, but a fumble at the Ole 23 enabled St. John's to get on the board and go ahead 7–6. St. John's scored again in the second period, but the PAT was blocked by Jed Downs. Mitch Long's sack of the Johnny quarterback provided the impetus for a 55-yard, 11-play drive,

Arvesen intercepts against Carleton, 1976, with help coming from Mylrea (35), Kunitz (54), and Simonson.

Porter going the last five on a bootleg with 38 seconds left, making it 13–13 at the half.

In the third period, VandenHeuvel recovered a fumble at the St. John's 16, setting the stage for what appeared to be the turning point in the contest — a failed fourth-down field goal attempt. Following two punt exchanges, a center snap went over the head of punter Randy Sanders, resulting in a safety and good field position for St. John's following the free kick. Buoyed by the turn of events, the Johnnies went 52 yards in 10 plays to lead 22–13. A 51-yard breakaway by Johnny fullback Schmitz closed out the scoring: St. John's 29, St. Olaf 13.

Dave Mylrea was named outstanding defensive player of the game, and Chevrolet gave a $1,000 scholarship to St. Olaf in his name.

A strong and opportunistic defense, a hallmark of this Ole club throughout most of the season, was the key to a 16–0 shutout of St. Thomas in the season finale. The secondary picked off four of the Tommies' passes — Nahorniak got two and Mylrea and Olson, one each. The Oles also recovered two fumbles and gave up only 138 total yards.

Randy Sanders closed out his Ole career by kicking field goals of 37, 36, and 25 yards and one PAT for 10 points. Sanders also punted 11 times, one of the kicks going for 58 yards.

Tim Bates' pinpoint pass to Lee Dunfee, kneeling in the end zone, was the only touchdown of the first half. But two of Sanders' field goals, one following a fumble recovery by Long and the other set up by Mark Porter passes to George and Remes made the score 13–0 at halftime.

Mark Porter holds, Randy Sanders converts, 1976

Randy Sanders, 1976

Coach Chuck Lunder retires at the end of the 1976–77 year.

The third period was a defensive standoff — no scores, no turnovers, six punts. Interceptions by Olson at the seven, Mylrea at the 27 and Nahorniak's second of the day, which he returned 44 yards to the St. Thomas 10, stymied the visitors in the fourth period. Nahorniak's interception and return set up Sanders's final field goal, which rounded out the scoring. It was a super day for the seniors and Coach Chuck Lunder to end their St. Olaf careers. The seniors were co-captains Long and Olson, Wilkens, Sanders, Ryland, Kruger, Lass, Thorfinnson, Mangrum, Bickel, Kroll, Kunitz, and Uecke.

The 7–3 season was good for a second-place tie in the MIAC. Coaches and fans remember this team for solid defense, consistently strong special teams and kicking game, and an offense that was able to rise to the occasion.

Randy Sanders, Mitch Long, and Roger Olson won all-conference recognition, with Uecke, Arvesen, Mylrea, and VandenHeuvel tabbed for honorable mention. Mark Arvesen was second among punters in the MIAC. Long and Olson shared MVP honors, while Mark Porter and Arvesen were named co-captains for '77. Olson, Mylrea, and Sanders were named to the All-Lutheran College team.

1976 Season Notes

Colorful hijinks have always been a part of the St. Olaf-Carleton rivalry. The 1976 game may have been notable for the chants: "Back to the books" (St. Olaf students); "At least we can read" (Carleton students); "Read the scoreboard" (St. Olaf students).

The JV squad had a memorable game with the University of Minnesota varsity reserves in Memorial Stadium. The Gopher reserves were competing for spaces on an upcoming travel squad. Coach Cal Stoll and his staff watched as the gallant band of Ole reserves went down 42–7 but not without a battle.

Six men were inducted into the Ole Athletic Hall of Fame at Homecoming. They were Peter Fossum '19, Clifford (Kippy) Gilbertson '31, Marshall (Mush) Haugen '48, Erv Mikkelson '56, Dave Hindermann '62, and Mark Aamot '63.

Add to memorable comments: Defensive back Mark Arvesen in the locker room after the Macalester game in which he ran back a punt for a touchdown, "We had enough practice [Mac punted 12 times] and we finally got it right on the ninth try."

The St. John's game program included a fine tribute to Chuck Lunder, who retired at the end of the 1976–77 school year. Jim Dimick's accolade included this statement:

"Chuck Lunder is one of the grandest men to ever don coaching togs anywhere. Chuck coaches the offensive line, but his value to the grid fortunes extends far beyond his work with his linemen. A warm, intelligent, personable individual who is respected and loved by all he serves. Those close to the scene realize it is people like Chuck Lunder who make the St. Olaf tradition what it is." The authors say "amen" to Jim's statement. An important trait in a coach is loyalty. Loyalty to the program you work with and to the institution you represent. Chuck rated at the top.

An autographed football was presented to Tim Quinlivan, a special guest at the annual banquet. Tim had started with the present seniors but was forced to leave school after he suffered major trauma as a result of an accidental fall in the St. Olaf Center.

1977

As the 1977 season approached, Tim Larsen '74, former captain and outstanding defensive lineman, joined the coaching staff in the absence of Jim Dimick, who was on sabbatical leave at the University of Arizona. With the retirement of Chuck Lunder, Rod Grubb took over the offensive line. Mark Gelle was in his second year as an Ole coach after being a volunteer in '76.

The outlook for the season was a solid defense and a capable offense a year older and wiser. The defense looked particularly strong with seven starters returning, six in the line and linebacker positions. That was tempered, however, by the loss by graduation of three three-year regulars.

Two non-conference games — Wartburg and Carleton — opened the season. True to predictions, the defense showed its stuff early against Wartburg.

Early in the second period, tackle Eric Ristau blocked a punt and Nate Bergeland recovered at the 30. Seven plays later, Bates rolled out and passed to Lee Dunfee for the score. Chuck Benson converted. The Knights evened the score at seven at halftime, and the third quarter was a defensive standoff. The speedy Dunfee returned Wartburg's first punt of the fourth period 56 yards to the 18-yard line. John Ederer scored from the two and repeated with less than a minute to play to make the final 19–7. Linebackers Nahorniak and Mylrea had 22 and 18 tackles, respectively, and Fiebiger led rushers with 79 in 22 carries.

The Metric Game (the Liter Bowl)

The 56th renewal of the Goat series had a special feature: it was the first metric football game and, as such, attracted nationwide attention (*Sports*

Metric Game fans, 1977

Illustrated and several national TV networks, among others). Termed the "Liter Bowl," it was the brainchild of Dr. Jerry Mohrig, professor of chemistry at Carleton. The size of the Laird Stadium grid was enlarged a little to account for the difference between yards and meters — length 120 meters, including end zones; width 50 meters; first down chains 10 meters. The only dimension that was not changed was

the height of the goal post crossbar, which remained at 10 feet. Player heights and weights in the game program were in kilograms and centimeters.

David Nelson, secretary of the NCAA rules committee, commented that, "the reason we (NCAA) don't change to metric … is … because none of us on the rules committee understand the metric system."

The slight differences in dimension didn't bother the Oles. Their experience and superior firepower overwhelmed the Carls 43–0. Dunfee scored first on a reverse from the 14-meter line and Fiebiger followed from the 12. Benson drilled a 34-meter field goal, and Bates scored on a sneak making it 22–0 at halftime.

At the start of the third period, Porter directed a 54-meter march, Ederer scoring. Steve Ostlie's 38-meter pass to Wally Hustad, and a touchdown

The Metric Game program, 1977

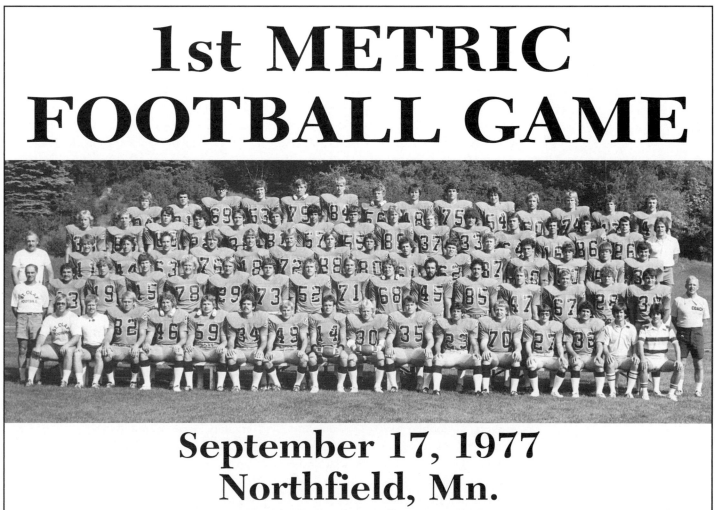

1st METRIC FOOTBALL GAME

September 17, 1977 Northfield, Mn.

Mark Arvesen, 1977 captain

Mark Porter, 1977 captain

run by Jim Dougherty closed out the scoring. The Ole defense turned in another great performance, limiting Carleton to zero meters rushing and only six first downs.

Heading into the league schedule, St. Olaf played host to visiting Augsburg. Though they started slow, the Oles went on to dominate the Auggies and carve out a 24–13 win. After stopping the first two Ole drives, the Auggies began one of their own from the 30. Steve Chiodo pulled down the Augsburg running back after 44 yards. A Rick Rost interception stopped them temporarily, but after a subsequent fumble recovery, they scored. With a lot of back and forth, a fumble recovery by Jed Downs, and some offense by Mark Quinnell and Bates, the Oles tied the score at 7–7 by halftime on a Bates pass to Steve McKay. Benson converted. In the second half, three Augsburg turnovers led to three Ole scores — two touchdowns by Bates and a field goal by Benson. With the score at 24–13, the final as it turned out, Arvesen, Chiodo, and Rost intercepted to kill Augsburg threats.

The following week, the Oles were knocked from the unbeaten ranks when Hamline took a 24–17 victory in St. Paul. The Oles jumped out to a 10–0 lead on a Benson field goal, following a Rost interception, and an Ederer off-tackle slash set up by Nahorniak's fumble recovery. At that point, Hamline went to the air — a good thing too (for them) since they gained only five yards net rushing. By the end of the third quarter, Hamline quarterback Wannebo had hit touchdown passes of 63, 13, and 66 yards, all to flanker McGovern — and the score was 24–10. The Oles drove 47 yards in seven plays to make it 24–17 and threatened twice more but couldn't hit pay dirt. Hamline frustrated the Oles with 241 yards through the air.

For the second week in a row, St. Olaf held well on the ground but was victimized by the aerial game. Under a heavy overcast and drizzle on a soggy Manitou Field, the Concordia Cobbers took a 17–6 decision. After Dave Mylrea intercepted to kill a Cobber threat in the first quarter, Concordia put it together in the second quarter and scored all of their points. Early in the period, the Cobbers marched to the Ole 10 where they were stopped and had to settle for a field goal. The next two Concordia possessions were backbreakers for the Oles — two drives, two scores — added up to a 17–0 halftime lead.

Following a scoreless third period, Rick Rost intercepted. The Cobbers got the ball back but had to punt. A bad snap from center gave the Oles the ball at the Concordia three and Ederer scored from there.

St. Olaf edged the Cobbers in rushing, 135 to 131 but yielded 126 yards through the air, while connecting for only 16 themselves. The defensive front of Bergeland, Ryland, and Ristau and Linebackers Mylrea and Nahorniak played great football.

Taking out two weeks worth of frustration, the Oles buried the Macalester Scots 67–0. St. Olaf scored twice in the first seven minutes and once more late in the first period and then twice in the second, once in the third, and four times in the fourth. Halfback Mark Quinnell led the offensive onslaught with 163 yards and three touchdowns on 28 carries. Other scores were by Bates, McKay, Ederer, Fiebiger, two by Mike Schrader, and one on an interception runback by Ed Voight. Other interceptions were by Steve Chiodo and Jed Downs and two by Carl Bergstrom.

Despite the score, the Oles had only 375 yards of total offense, testifying to the significance of the Mac turnovers — six interceptions and two fumbles.

In the Homecoming game versus Gustavus, the Oles played very well against a very good team but came up short 15–22. The Gusties drove 69 yards with the opening kickoff to jump out ahead 7–0. Following two punt exchanges, Steve Ostlie lofted a halfback pass to Steve McKay. Steve bobbled the ball momentarily, and the Gustie defensive back intercepted at the three. On second down, Rost tackled the ball carrier in the end zone for a safety. Arvesen brought the kickoff back to the Gustie 38, and the Oles scored in seven plays.

A replay of the Concordia game saw Gustavus score twice in the last two minutes of the half — the last being a 55-yard field goal as the half ended. Halftime score: 17–9. A third-period poocher punt by Arvesen was downed at the two. The Gusties fumbled on first down, Arvesen recovered, and Bates scored on a keeper. An Ole fumble led to a 50-yard Gustie drive and a field goal: 20–15. A magnificent goal-line stand turned back four Gustie attempts. The remaining 10 minutes were marred by five turnovers, three by the Oles. The loss dropped the Oles to 2–3 in the league, while the Gusties moved to 4–1.

Gaining some revenge for the 16–0 loss in '76, the Oles outplayed non-conference foe Bethel 25–13. The Royals struck first on an 18-yard pass, but from that point on, the Oles shut them out until late in the game when they connected on a 71-yard pass play. In the meantime, the Oles rang up 25 points on touchdowns by Quinnell, Mylrea (after a punt block by Nahorniak), Fiebiger, after a 78-yard, 15-play march engineered by Mark Porter, and a pair of field goals by Benson and McKay.

In the season's penultimate game at Collegeville, St. Olaf scored on its first offensive series, but couldn't make the lead hold up, and St. John's carved out a 21–7 win. The Oles' touchdown drive featured passes from Bates to

Todd Porter for 22 and Tom Fiebiger for 24 and the touchdown. Schmitz retaliated for the Johnnies with a 64-yard touchdown run on the first play from scrimmage. St. John's capitalized on a fumble recovery to score again in the first period and a final time in the third quarter, driving 59 yards in eight plays. On their last possession, the Johnnies drove 93 yards in 14 plays to the Ole one, where an outstanding goal-line stand prevented a fourth score.

The 1977 season finale was testimony to the character and competitiveness of St. Olaf as the Oles played St. Thomas to a 7–7 tie on a frozen Manitou Field. The first quarter was three downs and punt for both teams. The Oles, sparked by Bates's passing and Quinnell's running, had the better of things in the second quarter. A Bates to McKay scoring pass got the Oles on the board with 9:25 to play in the half. With 1:13 remaining, a 73-yard pass-run combination put St. Thomas ahead when the defender slipped on the frozen field.

The scoreless second half was a replay of the second quarter - - field position favored the Oles, but they were never able to get the big play to break the game. Defense again was outstanding.

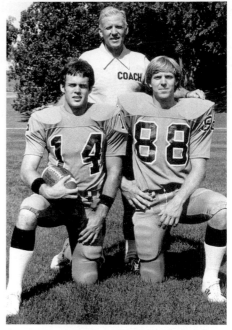

Coach Porter and sons Mark and Todd, 1977

Seniors playing their last game for St. Olaf were captains Mark Arvesen and Mark Porter, Carl Bergstrom, Dave Ryland, Tom Fiebiger, Bob Benes, and Gary Nelson. The group had been involved for four seasons and compiled a 20–16–2 record. All-conference selections were Arvesen and linebackers Mylrea and Nahorniak, the only players selected at that position. Honorable mention went to Nate Bergeland, Steve Lidke, and Tom Fiebiger. Dave Mylrea was voted most valuable. Mylrea and Arvesen also were named to the All-Lutheran College team. Players requested that student trainer Dave Seefeld receive the letter award in recognition of his dedicated service over four years.

Co-captains selected for 1978 were Rick Rost and Steve VandenHeuvel.

1977 Season Notes

Joe Soucheray covered the Metric game for the *Minneapolis Tribune*. Used to covering more high-powered contests, Soucheray wasn't especially charmed by the assignment. As it happened, Joe and St. Olaf Sports Information Director Bob Phelps were the last persons left in the Carleton press box at the end of the game. Soucheray's comment, "Well, look at

Bates running against Carleton, 1977, Moore and Multz move in.

John Nahorniak, linebacker, 1978

Dave Mylrea, linebacker, 1978

it this way: neither one of us will have to do this again next year."

Granskou, Skoglund Die

Two men who played leading roles in the growth and development of St. Olaf and its athletic program died during the 1977 season. The college's fifth president, Clemens M. Granskou, died Sept. 12, at the age of 82. A strong president and a consistent supporter of athletics, President Granskou was a frequent visitor at practice sessions, particularly after his retirement. His home was just across Lincoln Street from the practice fields.

Upon being awarded a St. Olaf monogram, Granskou quipped, "I will have Ella sew it on the seat of my pants as that is where I spent most of my time — sitting on the bench."[163]

The Oles were on the field at St. John's University in Collegeville in the next to the last game of the season when word came that Howell P. Skoglund had died in Sun City, Ariz., at the age of 74. Skoglund, a 1925 graduate and squad member, was a leading Twin Cities business executive and one of the five persons who founded the Minnesota Vikings of the NFL. Skoglund was a longtime member of the Board of Regents of St. Olaf, and he and his wife gave the naming gift for the Skoglund Athletic Center, constructed in 1968.

1978

To quote the St. Olaf press book, "The 1978 Ole gridders should again be strong defensively, as they have been the last two seasons, but may have to struggle to build an offense that will make them an MIAC title contender."

Gone were Mylrea, Arvesen, Bergstrom, and Ryland from the defensive unit, but returnees captains Steve VandenHeuvel and Rick Rost, along with John Nahorniak, Jon Anderson, Jed Downs, Eric Ristau, Dave Borgwardt, Nate Bergeland, and Steve Chiodo supported the statement about strength on defense. The offense had experienced regulars returning as well: Todd Porter, Brian Fenelon, and Steve McKay, ends; Steve Lidke, Kerry Multz, and Joey Langfeldt (who was on the '76 squad),

tackles; Brian Johnson and Mac Moore, guards, and Mark Simonson, center. Backfield returnees were Steve Ostlie, Tim Bates, Mark Quinnell, Mike Schrader, John Ederer, and Lee Dunfee. Some position changes — Terry Westermann to free safety, Ostlie to quarterback, and Bates to wingback — proved wise moves.

The Cornell College Rams, traditionally an offense-minded club, provided non-conference opposition in the opener. The Oles were weary after a hot bus trip to Mt. Vernon, Iowa, since the bus air conditioning had gone out. A good night's rest in an air-conditioned motel restored them somewhat, but the squad was still slow out of the gate and needed a 16-point third-quarter burst to pull away to a 23–7 victory.

The Rams scored in the first quarter on a 52-yard pass to Ram receiver Jake Remes, whose brother Steve played for the Oles a few years earlier. Bergeland started the third-quarter fireworks with a fumble recovery. An Ostlie to Mikkelson pass and McKay's PAT tied the score. On the next series, Downs trapped the Cornell quarterback in the end zone for a safety, and freshman Bob Klefsaas returned the ensuing free kick 55 yards for his first score as an Ole. Judicious use of personnel by the coaches, especially Grubb and Dimick working with the linemen, was a telling factor on a hot, muggy afternoon.

A second-quarter blitz powered the Oles over Macalester 55–13 in the home opener. Scoring on each possession in the quarter, five Oles had a hand in scoring 35 points, a record for one quarter. Schrader, Ostlie, Bates, Paul Estenson, and Fred Gelle scored six pointers, and McKay was five for five on conversions. The defense deserved equal credit, blunting the Mac offense and enabling the Ole attackers to take over consistently on the Mac side of the 50. Ederer, Klefsaas, and Robert Welch had second half scores.

The third game of the season gave evidence the Oles were for real. Traveling to Moorhead, St. Olaf dumped nationally ranked Concordia 26–17. A tenacious defense and a methodical offense got the job done. Dimick's "D" trucks and a secondary led by Westermann's two interceptions

The 1978 front five — Jed Downs, Eric Ristau, Jon Anderson, Nate Bergeland, and Steve VandenHeuvel

foiled the Cobber offense. They did manage to score first, however, capitalizing on two Ole fumbles. St. Olaf retaliated with an Ostlie to Bates scoring pass climaxing a 56-yard drive. Concordia's field goal made it 10–6 before Westermann's first theft led to a five-play drive with Bates scoring to put the Oles on top 13–10 at the half.

Klefsaas replaced the injured Ostlie at quarterback in the second half. His option running, coupled with the inside rushes of Schrader and Quinnell, had the Ole offense humming. Al Hodge's fumble recovery set up the next touchdown. With fourth and four at the Cobber 20, McKay lined up for the field goal, but Klefsaas, the holder, executed the fake, rolling around the right side and, aided by Porter's downfield block, took it to the two. Estenson punched it in from there to make the count 19–12. The teams traded scores in the fourth period. Mikkelson kept a nine-play, 79-yard march alive with a one-handed grab on a third-down play. Shortly thereafter, Klefsaas threw to Mikkelson for 27 and the score. A Steve Chiodo interception shut off the Cobbers late in the game. The Ole offense converted 11 of 17 third-down situations, and the defense limited the Cobbers to just 21 plays in the second half. A Concordia coach commented, "The Oles have the best pair of linebackers (Nahorniak and Hodge) we've played against."[164]

A 27–12 victory over Hamline put St. Olaf in sole possession of first place in the conference with a 3–0 mark (4–0 overall). Sustained marches of 80, 70, 70, and 54 yards all culminated in scores — Bates and Ostlie, on passes from Klefsaas; Schrader and Quinnell on runs. Sacks by Borgwardt and VandenHeuvel were typical of the defense that harassed the Pipers all afternoon. Rost's breakup of an attempted two-point conversion kept the score at 13–12 at one point before the offense took over in the second half and put the game away. Schrader's 104 yards and Quinnell's 103 were evidence of great offensive line play by Lidke, Multz, Moore, and others.

"Spurred on by one of the finest defensive performances in recent annals, the '78 Ole gridders battled a big, strong St. Thomas foe right to the wire and emerged a 16–14 victor in a real thriller." That eloquent statement in the *Viking Scorebook* by writer Bob Gelle summarized the game against the Tommies.[165] The defense held St. Thomas to minus 29 yards on the ground forcing them to the air where Ole defenders promptly stole four throws.

The Toms scored first when a high center snap led to an end zone recovery. The teams then battled inconclusively until a roughing penalty put St. Olaf in position for McKay to kick a field goal with no time remaining in the first half to make the score 7–3.

A potent defensive charge by the Ole front five resulted in negative yardage, and a partially blocked punt gave the Oles the ball at the Tom 43. Mike Schrader bolted up the middle and took it all in one bite. The Toms fought back, however, scoring on a halfback pass to preserve a 14–10 advantage with 11:05 remaining. Six plays later, the clock apparently went awry; it read 6:30 — six plays in four minutes 34 seconds! No way. After a lengthy coaches/officials meeting, one minute was put back on the clock. It proved significant.

After an exchange of possessions, the Oles started to march with Schrader and Estenson carrying a great deal of the load. The Oles converted on a fourth and inches play but fumbled the ball away at the 10. Before the home fans cheering had faded, the Toms returned the favor, Ristau recovering at the 13.

Anderson and VandenHeuvel pressure the passer, 1978

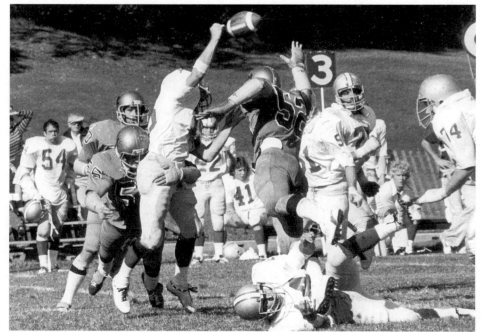

Steve VandenHeuvel, 1978 captain

Three plays put the ball at the six. Klefsaas rolled to his right and hit Dunfee in the corner of the end zone. With 56 seconds left, Tad Hauck intercepted St. Thomas's last-gasp pass to preserve the win.

There were heroes galore in this one, but no one displayed more courage than Jed Downs. After missing two weeks with mononucleosis, Jed played an inspired game after learning of his younger brother's tragic death in an automobile accident the night before.

The Oles' five-game unbeaten string came to an end the next week at St. Peter. Gustavus Adolphus recovered a St. Olaf fumble at the Ole 36 and moved in for a fourth-period touchdown and a 21–13 victory. Earlier, the strong Ole defense against the run forced the Gusties to go to the air early. Jay Schoenebeck scored for Gustavus in the first period, and Quinnell countered for the Oles three minutes later. Two long runs produced early second-half touchdowns. Straka went 75 yards for the Swedes, and Ederer broke free over the middle and went 66 yards for the Oles. Then came the fourth-quarter fumble which set up the winning points for the Gusties.

"For Men Only"

The Oles got back on the winning track with a classic 24–21 victory over the perennially powerful Johnnies in Collegeville. St. Olaf scored only seven points in the second quarter, but Coach Porter called those 15 minutes the turning point of the game.

"We intercepted them twice, recovered a fumble, and kept St. John's inside their 30 throughout that period. At that point, we felt we had begun to control the game and that if we didn't kill ourselves with mistakes, we could take it," Porter said.[166]

It is unfair to single out individuals, because the entire team played brilliantly, Porter said, but Steve Ostlie had his day. Playing "flawlessly," Ostlie completed 15 of 30 passes for 172 yards and the winning touchdown. Klefsaas, running at tailback, carried 27 times for 76 tough yards and completed five passes for 60 more. McKay had a 64-yard punt, two key receptions, and an important fourth down fake punt-pass to keep a drive going.

Rick Rost, 1978 captain

St. John's scored first, and on the next possession, the Oles were forced to punt, but McKay's boot put the Johnnies deep in their territory. They passed on third down, and Rost intercepted and brought it back to the six. Schrader scored and Langfeldt converted. A Dunfee interception kept the Johnnies backed up, but the Oles couldn't score again before intermission.

After St. John's scored to make it 14–7 in the third period, Nahorniak recovered a fumble at the Ole 41 to set up the second score. Ostlie engineered a 50-yard drive in four plays. Bates made a sensational diving catch at the two, Klefsaas scored and Langfeldt converted to knot it at 14. Langfeldt's field goal put the Oles up three, 17–14, but then St. John's struck with a first-down, 55-yard pass play. The Ole offense set out to get it back. A seven-play march produced the needed seven points. Ostlie threaded the needle on two pass plays to McKay, one of them on a hotly contested defensive pass interference call. At the close, the defense answered the call, putting St. John's in a fourth and 13 situation late in the game. Key plays were a quarterback sack by Bergeland and another fumble recovery by Nahorniak.

Though the score was close, statistics testified to Ole dominance — total offensive plays: St. Olaf 90, St. John's 55; second-half plays: St. Olaf 56, St. John's 24; fourth-quarter plays: St. Olaf 32, St. John's 9; St. John's rushing yardage 90, passing 109 (55 in one play). Nate Bergeland was named Conference Defensive Player of the Week.

This was a great triumph in St. Olaf football history. A large contingent of Ole followers whooped it up throughout the game and swarmed onto the field at the end. Coach Porter stood at the locker room door and shook each player's hand as he came in. "It was for men only out there today," Porter was heard to say.

As the squad showed up for practice on Friday before the Goat game, nary a helmet was to be found in the locker room. A burglary was reported, and the squad went on with the usual review practice. About halfway through the drill, a Carleton maintenance pickup pulled onto the track, loaded with the missing headgear.

The next day, the Ole defense was in command all the way, limiting the Carls to 88 yards total offense and not allowing them past their own 40 in the second half, en route to a 22–0 shutout, the fourth in a row. The result evened the Goat series at 28–28–1. Hodge led the defense with 10 tackles, and the forward five pressured the Carl quarterback throughout.

Three Langfeldt field goals and a pair of touchdowns were more than enough offense. An Ostlie to Fenelon 33-yard pass was the big play in the first touchdown drive with Klefsaas scoring from the seven. Early in the third period, Hodge intercepted and rambled into the end zone. The play was nullified by a clipping penalty, but Klefsaas scored four plays later. John Van Ginkel and Reed Johnson recovered fumbles in Carleton territory, but neither led to a score. Reserves played the final nine minutes to preserve the shutout.

St. Olaf narrowly missed another shutout as the team packed away victory number six in its quest for the MIAC crown, defeating Bethel 21–2. It was another sterling performance for the defense. The front five of VandenHeuvel, Ristau, Bergeland, Anderson, and Downs registered 12 quarterback sacks. As a group, the defense limited the Royals to minus 13 yards rushing and two pass completions for 16 yards, a total net of three yards.

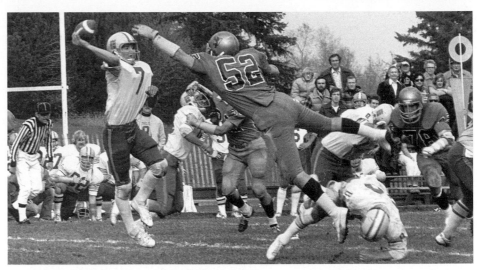

VandenHeuvel at his best against Bethel, 1978

On only one occasion did the Oles allow the Royals to penetrate deep into their territory. Midway in the first period, Steve Chiodo deflected a Royal pass and it fell into a receiver's hands as he lay on the ground. A second pass play netted a first down by inches at the two. Three running plays and an incomplete pass left the Royals still short of the goal. But on the second play after the goal-line stand, Ostlie was tackled in the end zone for a safety and the Royals' only points.

Schrader scored the Oles' first touchdown, prior to the Royal safety. It was set up by a 25-yard pass from Ostlie to Bates. The second tally came midway in the second period on a beautifully executed 65-yard pass play, Klefsaas to Mikkelson. Voight finished out the scoring with a 16-yard return of a pass interception.

A win was needed in the final game of the season against Augsburg for the Oles to claim a share of the MIAC championship with Concordia. They got it done on a bleak, windy November day on Manitou Field. After a slow start, a second-quarter splurge doomed the Auggies, 41–25. Augsburg scored first by virtue of a blocked punt and recovery in the end zone. The Oles retaliated early in the second period, moving 79 yards in six plays to tie the score. A shovel pass for 29 yards, a halfback pass for 36 and Schrader's nine-yard touchdown run were keys.

The Oles went ahead on the next Augsburg series when VandenHeuvel's hit on the Auggie quarterback resulted in a lame duck pass that Nahorniak picked off. After returning it 10 yards, John lateraled to fellow linebacker

The 1978 team, Rick Rost and Steve VandenHeuvel, captains

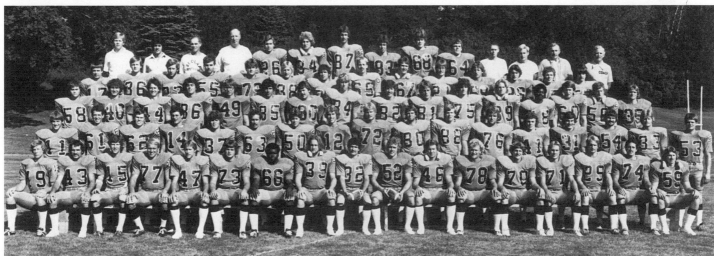

Steve Ostlie, 1978

McKinley Moore, "Big Mac," a great offensive guard, 1978

Hodge, who took it the rest of the way. Klefsaas ran for the two-point conversion to put the homefolks up 15–7.

With Ostlie handling the two-minute drill to perfection, St. Olaf moved 68 yards in 11 plays to lead 22–7 at the half. The Oles scored twice during a wind-aided third period — a 17-yard run by Schrader and 25-yard Klefsaas to Bates halfback pass. The final St. Olaf score was another by the defense. Dave Borgwardt picked off a short Auggie aerial and ran it in. Augsburg scored twice in the fourth period when the contest was out of reach.

The defense had limited Augsburg to 56 yards rushing, stole three passes, recovered two fumbles, and scored twice. The offense piled up 376 yards, including 177 on 15 pass completions.

In addition to the share of the MIAC crown, the win earned St. Olaf a berth in the NCAA Division III Midwest Regional playoff. The Oles, ranked eighth in the division, were to play the University of Minnesota-Morris on the latter's field.

After a difficult week of practice, due mainly to weather, departure day arrived and with it, six inches of snow. The Oles pushed their bus out of the parking lot and traveled west to Morris to find a snowless, but frozen, field. In an effort to make the field more playable, heated dry sand was top-dressed over the field. The warm sand brought the frost to the surface and then froze. The result was a field not greatly different from playing on asphalt. Game day brought a strong wind whipping sleety snow the length of the field.

The game could have been played on a 50-yard field as all 43 points scored came at the wind-aided end. A superior passing attack brought the Morris Cougars a 33–10 win. The Oles gained early momentum when McKay's punt rolled dead at the Cougar three. Bergeland and Nahorniak downed the runner in the end zone for a safety and a two-point lead. That was all the Ole scoring, however, until Klefsaas tallied on a 14-yard run in the final period. Meanwhile, Morris garnered three touchdowns and a field goal when they had the wind at their backs in quarters two and three. Both coaches agreed it was unfair to

ask teams to contest a playoff game in the condition of this day.

It had been a successful 9–2 season, a conference championship share, and first post-season playoff experience. Six men were selected to the All-MIAC team — Steve Lidke, tackle; McKinley Moore, guard; Nate Bergeland, defensive tackle; Steve VandenHeuvel, defensive end; John Nahorniak, linebacker, and Rick Rost, defensive back. Nahorniak was selected MVP, and Lidke and Mark Quinnell were named co-captains for 1979. Rost and Nahorniak were selected for the NAIA all-district team.

1979

Both expectations and goals were high as the Oles prepared for a conference title defense in 1979. Gone were top-notch defensemen such as Nahorniak, Downs, VandenHeuvel, and Ristau, but enough seasoned performers returned to support a feeling that the defense would again be formidable. Six defensive starters were back. Nate Bergeland, a premier defensive tackle, led the group, which also included Dave Borgwardt, Jon Anderson, Alan Hodge, Terry Westermann, and Tad Hauck.

Four of the seven offensive line positions were also expected to be manned by returning regulars, and all of the backfield slots saw returning regulars or sometime regulars. Captain Steve Lidke, one of the MIAC's outstanding linemen, returned at tackle, along with Bob Patterson and Greg Stangl. Ends Steve McKay, Todd Porter, and Brian Fenelon, center Mike Allen, and guards Jim Berdahl and Brian Johnson all returned. Captain Mark Quinnell led a backfield crew of Bob Klefsaas, Paul Estenson, Mike Schrader, and Tim Bates.

In the home and season opener, a sharp-shooting quarterback named Matt Dillon brought his Cornell Rams to Northfield on Defeat of Jesse James Days Saturday, shot the Oles out of their saddles, and rode off with a 37–25 victory. Dillon and his gang passed for 213 yards and four touchdowns. The Oles got on the board first, scoring on a 42-yard Klefsaas to McKay pass, and again on a Klefsaas keeper after a Hodge fumble recovery. The Rams

Mark Quinnell runs against Cornell, 1979

countered with a safety and then Dillon fired to Northfielder Jake Remes for a first-period score and two more in the second for 78 and 27 yards to take a 23–13 halftime lead.

St. Olaf dominated the third period with stout defensive play led by Bergeland, Anderson, and Hodge, shutting down Cornell without a first down until midway in the fourth period. Meanwhile, the Ole offense scored twice on a one-yard plunge by Kyllo and a 23-yard short side option keeper by Bates. Two interceptions by Cornell led to the decisive points. The first theft led to a short scoring pass, and the second resulted in a 37-yard return for the winning score.

Co-captain Quinnell was the Oles' leading rusher, racking up 104 yards on 20 carries. Klefsaas returned five punts for 134 yards and two kickoffs for 57. Bergeland was in on 15 tackles, including two quarterback sacks.

St. Olaf extended Macalester's losing streak to 43 games with a 21–7 win in an evening game in St. Paul. The defense again set the tempo, allowing only 58 yards rushing and no pass completions. Bob Ringham engineered a 55-yard march for the first touchdown. McKay scored the second touchdown, and Quinnell and Kyllo ran well behind an efficient offensive line. Ray Dunfee gave a

strong performance at wingback in place of the injured Bates.

At noon on the following Monday, St. Olaf was informed that ABC-TV had again requested permission to televise a game at Manitou field — the upcoming St. Olaf-Concordia game. It was a natural as St. Olaf and Concordia had been co-champions of the MIAC in '78, and both teams had been in post-season competition that year — St. Olaf in the NCAA Division III playoffs. Concordia had been the NAIA Division II national champions.

On a beautiful fall afternoon on Manitou Field, the Concordia Cobbers

triumphed 16–13 in a hard-fought contest. Concordia's traditionally strong kicking game accounted for nine points — field goals of 32, 40, and 43 yards. Jim Klug's inside running totaled 125 yards and one touchdown. He was selected offensive player of the game. Jon Anderson of St. Olaf was selected the outstanding defensive player as he spearheaded a stubborn Ole defense. Andy was assisted ably by Bergeland, who was in on 19 tackles. Klefsaas tallied St. Olaf's first touchdown on a seven-yard run set up by Marc Chiodo's interception and 45-yard return. McKay capped a 72-yard drive for the second score. All in all, a good football game well played by both teams.

Shaking off the Concordia defeat, the Oles carved out a 22–13 victory over Hamline in St. Paul with sophomores Dan Kyllo and Klefsaas leading the way. Kyllo averaged more than 5.1 yards per carry and scored the winning touchdown, while Klefsaas, piloting the team at quarterback, had 51 yards on the ground and 105 yards and a touchdown through the air. McKay had five receptions for 58 yards. Klefsaas led off the scoring with a three-yard keeper on the option. Borgwardt's fumble recovery set up a fine McKay reception and a Quinnell scoring run.

Linebackers Dan Backberg and Jeff Peterson with Coach Tim Larsen, 1979

Mark Quinnell, 1979 captain

Steve Lidke, 1979 captain

The third quarter was all St. Olaf. The offense moved the ball effectively, and the defense — led by Bergeland, Anderson, and Mike Jankowski — was devastating. Kyllo scored on a short run in the last period. Westermann handled a poor center snap, rolled out and passed to Fred Gelle for the final two points.

The "Big E," Paul Estenson, had his day as he rushed for 104 yards, added 74 more in kickoff returns and scored once, leading the Oles to a 31–20 win over St. Thomas on Parents' Day. The contest started out as though it might become a shootout as the teams traded early scores, but with the Oles up 14–7, the defense came alive and handled the Tommies the rest of the way.

Klefsaas scampered 26 yards for the first score, and Estenson tallied the second after three McKay receptions brought the ball to the three. The defensive play of the game was Brian Johnson's recovery of a wayward St. Thomas punt snap for a touchdown. When asked about his lineman's dream play come true, Johnson noted, "The play was nothing, but when I got off the ground, Bergeland almost killed me when he congratulated me."[167] Dunfee's field goal made the score 24–7 at the half. Late in the third quarter, Wally Hustad made an outstanding catch of a 12-yard Klefsaas pass to score. The Tommies scored two unanswered touchdowns to end the game.

The following Saturday, the Oles faced a huge challenge in St. Peter. The Gusties were the number-one ranked NAIA Division II team, scoring 50 points a game and totaling 556.8 yards per game, 424.2 rushing. It was an intimidating prospect, but two and a half hours of outstanding football later found the Oles with an 18–15 victory.

The triumph owed much to a dominating defense. Oles sacked Gustie quarterback Brad Baker 13 times (Anderson, four; Bergeland, four; Borgwardt, three; Jankowski, two) and held the opposing offense to 129 yards in total offense, nine first downs, and 85 yards rushing. Gustavus scored first on Jay Schoenebeck's 53-yard run off an option-pitch following a fumble. On the next possession, Baker was sacked, and he fumbled, the ball. Borgwardt recovered at the Gustie two. Kyllo scored.

Dan Backberg's fumble recovery at the Ole 22 stymied a dangerous Gustavus drive. Dunfee's field goal with 3:53 left in the first half put the Oles ahead for good.

Hodge recovered a Gustavus fumble at the 26 to start the second half. Klefsaas passed to McKay for 21 and then scored from the five on a rollout. Westermann took a play from the previous week's book, pulling down a high center snap on the conversion play and turning it into a two-point play when he threw to Estenson in the end zone to make the count 18–7. The Oles threatened again but a deflected pass was intercepted at the six, and Baker scored to make the score 18–13. A two-point conversion made it 18–15 with 4:26 left in the third period.

In the final quarter, the Gusties managed only one first down, while Baker was sacked four times for a negative 31 yards. The final Gustavus series is worth detailing. St. Olaf failed to gain on a fourth down play at the Gustavus 41 with 3:58 to play. On first down, Baker was dropped at the 35 by Jankowski. On second down, Anderson almost beat the snap to the quarterback and dropped him for another five-yard loss. Baker retreated to pass again on third down, and Anderson ran him down again for a loss of 13. Gustavus punted from the 18 and St. Olaf ran out the clock.

Bergeland's pre-game message on intensity and Robert Welch's comment, "regardless of odds," had something to do with the Oles' effort on this Saturday. Nate Bergeland was named the NAIA National Defensive Player of the Week.

Note

Prior to the next week's Homecoming game against St. John's, five men — Arnold Flaten '22, Harry Newby '34, Everett Nyman '39, John Hanson '52, and Duane Swenson '59 — were inducted into the Hall of Fame and the game-day program carried a good article by Jim Dimick featuring the "fabled backfield" of 1922–23 — Fevold, Glesne, Swanson, and Cleve.

One can wonder whether the monumental effort against Gustavus had something to do with the following week's

21–9 Homecoming loss to St. John's. In any case, it appeared at the time that the defeat ended any hope for a repeat championship. A bad start involving an offside penalty and a shanked punt gave St. John's the ball at the Ole 36, and they scored seven plays later to take a 7–0 lead. Hodge's fumble recovery stopped another St. John's drive at the 20. An 11-play march featuring the running of Kyllo, Quinnell, and Klefsaas culminated in a score to make the count 7–6.

A series of mistakes — an interception, a face mask penalty and a fumble — enabled the Johnnies to score again for a 14–6 lead with 35 seconds left in the half. A squib kick by St. John's backfired, and Klefsaas moved the Oles downfield quickly on passes to McKay and Porter. Dunfee kicked a 32-yard field goal with five seconds remaining to make it 14–9 at intermission.

A fine interception by Westermann at the goal line stopped one St. John's drive in the second half, but they came back with an eight-play, 68-yard march to score in the fourth period. Five Ole turnovers didn't help the cause in this contest.

Carleton had appropriated the Goatrophy two years prior to the annual game. It had not surfaced in the interim, but this was thought to be the year the Carls would legitimately possess the trophy. The Knights had

clinched their division championship in the Midwest Conference and were on a three-game winning streak. It didn't work out for them, however, as the Oles dominated play and carved out a 22–8 win. The Ole offense was on the field most of the afternoon and moved at will in the middle of the field, but fell short on several scoring opportunities — due partly to mistakes and partly to Carleton's goal-line defense.

An early fumble gave Carleton good field position, but a Marc Chiodo interception prevented a score. A 76-yard march by the Oles was stopped by a fumble, but a Dave Seymour interception finally set up the first Lion touchdown, Klefsaas scoring from the 21 after a short drive. Two penetrations of Carleton territory netted only a Dunfee field goal, and Carleton scored on a Ford to Davis pass to make the count 10–8 at halftime. St. Olaf dominated the third period and scored on a 14-yard Klefsaas to McKay pass.

Early in the fourth period, the Carls drove to the Ole eight only to be turned back by a strong defense, and the Lions promptly drove 92 yards in 16 plays, Kyllo scoring, to win going away. Some statistics: total plays — St. Olaf 90, Carleton 45; first downs — St. Olaf 22, Carleton 8. Carleton crossed midfield only three times.

The last home game for 21 seniors was an impressive 34–7 win over Bethel.

The lion assists an official with a call

An all-senior backfield started the game and demonstrated the value of experience. Estenson led the way with 173 yards and three touchdowns on 22 carries. He was to be named MIAC Offensive Player of the Week. Captain Quinnell took the injured Kyllo's fullback spot and demonstrated his versatility as a blocker and ball carrier. Bates was back at wing with his usual intensity, and Ringham engineered the offense with poise and intelligence.

The Royals found themselves down by 21 points with only 7:24 gone in the game. Estenson had scored three times and Dunfee had kicked three points. Klefsaas to McKay passes produced a second-quarter score and a

The 1979 team, Steve Lidke and Mark Quinnell, captains

Nate Bergeland, 1979

Cheerleaders and the crowd, 1980

28–0 halftime margin. The defense stood out, allowing Bethel to cross midfield only once and that was to the 45. Keith Tufte stole two Bethel passes, and the rest of the defensive secondary — Westermann, Hauck, and Jeff Thompson — complemented the upfront ironmen — Hodge, Anderson, Bergeland, Jankowski, and company.

Frequent substituting in the second half enabled all squad members to have quality playing time. Robert Welch finished out the Ole scoring with an option play in the fourth period. A 71-yard pass play was the Royals' only touchdown.

The victory over Bethel brought St. Olaf back into the title picture. With the right combination of wins and losses, the Oles could gain a share of the title.

On the frozen turf of Parade Stadium in Minneapolis and with updated progress of the St. Thomas rout of St. John's in the background, St. Olaf handled Augsburg 48–14 to claim a share of the MIAC crown with St. John's, St. Thomas, and Concordia. All had 6–2 records.

A late-season surging offense and the league's number one-ranked defense was too much for the Auggies, stifling them most of the afternoon. On the second play of the Lions' first possession, Klefsaas and Bates executed a perfect halfback option pass for 49 yards and the first score. Bates repeated later in the first quarter, taking a short-side option pitch from Ringham to score from the seven.

Delayed by a Westermann interception, the Auggies finally got on the board at 5:24 of the second period, only to suffer the perfect squelch when Klefsaas returned the ensuing kickoff 86 yards on a picture-perfect return pattern. Al Hodge's fumble recovery led to another quick Ole tally, and it was 27–14 at the half.

The Lions took the second-half kickoff and rode Ringham passes to Klefsaas and McKay to a score with 2:20 gone in the third period. The second score of the period came after McKay outwrestled two Auggie defenders for a lame duck pass launched by Klefsaas. Quinnell wedged it in from the one-foot line. An interception by Chiodo set up a final score by Estenson with 4:48 to play.

1979 ABC game broadcasters

The four-way tie for the championship — the first in the 59-year history of the MIAC — was a fitting climax for the squad and 21 seniors. Nate Bergeland, Steve Lidke, and Jon Anderson won all-conference recognition, and Bergeland also was named MVP. Voted co-captains for 1980 were Jon Anderson and Bob Patterson.

1979 Season Notes

Press interest in the ABC-televised St. Olaf-Concordia contest was so great and the demands of network television were such that an extra level was built onto the Manitou Field pressbox. Norm Madson's seasoned architect's eye (and knowledge) determined that there was unacceptable risk that the newly built addition could topple over backward if enough foot-stamping photographers were packed into it. What to do?

With only hours to go before the game, Madson and his carpenter crew were out behind the box propping it up from behind with 2' x 8' planks anchored in the turf and running up to the back of the new addition. It wasn't pretty, but it got the job done. Norm Madson was director of the physical plant and staff architect at St. Olaf from 1974 to 1993. He died of a heart attack at age 82 in February of 2003.

1980

Graduation had taken 21 seniors who had played a major role in back-to-back championship seasons, but a number of stellar underclassmen had also formed the core of those teams, and they were now in a position of leadership. The 1980 press book summed it up: "A small nucleus of excellent football players on offense and defense, plus a strong and experienced kicking game, will be plus factors."

Returning regulars on offense included Captain Bob Patterson, guard; Greg Stangl, tackle; Steve McKay and Brian Fenelon, ends; Bob Klefsaas, quarterback/tailback, and Dan Kyllo, fullback. Defensive regulars back were Captain Jon Anderson (the only all-conference performer), middle guard; John Ryden, tackle; Scott Maghan and Mike Jankowski, ends, and cornerbacks Mark Chiodo and Keith Tufte.

The opener was the non-conference Goat game. After six consecutive Ole wins, this was to be the "year of the Carls." Not quite. Riding the accurate arm of sophomore quarterback Bill Mickelson and a tremendous defense, the Oles buried a larger Carleton team 49–20. Mickelson completed six of 11 passes for 109 yards and two touchdowns, while the defensive unit had a banner day with three interceptions, two for touchdowns, two fumble recoveries, and a 40-yard punt return which set up another touchdown.

A confident band of Carls scored first on a 13-yard pass play, but then the Ole defensemen shut them down, allowing only one first down the remainder of the half. Meanwhile, Mickelson directed the Ole attack to two scores — the first a 46-yard pass to Klefsaas and the second a 21-yard

strike to McKay. Freshman Todd Nash converted two of his seven PATs.

After intermission, it was all St. Olaf. Dave Seymour returned an interception 48 yards for one score, while freshman Brad Wolner, replacing the injured Klefsaas, and the slashing runs of Kyllo keyed a 45-yard scoring drive. The defensive unit struck twice in the fourth period. A nifty punt return by Marc Chiodo set up a Mickelson to McKay scoring pass, and Tufte rambled 76 yards with an interception to score and put the game out of reach. Senior quarterback Bob Welch passed to Frank Kuzma for the final tally.

Defensive stalwarts Jon Anderson and Jankowski played brilliantly — a portent of things to come, while Kyllo with 78 yards and Wolner with 73 were the leading rushers.

Proving the Carleton win was no fluke, the Oles shut out St. Thomas 17–0 under the lights at O'Shaughnessy Field. The *Viking Scorebook* writer's summary: "Combining a great kicking game, a sound defense, and an opportunistic offense, the undermanned Ole gridders knocked off a favored St. Thomas 11 … in one of the major upsets in MIAC action in recent years."

The Tommies were tops in every statistical category except the kicking

game and the score. Big plays paid off for the Oles. The defensive unit, though giving ground between the 30s, was stingy in the red zone. They had three successful stands inside the 10, intercepted three passes, and recovered two fumbles to stifle a potent St. Thomas attack. It was the Lions' first shutout in two seasons.

The Ole offense got on the board early via Nash's 35-yard field goal following a fumbled punt recovery by Kyllo. An early second-quarter fumble recovery by Greg St. John at the Tommy 27 was followed quickly by Mickelson's pass to McKay in the left corner of the end zone. The Tommies mounted an 80-yard drive but were thwarted by a four-play goal line stand starting at the six. At the half, it was 10–0.

St. Thomas took the second half kickoff to the Ole 25 where the defense again held. Lightning struck as Mickelson hit McKay on a 71-yard scoring pass to close out the scoring. As the game wound down, two more goal-line stands by the Oles kept the Tommies at bay. Anderson, linebacker Jeff Peterson, tackle Scott Maghan, end Jankowski, and defensive back Chiodo (two key interceptions) were defensive standouts.

A courageous Lion eleven had a favored St. John's team on the ropes for

Oles converge on a loose football, 1980

Jon Anderson, 1980 captain

Bob Patterson, 1980 captain

three periods before two interceptions and two fumbles enabled the Johnnies to walk away with a 14–3 win. Nash's second-quarter field goal provided a 3–0 lead which held up until 5:54 of the fourth quarter. St. John's had punted out of bounds at the Ole 13. An Ole fumble gave the ball away at the Johnny 20, from where Raiala, fleet St. John's halfback, scored on a sweep. Raiala scored an insurance touchdown with two minutes left.

Kyllo pounded out 70 tough yards; Mickelson was nine of 15 passing for 97 yards. Tufte intercepted two passes and Seymour stole one. Jankowski and Anderson were leading tacklers.

The Homecoming game versus Augsburg was the occasion for honoring the 1930 football team — the undefeated MIAC champion and the second highest scoring college team in the nation. Eighteen players, two coaches (Ade Christenson and Cully Swanson), and the team trainer/manager gathered for the day. Players present for halftime introductions and a banquet later were Don Anderson, Irv Christenson, Al Droen, Clifford Gilbertson, Enoch Glesne, Johnel Golberg, Mel Hegdahl, Carl Iverson, Ken Ingvoldstad, Earl Johnson, Jerome Johnson, Hank Lecy, Lucius Lund, Harold Mickelson, Al Ness, Harmon Veldey, Cecil Tellekson, Terry Peterson, and Truman Solverude, manager.

The Ole squad's 23–7 triumph over Augsburg capped a gorgeous and festive afternoon on Manitou Field.

Steve McKay had a banner day on offense, hauling in six Mickelson passes for 106 yards and two touchdowns. On defense, Jankowski had 11 solo tackles and four assists as he harassed the Augsburg quarterback all afternoon.

Augsburg scored early in the first quarter, but the Oles tied it and went ahead on a pair of Mickelson to McKay scoring passes. A 42-yard field goal by Ray Dunfee made it 17–7 at halftime. The second half was a defensive standoff except for two more Dunfee three-pointers from 32 and 40 yards out. A tenacious pass rush by the front four produced five sacks. Dave Seymour's defensive secondary play — one interception, six solo tackles, five assists — was a strong point.

After considerable searching, a mid-season break in the schedule was filled with a home and home series with Michigan Tech University located at Houghton in Michigan's upper peninsula. A long, but scenic Friday bus trip with a workout at Mountain Iron High School brought the Oles to Houghton not sure what to expect from the Division II school.

Game day brought 37-degree temps and a homecoming crowd lubricated to fend off the chill. Initially, it looked like a long day for the Lions. The Tech Huskies moved 70 yards with the opening kickoff to go up 7–0. Klefsaas returned the ensuing kickoff to midfield. On the first play from scrimmage, the line opened a running lane, and Bob scooted the other 50 yards to score. The first of many yellow flags nullified the play, and the Oles settled for a 30-yard Dunfee field goal.

On the next Ole possession, Mickelson moved his team 93 yards in seven plays. The big gainer was a 68-yard halfback pass, Klefsaas to McKay, Steve taking the ball away from a defender at the 40. A strong pass rush forced a Tech fumble, recovered by Maghan, and the Oles scored in three plays, Klefsaas taking it in to make the score 16–7. Tech retaliated with a 15-play, 80-yard drive, featuring their option attack, and scored with 3:37 remaining to intermission. The Oles quieted the prematurely celebrating Tech fans with a beautiful six-play, 66-yard march to score with 55 seconds on the clock. It had been a 20-point second quarter.

Kyllo scored the only touchdown of the second half, finessing an all-out blitz with a 53-yard draw play to make the final 30–20. It was a great team effort with some real individual standouts: Kyllo 141 yards on 14 carries, Klefsaas 130 on 26 trips, McKay four receptions for 108 yards and a touchdown. Linebacker Jeff Peterson had 13 tackles, followed closely by Jankowski, Anderson, and St. John with 11 apiece.

A big, powerful Hamline squad dominated play in defeating the Oles 25–7 in a Parents' Day contest on Manitou Field. St. Olaf struck first on the Lions' third possession, going 83 yards in 13 plays, Klefsaas taking it in from the two. From that point on, however, it was all Hamline.

Utilizing outstanding offensive line play to advantage, the Pipers scored 18 points in the second quarter, the inside running game being their best weapon. With both squads stymied on the ground in the second half, the Pipers took advantage of a wind advantage and went to the air to score the game's final points.

A greater loss than being on the short end of the score in the Hamline game was the season-ending knee injury suffered by Steve McKay when he was tackled on a fake punt play. His pass receiving and punting had been major factors in the Ole game, and his loss was a significant blow. At the time of his injury, Steve held St. Olaf records for most passes caught in a season (36 in 1979), most yards receiving in a season (620 in '79), most receptions in a career (67) and most yards receiving in a career (1,610).

At Gustavus the following week, the Oles dominated the line of scrimmage completely for the first 27 minutes, but seven turnovers (four interceptions, three fumbles) nullified the strong play and the result was a 27–3 defeat. With three and a half minutes to play in the first half, Gustavus held the ball for 14 plays and gained only three yards. Klefsaas and Kyllo pounded out consistent yardage primarily behind the Oles' strong side of Patterson, Stangl, and Fenelon. The Oles reached four-down territory five times but could manage only a 22-yard field goal by Nash.

The Gusties scored three times in the second half via Ole fumbles at the 20 and the eight and an interception at the 47.

The defensive linemen, led by Anderson and sophomore tackle John Ryden, played at their season best. Freshman defensive end Al Lottmann sustained a leg fracture, making a thin squad thinner.

On a cold, bleak afternoon, the Oles closed out their home schedule by edging a good Bethel squad 10–9. St. Olaf had a considerable statistical edge, but five turnovers stopped potential drives and forced the defense to play in their own territory much of the afternoon. A staunch Ole forward wall, led by Jankowski, limited Bethel's running game to 29 yards, but a good short passing game accounted for 166 yards and most of their first downs.

Bethel opened the scoring with a 39-yard field goal, while three successive turnovers by the Lions stymied their offense before Marc Chiodo returned an interception to the Royal 30. Quarterback Bob Welch hit Frank Kuzma for a 29-yard gain, and Klefsaas dived in from the one. Nash's PAT made it 7–3.

With Mickelson at the controls, the Oles moved to the Bethel 16 but had to settle for a Dunfee field goal to extend the lead to 10–3. The Royals came roaring back and connected on a 40-yard scoring strike to close the margin to a single point. Bethel elected to go for two and the victory, but a strong Ole rush hurried quarterback Anderson's pass in what proved to be the play of the game.

Klefsaas ran for 127 yards, his second 100-yards-plus performance of the season, but injuries continued to take a toll as Fenelon, Dan Dimick, and Hustad turned up doubtful for the coming Concordia encounter.

The turnover nemesis continued to plague the Oles as they challenged league-leading Concordia in Moorhead. Four fumbles, one coming inside the Concordia 10 when the score was 6–0, was an example. Fortunately, the defensive unit again played strongly.

Reception by Ray Dunfee, Jon Saunders looks on, 1980

Bob Klefsaas, 1981 captain

Led by Anderson and Jankowski, they held the vaunted Cobber attack at bay for most of the game. Linebacker Dan Backberg was all over the field.

Cobber kicker Holter accounted for nine points on three field goals, while Concordia's sole six-pointer came at the beginning of the second half. The Lions' only counter came late in the game on a Dave Caldwell to Ray Dunfee pass with 3:56 remaining. It was a strongly contested game against the league's eventual champion.

The season's final game was against Macalester in St. Paul. An inspired Mac defense stymied the injury-plagued Lions for the first half, but after intermission, senior quarterback Bob Welch directed three scoring drives to squelch any hopes the Scots had, and the Oles rolled to a 21–0 shutout victory. Welch's touchdown targets were Fenelon, Kuzma, and Schrader, and Klefsaas racked up his third 100-yard game with 109 yards on 24 carries.

The Ole defensive unit completely dominated the Mac offense, allowing only 52 yards for the game. The Scots were able to cross midfield only once and that came on a fumbled punt reception. Jankowski, Anderson, Ryden, Maghan, and St. John led the front wall charge.

Eleven dedicated seniors prepared and played valiantly in a season in which injuries were key. Jankowski and Captain Jon Anderson had stellar seasons. Cornerback Marc Chiodo and linebacker Dean Monke also played vital roles. Brian Fenelon and Captain Bob Patterson had been three-year stalwarts. Wally Hustad and Dan Dimick will be missed in the offensive line. Steve McKay and backup Fred Gelle, along with senior backs Mike Schrader and Bob Welch, made important contributions to a 6–4 season and a 4–4 league mark, good for fifth place.

Middle guard Anderson, defensive end Jankowski, wide receiver McKay, and tailback Klefsaas were named to the MIAC all-conference team. Honorable mention selections were tight end Fenelon, guard Patterson, fullback Kyllo, tackle Stangl, and defensive back Tufte. Anderson also was recognized nationally with his selection to the Kodak All-America College Division II team — a highly select honor.

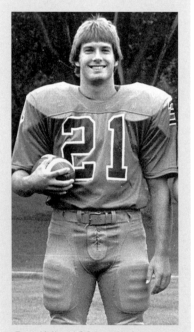

Dan Kyllo, 1981 captain

Anderson also was elected most valuable by his teammates, while Bob Klefsaas, Dan Kyllo, and Keith Tufte were named tri-captains for the 1981 season.

1980 Season Note

Professor Harlan Foss, longtime faculty member in the department of religion, who also served as dean of the college and acting president, was inaugurated as the seventh president of St. Olaf College during the fall 1980 season. Dr. Foss, who died in 1995, was a strong supporter of Ole athletics and followed the teams avidly.

1981

A squad of 70, including 29 letter winners, reported Aug. 24 to begin preparation for an 11-game schedule beginning with Carleton and including non-conference foes Luther and Michigan Tech. The squad had a good nucleus of experienced players — particularly in the offensive and defensive backfields — but a lack of interior linemen would prove a handicap as injuries took their toll during the campaign.

Outstanding returnees included captains Bob Klefsaas, Dan Kyllo, and Keith Tufte; offensive backs Ray Dunfee and Bill Mickelson, defensive backs Denny Fiedler and David Seymour, linebackers Jeff Petersen and Danny Backberg, center Tim Logemann, tackle Charles Viren, end Frank Kuzma, and defensive linemen John Ryden and Greg St. John.

With Klefsaas' run/pass option skills and leadership ability, it was decided to play him at quarterback and place promising sophomore Brad Wolner at tailback. Jon Nydahl was the strong side tackle with George Wood and Chuck Feske at offensive guards. The defense had Tufte and Bill Hybben at the corners, Fiedler at free safety, and Seymour at strong safety. Petersen and Backberg were the linebackers, and Ryden, Crawford, Lottmann, St. John, and Zima made up the front five.

Carleton stunned St. Olaf 20–12 in the opener at Laird Stadium. The Carls' passing attack and the Oles' lack of an effective running game spelled defeat on this day. The teams felt each other out in a scoreless first period until St. John blocked a Knight punt on the last play of the quarter. The block gave the Oles good field position and set up Todd Nash's 35-yard field goal. The Carls used an intercepted pass to advantage and moved for a score in the second period before Nash tallied a second three-pointer to make it 7–6 at halftime.

The Knights drove 80 yards with the second-half kickoff and extended their lead to 10–6 on a 22-yard field goal. Later in the third period, the Oles put together their best drive of the day, going 62 yards in 11 plays with Wolner scoring from the two. That made it 12–10 and marked the end of Ole scoring for the day.

Carleton dominated play in the fourth period with a 27–7 play advantage. A field goal and a touchdown on a questionable pass completion with 23 seconds remaining made the final 20–12 and the all-time series count St. Olaf 30 wins, Carleton 29, with one tie. Petersen went down with a knee injury.

On a typically hot and muggy early fall day in Decorah, the Oles upset a more physical Luther squad 14–2. Besieged with injuries, St. Olaf capitalized on three big plays offensively and battled tenaciously on defense to record their first win of the season. The first half was a scoreless standoff, both defenses dominating.

The Lions stopped the Norse on the first series of the second half, forcing a punt and taking over at their own 17. On the first play, Kyllo broke over the middle on a well-executed trap play and went 83 yards to score. Nash's kick made it 7–0. On the ensuing Luther possession, Backberg's jarring tackle forced a fumble recovered by Dan Otterson. Mickelson promptly found Kuzma open on a 49-yard pass play. Three plays later, Ray Dunfee threw a wingback reverse pass to Kuzma for the touchdown. Nash tacked on the PAT and it was 14–0.

Forced to a catchup passing offense in the fourth period, Luther fell victim to interceptions by Tufte and Dana Jensen. Three quarterback sacks

Karl Nienhuis scrambles against Concordia, 1981

by Lottmann also helped. Luther's two points came on a safety after a fumbled punt late in the game. Kyllo led the rushing attack with 102 yards, while Kuzma gathered in four passes for 90 yards and a touchdown. Freshman linebacker Todd Vitols was the tackling leader, followed by Ryden, Crawford, Jensen, and John Pellicci.

St. Thomas rolled into Manitou Field on a beautiful fall afternoon and wrested a 16–9 victory from the scrappy Oles in a well-played game. On their second possession, the Tommies marched 75 yards on five snaps to take a quick 7–0 lead. An unsuccessful field goal try and a goal-line interception blunted the Oles' two scoring chances. On an ensuing Ole series, a pass blocked at the line of scrimmage fell into a defender's hands, and the Tommies converted that break into a nine-play drive ending with a five-yard scoring pass.

The Oles' only touchdown came in the third period. Dunfee scored on a sweep after an alert Fiedler recovered a fumble at the St. Thomas 21. Nash's conversion made it 13–7. A magnificent goal-line stand gave the Oles the ball at the two when the Tommy running back fumbled after being hit hard by Crawford. Kuzma punted out of the

hole, but a too-many-men-on-the-field penalty on the kick allowed the Tommies within field goal range and they converted a 33-yarder to put the game away.

Ryden played another strong game — eight tackles, six assists. Sophomore Chris Sackrison had six and two, and Vitols had 11 good hits. The Fiedler-Seymour secondary combination had 21 tackles/assists. St. John, Lottmann, and Wolner were added to the injury list.

With a strong running attack, a powerful St. John's squad overpowered the injury-ridden Oles and won 23–0. A valiant Ole defense, playing much of the time in their own territory kept the opening quarter scoreless, but the Johnnies broke it in the second period and scored all their points.

Playing inspired football in the second half, the Ole defense held the Johnnies scoreless. St. John's threatened only once, and that drive was halted when freshman Mike Rinke intercepted at the goal line and returned it to the 30. Nydahl played admirably. Sanders had four receptions for 40 yards. Vitols, Fiedler, Ryden, Seymour, and Nelson led a valiant defensive group.

A meager crowd braved a wet, windy day at Parade Stadium to attend Augsburg Homecoming. The Auggies

Keith Tufte, 1981 captain

Dennis Fiedler, 1981

delighted the home folks by starting with a bang, returning the opening kickoff 88 yards for a touchdown in the first 15 seconds. Things went from bad to worse from the Ole point of view when the ensuing kickoff bounced off an Ole up man, and Augsburg recovered at midfield. A few plays later, an Auggie running back bolted 30 yards to score, making the count 14–0 Augsburg with 13:34 remaining in the first period. The Ole offense had yet to touch the ball. But it wasn't over.

Klefsaas was blindsided attempting to pass. The ball squirted out of his hands and an Augsburg linebacker caught it in the air and went 54 yards for the third touchdown. Augsburg had run fewer than 10 plays and led 21–0. With Klefsaas, Kyllo, and Wolner running the ball, the Oles finally scored, and Kyllo's two-point conversion run made it 24–8 at halftime.

A steady rain continued through a scoreless third period. Freshman twins Tyrome and Jerome Robertson combined to spark a final Ole drive. The final: Augsburg 38, St. Olaf 16. Bill Nelson and Todd Vitols played well for the Oles, and Dunfee was added to the injured list.

The following week, St. Olaf put together two goal-line stands and a sustained touchdown march after the second-half kickoff and went on to defeat Michigan Tech 14–0 for the second victory in the home-and-home series. Klefsaas passed five yards to Kuzma on the end of a 74-yard march, and Tyrome Robertson scored on a slant behind excellent blocking. Nash converted after both scores.

The offensive line had its best day of the season, enabling Wolner to rush for 113 yards and Klefsaas to gain 98 all-purpose yards on 17 rushes and seven passes. Defensively, tackles Ryden and Crawford were solid as was the secondary of Seymour, Tufte, Fiedler, and Jensen.

It was particularly gratifying to the coach to have a squad that was 0–3 in conference play defeat a Division II school for the second successive year. A discrete but important highlight.

Hamline's Norton Field was a quagmire from hard rains as the crippled Oles — with five defensive starters watching from the sidelines — put forth a valiant effort to prevail in the mud, 10–7. The Oles marched 70 yards with the opening kickoff, Wolner scoring, to take a 7–0 lead. They got the ball back toward the end of the first quarter and got close enough for Nash to kick a three-pointer to close out Lion scoring. A Fiedler interception thwarted Hamline's only first-half drive.

The Pipers' ball control offense gave them the upper hand in the second half, but they could score only once. An alert Ole secondary came up with three crucial interceptions — one each by Hybben, Jensen, and Tufte, Keith's coming on a last-second "do or die" situation.

Seymour had 15 tackles to lead the defense, with Ryden and Backberg chipping in 10 apiece. Klefsaas ran the option well, and Kyllo bulled for 117 yards on 18 carries. Wolner had 96 in 20 carries. One muddy, exhausted lineman said after the game, "This is a priceless feeling. I wouldn't sell this feeling for a million dollars."[168]

With Manitou Field resembling the Arctic tundra due to morning snow flurries, a powerful Gustavus squad used size and quickness to dominate St. Olaf and post a 23–0 shutout win. The Gusties went 55 yards for the first score and recovered a fumbled punt to capitalize again to make it 15–0 in the first period.

The Oles regrouped and played inspired ball the second half, the defense allowing only one first down in the third period and four for the half. An interception led to the final Gustie score.

The injury-riddled defense was led by Seymour, Vitols, Pellici, and Nelson, all with eight stops. Bill Nelson and Jensen each had an interception. Wolner worked hard for 88 yards.

Hall of Fame Induction — Home-coming lightened the Gustavus loss some-what as six men were inducted into the Hall of Fame and introduced at halftime. They were Carl Iverson '31, Fred Putzier '23, Dennis Runck '59, George Thronson '58, David Wee '61, and Lloyd Ellingson '32.

St. Olaf put together its best offensive performance of the season only to bog down on two fourth-period drives and wind up losing to Bethel 23–21. The Oles rolled up

449 yards in offense as the offensive line, led by Jon Nydahl, created good lanes for running backs Klefsaas, Kyllo, and Tyrome Robertson, who ran for 80, 79, and 78 yards, respectively. Mickelson had a good day, completing 12 of 23 passes. Klefsaas, in a receiving role, caught five of them for 96 yards and one touchdown.

The Oles led 13–10 going into the third quarter, but broken coverage on a Bethel pass play allowed one touchdown, and a quick, 60-yard thrust up the middle produced another and, as it turned out, put the game out of reach. Kyllo scored late on a three-yard run. The Oles had great play from the offensive line, and Mickelson had his best day as an Ole.

In the season's penultimate game, Concordia running back Reid Christopherson turned in a sparkling 249-yard performance, and the Cobbers rumbled to a 42–13 victory. The Ole game was not without its high points, however. Chief among them was an exceptionally gritty performance by Klefsaas, who replaced the injured Mickelson at quarterback. Bob completed 12 of 26 passes for 131 yards and one touchdown and ran 15 times for 46 yards, including an 18-yard scoring scamper. The senior may have had better days statistically, but never a better effort in spite of the odds. The crippled Ole offensive line was missing four regulars before the day was over.

Brothers Randy and Jeff Peterson, 1981

Christopherson ran for four touchdowns (62, 76, 55, and nine yards), accounting for more than half of the Cobbers' 419 yards rushing.

In the season finale, St. Olaf turned a 38-yard touchdown pass and two late interceptions into a 23–20 triumph over Macalester. Mac jumped ahead 7–0 on a 95-yard early drive, but Todd Nash answered with a field goal to make it 7–3 at the half. The teams exchanged third-quarter touchdowns (Kyllo for the Oles, Dennis Czech for Mac). But then the Oles, with Klefsaas at the helm, struck for the winning points on a 71-yard, seven-play drive culminating in Klefsaas' 38-yard pass to Kuzma. Interceptions by Seymour and Hybben preserved the win — an especially meaningful one as 11 key men were not in uniform.

The seniors — Klefsaas, Kyllo, Tufte, Logemann, Backberg, Wood, Viren, Crawford, Olson, and St. John — were challenged greatly by adversity in their last season but could take satisfaction in a 26–16 four-year record. Bob Klefsaas was named first-team all-conference and MVP. Dan Kyllo, Dave Seymour, and John Ryden were all-conference honorable mention. Seymour and Ryden were elected co-captains for 1982.

1982

Captains John Ryden and Dave Seymour led a contingent of 26 lettermen among the 72 candidates who reported for the 1982 season. Also among the returnees were several statistical leaders from 1981 — Bill Mickelson, passing leader; Frank Kuzma

The 1981 team, Bob Klefsaas, Dan Kyllo, and Keith Tufte, captains

139

John Ryden, 1982 captain

Dave Seymour, 1982 captain

and Jon Sanders, one-two in receiving; Brad Wolner, leading rusher; Paul Koehn, kick returner, and Ryden and Seymour, leading tacklers. The squad faced a challenging 10-game schedule of eight conference contests bracketed by non-conference foes Carleton and Luther.

On a hot, humid Saturday on Manitou Field, a tough, consistent defense led by Ryden and Seymour and aided by two key Carleton miscues enabled the Oles to post a 9–0 shutout and avenge the previous year's defeat.

The defense kept the Carls at least 30 yards away from paydirt all afternoon. Kuzma's punting also was a plus factor. He kicked 10 times for a 35.3 average, one boot going for 49 yards. Two errant center snaps led to all the Ole points. One sailed through the end zone for a safety. The other, in the fourth period, gave the Oles possession at the Knights' 27. From there, Mickelson hit Saunders for 19 and Tyrome Robertson scored three plays later. Seymour had a banner day with 10 tackles, a pass interception, and two pass breakups. St. Olaf led the Goat series 31–29–1.

It was a case of too little, too late as the Oles were upset by Macalester 20–12. Dennis Czech, a pint-sized Mac running back, was the kingpin in the Mac offense. He gained 158 yards, including a 63-yard scoring scamper early in the contest. The Scots capitalized on two Ole fumbles to score twice more to make the count 20–0 at the half.

The Oles roared back in the second half to score twice — Ray Dunfee from the six and a Dunfee to Saunders 76-yard scoring pass. In addition to the loss on the scoreboard, St. Olaf also lost Paul Koehn, who suffered a knee injury on the opening kickoff, and Mickelson on the second offensive series.

The following week in Moorhead, the Oles persevered through a long afternoon at Concordia's Jake Christiansen Stadium. The Cobbers, the previous year's NAIA national champions, ground out a 39–11 victory. The hosts struck first after recovering a fumble on the kickoff. The Oles forced two fumbles but could manage only a Dunfee field goal in the first half. After intermission, St. Olaf thwarted the strong

Cobber attack fairly well, and Seymour returned an interception for the only Ole touchdown. Brian Jacobs, in his first start at quarterback, passed to Kuzma for the two-point conversion. Defensively, Lotmann, Ryden, and Vitols led the charge. Randy Petersen and Jacobs were cited for their play also.

On a Parents' Day Saturday better suited to an amphibious landing than football, the Ole defense grounded Bethel's air attack and scored three touchdowns to lead the Oles to a 21–8 victory. The Lions intercepted five passes, recovered two fumbles and blocked two punts.

Seymour and linebacker Bill Nelson each scored via interceptions, and in the third quarter, John Pellici blocked a punt, which was then recovered in the end zone by Vitols for the third touchdown. A strong pass rush by Craig Dennis, Scotty Maghan, and ends Chris Sackrison and Kurt Hjerpe and the blitzing of linebackers Jeff Petersen, Bill Nelson, and Vitols were outstanding features. Unfortunately, it was to be the last victory in a disappointing season as the Oles closed out the campaign with consecutive losses to Hamline, St. Thomas, St. John's, Gustavus, Augsburg, and Luther.

For the second consecutive Saturday, weather was a factor. Slippery conditions and a strong wind blowing across Hamline's Norton Field in St. Paul figured prominently in Hamline's 21–3 victory. The Pipers scored early when a St. Olaf punt into the wind gave the Pipers the ball at the Ole 36. The Oles countered with a drive to the Hamline 22 before giving up the ball. Two plays later, Dennis Fiedler intercepted to set up a 32-yard Dunfee field goal — and the Oles' only points. From there, it was a defensive struggle, with the Oles unable to contain the 13 for 18 passing of Piper quarterback Kyle Aug.

St. Thomas, also with an outstanding passing game, was the Homecoming opposition. With 13:49 remaining, the game was still in doubt. Al Lottman covered a Tommy fumble, leading to a touchdown by Wolner to make the score 24–14 St. Thomas. The visitors tacked on 10 more points to post a 38–14 win. The Oles played with a high degree of intensity but could not

Coach Hauck consults with Dave Seymour, 1982

match the St. Thomas aerial game. Quarterback John Meutzel threw high and far to a trio of talented receivers — Hygins, Gustafson, and Graham. Maghan, Ryden, and Lottmann were cited for outstanding defensive play.

St. John's exploded for 17 points in the second quarter to lead 24–0 at halftime and coast to a 38–8 victory. The Ole defense played the Johnnies' ground game well but couldn't handle the aerial attack and gave up almost 300 yards passing. A bright spot was the defensive play of Craig Dennis and Captain Ryden. Mickelson returned to action having been out since the second game of the season.

In a good, hard-fought football game, Gustavus continued the long pass nemesis to break out of a 10–10 half-time tie and post a 21–10 win. Two pass plays and a pair of field goals accounted for the first-half scoring. Mickelson threw to Kuzma for 55 and a touchdown, while the Gusties countered with a 48-yarder. Dunfee kicked a 45-yard three-pointer with 31 seconds left in the half. Gustavus controlled the second half and scored on a 33-yard pass and a fourth-quarter field goal.

The frustration of a losing season continued with a 24–7 loss to Augsburg at Parade Stadium. Leading 17–6 with 12:46 to play, the Oles appeared to have the contest under control. Mike

Rinke had just returned his second interception 35 yards to score. But then the Auggies mounted a serious comeback. They put together a 79-yard drive in 10 plays to make the count 17–14, then tied the score with a 20-yard field goal with 2:56 remaining.

The Auggies' Jesse Quam recovered an errant Ole pitch, and Winter passed to Myers to put the ball at the St. Olaf three. Two plays later Nelson scored to pull out the victory.

Freshman Clay Anderson kicked two PATs and a 33-yard field goal, filling in for the injured Dunfee. Wolner, Vitols, Maghan, and Lottmann also were cited for their play.

In the season finale, it was just too much Larry Davis. Luther's 230-pound running back carried 35 times for 238 yards and two touchdowns as the Norse edged St. Olaf 21–14 on snow-covered Manitou Field. The contest was even except for two long runs by Davis, one for 70 yards and a touchdown on the fourth play of the game. Luther added a second score on a spectacular one-handed catch for 20 yards in the second period.

The Oles engineered a beautiful "hurry up" offensive drive culminating with Mickelson scrambling 20 yards

Chris Sackrison and Scott Maghan stop a St. Thomas runner, 1982

Bill Nelson, 1983

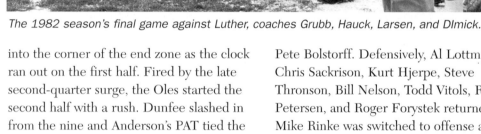

The 1982 season's final game against Luther, coaches Grubb, Hauck, Larsen, and Dlmick.

Bob Klefsaas '82, one of St. Olaf's finest backfield performers, returned as an assistant coach in 1983. In his playing days, Klefsaas operated at both tailback and quarterback, leading his teams in total offense for four seasons. He was a two-time All-MIAC selection.

into the corner of the end zone as the clock ran out on the first half. Fired by the late second-quarter surge, the Oles started the second half with a rush. Dunfee slashed in from the nine and Anderson's PAT tied the score at 14. The remainder of the game was a standoff until Davis slipped outside and went 53 yards for the winning points.

Sixteen seniors closed out their Ole careers. Frank Kuzma had his best day as an Ole, catching seven passes for 137 yards and punting well. Mickelson was 14 of 34 for 185 yards. Nelson and the Peterson brothers, Jeff and Randy, stood out on defense. Co-captain John Ryden was named first-team All-MIAC, with Dave Seymour, Kuzma, and Scott Maghan garnering honorable mention. Seymour was named most valuable for his outstanding play and leadership. Brad Wolner and Jon Nydahl were elected co-captains for 1983.

1983

Carleton, a charter member of the MIAC, rejoined the conference after an extended period in the Midwest Conference and celebrated 100 years of football.

At St. Olaf, 67 men, half of them letter winners, reported for practice on Aug. 22. Among the returning offensive regulars were co-captains Jon Nydahl and Brad Wolner, Olson, Kurt Johnson, Brian Jacobs, and

Pete Bolstorff. Defensively, Al Lottmann, Chris Sackrison, Kurt Hjerpe, Steve Thronson, Bill Nelson, Todd Vitols, Randy Petersen, and Roger Forystek returned. Mike Rinke was switched to offense as a split end. Freshman Greg Van Gilder broke into the starting lineup early.

A young Ole team traveled to Decorah and battled a talented Luther eleven on even terms for three quarters before succumbing 25–0 in the opener. The game was closer than the score suggests. A first-period safety put Luther up 2–0, and that remained the difference until 4:33 of the third period. A wind advantage and a superior kicking game enabled Luther to have consistently good field position. The Norse scored three touchdowns late in the game. Linebacker Nelson, a native of Decorah, played valiantly in his homecoming, as did Vitols, Hjerpe, Petersen, and nose guard Tim Osmondson.

The conference opener was played on a windy Saturday at Macalester in St. Paul.

Using the wind to advantage, the Oles scored on three of their first four possessions and went on to down Mac 19–0. Wolner broke the scoring ice with a 48-yard jaunt, closely followed by a 26-yard field goal by freshman Steve Wee, playing in his first football game. Bill Thomas' punt block set up Wee's kick. Two plays later, Forystek intercepted a Mac aerial and returned it to the hosts' 20. Bolstorff scored on a seven-yard keeper. It was 17 points in the first quarter. The final two points came when a high snap sailed over the Mac punter's head and out of the end zone for a safety.

A stingy Ole defense, led by Osmondson, kept Macalester at bay. Coaches of both teams noted that, "Osmondson was the best player on the field today."

The Ole defense acquitted itself well for the second week, but the offense was deficient in the scoring department, as the Lions lost to Concordia 14–9. St. Olaf scored first on a 43-yard punt return by Mark York. The Cobbers struck for touchdowns in the second and third periods before Wee's 42-yard field goal brought the score to the final count. The Oles moved the ball into Concordia territory three times in the final period but couldn't put points on the board.

Osmondson, Hjerpe, and Lottmann, along with linebackers Mike Zobel and Vitols, played well defensively. A bright spot on offense was the play of freshman quarterback Karl Nienhuis, who played three quarters.

The Bethel Royals scored 15 points in the fourth quarter to come from behind and edge St. Olaf 18–17 at Bethel. Three errors in the kicking game — a bad center snap on a PAT, a blocked punt, and a fumbled punt — spelled disaster for the Oles. A third-quarter highlight was Wee's 52-yard field goal, probably the longest in St. Olaf football history. (One account has Harry Fevold, in 1921, dropkicking a three-pointer from the 45, but in those days the goal posts were on the goal line, so Wee's 52-yarder, with the posts 10 yards deep, would have been longer.

The following Saturday, an out-manned St. Olaf 11 played favored Hamline even into the fourth period, when the Pipers put together a 17-play, 80-yard drive to post a 19–9 win. The Oles had scored first, taking the opening kickoff 79 yards with Brian

Jacobs going the last five. Hamline countered with two field goals and a touchdown to take a 13–6 halftime lead. Wee's 36-yard field goal brought the Oles within four at 13–9, but the Pipers then came through with the game-clinching six-pointer.

An undefeated St. Thomas squad scored two touchdowns in the first four minutes and then held off a scrappy St. Olaf 11 for the rest of the game to hand the visiting Oles a 14-0 defeat. A 68-yard interception return accounted for the first Tommy score, and the second came two plays after the Oles came up short on a fourth and a foot situation. On two occasions, St. Olaf missed field goal attempts, and a good looking halfback pass was inches from a touchdown as halftime approached.

Neither team penetrated the other's 25 the rest of the game.

The coach commented, "The most encouraging part of the game was that after a horrendous start, we could have folded our tents and come home, but we didn't. Our squad stayed in there and played good football, both offensively and defensively." Wolner had 100 yards rushing on a slippery field.

It began to have all the earmarks of a hardluck season, as St. Olaf outgained St. John's 377 to 371 and collected 22 first downs to the Johnnies' 12, but the score read St. John's 17, St. Olaf 12.

Both teams moved the ball well in the first half. The Oles took a 9–3 lead on Nienhuis' four-yard run. The St. John's passing attack turned out to be their salvation. The game's crucial

Captain Brad Wolner, runner, 1983

143

*Pete Bolstorff,
1983 quarterback*

*Brian Jacobs,
1983 quarterback*

moment came late in the third period with the score 17 to 12. The Oles marched and came up with a first down at the Johnny three. Four attempts to score were turned away by a gallant St. John's goal-line stand.

Tailback Jacobs fought for 60 tough yards; Nienhuis was seven for nine through the air before being injured late in the first half. Cornerback Brad Lemke was superb with a share in 13 tackles. Linebackers Zobel and Vitols were close behind.

St. Olaf started with a rush versus Gustavus, converting a fumbled opening kickoff into a touchdown and taking a 14–3 lead into the lockeroom at halftime. But the second half belonged to the Gusties as they came from behind to carve out a 17–14 win. Bill Thomas recovered the fumbled kickoff at the 19-yard-line, and five plays later, Jacobs tallied from the five. Two possessions later, Gustavus connected on a 23-yard field goal for their only points of the first half. Wolner rambled 69 yards — a beautiful run, his longest of the season — to score at 7:46 of the second quarter. With the Gustavus defense pinching in, quarterback Pete Bolstorff audibled and hit Wolner with a quick pitch to the outside.

After intermission, Gustavus blocked a punt and drove in from the six to close to within four, 14–10. They scored again on a 38-yard drive. It was an evenly fought contest decided by a blocked punt. Lemke, Nelson, and Peterson led the defense in tackles.

With six seniors playing their last game on Manitou Field, the Oles bolted to a quick lead and played relentlessly the rest of the way to down Augsburg 38–15. St. Olaf scored on its first three possessions. The first was on a Bolstorff pass to Kevin Hjerpe at 11:24; the second a run by Jacobs after a 67-yard, 13-play march; the third, again by Jacobs, on a sparkling 69-yard scamper at 2:32. Augsburg had added a second-period touchdown and a third-quarter field goal, but it was not enough to overcome that early Ole onslaught.

Bolstorff executed the option to perfection; Jacobs had 193 yards on 32 carries; Wolner added 114 in 25 carries. It was satisfying to have the running game get untracked. Al Lottmann went down with a

knee injury. Linebacker Zobel and freshman tackle Greg Van Guilder led the charge defensively, and Clay Anderson was four for four on PATs and also notched a 34-yard field goal.

The season finale — the Goat battle — had added significance this year because Carleton had rejoined the MIAC and it was a conference matchup. Behind a forward wall that controlled the line of scrimmage, Ole running backs Wolner and Jacobs picked up where they had left off the week before, continuing an outstanding running attack that keyed a 24–13 victory. Although a week's worth of snow had been brushed from the Laird Stadium field, the turf was slippery. The cold and snow was no deterrent to the determined Oles, however.

Two fumbles foiled sustained drives in the first quarter before Steve Wee's 34-yard field goal drew first blood. Carleton retaliated to go ahead 7–3. St. Olaf responded with a picturesque "two minutes to score" drive of 99 yards, culminating in Bolstorff's 26-yard scoring strike to Mike Rinke at 1:04. It gave the Oles a halftime lead and was the turning point in the contest.

Bolstorff and company took the second-half kickoff and marched 80 yards in nine plays, Jacobs scoring. A Bill Nelson interception gave St. Olaf good field position for a fourth-period touchdown. Carleton scored with three seconds on the clock. The Goat series now stood at 32–29–1, favoring St. Olaf.

Brad Wolner, the leading rusher in the MIAC with 900 yards, was named to the all-conference first team and was designated the St. Olaf MVP. Five Oles — Mike Zobel, Kurt Hjerpe, Jon Nydahl, Tim Osmondson, and Roger Forystek — were designated all-conference honorable mention. Tri-captains for 1984 were Brian Jacobs, Kurt Hjerpe, and Todd Vitols.

This group of Ole gridders did not have the greatest success in terms of scores, but they exemplified the qualities to be strived for in athletics. In describing them, it is well to include President Theodore Roosevelt's well-known comment on the character and value of athletic competition:

"It is not the critic who counts, not the man who points out how the strong man stumbled or where the doer of deeds could have done them better. The credit belongs to the man who is actually in the arena; whose face is marred by dust and sweat and blood, who strives valiantly; who errs and comes up short again and again; who knows the great devotions and spends himself in a worthy cause; who at the best knows the triumphs of high achievement; and who, at the worst, if he fails, at least fails while daring greatly, so that his place shall never be with those cold and timid souls who know neither victory nor defeat."

Quotable Quote

Randy Peterson, St. Olaf free safety: "Playing football at St. Olaf has been the most rewarding experience in my three years here. The other aspects of my college life have been great, but the things that make up St. Olaf football — the respected coaches, camaraderie with my teammates, the discipline of practice, and the opportunity to compete each Saturday — have made my years at St. Olaf unforgettable. I believe that I have been blessed by the Lord in being able to attend St. Olaf and receive a quality education, as well as being a member of the football family."

1984

Dr. Melvin George was named the eighth president of St. Olaf College in the summer of 1984. Dr. George had been vice president for academic affairs at the University of Nebraska and the University of Missouri and, just prior to his appointment at St. Olaf, had been acting president at Missouri.

Thirty-two lettermen and a host of talented first-year men greeted the coaching staff to prepare for a 10-game schedule in 1984. Tri-captains Brian Jacobs, Kurt Hjerpe, and Todd Vitols led a club with more experience than had been the case the previous two seasons; 13 seniors and 22 juniors had played extensively. All but two defensive

Brothers Kurt and Kevin Hjerpe, 1984

starters returned, and the offensive line included five returnees.

Joe Klinkhammer was added to the coaching staff, replacing Jim Dimick, who was on sabbatical. Joe, a Northfielder, was an all-conference defensive tackle at St. Thomas in 1982 and tried out with the Dallas Cowboys. It was good to have Joe on our side of the ball; he gave us fits when he played for the Tommies.

The season got off on the right foot. After falling behind Luther 10–0 at halftime, the Oles outscored the Norse 24–3 after intermission to record a 24–13 victory. A third-quarter one-yard touchdown run by Jacobs and a

beautiful 76-yard touchdown-scoring punt return by Mike Rinke put the Oles ahead to stay in the third period. Steve Wee's 41-yard field goal and a 34-yard Jacobs to Rinke halfback pass, following a Zobel interception, padded the margin.

Hjerpe, Van Guilder, and Osmondson led the defense, while Bolstorff, Jacobs, and Kurt Johnson were cited on offense. It was a good birthday celebration for Rinke, as he caught three passes for 69 yards to go with his scoring punt return.

The exhilaration of the come-from-behind win over Luther lasted a week — until bad breaks and big plays by the opposition (Macalester) spoiled the Oles' bid for victory in the conference opener. Putting together three long runs of their own and taking advantage of five Ole turnovers — three fumbles, two interceptions — the Scots fashioned a 23–14 win.

St. Olaf took an early lead on a Jacobs to Rinke halfback pass set up by Mark York's fumble recovery. Down 14–7 in the third quarter, St. Olaf marched 70 yards to tie the score only to have Mac retaliate with a 70-yard burst up the middle on the first scrimmage play after the kickoff to sew up the win.

The Ole offense accounted for 413 total yards with 260 coming through

1984 players. First row: Berletic, Jacobs, Bolstorff, Anderson, Hammond. Second row: Vick, Albrecht, Hjerpe, Nienhuis, Tobiason, Rogotzke.

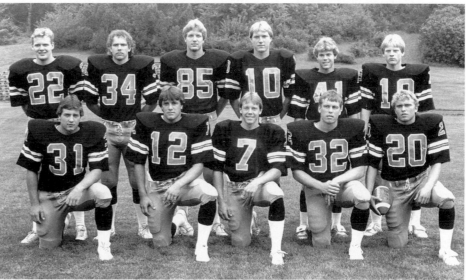

Joe Klinkhammer, assistant coach, 1984

Tim Osmondson, outstanding middle guard, 1984

the air. Bolstorff was 18 for 27 for 230 yards. Rinke had seven catches for 105. Olson and Kevin Hjerpe each caught four for 62 and 63 yards, respectively.

In a well-played, action-filled game in which the lead changed hands four times in the second half, St. Olaf lost its second consecutive conference game, this one to Gustavus 30–25. The Gusties opened with 10 unanswered points, but the Oles countered with 13 in the second quarter. The first score was a perfectly executed hook and ladder pass, Nienhuis to Rinke to Jacobs.

Early in the fourth period, Lemke recovered a Gustavus fumble, and on the first play from scrimmage, Nienhuis threw to Rinke for 34 yards and a touchdown and a 25–24 St. Olaf lead with 9:59 remaining. From that point, the Gusties marched 76 yards on 15 plays to sew up the victory. A last-ditch Ole scoring effort was killed by an interception. Coach's comment: "A good college football game with a good effort by the Oles."

Bethel came out throwing in the next game and took an early 7–0 lead. From that point on, however, it was all St. Olaf, as the Oles thrashed the Royals 33–7 for their first-of-the-season conference win. St. Olaf accumulated 341 total yards, scoring 19 points in the second quarter and 14 in the fourth.

Two big plays in the second quarter helped to jump-start the offense. The first was a 45-yard Nienhuis to Jacobs pass and the second a 35-yard halfback pass, Jacobs to Rinke. Brian Jacobs had a banner day; he rushed 26 times for 108 yards, caught four passes for 97, threw a 35-yard touchdown pass, and scored twice. His performance earned him MIAC offensive player of the week honors.

Defensively, the Oles limited Bethel to 71 yards behind great play by Hjerpe, Thronson, Osmondson, and others. Lemke, Thomas, and Mike Jacobs each had an intercepton to shut down a relentless Bethel passing attack.

A 28-point outburst in the last six minutes of the first half brought the season's second straight conference victory and the first win over St. John's since 1978 — a 31–0 shutout.

The 28-point explosion necessitates almost a play-by-play account: A 48-yard Nienhuis to Rinke pass set up the first Ole counter. On fourth and goal from the three, a fake field-goal pass from holder Brian Jacobs to Kevin Hjerpe scored. On the second play after the ensuing kickoff, the Johnny quarterback fumbled and the Oles recovered at the Johnny 29. Nienhuis threw to Rinke for the second touchdown with 5:13 left in the half — 14–0. Two series later, the Olaf defense forced the Johnnies to punt. Another Nienhuis to Rinke aerial clicked from 14 yards out to make the count 21–0 with 46 seconds left in the half. St. John's tried to come back with a deep pass on first down, but strong safety Roger Forystek picked it off and returned 32 yards to the Johnny 25. With five seconds left, Nienhuis connected on his third touchdown pass, this one to Kevin Hjerpe from the 13.

The Oles took the second-half kickoff and drove 80 yards before settling for a 29-yard Steve Wee field goal.

Despite the second-quarter pyrotechnics, which doubtless took a lot out of the Johnnies, it was the Olaf defense that rose to the occasion through the day, shutting out a typically strong Johnny offense, forcing three turnovers, and allowing only 130 total yards.

Coach's comment: "The first half was as good a half of football as we have played in a number of years. There wasn't any great strategy involved. We just had everyone executing and capitalized on our opportunities." Rinke was selected MIAC player of the week.

St. Olaf played a very strong St. Thomas squad tough for three quarters before giving up three fourth-quarter touchdowns to lose 35–15 at O'Shaughnessy Stadium in St. Paul. Down 7–0 in the first period, the Oles cut the margin to 7–3 on a 39-yard Steve Wee field goal, but a blocked punt allowed the Tommies their second first-quarter score. The Oles retaliated in the second quarter on an 84-yard touchdown pass, Bolstorff to Kevin Hjerpe, to make it 14–9 at the half.

After a scoreless third period, St. Thomas scored three times in the fourth.

Coach Porter with 1984 captains
Brian Jacobs (12), Todd Vitols (38),
and Kurt Hjerpe (90).

Mistakes in the kicking game and the failure to establish a consistent offense spelled downfall.

"Homecoming victory over Carleton brings 300th win" was the *Messenger* headline Oct. 26, 1984, as the Oles downed the Knights 24–19. It was the 300th football victory in St. Olaf history, going back to the first official team in 1919. A St. Olaf News Service release dated Oct. 22, 1984, highlighted this win and listed the won-loss records of the six head coaches since the start — Endre Anderson, Ade Christenson, Mark Almli, Helge Pukema, Tom Porter, and Dave Hauck.

St. Olaf drew first blood against the Knights with two first-quarter touchdowns. Linebacker Dave Olson intercepted an errant Carleton pass, and six plays later, Jacobs tallied from the three. Karl Nienhuis threw 40 yards to Todd Prieve and then scored himself from the five on a nicely executed option. Carleton retaliated to make the score 14–7 at the half.

In the third period, Paul Koehn's interception led to an Ole eight-play, 70-yard drive, Nienhuis throwing to Rinke for the score. Wee added the final

three points on a 29-yard field goal. Defensively, Ole linebackers Konat, Zobel, and Olson were standouts, while Koehn, Thomas, and Forystek registered interceptions. Rinke had another fine day offensively, catching five passes for 104 yards and a touchdown. Tailback Jacobs and fullback Berletic rushed for 102 and 49 yards, respectively.

Newspaper accounts of the contest were interesting. One noted that "personal foul penalties helped the Knights in their last two scoring drives, turning the game into a cliffhanger."[169] Another refers to "questionable calls" by the officials that "killed Carleton's chances in the second quarter."[170]

The annual "Lefse Bowl" between St. Olaf and Concordia was played on a rain-soaked Manitou Field and ended in a disappointing 10–10 tie. Two missed field goals on St. Olaf's first two possessions and another in the third quarter came back to haunt the Oles. Concordia scored with 2:12 to play in the first half, but St. Olaf stormed back with a perfectly handled two-minute drill to tie the score with 10 seconds left.

The teams traded field goals in the second half, the Oles' Steve Wee kicking a 37-yarder. St. Olaf had one last chance to break the deadlock, but it was killed by an interception.

Coach's comment: "Our defense played a great football game, but

offensively we could not sustain a drive except for our 11-play, hurry-up series just before halftime."

St. Olaf helped to dedicate Augsburg's new Anderson-Nelson gridiron and apparently found the artificial turf much to their liking. The Ole defense, in particular, came to play, recording six quarterback sacks, two interceptions, and three fumble recoveries and accounting for at least nine first-quarter points in leading their team to a 26–0 shutout victory.

Augsburg's fumble at the 15 on the opening kickoff set up Jacobs' score from the two. Forystek then intercepted and returned the ball 22 yards for a second score. Nose guard Osmondson continued the impressive defensive play with a quarterback sack in the end zone for a safety. In the second quarter, the Ole offense put togther a 57-yard drive capped by a 30-yard halfback pass, Jacobs to Rinke, for a 23–0 lead. Wee's 42-yard field goal in the fourth period rounded out the scoring.

The Ole defense allowed only 120 total yards. Van Guilder, Osmondson, and Konat had outstanding games.

In the '84 season finale, St. Olaf entertained MIAC champion Hamline and managed to put the only blemish on the Pipers' fine season. Hamline had won the MIAC crown, defeating St. Thomas the week before. They were 9–0 and ranked fifth nationally

The Goatrophy

Bruce Gutzmann,
1985 captain

Jon Nycklemoe,
1985 captain

and had a good chance for an NCAA Division III playoff spot.

On a snow-covered Manitou Field, the Oles stopped the Pipers' winning streak with a gritty game ending in a 7–7 tie. Hamline took the opening kickoff and drove 72 yards to score, riding the throwing arm of quarterback Kyle Aug. The rest of the half belonged to St. Olaf, however, as the defense tightened, allowing Hamline to cross midfield only one more time. The Oles repeatedly had good field position but were kept out of the end zone by two interceptions.

St. Olaf tied the score in the third period on a two-yard run by Nienhuis and Norman's PAT. Hamline made a serious bid in the last quarter, but Mark York's sack of Aug on a fourth and four situation stopped it. Both teams missed field-goal attempts in the fourth period and turnovers thwarted other efforts to score. Field conditions affected play but probably were not instrumental in the outcome.

First-team all-MIAC honors went to Kurt Hjerpe, defensive end; Brian Jacobs, tailback; and Mike Rinke, flanker. Honorable mention winners were Roger Forystek, defensive back; Kurt Johnson, center; Brad Lemke, cornerback; Tim Osmondson, nose guard, and Mike Zobel, linebacker. Jacobs and Rinke shared MVP distinction. Bruce Gutzmann and Jon Nycklemoe were elected captains for 1985.

1985

In a preview of the 1985 season in the *Viking Scorebook*, Sports Information Director Bob Klefsaas characterized the returning squad as one with "good attitude." As it turned out, they would need all the good attitude they could muster. Coming off a 5–3–2 season in which the squad had lost only one game of the last seven, expectations were high for the group, which included 15 seniors, many of them multi-year regulars. But from the start, the deck appeared stacked against them.

Victimized by turnovers (four lost) and other mistakes — a roughing the kicker penalty and safety from intentional grounding — the Oles fell behind Luther 22–0 in the opener. Rallying gamely in

the second half, the Oles finally hit paydirt in the third period on a one-yard run by Leif Syverson after an interception by Bill Thomas had given them a short field. Syverson then orchestrated an 87-yard drive and threw five yards to Scott Anderson for the second touchdown. With the defense holding, Syverson completed five of nine passes and scored on a sneak. The tying two-point conversion appeared good, but the Oles were whistled for motion.

Although short on the scoreboard, the Lions roared on the statistical charts — 317 yards of offense and 20 first downs to 176 and five for the Norse. But, as someone famously said, stats don't win games, points do.

Against the Macalester Scots the next week, the Lions scored first in the first and second halves, but in between, the Scots scored three times to hand the Oles their second setback by 20–10. In the first half, the Oles got fine punting from Greg Van Guilder and a 20-yard field goal from Steve Wee. In the second half, Roger Forystek returned a punt to the Mac seven-yard line, and a fourth down Syverson to Don Larson pass scored from the four. But Mac countered with two second-half touchdowns.

Zobel, Konat, and Osmondson led a strong defensive unit, and Tom Vick caught five passes for 36 yards.

The run of bad luck continued as the Oles let a 14–3 lead slip away as Gustavus triumphed 24–21 in St. Peter. Two second-quarter turnovers — a mid-air fumble recovery returned for a touchdown and a fumble recovery at the 29 — let the Gusties back in it. The Oles regained the lead in the second half. A 40-yard run by Mike Berletic set up a one-yard scoring sneak by Syverson. Norman's PAT put the Oles up 21–17. A completed pass on fourth down enabled Gustavus to protect the 24–21 margin.

The play of Berletic was one of the few bright spots as St. Olaf dropped its fourth game of the season 13–9 to the Bethel Royals. The Ole scoring consisted of three Steve Wee field goals of 43, 26, and 40 yards, the first two set up by interceptions by Mark York and Bill Thomas. Bethel came back to go ahead 7–6 before Steve hit his third three-pointer from 40 yards out with 17 seconds left in the half. Bethel's winning touchdown came on a 47-yard punt return in the third quarter.

Berletic caught two passes for 38 yards and rushed 30 times for 123 yards in the losing cause. The defense also played well, giving up only six first downs and 18 yards rushing and contributing four sacks and three interceptions.

Down in conference play 0–3 (0–4 overall) and going against league-leading St. John's, at 3–0, was a daunting prospect, but over the years Oles have shown remarkable ability to rise to daunting challenges, and so it was to be this time. Riding the strong right leg of Steve Wee and taking advantage of a brisk wind, the Lion gridders took out their frustrations on the undefeated Johnnies and spoiled their Homecoming with a stunning 15–10 upset at Collegeville.

Wee was a perfect five for five with kicks of 49, 50, 47, 54, and 32 yards. With the 54-yard kick, Wee surpassed his own all-time record of 52 yards, set against Bethel two years earlier. St. John's scored via a field goal

on their first possession, but then the courageous Ole defense shut down the vaunted Johnny attack, holding them scoreless until 3:15 of the final period. By then, the Lions were up 15–3.

Osmondson, Van Guilder, and Anderson led a determined pass rush resulting in four deflected passes and four interceptions. Paul Koehn had three picks and Tom Konat, the fourth. The defense allowed only 90 yards rushing, while on the Ole side, Berletic powered his way for 76 tough yards. Syverson completed six passes for 63 yards, and Dave Schooler made two spectacular catches to put the Oles within field goal range. All in all, it was a superb, hard-earned and much-needed victory.

The stage was set for St. Thomas the following week: a great win over St. John's, Homecoming, a good week of practice, and a great day to play. But the Tommies failed to cooperate. They reeled off 34 points in the first quarter and seven more in the second en route to a resounding 41–0 trouncing

of the Lions. The Tommies made a shambles of the Ole passing attack while showing a superb aerial game of their own, amassing over 300 yards passing. It was not a case of poor defensive play, but rather outstanding personnel and performance by the St. Thomas offense.

Bragging rights for Northfield and the Goat were prizes as the Oles traveled across the Cannon River to challenge the Carleton Knights at Laird Stadium. For the first time since 1981 and for only the third time in 21 years, the Knights came out on top decisively, 35–7. Carleton scored on a 10-play, 70-yard drive and another covering 75 yards in two plays to take a 14–7 halftime lead. St. Olaf's lone tally of the half, and the game, was a one-yard run by Forystek, capping an 11-play, 94-yard march.

Carleton put the game away early in the third period, scoring two touchdowns in five minutes.

To an objective observer, the Oles might have resembled a one-man band — named Roger Forystek. Forystek

Kurt Hjerpe harasses the passer, 1985

Roger Forystek, 1985

Steve Wee, place kicker extraordinaire, 1986

played all the way on defense and had one interception. He also played most of the game on offense and racked up 73 yards on 18 carries and, as noted, scored the lone Ole touchdown. Not content with that performance, Roger returned three punts for 51 yards. Despite the loss, the Oles still led the Goat series 33–30–1.

The following week, with the squad desperately needing a win, history repeated itself. The Lions virtually replayed their St. John's victory, holding a powerful Concordia club to 113 yards rushing and allowing only five pass completions, while picking off four Cobber aerials in posting a 12–2 victory in the annual Lefse Bowl. Thomas had two interceptions and Konat and Lemke, one apiece. The entire defensive unit was cited, but for the second consecutive week, Forystek, playing both ways, was the "best player on the field." Roger had nine unassisted tackles, rushed 32 times for 88 yards, caught one pass for 20, and returned five punts for 59 yards.

Wee's 40-yard field goal constituted the only points of the first half, and he connected again at the beginning of the second half, this one for 45 yards. In the first half, Wee's boot was set up by a beautiful 34-yard play-action pass, Syverson to Larson. It was only the second victory of the season but again against a league-leading club.

St. Olaf marched to its second win in a row — the first of the season at home — downing Augsburg 28–16. The Oles jumped out to an early lead, scoring two touchdowns in the first quarter and then adding a touchdown in each of the final two periods. Meanwhile, the Auggies reacted to the Lions' double-barreled first-period assault with 10 points in the second quarter. And they managed a fourth-quarter touchdown after the game appeared safely in the Ole bag.

Forystek on an 18-yard run and Berletic on a one-yard plunge scored the final two touchdowns. Defensive standouts for the Oles were Bill Thomas, with two interceptions to break Steve Ashley's long-standing single-season record, and Adam Elliott and Thomas Konat against the Auggie running attack.

A 9 a.m. game at the Metrodome versus Hamline was the season finale — and it

gave a bright feel to the season. Two electrifying kickoff returns by freshman Mike Eaton enabled the Oles to get out in front early and stay there. The game was a seesaw, "feel 'em out" battle in the first period. Hamline scored first at 12:04 of the second period. Eaton returned the ensuing kickoff to the Piper 24, and three plays later Syverson sneaked in from the four. Norman added the PAT. On the next series, Hamline recovered an Ole fumble at the 31 and cashed in with a field goal to make the count 10–7. But then Eaton worked his magic again, returning the kickoff 92 yards to score behind a great blocking pattern.

The Oles scored what proved to be the game winner with 6:59 left in the third period. Forystek bucked in from the two after a 72-yard, 13-play march. Syverson played his best game of the season, and Konat, York, and Scott Elrod shone on defense.

The season had stretches of 0–4 and 1–6 which pushed both coaches and players into periods of self-examination. There were ample opportunities to point fingers, but the squad showed a great deal of character. Klefsaas's preseason assessment of good attitude was ultimately borne out in the 3–0 season-closing run which took some of the sting out of the disappointing first half of the season.

Forystek and Wee were named first team all-conference with Berletic, Osmondson, and Konat on the second unit. Forystek was voted MVP. Captains-elect for 1986 were Greg Van Guilder and Mark Melin.

1986

The '86 season was one of ups and downs. It was the third game before the Oles scored a touchdown. A four-game losing string in midseason tested the squad's integrity. Closing out the season with a pair of wins evened the record and brought the third consecutive victory over St. John's.

The "blond haired and blue-eyed gridders" of St. Olaf and Luther waged a defensive "Battle of Norway" to initiate the season. Neither team could penetrate the other's defense for a touchdown, so it was up to the redoubtable Steve Wee to hit two field goals (24 and 23 yards) and enable

St. Olaf to rack up an opening-day win. St. Olaf led in offensive statistics, but it was the two defenses that dominated. Captains Melin and Van Guilder led the Ole defenders, while Berletic led all rushers with 100 yards. Dave Schooler had three key receptions, including a 30-yarder in the second quarter.

The second game of the season turned out to be an aerial circus, as St. Thomas passed for four-second quarter touchdowns on their way to a 41–0 rout of the Oles at O'Shaughnessy Stadium. Wee's fourth-quarter field goal attempt was the only St. Olaf scoring opportunity. "We caught a strong team on a hot day" was the coach's comment.

The squad shook off the Tommy defeat as the offense came alive and the defense made several big plays and the Oles edged Hamline 16–13.

Nose guard Adam Elliott's block of a Piper field goal attempt led to St. Olaf's first score — a 42-yard field goal by Wee — as the first quarter closed. After an exchange of turnovers in the second quarter, Chris Reinertson went to the air for his first MIAC touchdown pass — a 49-yard bomb to Schooler — to cap an eight-play drive. The Pipers retaliated but Elliott blocked the PAT to preserve a 9–6 Ole lead. Hamline took it back early in the third period to go up 13–9.

St. Olaf lost no time getting back in it as Reinertson led the Oles on their most impressive drive of the young season. He connected on five pass plays as the drive went for 81 yards in 15 plays, Berletic scoring. Norman's PAT closed out the game's scoring. John Borstad's interception stopped a late Piper rally. Bruce Hammond rushed for 110 yards in 25 carries, while Schooler had five receptions. Elliott was "the best player on the field."

After a lethargic first half, the Oles surprised the Bethel Royals with four second-half touchdowns, propelling themselves to a 38–19 win at Bramer Field. St. Olaf anticipated the Royals' strong aerial attack, which produced the game's first score and responded with an eight-play, 69-yard march, Berletic going the last four to score. Another Royal score with the PAT blocked by Elliott made it 19–10 at halftime.

The third-quarter splurge began as Matt McDonald led the Oles on a nine-play, 91-yard drive to score. On the following kickoff, a host of Oles nailed the Bethel return man causing a fumble. Mike Jacobs picked off the fumble in the air and scampered 15 yards to score. That bit of heroics, the two quick scores, rescued the Oles from being down 19–10 and put them ahead to stay at 24–19. The Royals had yet to run a play from scrimmage in the third period.

From that point on, the Ole defense kicked in and grounded the Royal aerial game. The fourth quarter also belonged to the Lions. McDonald connected with Berletic on a 30-yard touchdown pass and Hammond added the clincher on a 29-yard run. It was Bruce's second 100 yards-plus rushing game of the season.

Winless Gustavus surprised the Oles with a no-huddle offense and jumped to a quick 14–0 first-quarter lead. From that point, the two teams essentially played on even terms, but the Gusties managed to preserve their two-touchdown margin and carved out a 28–15 victory. A blocked punt by Gustavus and a bad long snap leading to a safety provided defensive scores for each team. A 19-yard halfback pass, Hammond to Don Larson, narrowed the gap in the third quarter, but the Gusties picked off two Ole passes in the fourth period to stymie comeback attempts.

The usual pomp and circumstance of the annual Goat game was washed away by a cold rain that soaked the Laird Stadium turf. The entire game was played on the south half of the field with the wind aiding whichever team had the advantage. The wind and rain, which worsened as the game progressed, made running difficult, passing near impossible, and fumbles frequent. St. Olaf had four.

The Knights scored first and missed the conversion. The six-point lead held, aided by a three-play goal line stand which ended with an Ole

The 1985 team, Bruce Gutzmann and Jon Nycklemoe, captains

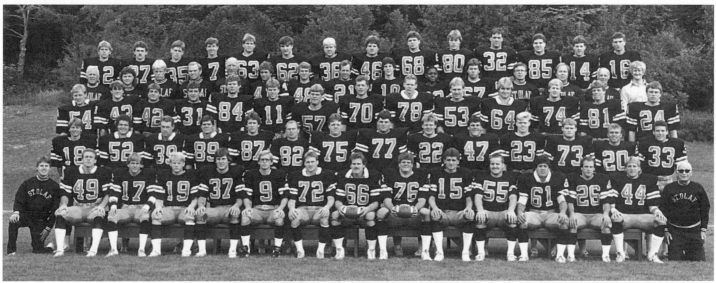

Greg Van Guilder,
1986 captain

Mark Melin, 1986 captain

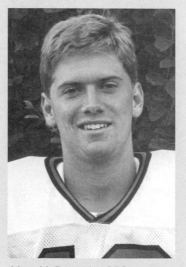

Matt McDonald, 1986

fumble at the two. A 45-yard Steve Wee field goal in the third period brought the final score to 6–3. Both squads' defensive units were spoilers for the day.

The following week, visiting Concordia ran off 32 unanswered points to dampen the enthusiasm of St. Olaf's Homecoming crowd. Two fourth-quarter Ole touchdowns were too little too late as the Cobbers routed the Oles 39–14. The Lions weren't able to respond effectively to the Concordia onslaught until the fourth period when freshman running back Kipp Heyer provided the Oles with their best play of the day — an 82-yard halfback pass to Steve Mathre for a touchdown. Speedster Steve scored again on a 52-yard pass from Brandt Colville. Hal Norman converted after both touchdowns. The potent Cobber offense racked up 612 yards — 304 rushing, 308 passing.

An interesting aspect of the game was the numerous Ole-Cobber relationships. Two former Concordia quarterbacks, Rod Grubb and Ron Rasmus, were St. Olaf assistant coaches. Ole quarterback Matt McDonald is a grandson of Jake Christiansen, Concordia coaching legend and former Ole gridder.

This was one of those seasons in which things get worse before they get better. Turnovers — four fumbles and two interceptions — led to a fourth straight defeat, a 25–35 loss to Macalester. Fumbling twice on their first three plays, the Oles literally handed the Scots the victory. After allowing Mac an early lead, the Oles charged back and scored on a 57-yard bomb, Reinertson to Schooler, with Norman kicking the point. A successful fourth and one play by the Scots kept a 72-yard drive alive and put them up 14–7. St. Olaf countered with an eight-play, 63-yard march capped by a Reinertson to Mathre 14-yard scoring pass.

The Lions played with greater intensity the second half. A 42-yard field goal by Wee and a one-yard blast and a two-point conversion pass, Reinertson to Anderson, brought St. Olaf to within three points but it wasn't enough.

Fortune finally turned the following week. Two first-quarter touchdowns were enough as the defense consistently closed the door on Augsburg in a 17–10 Ole win on Manitou Field. On the first possession,

the Reinertson to Anderson combination was good for 15 and a touchdown on the end of an 11-play, 60-yard march. The second possession resulted in an almost identical drive with Berletic scoring on a short run. With Norman kicking both points, the score was 14–0. An Augsburg fumble set up a 19-yard Wee field goal to close out Ole scoring

The strong Ole defense kept Augsburg at bay until midway in the third quarter when a field goal and a 94-yard scoring march produced 10 points. A fourth-down sack by Eric Peyton and Joe Snodgrass with 0:41 remaining killed a final Auggie drive.

On a snowy, blustery day in Collegeville, St. Olaf made history with a 16–14 conquest of St. John's. It was the third consecutive Ole victory over the Johnnies and was history making in the sense that no other MIAC team had made it 3–0 over the powerful Johnnies in the previous quarter century.

Adam Elliott led the defensive charge for the Oles. With the game scoreless late in the first quarter, Elliott blocked a field goal attempt setting the stage for a 14-play drive culminating in a two-yard scoring run by Berletic. The Johnnies answered the challenge on the ensuing kickoff with a 12-play drive to tie the count. The squads exchanged touchdowns in the third period. Reinertson passed to Heyer for the Ole score, Norman converting. A superb 25-yard reception by Schooler on a third-and-long situation kept the drive alive.

After several exchanges, Van Guilder nailed a 46-yard punt that stopped dead on the St. John's one-yard line. A high center snap resulted in a safety giving the Oles the victory. A last-minute St. John's field goal attempt was wide right.

Outstanding on Ole defense were Elliott, Van Guilder, Melin, Dale Evenson, and Mike Jacobs. Offensively, the entire line played outstanding football with 148 yards rushing highlighted by Heyer's 66. It was a strong finish to an up and down season.

John Borstad and Adam Elliott were named first-team all-conference with Berletic on the second 11. Schooler, Cory Watson, Van Guilder, Melin, and Brian Putz garnered honorable mention. Elliott was named most valuable and co-captain, with Eric Peyton, for the 1987 season.

Mark Fredrickson received recognition with his selection to the MIAC all-conference academic team.

Ole Footballers Make History; Return to "Old Country"

Athletic history was made when a portion of the 1986 St. Olaf football squad (28 players) made a goodwill excursion to Norway in May and June of 1987. The trip marked the first visit to Norway by an American football team.

After a stop and workout in Bergen, it was fitting that the first official visit was to the city of Voss. Voss was the birthplace of Knute Rockne, the legendary Notre Dame coach, and the Oles' stop there was on the 100th anniversary of Rockne's birth. The Oles conducted a clinic for a near-capacity crowd at the beautiful Voss stadium. Members of the Rockne family were in attendance. An autograph session followed and was repeated on the train trip from Bergen to Oslo the next day.

In Oslo, the squad met and had home-stay experience with members of the Westside Vikings, opponents in the two-game series played. The home-stay provided personalized views of Norwegian life and culture. The Westside Vikings and members of their families provided a bus sightseeing tour of Oslo, which was followed by an exceptional smorgasbord banquet and dance. An ex-Ole footballer living in Oslo, Mark Wangsness, met the train at the station and assisted with the clinics and games.

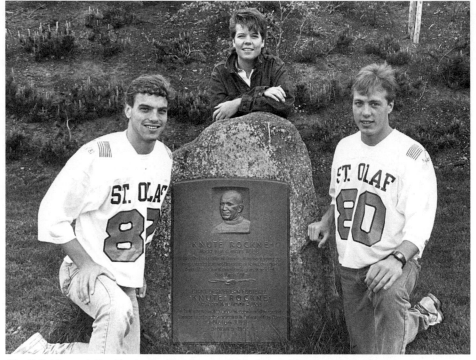

Northfielders at the Knute Rockne memorial in Voss, Norway, Mark Thornton, Laura Porter, and Steve Mathre, 1987.

Game Highlights

The first points scored by the Oles came courtesy of the defense when defensive back Erik Mikkelson '89, stormed through to tackle the punter in the end zone for a safety.

Quarterback Chris Reinertson '89, had a great passing effort, tossing two touchdown passes and running for another score in the opening game and adding three scoring passes in game two.

Brad Wolner '84, joined the team in Oslo to help fill a shortage in running backs. He showed he hadn't lost the scoring touch when he ran for four touchdowns in the second game.

Defensively, the Oles had strong efforts from Greg Van Guilder '87, Dale Evenson '87, Mikkelson and Leif Espeland '88, and Adam Elliott '88.[171]

The games versus the Westside Vikings were not competitive, St. Olaf winning 65–0 and 66–0. The Norwegians did not have ball-handling skills — passing and catching. If you put a round ball on the ground, it was a different story.

The Norwegian excursion ended with an overnight fjord steamer trip to Copenhagen, Denmark, for a few days of sightseeing before heading home.

The team that traveled to Norway, May 1987.

Adam Elliott,
MVP 1986 and 1987

Kurt Johnson, 1987

1987

With 33 lettermen and a good number of experienced underclassmen returning, the coaching staff felt there was a good prospect of filling in for departed seniors. The defense would again be strong with co-captains Elliott and Peyton back. Warden, Espeland, and Shaffer would furnish size. The offense had experienced quarterbacks in Reinertson and McDonald and hard-blocking Mike Berletic. Seniors Scott Anderson and Don Larson, along with underclassmen Steve Mathre and Brent Kvittem, made a good receiving corps. Brian Putz, Bart Halling, Eric Engwall, Stu Cox, and John Carlson were proven offensive linemen.

The season opened with the Oles on the wrong end of two shutouts. Luther prevailed 10–0 as the Oles fell victim to a rash of turnovers. Luther scored early in the second quarter. Finding little success on the ground, the Lions went to the air and were intercepted twice before halftime. The third quarter was troublesome for both teams, filled with fumbles, interceptions, and penalties. Warneke and Tostrud had interceptions for the Oles, but they couldn't capitalize. A fourth-quarter field goal by Luther sealed the victory for them. Shaffer's punting was a bright spot for St. Olaf.

Manitou Field was the site of a grueling defensive battle with St. Thomas. A 41-yard touchdown strike on their second possession was enough for the Tommies as they slogged to a 17–0 win.

Relentless defenses by both teams resulted in four turnovers and several squandered scoring opportunities. The Oles failed to capitalize on a blocked punt by Elliott and an interception by Kent Meyer. The latter led to the Oles' best drive of the day, but it fizzled at the Tommies' five with a misguided pitch. Yet another scoring chance was stopped by an interception in the end zone. St. Olaf had the better effort on defense, but the Tommies' offense and kicking game were superior. Chris Reinertson and Mike Warden incurred injuries.

The Oles finally got on the scoreboard in the season's third game against Hamline, but it was in a losing cause. In the fourth period, McDonald threw a 48-yard scoring strike to Larson. The rest of the game belonged to the Pipers, however, as they scored three times in each half to pack away a 37–6 win.

Victory came in the fourth game of the season. St. Olaf built a 21–7 first-half lead and relied on its defense in the second half to score a 21–13 homefield triumph over the Bethel Royals. Ten-yard runs by McDonald and Peloquin provided the Oles with a 14–0 cushion before the Royals got back into it with a 44-yard fake punt pass play.

The Oles put the game away with a 97-yard march, aided by a 26-yard pass to Larson. Peloquin scored from the two on fourth down to make the count 21–7 before the Royals scored an inconsequential touchdown. Earlier, a Mike Warden fumble recovery at the six-yard line stopped a Royal threat. An Ole defense that allowed only 17 yards rushing helped mightily.

Dave Moen was three for three in PATs. McDonald was added to the injury list with a broken arm.

The Oles started well the next week against Gustavus, building a 10–0 lead and taking it into the fourth period, but it wasn't quite enough. Tony Grundhauser recovered two Gustavus fumbles and each led to an Ole score. The first set up a Dave Moen field goal and the second led to a 31-yard Novak to Mathre touchdown pass. Three Gustavus scores in the second half brought the Gusties the come-from-behind win.

In the annual Goat battle the following week, the Oles were unable to corral Knight quarterback Tim Nielson and the Carleton running game in general. Dave Tobiassen scored first for St. Olaf on a seven-yard run. The 6–0 lead didn't last long, however, as the Knights promptly marched the ball to score and take a 7–6 lead.

In the second quarter, Nielson carried on five out of six plays and scored on a 25-yard run. St. Olaf's attempt to counter was subverted when Novak's pass was picked off in the end zone, and Carleton stretched the lead to 21–6 with a three-yard run.

The Oles narrowed the gap in the second half with a 14-play drive, including two passes to Larson, culminating in a Novak to Kvittem scoring pass. Two fumble

154

recoveries by Elliott kept Ole hopes alive, the second leading to a Novak to Larson touchdown pass. But Nielson and the Knights were not to be denied. They scored a touchdown and a field goal in the fourth period to ice the victory, 31–18.

For the third consecutive game, a strong fourth period spelled defeat for the Oles. With the score tied at 10 going into the final period, the Concordia Cobbers got a good break and rode its momentum for three fourth-quarter scores and a 31–10 win.

A Novak to Larson scoring pass, a two-point conversion pass to Kvittem and a blocked punt leading to a safety had given the Oles the 10–10 tie. On the first possession of the fourth quarter, an apparent completion at the Cobber 17 on a pass to Mathre was ruled a fumble. Concordia promptly reeled off 82 yards for the go-ahead touchdown. That momentum propelled them to two more quick touchdowns to wrap up

the victory. Shaffer's punting kept the Cobbers in check for much of the game.

Before a large Homecoming crowd, St. Olaf scored in the final minute to take a 28–21 thriller from Macalester. The Scots posted two quick scores early courtesy of a pass interception and an interference call. But then the Lions roared back from that 14-point deficit. With Berletic and Pelloquin carrying much of the load, St. Olaf launched a 69-yard drive, Pelly completing it with a 36-yard touchdown run. In the third quarter, Jon Tostrud intercepted at the Scots' five. On the subsequent Ole drive, Peloquin broke loose for a 44-yard scamper and then scored from the two. Moen's converion made it 14–14.

The teams traded touchdowns, Berletic scoring for the Oles on a pass from Novak. With minutes remaining in the contest, the Lions drove with Novak throwing to Larson and Berletic for 14 each and Kvittem

for 19. Berletic ran it in from the two for the winning points with 38 seconds remaining.

Having found the winning combination after several games' drought, the Lions exploited it the following week as they laid a 28–0 shutout on Augsburg in Minneapolis.

The Oles blocked two punts and turned both into scores to take a 14–0 first-quarter lead. Brian Danielson got the first block; Kirk Meyer scooped it up and ran 31 yards for the first touchdown. Leif Mostrom blocked an Auggie punt at the 45. Chris Novak ran an option for 12 and Berletic scored. A third Augsburg turnover, a fumble at the 10, led to Larson's short run for the score.

Taking over on downs at their 32 in the fourth period, the Lions scored one final time. Novak threw short to Berletic and then hit Mathre for 51 yards and the touchdown. Carlson's fourth PAT made the score 28–0.

Adam Elliott recovers a Carleton fumble, 1987

Steve Shaffer, 1988 captain

Tony Miller, 1988 captain

Strong defensive play and good punting kept the Oles in the season's finale against St. John's for three quarters, but the Johnnies broke out for a 28–2 victory. The Lions' only points came on a safety late in the contest after Shaffer's punt had pinned them at their one-yard line. A Tony Grundhauser interception and Tony Miller's blocked punt went for naught.

A 3–7 season was disappointing, but some positive feelings remained. The squad prepared well and competed strongly. One cannot help believing that the loss by injury of key personnel for all or part of the season may have played a critical role in the season's outcome.

Adam Elliott, middle guard, and Brian Putz, offensive lineman, won first-team all-MIAC recognition. Fullback Mike Berletic and defensive end and punter Steve Shaffer were named to the second 11, and ends Brent Kvittem and Don Larson were tabbed for honorable mention.

Elliott was named most valuable — only the third player in St. Olaf history to be a two-time MVP. The other two were Dave Krahn, 1965 and 1966, and Ole Gunderson, 1970 and 1971. Co-captains named for 1988 were Steve Shaffer and Tony Miller.

1988

Only seven seniors were on the '88 preseason roster, but 24 juniors provided needed experience, as many had played regularly in past seasons. Another plus was the addition to the coaching staff of Mike Allen as receiver coach. A Northfielder, Mike was an outstanding regular center on the '78 and '79 MIAC champion teams.

With St. Olaf leading the all-time series with Luther 20–12–2, the Norse provided the non-conference opposition in the home opener, the beginning of a 10-game season. Big plays, a number of third-down conversions, and a strong goal-line stand in the second quarter propelled the Oles to a 17–10 victory.

The Oles went up 7–0 in the first period on a 62-yard drive, Chris Novak passing to Steve Mathre for the last 27 yards. Mathre scored again in the third period on a 20-yard pass from Reinertson.

Among the Oles' big plays were an interception of a third and 10 pass by co-captain Tony Miller, a blocked 44-yard Luther field goal attempt in the fourth period, and a quarterback sack by Brian Danielson with 51 seconds remaining. The lone Norse touchdown came early in the second period on a fourth-down play after three previous attempts from the one had failed. It turned out to be the game's turning point. That brave stand, even though it eventually yielded a touchdown, inspired the team for the remainder of the game.

Co-captain Steve Shaffer and Mike Warden led the defense; Tim Peloquin was the leading rusher, and Shaffer's strong punting was a definite asset.

A game-saving tackle at the one-yard line as time expired helped Macalester secure a 14–7 victory over St. Olaf in the second game of the season.

Finding it tough to run against a strong Mac defense, the Lions resorted to a fake field goal play, Reinertson passing to Peloquin for the game's first score. That lead held up into the second half, when the Scots scored twice. The final play of the game, a 12-yard pass from Reinertson to Mathre, was stopped at the one.

Defense was the Oles' strong point. They accumulated six sacks and held Mac to 174 total yards, 60 coming through the air. Though they scored twice in the second half, the Scots were able to come up with only one first down. Danielson blocked a fourth-quarter field goal attempt to keep the contest close.

Note: The *Messenger* for Oct. 21, 1988, reported that St. Olaf would not have the traditional Homecoming queen and court as in past years. "It would cost too much and the selection process was unrepresentative," the paper said.

In the annual Goat game, Carleton's defense intercepted four Ole passes, recovered two fumbles and scored a safety to keep St. Olaf outside the Knight 22-yard line until the final four minutes of the game. For the second consecutive season, Carleton's stellar quarterback, Nielson, was the offensive spark. His three touchdown passes were key in the 25–7 Carleton triumph.

Despite the relatively one-sided score, the Ole defensive line played well. Carleton had only 127 yards rushing on 51 attempts. Warneke and Warden were defensive standouts. Freshman quarterback Kirk Aamot finished the game for St. Olaf. He was six of 10 passing and led the only Ole scoring drive.

A missed 37-yard field goal by Bethel with 20 seconds remaining allowed St. Olaf to win a thriller, 17–15 at the Royals' Arden Hills field. Unable to capitalize on early scoring chances, the Oles entered the fourth quarter down 7–3. Then, a one-yard run by Steve Schmidt capped a 10-play, 55-yard drive, and Schmidt scored again on a beautiful 26-yard run during which he demonstrated good open-field elusiveness. A 25-yard second-quarter field goal and two PATs by Steve Hoeman were essential to the win.

Bob Ehren and Jon Tostrud picked off Royal passes, and the defense was strong for the second Saturday, yielding a mere 78 yards rushing.

Returning to Manitou Field, the Oles nearly pulled off a second come-from-behind win, this one would have been an upset of the undefeated Hamline Pipers. But Hamline's four-yard touchdown pass with 3:17 to play lifted them to a 22–17 victory. The Oles had rallied from a 14–7 fourth-quarter deficit and took a 19–14 lead before Hamline's game-saving touchdown.

Tim Peloquin had a monumental performance — contributing 194 total

Tim Peloquin, 1988

yards and three touchdowns. He gathered in a 77-yard pass from Aamot for his final score. The others came on a 50-yard run and a 48-yard pass from Karl Bowman. Bowman led the Oles to within 27 yards of a win, but Peloquin's last second halfback pass was intercepted.

Ehren, Warden, and Kick Meyer were cited for their defensive play.

The Oles continued their established pattern of play the next week at St. Peter against Gustavus. A strong fourth-quarter comeback fell just short, and the Gusties escaped with a 33–30 win. The Lions had been down 30–6 going into the fourth period. Bowman marched his team 35 yards and threw to Mathre for 26 and the touchdown. Trying to make up for lost time and opportunity, Bowman went to the air again and registered scoring strikes to Peloquin

and Mark Thornton. But that late three-touchdown assault wasn't quite enough. First-half scoring included a 77-yard touchdown pass, Novak to Mathre, and a 27-yard Hoeman field goal.

Shaffer led the defense with 16 tackles and an interception. Jon Tostrud and Jon Dahl were also tackle leaders. Playing catchup football, the Oles accumulated 358 yards through the air. On the debit side, Chris Wolner suffered a season-ending knee injury.

Trailing 3–0 with less than a minute to play against league-leading Concordia, St. Olaf marched to the Cobber 24 only to have the drive stall on four consecutive pass plays. Reinertson's third-down pass into the end zone appeared to be good but fell incomplete. After the change of possession, the Cobber quarterback slipped to the outside and, with 24 seconds to play, rambled 72 yards to clinch a 10–0 victory.

With the defensive squads of both teams in control of the game early, the only scoring other than the clinching touchdown was a 20-yard field goal by Concordia with 1:30 left in the third period. The Ole defense embodied the football adage that a good defense bends but doesn't break. While allowing 472 yards, the defense had three sacks and recovered three fumbles. Greg Geary, Steve Shaffer, and Joe Snodgrass had super games.

Shutting out the Augsburg Auggies for three periods while scoring twice, the Lions posted their third win against

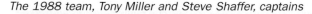

The 1988 team, Tony Miller and Steve Shaffer, captains

Chris Novak, 1988

*Brent Kvittem,
outstanding end, 1987–89*

five setbacks. Rob Warneke's interception of an Auggie pass at their 43 set up an eight-play scoring march, Reinertson throwing nine yards to Troter Bauer for the touchdown with 7:53 to play in the first period. Hoeman's conversion was good, and the count remained at 7–0 into halftime. The Oles capitalized on another break to score again in the third period. A fumbled pitchout set up a Steve Schmidt touchdown.

Augsburg came back strong in the fourth period, scoring twice, but Hoeman's 15-yard field goal coming between the two preserved the 17–13 win.

In the last home game of the season, a modest crowd sitting through a light snow was treated to one of St. Olaf's best offensive displays. The Oles scored 17 points in the first quarter and led St. John's 23–14 at halftime. Unfortunately, the Ole offense cooled with the temperature, and the Johnnies, scoring 21 points after intermission, squeezed out a 35–30 win.

St. John's struck first, recovering a blocked punt in the end zone for a 7–0 lead. But then the Lions scored 17 unanswered points. Reinertson hit Bauer and Mike Mercer on toucdown throws of 11 and 89 yards respectively, and Steve Hoeman added a 10-yard field goal. Dana Henrickson's recovery of a Johnny fumble set up Mercer's one-yard touchdown run to close out first-half scoring.

Despite a second-half scoring spree by the Johnnies, the Oles didn't go down easily. Peloquin scored on a five-yard run with 6:46 left in the game, but two additional possessions failed to generate a score.

Captains Shaffer and Miller, along with Snodgrass, led the defense. Reinertson passed for 219 yards and two touchdowns, while Mercer, with 180 total yards, had a good day.

The season ended on a high note at the Hubert Humphrey Metrodome in Minneapolis as St. Olaf downed St. Thomas 22–15 in what Tony Miller described as "the most fun game I ever played in."

It was a game filled with excitement, both teams having good success offensively. The Lions led 7–0 at the half due to a clutch 19-yard pass, Reinertson to Mathre, with seven seconds remaining.

Leading 7–6 in the third period, the Oles padded the lead on another Novak to Bauer pass, this one for three yards. Then with 5:04 to play, Novak calmly led his team on a seven-play, 70-yard scoring drive featuring a fourth and 12 conversion pass to Kvittem and a 14-yard scoring strike to Mercer.

Both quarterbacks played well. Reinertson passed for 242 yards and two touchdowns, while Novak threw for the other. Mathre caught nine balls for 120 yards and a touchdown. The defense shone as well, holding a potent St. Thomas offense to 15 points, nine of them on field goals. The Oles had three sacks, two by Tom Miller.

Three Lions — Steve Mathre, Steve Shaffer, and Rob Warneke — received first-team all-conference recognition. Mike Warden and Joe Snodgrass were named to the second team. Shaffer was designated MVP. Captains elected for the 1989 season were Warneke and Tom Miller.

1989

After downing Luther 20–13 in the season's opening contest, the Oles took the measure of Macalester in the first MIAC contest of the 1989 season, 27–8. Peloquin's second-quarter burst followed a 27-yard scoring pass from Karl Bowman to Mark Thornton and gave the Oles a 13–0 advantage.

After Mac got on the board with eight points, St. Olaf put the game away with two third-period touchdowns — an 11-yard Bowman to Kirk Aamot aerial and a two-yard run by Steve Schmidt.

A dominant Lion defense didn't allow a first down in the third quarter, and the secondary had a field day, picking off five Scot passes. Bob Ehren had two, and Kent Meyer, Rob Warneke, and Joel Magrane, one each. Although the Scots ran eight plays inside the Oles' 10-yard line, the defense kept them away from paydirt.

With the series tied at 33–33–1 and the Oles winless against the Carls since 1984, the annual battle for the Goat came early in the 1989 season. The Oles were ready and jumped out to a 14–3 first-quarter lead and went on to a 27–22 win. Peloquin scored the first two touchdowns — an eight-yard run and a 29-yard pass from Bowman. Hoeman converted after both scores.

Chapter 7: The '90s and Beyond

1990

Twenty lettermen were graduated from the 1989 squad, leaving both challenge and opportunity for those remaining and others moving in. Hardest hit were the offensive line and defensive backfield. A coaching change also was added to the mix. Chuck Larsen, an Augsburg grad and longtime coach at Morristown High School, joined the staff, filling in for Rod Grubb, offensive line mentor, who was on sabbatical.

The season got off to an exciting and successful start — a dramatic, come-from-behind 22–21 win over Luther. The Oles bounced back from a 21–10 halftime deficit, scoring the game winner on a fourth and goal plunge by Steve Schmidt.

Kirk Aamot, starting only his second game at quarterback in nearly two seasons, was involved in more than 300 yards of total offense. He completed 15 of 23 passes for 243 yards and a touchdown and rushed for another 66. Mike Mercer, converted from fullback to wide receiver, caught five aerials for 113 yards and one touchdown. Defensively, Adam Barner picked off two Luther passes.

Gathering momentum the following Saturday against Augsburg, the Lions scored on their first drive and won going away, blanking the Auggies 34–0 for a second consecutive season. St. Olaf scored on drives of 48, 31, 79, 92, and 18 yards, outgaining their opponents 370 yards to 145. Tim Peloquin scored the first touchdown on a six-yard scamper. Barner's third interception in two games set up Steve Schmidt's 21-yard touchdown run for a 14–0 first-quarter lead.

Any hope of an Augsburg rally was smothered when Aamot led the offense on a 12-play, 79-yard drive to open the second half. The Lions followed with a 72-yard, 11-play march with Aamot going the last 20 on a keeper. The final Ole touchdown came via a 14-yard scoring pass, Dave Schmidt to Dave Keenan.

The strong St. Olaf defense allowed Augsburg inside the Ole 35 only once. Defensive standouts were Kent Meyer, Howard Rogotzke, and Barner, who picked up a second interception to swell his total to four in two games.

St. Olaf and Gustavus opposed each other in the third game, both sporting 2–0 records. In a hard-fought, if not well-played, game, Gustavus came out on top 26–13. The contest was marred by and probably decided by the

play of the special teams. There were three blocked punts, four errant long snaps, three penalties for roughing the kicker, and two botched punt plays which resulted in first downs for the kicking team.

One of the errors led to the first score of the game. Late in the first quarter, Lion nose guard Todd Organ blocked a Gustavus punt following a center snap which sailed over the punter's head. The Oles then rushed six times with Schmidt going the final yard. A high snap on the conversion attempt kept the score at 6–0.

The Gusties mounted an 80-yard scoring drive to make the count 6–6 at the half.

The third period proved to be the Oles' downfall. A blocked punt was recovered by Gustavus in the end zone. On the next possession, an interception set up an eight-play scoring drive. A roughing penalty kept the St. Olaf march alive, and the ensuing touchdown brought the score to 18–13.

Trailing 26–13 with less than three minutes to play, the Oles faced a fourth and five. A bad snap forced punter Judd Sather to retreat deep into his own territory to retrieve the ball. Judd

The 1990 team, Tom Porter's last as head coach; Jon Tostrud, Kent Meyer and Kirk Meyer, captains

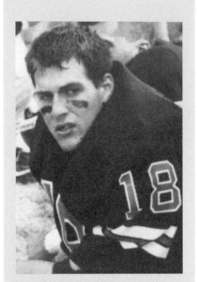

Jon Tostrud, 1990 captain

Kent Meyer, 1990 captain

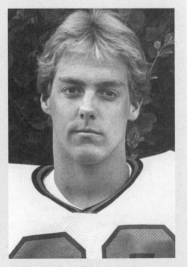

Kirk Meyer, 1990 captain

managed to recover and make a 53-yard pass-run completion to Barner. Jubilation turned to frustration when Aamot was sacked to end the scoring attempt.

Organ, Rogotske, and Kent and Kirk Meyer were defensive standouts.

The Oles got back on the winning track the following week, picking up their third win of the season against one setback. Dominating the game from the opening whistle, the Lions cruised to a 43–8 victory over Macalester in a night game on Snelling Avenue in St. Paul. It was a contest in which the entire travel squad had meaningful playing time and all played well. By half-time, the Oles had outgained the Scots 247 to 52. At the finish, the Oles' yardage advantage had climbed to 463 to 180.

Todd Organ opened the scoring three minutes into the game when he sacked the Mac quarterback in his end zone for a safety. The Ole offense scored later in the period when Peloquin pulled in an Aamot pass and ran it in. Steve Hoemann converted.

Mac mounted its best drive of the half, entering Ole territory for the only time but were forced to punt. The kick was downed inside the Lion 10. A holding penalty moved the ball to the three. On the next play, Aamot faked to his fullback and bootlegged around the right side. Finding nothing but daylight, he sprinted 97 yards for the touchdown. A 94-yard scoring drive featuring Aamot passes to Brett Lillimoe, Andy Butler (2), Tim Peloquin, and 15 yards to Mike Mercer for the touchdown brought the halftime count to 22–0.

The Lion reserves played most of the second half. A backfield of Trygg Wangsness, Dave Keenan, Jayson Green, and Keith Karpinski, along with good line play, accounted for two scores.

St. Thomas came to town for the fifth game of the season, and for the second time, the Lions lost out on Manitou Field. It was a scoreless standoff for two periods, and even after that, the Oles played the Tommies on even terms except for three pass plays — and all of them went for touchdowns. The final was 21–0.

St. Thomas scored once in the third period and twice in the fourth. After that the Oles put together a 50-yard drive

Ade Christenson makes his last visit to Manitou Field, 1990, pictured with Chuck Lunder (left) and Tom Porter.

before losing the ball on downs. The offense had also crossed the St. Thomas 40 five times and was inside the 30 three times, but four interceptions and seven sacks turned aside the scoring threats.

Leading the defensive effort against the larger St. Thomas front line were Rogotzke, Kirk Meyer, and Jon Dahl.

A stretch of 21 unanswered points and the play of an all-freshman backfield rallied St. Olaf to a 24–19 upset of undefeated and league-leading Bethel. The Royals' passing offense dominated the first half, scoring twice through the air, to lead 12–0. Late in the half, however, the freshman backfield of Karpinski at quarterback and Green and Keenan at the running backs took over. On their first play, Keenan exploded up the left sideline and went 65 yards untouched for a touchdown. The run not only closed the gap to 12–7 but shifted the momentum of the game.

The Oles came out strong in the second half. On the first possession, Karpinski completed passes to Butler and Bauer and finally a 30-yarder to Mercer to move the Lions into the lead at 14–12. Linebacker Howard Rogotzke, team leader with 15 tackles, intercepted his first pass of the season to set up another St. Olaf scoring drive. The third touchdown came on a third-and-goal pass to Butler.

Bethel fought back with a 58-yard scoring march to narrow the gap to 21–19, but on the next drive, Hoemann's field goal brought the count to 24–19. Bethel's final scoring opportunities were thwarted by Ole interceptions, the first by Bjorn Larson and the other by Dan Calhoun, who wrestled the ball from the hands of the Bethel receiver.

Going into the last four games of the 1990 season, the Oles sported a good 4–2 record, but the odds were against its continuing, because the heavies of the league were now up. And that's the way it played out. Concordia and St. John's, traditional MIAC front runners, thumped the Oles soundly 24–7 and 45–6. Carleton and Hamline, who often wound up in the middle of the pack or below, also came out on top, but somewhat more moderately — 37–20 and 21–6.

Playing an undefeated team for the third time in as many weeks, the Lions lost to Concordia 24–7. The Cobbers dominated in all phases of the game, holding St. Olaf to 127 yards, only 23 on the ground. Mercer accounted for most of the offensive yards, catching five passes for 83 yards and the lone Lion touchdown.

On the following Saturday, the St. Olaf record dropped below .500 as St. John's rambled to a 45–6 win, racking up 519 yards, the most any team had managed against the 1990 Oles. It didn't start out that way. Though up against a stiff wind, the Lions outgained the Johnnies in the first period but were still down 10–0. After the teams changed ends of the field, the Johnnies increased the lead to 22–6 at halftime. The Oles' lone counter came on a 59-yard touchdown drive with Aamot passing to Peloquin for 22 and Mercer for 15 and, finally, a six-yard scoring swing pass to Peloquin. St. John's picked up the pace in the third period, scoring on five consecutive possessions.

Under climate and field conditions that were as bad as they come — a sloppy, wet snow — three bizarre plays early in the game set the tone for a 37–20 Carleton victory. The first of the strange plays occurred when Aamot, running a keeper, fumbled after gaining a first down. A Carleton defensive back scooped up the fumble (a new rule permitted defense to advance a fumble) and ran 72 yards for a touchdown and a 6–0 Carleton lead. Later in the quarter, a 38-yard Carleton pass was deflected by two Ole defenders before finally finding its way into the hands of a Knight receiver — 14–0 Carleton.

In the second quarter, Karpinski led a seven-play, 57-yard march featuring passes to Troter Bauer and Brett Lillemoe and, finally, to Mercer for the touchdown. The two-point conversion try led to the third unusual play. The conversion pass was intercepted and returned 100 yards, with the assistance of a lateral, resulting in a two-point score for the Knights.

Carleton scored 21 unanswered points in the third quarter, and St. Olaf scored the last 14 — Bauer and Mercer on 14-yard and 12-yard receptions, respectively, both on passes from Aamot.

Offensive mention went to Keenan for his ball carrying on a greasy field. In a heavy-hitting defensive game, Chris Nelson, Jon Dahl, and Kirk and Kent Meyer stood out.

Hamline's ball-control offense and stingy defense spelled defeat for the Oles in the season's final game at the Metrodome. Six turnovers, including five interceptions in critical situations, made third-down conversions rare. Hamline rushed the ball 66 times, compared to 25 for the Oles, and outgained St. Olaf on the ground 285 to 57.

After a scoreless opening period, Hamline scored twice in the latter half of the second for a 14–0 halftime lead. The third quarter was scoreless, like the first, but early in the fourth, the Lions narrowed the gap to 14–6 when Karpinski and Mercer hooked up on an 80-yard touchdown pass play. The Pipers iced the contest with a time-consuming, 13-play drive to make the final count 21–6. Two final St. Olaf possessions were stalled by turnovers.

Todd Organ, Howard Rogotzke, and Dave Bergh played significant roles in a defense that played with intensity and aggressiveness.

Coach Porter directs from the sidelines, 1990

Captain Don Canfield, 1962

Head Coach Don Canfield, 1991

In some ways the 4–6 season — with the heavies coming at the end as noted — was disappointing, but it was also gratifying in that the intensity and level of play of the squad did not drop off. It simply was a case of encountering stronger opponents.

Mercer and Kirk Meyer won all-conference first-team recognition, while Kent Meyer, Andy Butler, and Howard Rogotske were named to the second team. Honorable mention went to Peloquin and Dahl. Jon Tostrud was voted most valuable.

A new award inaugurated this year — the Major Ben Danielson Award — was presented to Coach Porter by Brian Danielson and Mary Danielson Gates. Ben Danielson played end for the Oles in 1962, '63, and '64 and was graduated in 1965. A fighter pilot, Danielson was shot down and killed in the Vietnam war.

Porter Steps Down; Canfield Named Successor

The 1990 season marked the end of an era as Coach Tom Porter retired after 32 years at the helm of the St. Olaf program. A search for a successor was conducted during the late fall of 1990.

In the period of 1958–1990, Porter's teams compiled a won-lost-tied record of 171–117–5 and won six Midwest Conference championships and two MIAC championships. Porter's 32-season tenure makes him the longest-serving head coach in St. Olaf history, and his record of 171 wins makes him the mentor with the most victories.

A search committee with representatives from all sectors of the college community recommended and the college appointed Don Canfield, 1964 grad and former standout guard/linebacker and co-captain, to succeed Porter as head coach. Canfield brought a background of high school and college coaching, most recently 18 years as head coach at Wartburg College in Waverly, Iowa, where he compiled a 64–33 record which included two Iowa Conference titles and a 1982 berth in the NCAA playoffs.

The appointment was effective Jan. 1, 1991, in order to allow Canfield to become well acquainted with returning squad members and for them to get to know their

Ben Danielson '65, namesake of the Major Ben Danielson Award presented to Coach Tom Porter in 1990.

new coach. The mid-year appointment also allowed Canfield to direct the recruiting program for the coming season.

1991

A good group of underclassmen, many of whom had played significant roles as frosh the previous season, greeted Coach Canfield. The squad and its new coach got away to a quick and successful start with victories over Luther, 22–21, and Augsburg, 35–13, before falling to Gustavus 28–13. The latter game marked the emergence of a potentially great passing combination in quarterback Keith Karpinski and receiver Tom Buslee. The duo scored once and gave significant promise for the future.

Prior to the Gustavus game, groundbreaking ceremonies took place at the west end of Manitou Field for the new $2.2 million Manitou Fieldhouse, construction to begin the following month.

Quickly getting back on the winning track, Canfield's Oles bombed Macalester 62–0 and edged St. Thomas 26–25. Particularly noteworthy in the St. Thomas game was Karpinski's two-minute drill, climaxed by Keith's finding Mike Mercer in the end zone. "Mike's catch was just phenomenal!" Canfield said.

Continuing their upset play, St. Olaf downed an undefeated and ranked Bethel Royal squad 17–6. The Royals had not lost a home game in two seasons. The Oles upped their record to 6–1 with a 24–13 win over Concordia before losing to St. John's 67–19. Between the Concordia and St. John's games came the Halloween storm which dumped 15 inches of snow on most of Minnesota and caused first postponement and then cancellation of all games, including the Goat game, breaking a St. Olaf-Carleton string going back to the World War II years.

Undeterred by the St. John's defeat, the Oles bested Hamline 26–23 in a closely contested game. It was another nailbiter, as Karpinski drove the offense 60 yards late in the game and spiked the ball with two seconds to play. On the next play, Keith drilled the ball 11 yards to Steve Schmidt in the back of the end zone to seal a come-from-behind win. It put the Oles in second place in the conference with a 6–2 record.

Winning first-team all-conference recognition were Andy Butler, Mercer, Judd Sather, Chris Nelson, and Steve Schmidt. Schmidt also was named most valuable, and first-year coach Canfield was named MIAC Coach of the Year. Organ, Butler, and Jim Starr were named captains for 1992.

Manitou Field Facilities Upgraded

The Manitou Field athletic facility, to be dedicated in 2002 as part of the Ade Christenson Athletics Complex, was completed in August 1992. It was funded in part by the Vision Campaign capital fund drive and a special campaign spearheaded by former athletic director and coach Bob Gelle. The $2.2 million fieldhouse was part of a two-phase project. Phase two was to include the building of an all-weather track and reconstruction of the football playing field and two practice fields. New bleachers and press box followed in 2003.

1992

The '92 squad finished an up-and-down season in grand style as they ended a four-game losing streak with two end-of-the season victories.

The sting of a season-opening 31–13 loss to Luther was soothed somewhat by a hard-fought, well-earned win over St. Thomas in the home opener. The Ole defense dominated the line of scrimmage with outstanding play from Todd Organ, Bill Kelly, and Jim Starr keying a 14–7 victory. Offensively, Keenan was the workhorse with 137 yards on 36 carries. Both touchdowns came via the Karpinski to Buslee passing combination.

A superior St. John's team evened the Oles' MIAC chart at 1–1 with a 62–7 win. The Johnnies tallied four first-quarter touchdowns en route to a 35–7 halftime lead. They padded the margin after intermission.

What began to look like a one-week-down, one-week-up season continued as the Lions posted a convincing 47–0 win over Macalester. The triumph was spearheaded by a defense that forced seven Mac turnovers. The offense took full advantage of the turnovers to register the shutout. The Ole scorers started early with two running touchdowns by Keenan and one by Joel Magrane on a pass from Karpinski. Darrell Erickson added a 25-yard field goal to put his team up 26–0 at halftime. The Oles tacked on three more touchdowns in the second half as the defense continued to dominate.

The Oles ran off a cliff the following week, beginning a four-game losing string with a 14–9 loss to Gustavus. Carleton posted a 21–9 win the next week, followed by Hamline's 17–14 victory and Concordia's 45–21 triumph.

Gustavus won on a late-game drive. Trailing 14–7, the Oles had a chance to tie or go ahead only to lose the ball on downs at the Gustavus 14. The Gusties ran the clock down before taking a safety to avoid punting.

Turnovers plagued the Oles in the Goat game, played before a large homecoming crowd at Manitou Field. The Carls built a 21–3 halftime lead that proved insurmountable. The Oles' only touchdown came on a Karpinski to Keenan pass. Dave had 223 total yards but only 32 came on the ground. John Best, Rob Baker, Brad Fuerst, and Todd Organ were noted for fine line play. Karl Sherve, Jason Laukkonen, Starr, and Sather were the leading tacklers. With the loss, the Goat series stood at 35–34–1 in favor of Carleton.

The losing skid continued as Hamline eked out a 17–14 win and Concordia won more convincingly, 45–21. The Hamline game was very tight and the Oles led 14–10 in the fourth, only to have the Pipers score late in the game to register a come-from-behind victory. Keenan scored both St. Olaf touchdowns.

Manitou Field, 1991

Playing, Coaching Legend Christenson Dies

Ade Christenson died June 18, 1993, at his home in Northome. He was 93. Ade served the St. Olaf physical education and athletic departments for 38 years. He was appointed to the faculty in 1927 and named head football coach in 1929. He coached, with the exception of a few years during World War II and the 1949 and 1950 seasons, until he retired from coaching in 1958. Ade was an innovative coach with great imagination, particularly for the offensive phase of the game. He was an ardent proponent of athletic competition for its own sake rather than just for the won-lost record.

For further reading about Ade, his life, and philosophy, see *The Verdict of the Scoreboard* by Ade Christenson, The American Press, N.Y., N.Y., 1958; and an essay, "Adrian (Ade) Christenson" by Tom Porter, *Called to Serve*, Pamela Schwandt, ed., St. Olaf College, 1999.

St. Olaf fell behind Concordia early and trailed 17–0 midway in the second period. But then a hook and ladder play, Karpinski to Buslee to Keenan, was good for 62 yards and a touchdown. Then Karpinski drilled a 38-yard pass to Magrane to set up his own one-yard scoring run, and soon after, Organ's punt block was returned by Scott Cybyski for a third touchdown and a 21–17 Ole lead at halftime. But in the second half, the Cobbers went back to basics and their powerful ground attack dominated and brought them the triumph.

The four-game skid, marked by many "close, but no cigar" situations, finally came to an end as the Lions downed the Bethel Royals 27–20. The game had all the earmarks of a breakout as several long-standing records fell. The Oles racked up 458 yards in total offense; Karpinski completed 19 of 29 aerials for 335 yards and three touchdowns. Keenan caught 10 passes for 247 yards and two touchdowns and had 328 yards of total offense for the day. His 10 receptions broke the previous single-game mark of nine. Tom Buslee caught five to break the single-season record of 40. Kyle Paulson rushed for 90 yards.

Mike Fossum, Brad Fuerst, and Rob Baker were cited for their offensive line play, while Erickson's and Sather's kicking contributed greatly to the day's success.

A thrilling 20–18 victory over Augsburg in the Hubert Humphrey Metrodome ended the season on a positive note. After trailing 12–0 at halftime, the Ole offense came alive. On the first play of the second half, Buslee caught a 20-yard pass from Karpinski to set a new career receiving record of 1,220 yards. Paulson and Keenan scored second-half touchdowns to put the Oles ahead 13–12.

The Lion defense stopped the Auggies when the punter bobbled the snap, and St. Olaf took over at the Auggie 11. Two plays later, Karpinski hit Buslee for 10 and the touchdown. Augsburg struck back hard and scored on a 90-yard pass play to cut the Ole lead to 20–18. And still the Auggies were not through. With time running out, they drove to the Ole 31. Cybyski blocked a field goal try, but the rebound was recovered by Augsburg. A second field goal attempt fell short as time expired.

Keith Karpinski, 1991

Karpinski finished the season with 1,345 yards passing for a new St. Olaf record. First-team all-MIAC honors went to Buslee, Keenan, and Sather. Fuerst, Laukkonen, and Organ were named to the second team, while Karpinski, Fossum, and Starr were awarded honorable mention. Keenan was named MVP and was elected co-captain with Sather for the 1993 campaign.

1993

St. Olaf opened the season on a successful note, defeating Luther 23–14. Jason Harris, Brad Laukkonen, and Trevor Olson, along with Eric Lien and Craig Crosby, led a tenacious defensive unit that held the Norse to under 200 yards in total offense. Buslee snagged 11 passes for 165 yards to smash Keenan's previous single game record of 10 catches set against Bethel the previous season. Karpinski racked up 235 yards passing and Paulson had 105 yards rushing for a team total of 421 yards.

Reality intruded the following week as St. Thomas put the clamps on the explosive Ole offense and came away with a 35–12 win. Poor field position, turnovers, and breakdowns in the kicking game by the Oles helped the Tommies. Each of the

St. Thomas scores came off St. Olaf errors. Two interceptions were returned for touchdowns, a failed fake punt and a fumbled punt afforded St. Thomas good field position. Buslee repeated his feat of grabbing 11 passes, while Karpinski threw for 275 yards. Sather, Laukkonen, Harris, Crosby, and Stenson were cited for their defensive play.

The carnage continued as St. John's accumulated 28 first downs and 549 yards of offense in battering the Oles 71–10. While the Ole offense sputtered throughout the afternoon, the Johnnies scored twice on punt returns and blocked a punt to set up another.

Hit hard for two Saturdays, Coach Canfield's Oles bounced high on the succeeding two outings, downing a struggling Macalester team 28–15 and defeating Gustavus 26–23 on a beautiful Manitou Field afternoon — and it was Homecoming to boot.

Despite having two punts blocked, one for a safety, the Oles scored twice in each half against Gustavus with impressive drives of 89, 67, 49, and 58 yards. Freshman Eric Anderson had 113 yards on 29 carries, while on defense, Chad Engelbrecht had a good day. Another freshman, Tony Bolstorff, had an impressive debut with 19 tackles.

The Oles dominated in the first half and led 14–3 at halftime. The second half, however, was a nail-biter for the home team. Gustavus went ahead 15–14 with 9:15 remaining and it was dog-eat-dog from there until with 1:33 left, Karpinski found Buslee open for the winning six-pointer.

Keenan had 235 total yards, while Karpinski passed for 230 and three touchdowns. Anderson rushed for 93, and Laukkonen, Olson, Zorn, Crosby, and MacGuffie were defensive standouts. Sather had probably his best day as an Ole with 19 tackles, two pass deflections, one caused fumble, and a 40-yards-plus punting average.

"Offense shines, Defense Sputters in a Wild One," was the *Messenger* description of the 51–48 loss to Carleton in the annual Goat game. The teams combined for 1110 yards of total offense — St. Olaf 552, Carleton 558. Karpinski had 390 of his team's total — 347 passing and 48 rushing. Buslee had 11 receptions for the third time in the season, while John Best had three touchdown catches. Keenan had 251 all-purpose yards; Anderson averaged 5.1 yards per carry. It was tons of offense for the Oles but not enough to offset the Carls' 51 points. The series stood at 36–34–1 in favor of the Knights.

Karpinski had another banner day versus Hamline, completing 30 passes to eight different receivers, but the Oles could manage only 13 points in a heartbreaking 21–13 loss to the Pipers.

The pain from the Hamline loss was dulled the following week as the Lions downed Concordia 58–34 in a triumph Coach Canfield termed "the biggest of the season."

The offensive spotlight again was on Karpinski and the receiving corps of Buslee, Best, and Keenan. Keith was 23 of 35 for 448 yards, another St. Olaf record. Mike Fossum led a strong offensive line, while MacGuffie, Zorn, and Sather keyed the defense in holding the potent Cobber rushing attack in check.

In an exciting game in which defenses were outstanding, the Bethel Royals edged the Oles 17–15. Defensively, St. Olaf held Bethel to three points in the second half, but they had only four first downs and 79 yards of total offense themselves. Laukkenon had a team-leading 19 tackles, followed by his fellow linebacker, Bolstorff, with 16.

The season ended with a heartbreaking 26–24 loss to Augsburg. Karpinski, who rewrote the Ole record book the last two seasons, took over every passing and total offense record. His 218 yards in the Augsburg contest put him over 5,000 yards in career passing. John Best was Keith's main target against the Auggies, grabbing eight for 131 yards.

Karpinski, Buslee, and Sather garnered first-team all-conference slots with Fossum, Keenen, and Laukkonen named to the second 11. Honorable mention went to Best, Bolstorff, and Kyle Paulson. Tom Buslee was voted most valuable. Captains selected for 1994 were Laukkenon and Eric Lien.

1994

Six turnovers overshadowed a strong defensive effort in the season and home opener against the Hamline Pipers. The four fumbles and two interceptions were too much to overcome, resulting in a 19–6 loss. Hamline had a 12–0 lead before Kevin Cook connected on his two field goals (49 and 47 yards), the second with only two seconds

Team celebration in front of the new fieldhouse

remaining in the first half. After that, the Ole defense took control of the game, but four fumbles in the last five possessions doomed the Oles' chances.

The following week, St. Olaf reduced their turnovers to one interception and came from 13 points down to edge St. Thomas 20–19 at O'Shaughnessy Stadium. Cook was again the "ice water man" as he drilled a 24-yard field goal with 12 seconds remaining to win the contest. Clock management and good defensive play were also important. St. Olaf had the ball for 21 minutes in the second half, allowing a talented St. Thomas offense only three possessions. For the Oles, senior quarterback Jim Wiberg entered the game in the second quarter and completed 12 of 25 passes for 193 yards. For that heroic effort, Wiberg was named MIAC Player of the Week. The entire defense was also outstanding.

Four Kevin Cook field goals (37, 30, 34, 42) were not enough offense, and the Oles dropped a 14–12 decision to Gustavus. Offensive drives resulted in field goals, not touchdowns. The Lion defense bent but didn't break for most of the afternoon, allowing the Gusties only the 14 points, despite two 100-yard rushers. Junior linebacker Craig Crosby and senior defensive end Eric Zorn led the defense.

Carleton ran its edge in the Goat series to three, 37–34–1, by pinning an 18–6 defeat on the Lions to make the season record 1–3. The Carls passed for 354 yards and two touchdowns even though the Oles picked off four aerials, Chad Engelbrecht getting two. Big plays, made and not made, were a factor. St. Olaf failed to capitalize from the Knights' 11 midway in the first quarter. With four seconds to go in the half, Carleton completed a touchdown pass for a 12–0 margin at intermission. The injury list grew as six regulars were sidelined.

The Oles got back on the winning track with a 35–25 conquest of Macalester, but the following week, they were outclassed by Concordia.

Whitey Aus, player 1956–58, athletic director, 1991–94

Statistics don't always tell the story, but they largely explained the 38–0 setback at the hands of the Cobbers. Outgained by 521 yards to 143, 24–9 in first downs, and, in time of possession by over 10 minutes, it was a case of the Oles simply meeting a superior football team. Concordia also displayed superiority in defense, limiting St. Olaf to fewer than 200 yards.

St. John's jumped to a 20–0 first-quarter lead via two big play touchdowns and never looked back in rolling over St. Olaf 40–15 in Collegeville. The Oles felt they had gained momentum going into halftime, but the Johnnies countered in six plays before halftime and then scored twice more in the third period. The Oles added a consolation touchdown in the fourth on Mike Wylde's five-yard run. John Best had a good game as a blocker and also hauled in seven receptions. Freshman Chad Durgin also performed well.

In the face of a season in which wins were hard to come by, Coach Canfield credited captains Lien and Laukkenon, with senior teammates, for exceptional leadership in a difficult situation.

The struggle continued as Bethel handed the Oles their third straight loss, 41–20. The Oles made plays that often

would have won ball games. Travis Zorn returned an interception for a touchdown and a 7–0 lead, Ryan Bartold had his best day as an Ole, and Best grabbed 10 passes for 100 yards. But the team also lost chances to score with turnovers, two interceptions, and two fumbles.

For the first time in the '94 season, St. Olaf scored 20 points in a quarter and led Augsburg 20–13 at halftime of the season finale at the Metrodome. But typical of this difficult season, the Auggies roared back after intermission to post a 34–20 win. Best went out in style with nine receptions for 94 yards. Ohm completed 16 of 30 passes for 186 yards. Defensively, Zorn blocked a punt and picked off one Auggie pass. Crosby also had an interception and was the leading tackler.

John Best was voted most valuable. Craig Crosby and Trevor Olson were named captains for 1995.

Huyck Named Interim Athletic Director

Bill Huyck, longtime Carleton coach of track and field, was named interim athletic director at St. Olaf following the resignation of Whitey Aus.

1995

Coach Canfield and his staff were optimistic for the upcoming season — and with reason. There was good leadership in Crosby and Olson and talented performers on both sides of the ball. On defense, returnees included MacGuffie, Lund, Cybyske, Harris, Zorn, Engelbrecht, and Enestevdt, while on offense, Ohm, Lillimoe, Best, Bass, Epley, and Baker were back.

Luther posed the first challenge. The defense held firm from the start, but it was well into the second half before the offense got untracked. Durgin scored the first touchdown of the season. Veteran kicker Kevin Cook added field goals of 28, 31, and 35 yards and two PATs.

The defense played setup, contributing to five Luther turnovers, including interceptions by Zorn,

Engelbrecht, and Kodl. Kodl returned his theft for a touchdown. The line hounded the Norse quarterback throughout the afternoon. All contributed to the 23–0 final score — the first shutout since 1991.

The Hamline Pipers were next, and the Ole defense took up where it left off. Linebacker Omann's fourth-quarter interception return for a touchdown tied the score at 20. Cook calmly split the uprights for a 21–20 victory. A 48-yard scoring bomb from Ohm was a key contributor in the cause.

A quarterback with a hot hand and an opportunistic St. Thomas squad invaded Manitou Field and walked away with a 35–14 win. Esterly, the Tommy quarterback, completed an amazing 21 of 23 passes for 275 yards. Esterly's success, combined with five St. Olaf turnovers, spelled disaster for the Lions. A quick start and strong first half play provided St. Thomas a 28–0 lead at intermission.

The Oles retaliated in the second half. Pass receptions by Best and strong running by Wylde keyed the comeback, and Wylde and Ohm scored to cut the margin to 28–14. The Tommies put seven more on the board, however, to put the game out of reach.

In a turn-around game from the previous week, the Ole offense piled up 410 yards, committed only one turnover, and went on to thump Gustavus 28–22. In a game summary headline, the Mess noted, "Ohm leads St. Olaf offense to best game of season; Albrecht makes game-saving interception at goal line."

It was a windy day at Hollingsworth Field in St. Peter and prospects looked just as bleak for the Oles when the Gusties scored twice for a 13–0 lead. But St. Olaf got on the board with a five-yard run by Wylde and slipped into the lead at halftime when, with 32 seconds left, Bass made a spectacular catch of Ohm's pass between two defenders.

The Gusties regained the lead at 22–20 in the third period, but the Lions roared back. Ohm directed a 50-yard march and sneaked in the ball himself to tie the score and then passed to Lillimoe for the two-point conversion. A final Gustavus drive brought them to the Ole five with 30 seconds to play, setting the stage for Engelbrecht's diving, and, as it turned out, game-saving interception in the end zone on a third-down play.

St. Olaf's slow start in the Carleton game was a repeat of the previous two contests. The Knights scored in each of the two first-half quarters to go ahead 14–0. But the Ole offense got untracked in the second half and went ahead 15–14. Ohm scored on two sneaks, the later set up by a fourth and 15 pass/run Ohm to Bass. A two-point conversion put the Lions back in the lead. With minutes remaining, Carleton drove downfield. A fourth-and-11 pass completion kept the march alive, and a few plays later, the Carls scored to take the contest 21–15. The victory extended the Knights' series lead to four, 38–34–1.

Continuing the win one, lose one, win one pattern, the Lions started fast and played strongly throughout in downing Macalester 35–18. Three Scot fumbles providing good field position were quickly turned into scores to the delight of the overflow Homecoming crowd at Manitou Field.

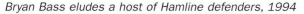

Bryan Bass eludes a host of Hamline defenders, 1994

President Foss Dies in Arizona

Harlan Foss, the seventh president of St. Olaf College died Dec. 20, 1995, in Arizona at the age of 77. Foss had suffered from cardio-vascular illness for a number of years, but had been dealing with it very well until shortly before his death. President Foss, a 1940 graduate of St. Olaf, was an avid follower and supporter of Ole athletics.

Death Takes Coach Canfield

Shortly after the close of the 1995 season, Coach Don Canfield was diagnosed with colon cancer. After a courageous battle, Don died in May of 1996. He was 55. Don has been missed sorely by his wife, Jeanne; daughter, Amy, and son, Mark, as well as by his colleagues and friends at St. Olaf and Bethel Lutheran Church and, especially, the men who played for him.

Captain Eric Anderson, quoted in the Sept. 20, 1996, issue of the *Manitou Messenger*, said, "He was a good coach. He was a good guy both on and off the field. He taught us about both football and life. He was more than a coach."

Those 21 points in the first quarter was a season first. An Ohm to Best pass increased the lead to 28–0 at halftime. A 70-yard pass/run play, Ohm to Bass, was good for a third-quarter score and a 35–0 margin. With the game seemingly safely in the win column for the Oles, the Scots scored three times in the final period.

Concordia's potent offense made for a long trip home from Moorhead following a 48–16 defeat at the hands of the Cobbers. Kevin Cook's three field goals (42, 36, and 33 yards) gave the Oles a 9–6 halftime lead. But in the third quarter, Concordia's power began to tell, and the Cobbers finished that period with a 34–9 advantage. Concordia scored twice and the Oles once in the fourth quarter to make the final 48–16.

The Cobbers' league-leading defense against the run stymied the Ole ground attack, limiting it to 10 yards. Consequently, Ohm passed 47 times and completed 25. Lillimoe caught eight and Best, six to lead the receivers.

The St. Olaf Lions returned home to play their best game of the season, stunning undefeated St. John's 24–21. Senior Mike Wylde summed up the team's play, "We played a perfect game."

St. John's scored first, but St. Olaf countered on a five-yard touchdown pass, Ohm to Best. A second-quarter three-yard run by Durgin and the two PATs by Cook made it 14–7. In the third quarter, Cook added a 24-yard field goal. Two touchdowns by St. John's, the second with only 52 seconds remaining, gave the Johnnies a 21–17 lead, a seemingly winning cushion. But, on the first scrimmage play after kickoff, Ohm unleashed a 66-yard bomb to Bass, and the Oles were suddenly at the Johnny 15. With 22 seconds on the clock, Ohm scrambled left and made a quick toss to Lillimoe. Tait broke free from a crowd of Johnny defenders to make the game-winning catch. Cook's PAT produced the three-point margin.

A strong Bethel squad pounded St. Olaf 42–7 at the Metrodome. The Royals built a 14–0 halftime lead and ran it to 42 before the Oles could retaliate. Highlights of the Bethel explosion in the third period were two Lundeen to Lundeen (brothers) pass plays and a

Interim Head Coach Rod Grubb, 1996

63-yard run. Ole sophomore quarterback Peter Schultz led a late Lion surge. Josh Anderson's catch of a tipped ball was the sole Ole tally.

Playing in the Metrodome for the second consecutive week, the Oles ran into a tenacious Augsburg squad and went down to defeat 20–12. St. Olaf came out slow, but the Auggies came out shooting, and they quickly built a 20–0 first-half lead. Ohm found Lillimoe for a five-yard scoring pass late in the third period, and after being stopped at the five on another drive, the Ohm to Lillimoe combination produced again. A two-point conversion attempt failed.

The season ended with a 5–5 overall record and 4–5 in the MIAC. John Best was voted most valuable, and Eric Anderson and Joshua Holmes were named captains for 1996.

Rod Grubb Named Interim Head Coach

In addition to the personal anguish it brought, Coach Canfield's untimely death *[see sidebar]* posed a practical problem for St. Olaf: where to find a coach with the 1996 season fast approaching. College and athletic administrators turned to Rod Grubb, and he graciously agreed to step into a difficult situation.

Rod had served St. Olaf since 1968 as professor of political science and, for many years, chairman of the department. He had coached at Concordia and St. Olaf for a total of 27 years. As a student, Rod was Jake Christiansen's quarterback at Concordia and had been a coaching colleague of Tom Porter, Dave Hauck, Bob Gelle, Jim Dimick, and others at St. Olaf.

1996

The Oles squeaked by traditional rival Luther in the season opener by a tight 29–28. In what must have been a shock to Coach Grubb, the Norse scored on the first play of the game — a 76-yard breakaway. Recovering quickly, the Lions put together two drives, both ending with Haakon Nelson field goals. A 60-yard Chuck Ohm to Ivan Carter touchdown pass and a Dustin Ferrell run made for a seemingly comfortable 22–7 halftime lead.

Luther roared back after intermission and scored three unanswered touchdowns to take a 28–22 lead. Not to be denied, the Lions scored on another Ferrell run, and Nelson's PAT brought the one-point victory.

Perennial MIAC favorite St. John's was next up, and the Johnnies had a special motivation — avenging the previous season's 24–21 loss to the Oles. The first quarter was scoreless, but the opportunistic Johnnies intercepted twice and scored three times in the second to take a 21–0 halftime lead. St. John's added a pair of touchdowns in the second half and the Oles' Ferrell scored once to make the final 36–7. It was a game in which St. Olaf played better than the week before against Luther but not good enough to handle a stronger opponent.

The trip to Moorhead again proved to be a long day in more ways than one as Concordia muscled its way to a 20–7 win. Proving themselves the better "mudders," the Cobbers built a 20–0 halftime lead on a rain-soaked field. Dustin Ferrell scored on a short run for the only second-half tally. For the Oles, it was a game of halves — not good the first half, well-played the second.

Bouncing back, the Lions nudged Augsburg 30–27. Junior free safety Chris Hallgren was selected MIAC Defensive Player of the Week for his play against the Auggies.

After dropping a 30–6 decision to Bethel, the Oles returned home to face the Hamline Pipers for Homecoming. In connection with that Oct. 12 clash, a grove of five trees and two benches on the north side of Manitou Field were dedicated as a memorial to the late Coach Don Canfield. The project of the memorial grove overlooking the 50-yard line was conceived and funded by Don's teammates and classmates in the class of 1963, and by members of the Canfield family.

The Lions battled the Pipers to the final gun before going down 24–22. It was a case of not cashing in on first-half opportunities. Despite racking up 250 yards of offense, the Oles failed to put points on the board. In the meantime, Hamline built a 21–6 advantage.

The Oles finally found the offensive payoff punch and scored twice and converted a two-pointer to take a 22–21 lead. A late 32-yard field goal by Hamline was the decisive difference.

Carleton scored 28 unanswered points, including 21 in the second quarter, on the way to a 42–9 triumph in the 74th renewal of the battle for the Goatrophy. The game started out to be a thriller. Ole linebacker Amann recovered a fumble, and quarterback Ohm passed to Carter to put the ball at the Carleton five. The Knights stiffened and forced the Oles to settle for a 22-yard Nelson field goal. The Oles threatened again in the second quarter, but the Carls intercepted in the end zone. The theft provided the impetus for the Carls' 28-point run to halftime.

St. Olaf's chances for a rally in the third period were squelched when Carleton recovered a blocked punt at the Ole one. The Knights drove in for the score, but St. Olaf responded with a 10-play, 69-yard scoring drive, directed by Ohm. However, as they say, it was too little, too late. The Goat game series record stood at Carleton 39, St. Olaf 34 and one tie.

St. Olaf hung tough for three quarters before St. Thomas pulled away for a 49–26 triumph. After trading early scores, the Oles blocked a punt and took only three plays to score, Ohm passing to Morsden for 49 and the score to give the Oles a 13–7 lead. An end-zone interception ruined Ole hopes for a score before halftime. The

Longtime equipment manager Percy Johnson confers with Tom Porter at Johnson's 80th birthday party, 1997 (photo courtesy of Mildred Johnson)

Paul Miller, head coach 1997–2001

Tommies were up 21–13 at intermission. Anderson punched in for a touchdown in the third period, but the Tommies countered and then won going away.

Macalester, with one of its better teams, registered a 31–17 victory in St. Paul.

The season finale was a 20–14 loss to Gustavus at the Metrodome. The squads, both fighting for a second conference win, exchanged early scores. Gustavus added a field goal before Ohm launched a drive in which he completed five of seven passes culminating with a seven-yard scoring strike to Anderson and a 14–10 halftime lead. A Gustavus touchdown put them in the lead 17–14, and then a final field goal produced the 20–14 final.

A significant difference in the contest was Gustavus' 333 to 126 advantage in rushing yards. Ohm was 21 of 36 through the air for 250 yards and a touchdown. Anderson caught eight of Ohm's throws, Carter and Marsden, five each. Ryan Fleming punted seven times

for a 44.1 average. Durgin, Asleson, Omann, and Kern led the defense.

Eric Anderson was voted MVP, and Durgin, Nicholas Johnson, Christopher Kodl, Peter Schultz, and Darik Steinbach were chosen captains for 1997.

Paul Miller Named Coach

After a thorough search, Paul Miller, a South St. Paul native and graduate of the University of Minnesota at Morris, was appointed head coach. Miller brought an extensive and highly successful coaching background at the high school and college level, most recently at Twin Cities suburban Apple Valley High School. Miller embodied a positive, enthusiastic, and highly organized manner of coaching, and he assembled an excellent staff of assistants.

1997

Following an intensive, well-conducted, three-week preseason camp, the Oles opened the '97 season hosting a good

Luther team. St. Olaf ended its 46-game series with the Luther Norsemen on a sour note, losing 19–12. The contest marked the end of the current series because of Luther's expanded schedule in the Iowa Conference. It would be resumed, at least temporarily, in 2003.

The Norsemen opened the scoring with 4:05 left in the first period, but then Ole quarterback Pete Schultz completed four consecutive passes, the last one to Ryan Hollom for 11 yards and the first St. Olaf score of the season. Haakon Nelson hit a 25-yard field goal in the third period to give the Lions a 9–6 lead. Jerod Schoenecker's 21-yard interception return set up Nelson's kick.

Luther retaliated with an interception for a touchdown. Nelson's second three-pointer narrowed the gap to 19–12, but that's the way it ended.

The MIAC opener against perennial power St. John's opened a few eyes around the league as the Ole defense was exceptionally tough in a 21–7 loss. Chris Hallgren picked off a Johnny pass on their first drive. His second first-quarter interception and 85-yard return for a touchdown put the Oles ahead 7–0.

St. John's put up 21 unanswered points in the second quarter as their special teams stepped up. That ended the scoring. The Ole defense allowed St. John's rushers an average of only one yard per carry for a total of 39. Jesse Bengston and Sven Bjorklund led the charge that sacked the Johnny quarterback eight times.

Meeting the conference toughies back to back, the Oles faced a powerful Concordia squad at Manitou Field. Overdoing the gracious host role, the Oles fumbled the opening kickoff, enabling the Cobbers to score in five plays and take an early lead.

In a turnabout from the St. John's contest the previous week, the Lions had problems with the Concordia rushing attack; the Cobbers rolled to 16 first downs and 346 yards on the ground. They led 24–0 at halftime en route to a 38–0 shutout.

The ' 90s and Beyond

Augsburg handed St. Olaf a second straight shutout in Minneapolis. The Auggie aerial attack with quarterback Lamker thowing principally to flanker Hvistendahl did much of the damage. Hvistendahl caught 15 passes for 207 yards and three touchdowns early in his career as a premier receiver in the MIAC. The Auggies broke the game open in the second quarter with three touchdowns, taking a 28–0 lead. St. Olaf managed only 196 yards in total offense and had three passes intercepted. The final was 42–0.

Facing a must-win situation versus Macalester at Homecoming, the defense played well and the offense came alive and the combination was good for a 19–3 victory. An initial safety was followed by a four-yard touchdown pass, Schultz to Cahoon, for a 9–0 lead. Nelson's field goal made it 12–0. A Schultz pass to Cahoon and runs by Walters and Winkler were highlights of a 73-yard drive climaxed by Hollom's 21-yard touchdown reception in the corner of the end zone. The Oles had 13 tackles for loss, including five sacks, two by Bjorkland. The offense gained 294 total yards.

St. Olaf and Hamline played to a 21–21 tie in regulation time, but the Pipers scored on a five-play drive in overtime to take a 27–21 victory.

The teams traded touchdowns early, Schultz scoring on a one-yard sneak

for the Lions. The Ole offense stalled, but just prior to intermission, Hollom returned a Piper punt 91 yards for a touchdown. Nelson's second PAT gave the Oles a 14–7 lead. Ryan finished the day with three pass receptions for 36 yards, two kickoff returns for 63 and 97, and three punt returns, including the 91-yarder for a touchdown. That performance earned him MIAC Special Teams Player of the Week honors.

The Bethel Royals overwhelmed St. Olaf 52–10 in a game played on Manitou Field. Haakon Nelson gave the Lions a brief 3–0 lead with a 27-yard field goal, but the Royals countered immediately with a 36-yard touchdown pass and increased their lead to 16–3 at the end of one quarter. Paul Minkler returned the ensuing kickoff 85 yards for a score, cutting the Bethel lead to 16–10. The second half was all Bethel; the Royals scored 36 points on five touchdowns, two by their defense.

With the Goat series standing at 39–34–1 in favor of Carleton and the Carls having won the last six games, the pressure was on to snap that string. A scoreless first half made it look as if no one would win. But then Hollom electrified the Laird Stadium crowd with an 85-yard return of the second-half kick-off for a touchdown. Carleton countered with a touchdown and a field goal to take a 10–7 lead, but this was to be the Oles' year. They drove 73 yards to

The eagle again faces St. Olaf, 1997

regain the lead on Minkler's 12-yard run. Nelson's conversion made it 14–10.

A Carleton threat was killed by Tollefson's interception at the St. Olaf two-yard line. The Oles took a safety, making the count 14–12, and kicked it away. The Knights brought the ball back to the Ole 13 with 12 seconds remaining. Their attempted field goal was wide left; the string was broken; the eagle would be turned.[172] The series count was narrowed to 39–35–1, still in favor of the Carls.

A good start against St. Thomas didn't hold up, as the Tommies were victorious 28–3. A good play call by Coach Miller put the ball on the St. Thomas 24-yard line in position for a Nelson field goal and a 3–0 lead. An Ole fumble and a stiff St. Thomas defense didn't allow the Ole offense to get on track. St. Thomas built a 14–3 halftime lead and increased it in the fourth period.

The finale against a strong passing Gustavus team was played in the Metrodome. St. Olaf scored first, marching 66 yards in seven plays, Schultz scoring on a sneak. But that was the extent of the Ole offensive punch; the Gusties were just beginning. A field goal and a pass play brought the halftime count to 10–6. Two more Gustie aerial scores made the count

Oles celebrate the return of the Goat, 1997

Paul Minkler advances the ball against Augsburg, 1998

24–6, and the final score was 37–6. A bright spot for the Oles was Minkler's 105 yards rushing, his first 100-plus rushing day.

Seniors who played their last game for St. Olaf were quarterback Pete Schultz, wide receiver Ivan Carter, tight end Rich Cahoon, offensive linemen Nick Johnson, Alfred Furth, and John Grombacker, linebacker Jesse Bengston, and defenders Chad Durgin, Chris Kodl, and Chris Hallgren. A young team in Coach Paul Miller's first season played good football. As Cully Swanson might have said, "Youse can tell by how they play that they have been coached well."

All-conference honors went to Ryan Hollom, Jesse Bengston, Rick Cahoon, and Chris Hallgren. Bengston was voted most valuable. Captains elected for the 1998 season were Paul Minkler, Darik Steinbach, Peter Schultz, and Ben Diederich.

1998

Coach Miller and his staff started their second season with a good mix of returning squad members and an outstanding recruiting class. Schultz, Hollom, Minkler, Hildebrandt, and Nelson were among the returnees. Flugum, Ryan, and Sprout were promising first-year men.

The season opener against Carthage at Kenosha, Wis., was sobering. A large and powerful Redmen squad handled the Oles 23–0. St. Olaf sustained a number of injuries, which contributed to the outcome.

Injuries continued to plague the Lions in the home opener against St. Thomas, but the team was more competitive than it had been against Carthage. The Tommies prevailed but only by 9–6. St. Olaf was held to seven yards and no first downs in the first half and went to the locker room on the short end of a 9–0 score.

Halftime adjustments and a more physical style of play on the part of the Oles tightened the contest after intermission. Fried picked off a St. Thomas aerial and sprinted 80 yards to score. It was Fried's second important defensive play. He had recovered a fumble in the first half. Schultz led his Ole mates on a march late in the game, and they had a chance to win it, but a field-goal attempt was tipped at the line of scrimmage and went wide.

Defending MIAC champion Augsburg brought a championship swagger and a talented passing combination to Manitou Field in the season's third encounter. They jumped to a 14–0 advantage in the first five minutes, but a beautiful pass-run play,

Schultz to Sprout, provided the Oles their first points, and a goal-line stand forced Augsburg to settle for only a field goal before intermission. The Oles were down 17–7 at halftime.

A rejuvenated Ole squad, led by halfback Jay Larsen, made a game of it the second half. Larsen scored twice, the first time on a 10-yard run. Haakon Nelson added a 30-yard field goal to narrow the count to 24–17, before Larsen struck again to tie the score. The Auggies' Drier sprinted 62 yards untouched to enable the Auggies to emerge 31–24.

Coach Miller commented, "Our guys got us to the fourth quarter; now we are just going to have to learn how to win."

It didn't happen the next week as the Lions dropped another close one, 33–28, to Bethel. The Royals scored first when the Oles were unable to capitalize on a recovered fumble on the opening kickoff, but Schultz's pass to Marc Davies got the Oles on the board, and they went ahead on a Schultz to Sprout pass. The Royals spurted for 20 second-quarter points to go up 27–21 at the half. They added a six-pointer before St. Olaf capped a 78-yard march with a 22-yard Schultz to Hollom pass. But again it was it was not quite enough.

Hollom caught six passes for 76 yards, while Larsen rushed for 92 yards. Quarterback Schultz had his best game of the year, completing 14 of 21 pass attempts, three for touchdowns. On the defense, Diederich, Young, Bjorklund, and Kukkenon had outstanding games.

A good-sized Concordia squad spoiled the Ole Homecoming with a 35–21 win. The Cobbers built a 20–0 lead, while the Ole offense, which had shown signs of explosiveness against Bethel, was held without a first down until just before halftime when Schultz passed to Davies to score with 0:27 to go in the half.

The teams traded touchdowns in the third period, Minkler scoring for St. Olaf, and again in the fourth when Schultz passed to Davies for 36 and a score with 6:12 remaining. Diederich and Bergan were among the leading Ole tacklers, accounting for five quarterback sacks.

A blocked PAT in overtime enabled the Hamline Pipers to squeak past the Lions 14–13. Hamline scored first, and the Oles matched that effort, and that concluded scoring in regulation time. The Oles scored first in overtime, but the point-after attempt was blocked. The Pipers countered and their PAT just cleared the oustretched hands of Ole defenders with enough lift to clear the bar.

Schultz passed for 145 yards and a touchdown. Hollom caught four aerials and piled up 172 yards of total offense. Defenders Diederich, Vatland, and Bergan were outstanding.

Winless in six outings, the atmosphere had to be somewhat grim going into the battle for the Goatrophy, but the pall was lifted as the Oles, benefiting from several outstanding individual performances, outpointed the Knights 21–7. In his first two seasons as Ole coach, Paul Miller would go 4–16, but

two of the wins were against Carleton. In his five years at the Ole helm, Miller and his charges would never lose to Carleton. Talk about having a team's number!

In this contest, a number of Oles stepped up to give best personal performances of the season. Ryan had six solo tackles and two interceptions to garner MIAC Defensive Player of the Week honors. Punter Hildebrandt had one for 55 yards at an important point in the game, and three of his kicks were inside the opponent's 10, a performance good for MIAC Special Teams Player of the Week. Schultz completed 14 of 17 throws for 190 yards and two touchdowns. Hollom caught six of Schultz's throws for 90 yards and a touchdown. Diederich had 12 tackles and Bergan, 10, including a huge sack near the end of the game. The defensive secondary had four interceptions, one returned for a touchdown by Vatland. Carleton's lead in the Goat series was narrowed to 39–36–1.

The elation over the Carleton victory diminished quickly the next

Saturday as conference-leading St. John's shut out the Oles 35–0.

The losing skein continued the following week against Gustavus. St. Olaf struck first with a 67-yard bomb, Schultz to Sprout. Gustavus retaliated quickly as quarterback Southworth threw three touchdown passes in five minutes to put the Gusties up 21–7. The Oles fought back, Schultz again finding Sprout, this time for 63 yards and a score. Not to be held down for long, the Gusties added three second-quarter touchdowns to take a 42–14 margin to the clubhouse at halftime. The Oles couldn't score in the second half, while Gustavus added another to make the final 49–14.

The Oles apparently found the confines of the Metrodome to their liking — at least this season. The annual MIAC Showcase there had Macalester as the St. Olaf opponent. The Lions reeled off three first-half touchdowns to take a 19–7 halftime lead. Schultz threw for all three counters — 20 yards to Ryan for the first, 67 yards to Sprout for the second,

The Oles take the field, 1998

Joe Hammond, 1999 MVP

Brian Sprout, 1999

Haakon Nelson, 1999

and back to Ryan, this time for 15 yards, for the third. All three completed drives of more than 50 yards.

The Oles and Scots traded touchdowns in the third period, and in the fourth, hard-running freshman Manuel Spreigl scored his first collegiate touchdown with 4:11 to play. The 33–14 win gave the Oles a 2–8 season — a won-lost record that belied the improvement made by this squad.

It was the last game for 12 seniors — Minkler, Steinbach, Schultz, Olson, Tollefson, Moseman, Manning, Evans, Bergan, Walters, Haugo, and Duce. Ryan Hollom, Jeremy Young, and Steve Ryan were named to the MIAC first all-conference team, while Sven Bjorklund, Brian Sprout, and Jeff Flugum were on the second team. Tabbed for honorable mention were Peter Schultz, Dave Bergan, Ben Diederich, and Dave Hildebrandt. Schultz was voted most valuable. Bjorklund and Diederich were named captains for 1999.

1999

Entering his third season, Paul Miller had a young and emerging squad. The past two seasons had seen well-coached teams that with a break or two would have posted better records. The first two games of '99 were disappointing, but there were encouraging signs.

Playing the second game of a home-and-home series with the Carthage Redmen, the Oles put up a safety and field goal early and led into the late stages of the contest. At that point, a Carthage drive broke a 14–14 tie and gave the Redmen a 21–14 victory.

St. Thomas, the MIAC opener opponent, walked away with a 33–3 victory. The Oles showed improvement but could not generate enough offense.

An offensive explosion, led by quarterback Joe Hammond in his first collegiate start, was not quite enough to down the high-flying Augsburg Auggies in a night game in Minneapolis. Hammond threw for 330 yards and two touchdowns, and Manuel Spreigl rushed for 104 yards on 15 carries. Brian Sprout caught two Hammond passes, one for a 52-yard touchdown, and sophomore Steve Ryan chipped in with five catches for 99 yards. It all added up to 480 yards of

total offense, but the Auggies managed to emerge on top, 30–27.

While the focus was on the offense, the defense played valiantly. Led by Lafferty, Young, Bjorklund, Picchietti, and Diederich, they held the Augsburg rushing attack to 75 yards.

The Oles persevered through two more losses, to Bethel and Concordia, before getting into the win column with a 25–20 victory over Hamline at Manitou Field.

Turnovers continued to be a thorn in the losing Homecoming battle with the Bethel Royals. Typical of the day was a good Ole drive which was ended by a fumble at the Bethel three. On the next play, a perfectly executed Bethel sweep went 97 yards for a score and a 27–6 lead. The final was 39–13. A bright spot for the Oles was Sprout's six receptions for 106 yards.

Playing their best football of the season, the Oles battled undefeated Concordia to a standstill before losing 17–10 at Jake Christiansen stadium in Moorhead. Hammond led the St. Olaf attack, completing 15 of 27 passes for 209 yards. Ryan was his favorite target. The sophomore grabbed six throws for 121 yards.

Hammond's three-yard touchdown run and a 28-yard field goal by Nelson gave the Oles a 10–7 halftime advantage, but an early third-quarter Concordia interception and a long 14-play march by the Cobbers enabled them to take the 17–10 win. A strong Ole defense was led by Young. Hollom had a 75-yard pass reception.

All phases of the Ole game finally came together, and the Hamline Pipers were the victims, as the Lions posted a 25–20 win at Manitou Field. Running back Spriegl carried 31 times for 127 yards; linebacker Greg Medeck made two big defensive plays; Dan Patnode blocked a punt, and senior kicker Haakon Nelson contributed two second-half field goals.

The Oles' ability to control the ball played an important role in the win, as they ran 82 plays to the Pipers' 65 and took advantage of four Hamline turnovers.

Using the Hamline victory as a springboard, the Oles made it three in a row over the Carleton Knights in the annual Goat battle. Carleton jumped to an

Brian Sprout runs against Hamline, 2001

early 10-point lead, but the Lions answered with 17 points, good for a seven-point halftime lead.

As usual, the game featured great individual efforts and emotion. In the second half, Patnode blocked a Carleton punt to set up a St. Olaf score, and a late interception by Jason Carlson sealed the victory. Young and Bjorklund pressured the Knight quarterback all afternoon — each credited with two sacks. The victory narrowed the Carleton advantage in the series to two games, 39–37–1.

Buoyed by a two-game win streak, the Oles marched into Clemens Stadium in Collegeville and stood toe to toe with the 15th ranked Johnnies before losing 21–14 in a well-played game.

The Oles moved the ball well against the Johnny defense, but they also stymied themselves with five turnovers. A 14-play, 72-yard drive, with Cordell Hunkins scoring, tied the game at seven. Two plays after a St. John's turnover, Hammond threw to Sprout for a 17-yard touchdown and Nelson's PAT gave the Lions a 14–7 lead. The second half was an epic defensive battle, but the Johnnies scored twice to take it.

It was a great football game and a tough loss, but there were some bright spots: Hammond was 21 of 28 for 207 yards, Sprout racking up 118 of them. Defensively, Carlson had two

interceptions and 12 tackles, while Bjorklund had two sacks. Nickel's punting was outstanding.

In the 46th meeting of St. Olaf and Gustavus, the Gusties won 36–17 and kept their MIAC title hopes alive. The game was closer than the score might indicate. St. Olaf led 10–0 after the first quarter on a 39-yard Nelson field goal and an 11-yard Hammond to Ryan aerial. The Gusties responded with 22 unanswered points, but the Oles fought back, cutting the lead to 22–17, as Hammond found Ryan again for a touchdown, this one from 34 yards out.

Gustavus scored the last 14 points. St. Olaf had two fourth-quarter chances with drives deep into Gustie territory, but each time an interception blunted the thrust.

The offensive firepower that had been lurking all season, but only evidenced sporadically, exploded again in a 47–14 win over Macalester in the season's final contest at the Metrodome. Hammond had the hot hand again, completing 18 of 26 throws for 354 yards and five touchdowns, not surprisingly earning him MIAC Offensive Player of the Week honors. Ryan caught six for 141 yards. Freshman Tim Baer came off the bench in relief of the injured Spriegl and scored his first touchdown in the third quarter.

Nine seniors closed out their St. Olaf careers: John Kukkenon, Sven Bjorklund, Ryan Hollom, Scott Syverson, Cory Ristau, Andy Masis, Tom Erickson, Ben Diederich, Aaron Crowser, and Haakon Nelson. Joe Hammond was tabbed most valuable player.

The 1999 season was one of highs and lows. Defeating Hamline after five heartbreaking losses was a plus. Keeping the Goat for a third consecutive season had meaning for the seniors. The sting of tough losses to Concordia and St. John's was somewhat offset by the knowledge that the squad had played well in defeat.

2000

The first season of the new millennium was also the first in which Coach Paul Miller's Oles would be a veteran team. Numerous juniors and seniors who had performed as regulars returned. That experience showed in the opener, a 21–9 victory over Martin Luther College. Hammond and Spriegl, two of the chief offensive weapons, took up where they had left off. Hammond hit on 14 of 21 passes for 223 yards, while Spriegl piled up 124 yards rushing and scored one touchdown to earn MIAC Offensive Player of the Week designation. Doug Wolgamot led a stout defense that limited the Knights to 285 total yards; the Oles had 411.

St. John's struck early and often in defeating the Oles 42–6 in the conference opener. The Johnnies blocked a St. Olaf punt and took it in quickly. They crossed the final stripe four more times to lead 35–0 at halftime. The lone Ole tally came late in the game when Spriegl scored from the five. The Oles suffered a major blow in the

Defensive back Matt Hofkens intercepts against Augsburg, 2001

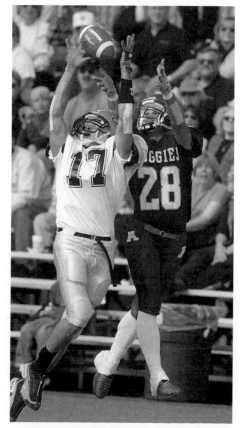

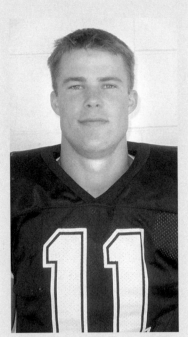

Steve Ryan, 2000 MIAC Most Valuable Player, the first Ole to win that distinction.

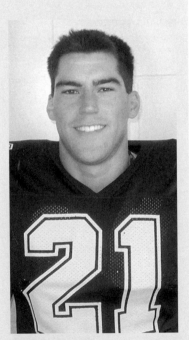

Manuel Spreigl, 2000 St. Olaf MVP

second half when Hammond left with a separated shoulder.

Freshman Brian Senske stepped into the quarterback position after Hammond's injury and had a bravura performance in his first college start, leading the Oles to a 28–18 win over the Hamline Pipers. Senske was 17 of 28 passing for 260 yards. Adding to an outstanding offensive game, Spriegl ran for 174 yards from scrimmage and scored twice. Total offense for the Oles was 508. Defensively, Wolgamot shone again with two interceptions. Cory Dingle had one.

On a beautiful Homecoming day on Manitou Field, the Oles came into their own in dismantling Augsburg 28–6. While the offense equaled its season's high, it was the defense that led the way, limiting a potent Augsburg attack to two field goals. Young, Moseman, and Hoagberg kept the Auggie quarterback, Tetzloff, scrambling all afternoon. Jake Roth and the secondary also played a major role in limiting the Auggie offense. Spriegl had 199 yards rushing, including a 67-yard jaunt in the third quarter. Senske continued his outstanding play, and Ryan caught a 40-yard pass for a touchdown in the third period.

A 32–2 defeat by Bethel was a blip, albeit a major one, as the Oles rolled inexorably toward their first winning season since 1991. The nationally ranked Royals mounted an error-free attack, while the Oles got into scoring position on five occasions but came up virtually empty.

Good fundamental football produced a 24–15 win over St. Thomas and put the Oles in third place in the MIAC standings. Defeating the Tommies was well and good, but more impressive was the manner in which it was done — not with finesse or trick plays, but with solid, physical play.

The offensive line of Ward, Flugum, Landsteiner, Hubbard, and Rafe consistently opened running lanes for Spreigl and Jay Larsen, who had 134 and 68 yards, respectively.

Senske's passing, 10 of 20 for 241 yards, added to the heroics by Spreigl and Larsen, made for a devastating two-pronged attack. Linebacker Lafferty and defensive back Thomas kept the St. Thomas running offense in check.

The Troll trophy, emblematic of victory in the annual St. Olaf-Concordia battle, accompanied the Oles on the ride back from Moorhead after a thrilling come-from-behind victory over the Cobbers.

Prospects looked dim after the Cobbers went up 21–0, but the Ole defense stiffened and allowed the hosts only 44 total yards in the second half. Meanwhile, the Lions gradually made up the deficit. They still trailed 24–19 with just over two minutes to play. Senske led his team in a brilliant two-minute drill, culminating with a 12-yard scoring strike to Ryan with 20 seconds left. "We made big play after big play on the drive," Jake Roth explained.

A 34–10 victory over Macalester assured the Oles of a winning season. The big offensive line that had made the running game go against St. Thomas did it again as the Oles totaled 189 yards rushing. They also protected Senske well. Mac had an early 3–0 lead, but a 15-play drive with Spreigl scoring from three yards out put St. Olaf in the lead for good. A three-man rush kept the Scots in check all afternoon.

In the annual Metrodome game, the Oles and Gustavus hooked up in a remarkable offensive show — 891 yards of offense: eight touchdown passes and 77 points — but the Oles came out on the short end of the count, 42–35.

Senske hit on 18 of 30 passes for 229 yards and three touchdowns. Ryan caught nine for 118 yards, and Spreigl rushed for 105. Defensively, Lafferty and Meyers led in tackles.

The Carleton clash was much more than another chapter in the storied Ole-Carl rivalry. In defeating the Knights 42–35, the Ole seniors joined the 1980 class as the last to defeat Carleton four consecutive years.

Spreigl set a conference record by scoring six touchdowns and amassing 253 yards on 37 carries. One was a 98-yard jaunt set up by linebacker Lafferty's third-quarter interception. As in the past, Spreigl's success was helped greatly by outstanding line play. The defense, led by linebackers Lafferty and Medick, kept an ever-dangerous Carleton passing game at bay.

The Ole win narrowed the Carleton margin in the series to a single game, 39–38–1. It was a great way to end a 7–3 season, 6–3 in the conference, good for third place.

It was a tough way for Carleton coach Bob Sullivan to end his outstanding Carleton career. Sullivan had done an admirable job of turning out respected, well-coached squads at Carleton for 21 years.

Manny Spreigl was named MVP of the 2000 squad, and Steve Ryan became the first Ole to win the MIAC MVP honor. Captains who showed great leadership were Jeff Flugum, Joe Hammond, Chris Nickel, Brian Sprout, and Jeremy Young.

2001

Coming off the 7–3 2000 season and with 17 regulars returning, the hopes and expectations for 2001 were high. Offensive leaders such as Ryan, Spreigl, Sprout, and Senske were back, as was Hammond, following the shoulder injury which had cut short his 2000 season. Linebackers Lafferty and Meyers, along with four-year starting defensive backs Dingles and Vatland, returned as defensive stalwarts.

The home and season opener was a confident 35–21 triumph over Martin Luther. Big plays and sustained marches characterized the win. Hammond and Senske, sharing the quarterback duties, threw for a combined 317 yards and four touchdowns. Brian Sprout made his comeback from a sidelined 2000 season a good one with five receptions and two touchdowns. Tight end Marc Davies scored the season's first touchdown on a five-yard pass from Hammond. Senske's first offensive play was a 53-yard touchdown pass to Ryan. The Oles led 28–7 at halftime and cruised from there. All units played good, solid football.

The conference opener was a momentous game as St. Olaf defeated St. John's 31–28 at Collegeville. Sean Kooman's 22-yard field goal with 41 seconds left broke the 28–28 tie. The win was the Oles' first over St. John's

Manuel Spreigl in action, 2001

since 1995 and the first at Clemens Stadium since 1986. Kooman's kick was preceded by a 75-yard, 16-play drive that ended with a spectacular reception by Jeff Schmidt.

St. John's had come back from an early 13–0 Ole lead, but stout defensive play made them earn every point. The Oles rolled up 497 yards on 97 plays, compared to the Johnnies' 313 on 51 plays. Longtime Ole play-by-play announcer Mike Morrisey of KDHL radio summed up the situation. Quoted in the *Manitou Messenger* for Sept. 21, 2001, Morrisey said, "My life is now complete; the Oles win in Collegeville." Ryan and Kooman were selected as MIAC Players of the Week.

St. Olaf moved to 3–0 with a unique 33–12 win over the Hamline Pipers. The game was stopped by the officials midway through the second quarter because of lightning and thunderstorm conditions. The score was tied at 6–6. By NCAA rules, games are suspended when lightning is present. If the conditions persist for more than 30 minutes, play is suspended until the following day. In this case, the weather was unrelenting, so the remainder of the game was postponed until Sunday afternoon.

When the game resumed, the Oles struck quickly to move to the convincing win. Senske hit Ryan twice on scoring strikes, the first a beautiful

Paul Miller resigns in 2001 as head coach after five seasons at St. Olaf

Head Coach Chris Meidt, 2002

62-yard bomb, and then Spreigl ran in from the seven.

The three season-opening victories were followed by three disappointing losses — a 20–0 shutout at the hands of Augsburg, a 38–6 blowout by the Bethel Royals, and a 28–16 loss to St. Thomas.

Augsburg took advantage of six St. Olaf turnovers — four fumbles and two interceptions — and sacked Senske six times in limiting the Ole attack to only 193 yards. A mishandled punt led to one Auggie score, and an interception set up another. Ole punter Nate Johnson was forced to kick nine times. Meyers, Vatland, and Lafferty led in tackles.

The defending conference champion and nationally ranked Bethel Royals were at the top of their game in spoiling the Ole Homecoming with a 38–6 thumping. The Royals scored twice before Spreigl's run gave St. Olaf its only points of the day. The tough Bethel defense limited the Oles to 228 yards of total offense. Senske left the game in the second quarter and did not return.

St. Thomas handed the Oles their third straight loss, 28–16, at O'Shaughnessy Stadium in St. Paul. The Oles came out of the blocks with a rush and took a 3–0 lead on Kooman's 32-yard field goal. After St. Thomas retaliated to go ahead 7–3 at the half, Hammond returned from a hand injury and hit Ryan on a 53-yard pass play. The Tommies came right back with a 64-yard march for a score and won going away.

The Oles lost linebacker Bill Germscheid with a concussion on the second play of the game. Owen Buckmaster replaced Germscheid and recorded eight tackles and a sack for a loss of 11 yards.

As if to get the bad taste of that game out of their mouths, the Oles edged Concordia for the second consecutive year, 34–33.

Moving quickly to continue their winning ways, the Oles disposed of the Macalester Scots 35–18. Spreigl had another banner game, 168 yards and four touchdowns, and senior wide receiver Brian Sprout also had a big day with 121 yards receiving and one touchdown.

Paul Miller Resigns in Fifth Season

With two games to go in his fifth season as head man of the Oles, Coach Paul Miller announced his resignation effective at the close of the season. The Nov. 2, 2001, *Messenger* carried the news and the regrets of Cindy Book, director of athletics.

"We are very sad that Paul is leaving St. Olaf," Book said. "He has done a tremendous job of helping our football program return to its winning tradition."

Miller had compiled an 18–29 won-lost record, but it was not indicative of the outstanding coaching job Paul and his staff had done. In an MIAC conference ever increasing in strength, Paul had turned out St. Olaf squads that were always well prepared and competitive.

Going out with a bang, Coach Miller presided over his Oles' fifth consecutive win over Carleton by a decisive 28–6. Ryan scored twice in the first quarter on passes from Hammond. Spreigl scored on a five-yard run in the third period and on an 18-yard screen pass in the fourth. The Knights didn't score until 5:48 of the final period.

The victory evened the Goat series at 39–39–1. In his tenure at St. Olaf, Paul Miller's teams had erased a five-game deficit.

A season-ending loss to Gustavus was almost an anti-climax. It was not the way 26 seniors and Coach Miller wanted to end their St. Olaf careers, but the Gusties and a hot quarterback put together a 37-point first half and won 51–27. Spreigl ended the game with 141 rushing yards and two touchdowns to cap a brilliant season — 1,045 yards and 17 touchdowns, surpassing 3,000 yards for his career. Sprout had 62 yards receiving and Ryan 42 for the day and 945 yards and nine touchdowns for the season. Lafferty, Meyers, and Busselman were leading tacklers for the season. It was a 6–4 season and a 4–4 conference mark, good for fifth place.

Jeff Flugum, Matt Lafferty, Steve Ryan, and Manuel Spreigl won all-conference recognition with Jim Struble, Dan Meyers, Marc Davies, and Jake Landsteiner tabbed for honorable mention. Spreigl was again named MVP.

Cordell Hunkins outruns the Augsburg defense, 2002

2002
Chris Meidt Named Head Coach

After Paul Miller's departure, the college named Chris Meidt, former standout quarterback and graduate of Bethel College, the next head coach of the football Oles. Meidt had solid coaching experience — seven years as offensive coordinator at his alma mater, during which Bethel won back-to-back MIAC championships in 2000 and 2001. Meidt's playing/coaching background and personal character made him a good fit for St. Olaf.

Coach Meidt inherited a corps of experienced regulars, notable among them quarterback Brian Senske, Matt Lafferty, Cordell Hunkins, Tim Baer, and Chad Thomas. The new coaching staff and squad made good preseason progress and opened the season on an up-note with a 57–14 victory over Carroll College of Waukesha, Wis. The Oles had 438 yards of total offense against Carroll, and Senske picked up where he had left off as a sophomore, completing a dozen passes for four touchdowns.

The annual Goat game came early in the schedule, but Meidt and the Oles were pumped from the win over Carroll and shut out the Knights 49–0. The offense surpassed the pace set in

the first game, amassing 440 yards. The Oles jumped to a 21–0 first-quarter lead on touchdown passes to Hunkins and Bass. The defense was equally impressive, allowing only 38 rushing yards. With the victory, St. Olaf went back ahead in the intracity series, 40–39–1.

Continuing their winning string, the Oles edged Augsburg 23–21, avenging a 2001 defeat. The Oles built a 10–0 halftime lead, but after intermission, the contest turned into a real

battle. The Auggies scored twice in the third period, but the Oles added a pair of touchdowns of their own in the final period to take the win.

Athletics Complex Named for Christenson

A special ceremony at halftime of the Augsburg game honored legendary pioneer coach/administrator Ade Christenson by naming the entire campus east-side athletic facility the Ade Christenson Athletics Complex. The extended Christenson family was present for the naming ceremony. A comprehensive article, "Ade Christenson Athletics Complex," is included in the Sept. 27, 2002, issue of the *Manitou Messenger.*

An early 13–0 lead was encouraging but unsustainable as the Oles battled through rain and wind against an unstoppable St. John's squad. The Johnnies started slow but gained momentum and carved out a 59–20 victory. The defense got the Oles off to a great start as interceptions by Chad Thomas and Kipp Pennou led to scores, Pennou's an 82-yard return for a touchdown. Another defensive stand-out was freshman John Davis with two steals. Turnovers played a pivotal role, and St. John's capitalized on each one.

Frank Bass advances following a reception, 2002

A large and boisterous Homecoming crowd was not enough encouragement as St. Thomas further dampened a wet afternoon with a 35–15 win. The Tommies took a 14-point lead into halftime and extended it after intermission. A bright spot for the Oles was an 89-yard interception return for a touchdown by Lafferty.

Coach Meidt's former team, the Bethel Royals, evened the Oles' season mark at 3–3 by scoring last to eke out a 36–32 win in a shootout. The two teams totaled over 800 yards of offense. For the Oles, Senske threw for 278 yards, while Jason Moore carried 18 times for 67 tough yards. Hunkins pounded the Bethel defense for three touchdowns, and Frank Bass had a record-setting

day, grabbing 14 passes for 197 yards. Bethel's running attack, featuring Mike Johnson, was nearly unstoppable.

Rebounding from the Bethel loss, the Oles put together a two-game winning streak, downing Hamline 48–12 and Macalester 34–6 to run the season mark to 5–3. Both games were highlighted by strong defensive play on the part of the Oles.

The last home game of the season versus Concordia was similar to the Bethel game — an Ole offense riding the accurate arm of Senske competing with the ball control ground game favored by the Cobbers. Senske passed for 275 yards, including 12 completions to Bass. Concordia's backs rushed for nearly 400 yards in the 24–14 Cobber

victory. Chad Thomas led a tough Ole defense with 10 tackles.

The season finale, an 8 p.m., game against Gustavus at the Metrodome, saw the Oles lose a heartbreaker 24–23 in the final minutes. After stopping the Gusties twice in the red zone in the last seven minutes, the Oles didn't hold on the third attempt. An eight-yard pass and a successful PAT were the difference.

In a valiant effort, Senske passed 36 times and completed 19 for a season-high 312 yards. Bass had his fifth straight 100-yards-plus game with 11 receptions. Bass was named the MIAC Offensive Player of the Week.

The Gustavus loss ended a streaky season — three season-opening wins followed by three losses, then two wins and a pair of losses. It added up to a .500 season overall, but only 3–5 in the MIAC.

Lafferty and Meyers won first-team, all-conference recognition, while Tilman Achberger, Senske, Bass, Dave Busselman, Chad Thomas, and Nate Johnson were designated second teamers. Honorable mention went to Matt Deon, Bill Germscheid, Hunkins, and Paterson. Voted MVP was Frank Bass. Germscheid and Senske were named captains for 2003. Acting as captains for the 2002 campaign were Neal Olson, Jeff Schmidt, Owen Buchmaster, Chad Thomas, Tim Baer, Reggie Fuller, Cordell Hunkins, and Matt Lafferty.

2003

As Chris Meidt entered his second year at the helm, optimism was high that the squad could improve on the 5–5 2002 finish. The difference between 5–5 and 8–2 could be attributed to the last minutes of a few games. Senior quarterback Brian Senske returned to pilot an explosive offense.

Receivers Paterson, Lund, and Fritze would again be good targets for the all-time leading St. Olaf passer, Senske. Co-captain Bill Germscheid was back to lead a defense that included experienced players such as Achberger, Busselman, Dean, and Chapman.

Brian Senske, 2002, owner of all St. Olaf passing records except one

Tilman Achberger leads Bobby Andrade against Carleton, 2003

The season opened on a down note as Luther took a 23–10 decision in Decorah. The Norse jumped to a two-touchdown lead in the first quarter. The Oles fought back with Dan O'Malley's 37-yard field goal in the second period and pulled within four points on an 80-yard drive capped by Aaron Stinar's score from the one.

Late in the third period, Luther completed a short pass that turned into an 83-yard touchdown play, due to missed tackles by the Oles. The Norse tacked on a field goal early in the final period.

Quarterback Senske led the Ole attack with 205 passing yards on 16 completions. Kyle Fritze caught four of Senske's throws for 80 yards to lead the receiving corps. Germscheid paced the Ole defense with 14 tackles; Matt Willis had 10.

The season equalizer came in the home opener the next week as the Oles downed Carleton 40–16 for their seventh consecutive victory in the intracity series. To add to the rivalry, local industry Malt-O-Meal sponsored a Cereal Bowl traveling trophy to augment the Goat.

Senske directed the Oles on an early 80-yard drive and took it in himself to put St. Olaf ahead. The Knights answered on their first drive of the second quarter, but by halftime, it was 26–9, and the Oles had the

game well in hand. Stinar scored his second of the day, and a Senske pass to Lund ended the Ole scoring. The win opened a two-game margin for the Oles in the 81-game series, 41–39–1.

Augsburg scored 18 unanswered second-half points to overcome an 11-point St. Olaf lead and defeat the Oles 31–24 in Minneapolis. The Oles outgained the Auggies with 360 yards of offense but couldn't find a way to keep their opponents out of the end zone. Trailing 13–0 in the second quarter, St. Olaf scored three times to go ahead 24–13 on touchdowns by Stinar and Lund and an O'Malley field goal. But then Augsburg turned on the power and scored three times to put the game away.

A Homecoming crowd packed the Manitou Field stands at the Ade Christenson Athletics Complex. Unfortunately, nationally ranked St. John's detracted from the spirit of the day as they amassed 553 yards of offense (379 rushing) to down St. Olaf 45–6. The Johnnies led 24–6 at the half and added 21 in the second half while holding the Oles scoreless. A 71-yard drive with Bobby Andrade scoring late in the second quarter was the lone St. Olaf tally.

A dominating Ole defense allowed St. Thomas a mere 58 yards and one first down in the first half while cashing a 27-yard O'Malley field goal for a 3–0 lead. But it all went for naught as the Tommies' offense came to life in the

second half and converted two of three interceptions to take a 14–3 lead. Stinar's six-yard run on the end of an 83-yard drive narrowed the gap, but the hosts scored twice more to pull away to a 27–9 victory.

St. Olaf won the statistical battle but lost the war, 33–7, in a mudfest with the Bethel Royals. The difference in the game was in the play of the special teams. An Andrade punt return was called back by penalty, and Bethel blocked a punt to set up a score.

With only one win in five outings, the smoldering Oles scorched Hamline 43–13. The game produced two MIAC Players of the Week — quarterback Senske on offense and punter Johnson on special teams. Senske passed for 253 yards and three touchdowns. Johnson averaged 44.5 yards per punt and 57 yards on six kickoffs.

After putting on a dazzling aerial display against Hamline, the Oles unleashed a 358-yard ground attack to subdue Macalester 47–14 and take their second victory in a row.

The Oles had 597 yards of total offense, the most impressive note being the 320 all-purpose yards racked up by freshman Nick Rost. Rost had 131 yards receiving, 93 rushing, and 96 in kick returns — punt and kickoff.

The two-game victory string was shattered abruptly the following week. The Concordia Cobbers piled up 531 yards of offense, the Oles obviously

Coach Meidt and offense, 2003

unable to blunt a high-powered attack.

Concordia scored 24 unanswered points in the first half. The Oles finally got on the scoreboard in the third period when Stinar scored on a 10-yard run. A Senske to Fritze pass was good for the two-point conversion. The Cobbers answered with a touchdown of their own and added a three-pointer to take a 33–8 lead. They added seven more in the fourth period before the Oles countered with a 37-yard pass from quarterback Jason Wilsey to Rost.

Running back Andrade led Ole rushers with 63 yards on 17 carries. That performance put Andrade over 1,000 yards from scrimmage for the season. Senske was eight of nine for 59 yards. Wilsey was four of five for 60 yards and a touchdown. Rost led all receivers with eight catches for 89 yards and a touchdown.

The Ole defense came to the fore in the season's final game. Senior co-captain Germscheid, in particular, had a memorable performance in the final

Tilman Achberger snaps the ball for Dan O'Malley (photo courtesy of Ann Germscheid)

game of his career. Germscheid recovered a fumble and returned it 19 yards for a touchdown, intercepted two passes, taking one in to score from 42 yards out, had four tackles and one sack.

The Gusties scored first, but the Oles retaliated with a 14-play, 87-yard march, culminating in a 17-yard Senske to Fritze pass. Rost rushed for a two-point conversion and an 8–7 lead. Stinar's 10-yard run and a 59-yard bomb, Senske

to Paterson, padded the lead. Gustavus pulled to within nine at 22–13, but could get no closer as St. Olaf tacked on three more touchdowns to put the game out of reach. The final was 41–27.

The victory snapped a long string of Ole losses to Gustavus. It also marked the first win at St. Peter since 1985. Bill Germscheid was named MVP, and seven men were named to the All-MIAC second team — Brian Senske, Bobby Andrade, Matt Schraan, John Davis, Tilman Achberger, Bill Germscheid, and Dave Busselman.

Brian Senske ended his senior season and his career owning all St. Olaf passing records except one — single-game yardage. His career passing total of 6,780 yards and single season total of 1,422 were both new St. Olaf marks. Both topped the previous marks set by Keith Karpinski. Karpinski remains the single-game passing yardage record-holder with 448 set in 1993. Pete Cathcart, Charlie Krois, Matt Bucka, and Kyle Fritze were named captains for 2004.

2003 seniors with the Goatrophy and the Cereal Bowl (photo courtesy of Ann Germscheid)

PART III — REFLECTION

Chapter 8: Telling the World

As the Vikings or the Lions or the Oles have triumphed or gone down to defeat on the field, St. Olaf has always maintained a healthy respect for the importance of letting people know about it — win or lose. The theory is that if "they" know us for our athletes' accomplishments, good sportsmanship, and wholesome effort, the reputation of the college will be enhanced, even though athletics is not our main business here.

It has also been considered important to cultivate the respect of the professional press people — writers and broadcasters — who actually produce the "first draft of history," as someone has called the daily press. The best way to do that, everyone agrees, is to be right, to be dependable, and to be available. If one earns that reputation, the men and women of the press will often beat a path to that person's door. Consequently, accuracy, dependability, availability have been the watchwords of the men and women who have publicized football on Manitou Heights.

The duties of those people have varied with the years and the needs and the people involved. Some sports publicists at St. Olaf have traveled with the teams; some haven't. Others have served as maitre d' in the press box, kept and distributed statistics, taken pictures. Some haven't. Some have reported scores and action in great detail; others have delegated those

duties to student assistants. But all of them have operated with those watchwords — accuracy, dependability, availability — clearly in mind.

The decade of the 1960s could be characterized as a great leap forward in the publicizing of St. Olaf athletics, in particular football and basketball. And three people were especially instrumental in it. They were Hal Bly, news service director and sports information director; Jack Laugen, assistant vice president for college relations, and Fred Gonnerman, director of information services.

All three men were involved in negotiations which led to play-by-play broadcasts of St. Olaf football and basketball games by KDHL Radio in Faribault. That practice continues today and is an important factor in keeping the sound of Ole athletics before the regional audience.

Bly was the moving force behind a coup that was the envy of many Minnesota colleges circa 1967. Hal observed that the small colleges didn't get much coverage in the metro dailies. He approached the *Minneapolis Tribune* and the *St. Paul Pioneer Press* and asked if he got them a good action picture of Saturday's St. Olaf grid game, would they use it in their Sunday morning editions. They said, "If you get it here by 5, we'll see …"

Bly instigated a plan which worked to the great advantage of

St. Olaf for the next decade or so. Student photographers shot action during the first half of home games, dashed back to the darkroom in the administration building, developed the film, quick dried it with hair dryers, and got prints back to Bly in the press box by game's end — around 4 p.m. Bly wrote cutlines for the pictures and sent a student to Minneapolis and St. Paul with pictures.

St. Olaf was the only Division III college in the state to have an action photo in the two dailies every Sunday after home games well into the 1970s — when competition forced the dailies to discontinue that coverage.

As luck would have it, the value of that exclusive St. Olaf picture coverage in the Twin Cities dailies was enhanced by what happened on the field. It was an era of dominance by the Oles in Midwest Conference football — the era of three consecutive Midwest Conference championships (1969, 1970, and 1971) and title contention in virtually every other season.

The athletes and coaches on the field produced a superlative product, and it was the talent and hard work of Bly, Gonnerman, and Laugen and others who preceded and followed them, that made the world aware of it in creative ways. It was another example of great teamwork, and St. Olaf was the beneficiary.

Clint Sathrum in action, 1953

The old Manitou Fieldhouse, circa 1987

*An aerial view of the Ade Christenson Athletics Complex, featuring the new Manitou Field and Fieldhouse, 2000
(photo by Mike Mihelich '82)*

Chapter 9: A Personal Note From Coach Porter

The summary of St. Olaf football, from the early student interest to the first official intercollegiate team in 1919, to the past season of 2003. Why write about it?

After spending forty years of my life on the firing line of athletics, it seems only natural that I should try to give recognition to the game itself and to those from whom I have benefited and with whom I shared the experience.

The game, and all it involves, is important. It is important to those players and coaches who have experienced the joy of victory, the agony of defeat, and, above all, the camaraderie of always striving to do their best and enjoying the struggle of athletic competition. It is important, also, to the institution represented by those players and coaches who, in this case, comprised the teams that carried the St. Olaf banner.

So, we have tried to recognize the game for the benefits it can impart to people, to institutions, and to society and then to give credit to all those players and coaches who participated at St. Olaf, especially those legendary men in the early years who saw the potential and followed through on their vision.

Among those adventurous, and in many ways audacious, souls were Endre Anderson, Ade Christenson, Cully Swanson, Frank Cleve, Bernie Cole, Mark Almlie, Syl Saumer, John Kirkeby and many, many others. Their names deserve to be set in type, if not etched in stone, for the contributions they have made, so that those who follow can realize the foundation and traditions from which they benefit.

Football at St. Olaf and at other NCAA Division III colleges is the remnant of what intercollegiate athletics was meant to be: amateur athletics for the student athletes and their student

friends and their faculty and staff members, athletics as a part of the college educational experience.

As Ade Christenson once stated, "I like to think of football as a course in the total educational curriculum, and even though this course is different in that you are scored in public, weekly examinations only on the basis of win or lose, the possible achievement is far more than that alone. The increasing capacity as football players, AND AS MEN, is the ultimate goal of this great sport, just as surely as is the immediate and strived for goal of victory."

So, our attempt here has been to trace the history and the context of football at St. Olaf as a way of paying tribute to the game and the people. We have tried to include many names, all the time realizing that there are many others just as important, just as worthy, just as significant but whose inclusion, for a variety of reasons, didn't fit the requirements of the narrative.

At the end of a successful 80-yard offensive drive, it is easy to recognize and mention who scored the touchdown, who kicked the PAT, who made a contributing pass, catch, or run. But, football being the ultimate team game, it is an axiom that the players in the

"trenches" certainly had done their job on that drive — made their blocks, protected the passer — even though they are not always recognized or their names noted. I certainly realize this, because I was one of those people.

The same holds true for the value of assistant coaches. The win and loss results are wrongly identified with the head coach. All players and coaches are involved in the results, positive or not. Loyalty is a strong factor in a football program — loyalty to oneself as a player or coach, loyalty to the principle of giving one's best, loyalty to one's team and the college. Therefore, we have included, in the Appendix if not in the narrative, names of all assistant coaches and all men who have played football for St. Olaf College.

Allow me to close with the following statement from an unknown author. I received it in a down time of a season. It puts the roles of the coach and the player in the proper perspective and implies, perhaps, the ultimate rationale for this book:

"When I grow tired, as I occasionally do; when I got discouraged, as once in a while happened, there was one never-failing source of inspiration upon which I learned to rely and which always sent me back into the fray with renewed strength and determination.

"It was a very simple thing. I would merely close my eyes and call up from the depths of memory of former teams the myriad faces which have passed before me for so many years. The bright, fresh, questing faces of the young men with whom I have lived and worked."

— *It has been worthwhile.*

Promoting the game against Luther, 1923

Intensity on the sidelines in the 1970s

PART IV — APPENDIX

Footnotes

Chapter 1

1. Roberts, J.M., *History of Europe* (1997, Penguin Grp.) p. 364.
2. *Ibid.*
3. Encarta, 2001.
4. Boorstin, Daniel, *Timetables of History* (1995, Simon & Shuster) pp. 388–89.
5. Danzig, Allison, *The History of American Football* (1956, Prentice Hall) p. 5–11. The facts and some language involving the transformation of rugby to football and its establishment in the U.S. are taken from this volume.

Chapter 2

6. Shaw, Joseph M., *History of St. Olaf College, 1874–1974* (1974, St. Olaf College Press, Northfield, Minn.) p. 49.
7. Shaw, op.cit., p. 50.
8. Wessing, C.M., Manitou *Messenger*, (MM) Vol. V, No. 7 (October 1891), p. 109.
9. *MM*, Vol. VII, No. 7 (October 1893), p. 105.
10. *MM*, op. cit. p. 124.
11. *Ibid.*
12. *Ibid.*, p.116.
13. *MM*, Vol. 10, No. 7 (Oct. 1896), p. 100.
14. *Ibid.*
15. *Ibid.*, p. 107.
16. Viking (yearbook) 1904, P. 164.
17. *Ibid.*, p. 166.
18. *Ibid.*, p. 156.
19. *Ibid.*, p. 152.
20. Danzig, *op.cit.*, p. 29.
21. St. Olaf *Catalog*, May 1908, pp. 20–21.
22. *MM*, Vol. 29, No. 6, Dec. 1911, p. 247.
23. *Ibid.*, p. 155.
24. *MM*, Vol. 27, No. 4. Dec. 1914, pp. 258–260.
25. *MM*, Vol. 29, No. 5, Nov. 1915, p. 195.

Chapter 3

26. Faculty Meeting Minutes, Oct. 12, 1917, p. 204.
27. Letter from President Lauritz Vigness to Rev. N.E. Boe, Oct. 24, 1917.
28. *MM*, Vol. 31, No. 15, Oct. 16, 1917.
29. Faculty Meeting Minutes, Oct. 25, 1917, p. 205.
30. Faculty Meeting Minutes, Nov. 8, 1917, p. 206.
31. Letter from President Vigness to Rev. J. A. Aasgaard, Jan. 9, 1918.
32. Faculty Meeting Minutes, June 21, 1918.
33. *MM*, Vol. 32, No. 2, Oct. 22, 1918.
34. *Viking*, 1919, 1920, 1921.
35. *Ibid.*
36. *MM*, Vol. 32, No. 20, April 29, 1919.
37. *Ibid.*, p. 1.
38. *MM*, Vol. 33, No. 1, Sept. 18, 1919.
39. *MM*, Vol 33, No. 3, Sept. 30, 1919.
40. *Ibid.*, No. 6, Oct. 21, 1919. p. 1.
41. *Ibid.*, No. 7, Oct. 28, 1919., p. 1.
42. *Ibid.*, No. 9, Nov. 11, 1919. p. 1.
43. *Ibid.*, No 12, Dec. 2, 1919. p. 1.

Chapter 4

44. Hollingsworth, Lloyd, *Gustavus Athletics: A Century of Building the Gustie Tradition 1880–1980* (1984, Gustavus Adolphus College Press) p. 77.
45. *Ibid.*, p. 78.
46. Jarchow, Merrill E., *Private Liberal Arts Colleges in Minnesota* (Minnesota Historical Society) p. 53.

Chapter 5

47. *MM*, Vol 34, No. 4, Oct. 5, 1920, p.1.
48. *Ibid.*, No. 6, Oct. 19, 1920, p. 1.
49. *Ibid.*, No. 7, Oct. 26, 1920, p. 1.
50. *Ibid.*, No. 8, Nov. 2, 1920, p. 1.
51. *MM*, Vol. 35, No. 5, Oct. 25, 1921.
52. *Ibid.*, No. 7, Nov. 8, 1921.
53. *Ibid.*, No. 10, Nov. 29, 1921.
54. *Ibid.*, No. 30, May 30, 1922.
55. *MM*, Vol. 36, No. 12, December 1922.

56. *MM*, Vol. 37, Welcome Extra, Sept. 12, 1923.
57. *Ibid.*, No. 5, Oct. 16, 1923.
58. *Ibid.*, No. 9, Nov. 13, 1923.
59. *Ibid.*, No. 11, Nov. 27, 1923.
60. *MM*, Vol. 38, No. 2, Sept. 16, 1924.
61. *Ibid.*, No. 1, Sept. 9, 1924.
62. *Ibid.*, No. 3, Sept. 30, 1924.
63. *Carletonian-Manitou Messenger* extra edition, Oct. 25, 1924.
64. *MM*, Vol. 38, November 1924.
65. *Ibid.*, No. 10, Nov. 18, 1924.
66. *Ibid.*, No. 31, May 1925.
67. *MM*, Vol 39, No. 6, Oct. 20, 1925.
68. *Ibid.*, No. 7, October 27, 1925.
69. *MM*, Vol. 40, No. 4, Oct. 5, 1926.
70. *Ibid.*, No. 5, Oct. 12, 1926.
71. *Ibid.*
    Georgina Dieson-Hegland, in her 1950 publication, *As It Was in the Beginning*, notes that after the St. Olaf-Shattuck game of 1893, "one of the players became sick with typhoid fever," an epidemic broke out at St. Olaf, and two students died. "Logically or not, this epidemic seems to have put an end to football at St. Olaf — until the year 1919," Mrs. Hegland wrote. Dieson-Hegland was graduated from St. Olaf in 1904. She then served as preceptress in Ladies Hall and later was a member of the faculty teaching Latin and German.
72. *Ibid.*, No. 8, Nov. 2, 1926
73. *Ibid.*, No. 11, Nov. 23, 1926
74. *Ibid.*, May 24, 1927.
75. *MM*, Vol. 41, No. 1, Sept. 27, 1927.
76. *Ibid.*, No. 4, Oct. 4, 1927.
77. *Ibid.*, No. 5, Oct. 11, 1927.
78. *Ibid.*, No. 8, Nov. 8, 1927.
79. *MM*, Vol. 42, May 22, 1928.
80. *Ibid.*, Sept. 18, 1928.
81. *Ibid.*, No. 22, March 19, 1929.
82. *Ibid.*, April 23, 1929.
83. *Ibid.*, No. 30, June 4, 1929.
84. *Ibid.*, No. 15, Jan. 29, 1929.

85. *MM,* Vol. 43, Oct. 1929.
86. *Ibid.,* Nov. 26, 1929.
87. *MM,* Vol. 44, No. 2, Sept. 16, 1930.
88. *Ibid.,* No. 4, Sept. 30, 1930.
89. *Ibid.,* No. 5, Oct. 14, 1930.
90. *Ibid.,* No. 6, Oct. 21, 1930.
91. *Ibid.,* No. 7, Oct. 28, 1930.
92. *Ibid.,* No. 9, Nov. 8, 1930.
93. *Ibid.*
94. *Ibid.,* No. 10, Nov. 18, 1930.
95. *MM,* Vol. 45, Oct. 6, 1931.
96. *MM,* Vol. 46, Oct. 4, 1932.
97. *Ibid.,* March 28, 1933.
98. *Viking,* Vol. 19, 1933–34.
99. *MM,* Vol. 48, No. 5, Oct. 10, 1934.
100. *Ibid.,* No. 10, Nov. 21, 1934.
101. *Ibid.,* No. 24, April 10, 1935.
102. *MM,* Vol. 49, No. 7, Nov. 1, 1935.
103. *Ibid.,* No. 19, March 18, 1936.
104. *Ibid.,* No. 21, March 31, 1936.
105. *MM,* Vol. 50, No. 7, Oct. 27, 1936.
106. *Ibid.,* No. 12, Dec. 15, 1936.
107. *Ibid.,* No. 14, Feb. 2, 1937.
108. *Ibid.,* No. 26, May 11, 1937.
109. *MM,* Vol. 51, No. 3, Sept. 28, 1937.
110. *Ibid.,* No. 21, April 5, 1938.
111. *Ibid.,* No. 22, April 12, 1938.
112. *MM,* Vol. 52, No. 5, Oct. 18, 1938.
113. *Ibid.,* No. 8, Nov. 15, 1938.
114. *MM,* Vol. 53, No. 2, Sept. 26, 1939.
115. *MM,* Vol. 54, No. 1, Aug. 30, 1940.
116. *Ibid.,* No. 9, Nov. 15, 1940.
117. *MM,* Vol. 55, No. 7, Nov. 14, 1941.
118. *Ibid.,* Nov. 28, 1941.
119. *MM,* Vol 56, No. 7, Dec. 11, 1942.
120. *Ibid.,* No. 9, Jan. 15, 1943.
121. *MM,* Vol. 57, No. 4, Nov. 5, 1943.
122. *MM,* Vol. 58, No 4, Nov. 10, 1944.
123. *Ibid.,* Oct. 27, 1944.
124. *MM,* Vol. 59, No. 3, Oct. 12, 1945.

125. *MM,* Vol. 62, No. 20, March 18, 1949.
126. Shaw, *op. cit.,* p. 411.
127. Interview, Al Finholt, Feb. 9, 2002.
128. *MM,* Vol. 65, No. 19, March 7, 1952.
129. *Viking,* 1953. p. 188.
130. *MM,* Vol. 66, No. 7, Nov. 7, 1952.
131. *MM,* Vol. 67, No. 8, Nov. 6, 1953.
132. *Ibid.*
133. *Ibid.,* No. 12, Dec. 11, 1953.
134. *MM,* Vol. 69, No. 4, Oct. 14, 1955.
135. *Ibid.,* No. 9, Nov. 18, 1955.
136. *MM,* Vol. 70, No. 8, Nov. 16, 1956.
137. *MM,* Vol. 71, No. 9, Nov. 22, 1957.
138. *Ibid.,* No. 13, March 21, 1958.
139. *MM,* Vol. 72, No. 17, Oct. 9, 1959.
140. *Ibid.,* No. 22, Nov. 13, 1959.

Chapter 6

141. *MM,* Vol. 73, No. 16, Oct. 14, 1960.
142. *MM,* Vol. 74, No. 17, Oct. 20, 1961.
143. Telephone conversation with Dale Liesch, April, 25, 2002.
144. *Viking,* p. 143.
145. *MM,* Vol. 74, No. 21, Nov. 17, 1961.
146. *MM,* Vol. 75, No. 17, Oct. 12, 1962.
147. *MM,* Vol. 76, No. 15, Sept.1963.
148. *Ibid.*
149. *MM,* Vol. 78, No. 21, Nov. 12, 1965.
150. *MM,* Vol. 79, No. 20, Nov. 18, 1966.
151. *MM,* Vol. 81, No. 15, Sept. 27, 1968.
152. *MM,* Vol. 82, No. 17, Oct. 17, 1969.
153. *MM-Carletonian* joint issue, Nov. 17, 1969.
154. Bob Phelps, St. Olaf news release, Nov. 15, 1970.
155. *MM,* Vol. 83, No. 18, Nov. 20, 1970.
156. "Oliver Towne" column, St. Paul *Dispatch,* Nov. 13, 1970.
157. Rolf Mellby, *Viking Scorebook,* Vol. 21, No. 7, Nov. 1, 1971.

158. Bob Phelps, St. Olaf news release, Nov. 8, 1971.
159. *MM,* Vol. 85, Nov. 14, Oct. 6, 1972.
160. Clifton Fadiman, ed., *The American Treasury 1455–1955* (New York, Harper, 1955) p. 273.
161. Postgame comment, Sept., 27, 1975.
162. *Viking Scorebook,* Vol. 26, No. 11, Nov. 9, 1976.
163. *Viking Scorebook,* Vol. 27, No. 3, Sept. 20, 1977.
164. Concordia sports information release, Sept. 26, 1978.
165. *Viking Scorebook,* Vol. 28, No. 6, Oct. 10, 1978.
166. Bob Phelps, postgame news release, Oct. 23, 1978.
167. *MM,* Vol. 93, No. 4, Oct. 11, 1979.
168. *Viking Scorebook,* Vol. 31, No. 8, Oct. 20, 1981.
169. *Northfield News,* Oct. 25, 1984, p. 26.
170. *Ibid.,* p. 16.
171. *St. Olaf* magazine, Vol. 35, No. 5, Aug. 1987, p. 41.

Chapter 7

172. In the early years of the St. Olaf-Carleton rivalry, a tradition was begun whereby the brass eagle on top of the Civil War statue on Bridge Square would be turned to face the campus whose team had won the annual battle for the football Goatrophy. In 1997, the victorious Ole gridders, muddy cleats and all, trooped en masse to the square to make sure the eagle faced the west. After all, it had been six years.

Team Photo Identifications

1904 class team *(page 4)*
Photo identifications not available.

1910 class team *(page 3)*
Photo identifications not available.

1912 class team *(page 5)*
Photo identifications not available.

1919, first intercollegiate team *(page 11 and back cover)*
Top row: Holter, Havig, Flaten, Swenson, Thune, A. Cole, Halvorson, Baumann, Glesne, Hoidahl, Thompson, C. Cole, Voldahl.
  Bottom row: Peterson, Nelson, Marvick, Coach Anderson, Captain Veldey, Dr. Cooke, Grose, Eide, Lee.

1920 *(page 15)*
Photo identifications not available.

1922 *(page 19)*
Top row: L. Fosshage, E. Isvik, H. Pearson, H. Burtness, M. Sampson, B. Olson, A. Tapager, K. Syverud, W. Johnson, M. Melby, G. Thornberg, M. Simundson, O. Bolstad.
  Middle row: Manager A. Christensen, F. Putzier, M. Cole, O. Thorson, R. Lunde, O. Premo, O. Jenson, Captain I. Swenson, Coach E.B. Anderson.
  Bottom row: C. Swanson, H. Fevold, F. Cleve, I. Glesne.

1923 *(page 21)*
Top row: Coach E.B. Anderson, O. Kosmo, O. Bolstad, F. Fremouw, A. Lium, H. Burtness, S. Anderson, E. Excog, V. Anderson, Manager A. Christenson.
  Middle row: A. Tunem, F. Cleve, Captain M. Cole, H. Pearson, R. Olson, O. Bongsto, O. Jensen, J. Christiansen, E. Reinertson.
  Bottom row: E. Vig, M. Erickson, E. Enger, C. Swanson, H. Fevold, I. Glesne, M. Simundson, M. Melby.

1928 *(page 27)*
Standing: Aamot, Johnson, Flaten, Lundgren, Engabritson, Engelson, McKenzie, Barsness, Grebstead, Velde, Hagen, Dybdal.
  Kneeling: Ramseth, Wangness, Golberg, B. Larson, T. Larson, Stageberg, Stolen, Almli, Rorstad, Olson, E. Johnson.
  Sitting: Quam, Mickleson, Ingvolstead, Meyners, Captain Obermeyer, Enderson, Netland, Engleson, McKenzie, Gilbertson.

1929 *(page 29)*
Back row: Coach Christenson, Earl Johnson, Edmund Johnson, Wangsness, Kjeldgaard, L. Johnson, Engleson, Lund, Ingvoldstad, Underdahl, Glesne, Eckegren, Line Coach Fryckman.
  Middle row: Velde, Gilbertson, Siemers, Droen, Hildebrandt, Almli, Saumer, Quam, Olson, McKenzie, Rorstad.
  Front row: Tellickson, Meyners, Nesset, Schiotz, Iverson, Tronnes, Mickelson, Golberg, Hegdahl, Opperud, Engebretson, Ellingson, Larson, Swanson.

1930 *(page 31)*
First row: Assistant Coach Pulkrabek, H. Christianson, Iverson, Gilbertson, Saumer, Ingvolstad, Nordstrand, Ellingson, Droen, Larson, Mickleson, Hegdahl, Lecy, Hildebrand, Coach Christenson.
  Second row: Fogg, J. Christenson, D. Anderson, Quam, Soli, Newby, Glesne, L. Lund, Telleckson, Shoitz, Veldy, R. Olson.
  Third row: J. Johnson, Wee, C. Johnson, Peterson, Emerson, Jensen, Ekegren, Grober, Vikre, Ness, Maring, Golberg.

1932 *(page 35)*
First row: Nordstrand, Lecy, Droen, Summers, Peterson, Saumer, Shoitz, Ellingson, H. Christenson, I. Christenson, Newby.
  Second row: Assistant Coach Olson, Tolleckson, Ekegren, Ness, Glesne, Larson, L. Lund, Santleman, E. Johnson, Soli, Grove.
  Third row: Assistant Coach Swanson, H. Swanson, Sorem, Larson, Graber, Jensen, Erickson, R. Lund, Bonniwell, C. Johnson, Passolt, Seig, Berg, J. Johnson, Coach Christenson.

1935 *(page 37)*
Photo identifications not available.

1936 *(page 39)*
First row: Kinden, Herfindahl, Anderson, Boe, Schwake, Emerson, Pitts, Torgerson, Nyman, Baldwin, Juel.
  Second row: Love, Heinel, Nanzer, Fortier, Comer, Ramseth, Captain Kirkeby, Rosendahl, Nelson, Thorsen, Peterson.
  Third row: Coach Christenson, McGrath, Berg, Eliason, Sundahl, Haugen, Juel, Skoglund, Klemp, Bloomquist, Barry, Hinds, Glesne, Assistant Coach Iverson.

1939 *(page 45)*
Photo identifications not available.

1946 *(page 51)*
Front row: Mel Edman, Ralph Gordon, Ron Hendriksen, Jim Kallas, Ed Morehead, Captain Stan Tostengard, Al Lehrke, Royal Peterson, Bob Zimmerman, Don Larsen, Kermit Halverson, Marshall Haugen, John Sibole.
  Second row: Howie Rose, Bill Dion, Arnold T. Nelson, Glen Swenson, Gus Stromner, Ralph Bailey, Walt Nelson, Paul Larson, Bob DeWyze, Fritz Christofferson, Marlyn Dahlen.
  Third row: Glen Reichel, Art Frederickson, Gordon Peterson, Arnold W. Nelson, Wheeler Curtis, Bill Scrimgeour, Leonard Bunge, Carl Larson, Lawrence Anderson, Ellsworth Buskirk, Adrian Christenson.
  Fourth row: Robert Strand, Vern Lace, Leonard Hedahl, Stan Nelson, Jim Burtness, Bill Carroll, Ed Thompson, Ira Swartz, Charles Mandell, Gerry Johnson.
  Fifth row: Newell Nelson, Dick Thorp, Dennis Mydland, Ardell Thompson, Berkley Hanson, Omar Juveland, Lyle Brassington, Alfred Anderson, Warren Nelson.
  Top row: Head Coach Ade Christenson, Assistant Coach Mark Almli, Line Coach Art Sand, Assistant Coach Dick Thompson.

1951 *(page 61)*
Row 1: Marv Larsen, Russ Mauer, Dick Ovington, Jim Rotramel, Arnie Thowsen, Harlan Hogsven, Paul Forsberg, George Trout, J.D. Hanson, Bob Tengdin, Don Maland, Larry Kallandar, Jim Devens.

 Row 2: Assistant Coach Sherm Brown, John Gustafson, John Pickner, Jim Varland, Dick Werdahl, Roger Oie, Burt Grover, Keith Ingbritsen, Bob Wilkens, Doug Olson, Clint Sathrum, Willie Mesna, Coach Ade Christenson, Assistant Coach Frank Wrigglesworth.

 Row 3: Steve Swanson, Al Anderson, Frank Peterson, Ray Runkel, Chuck Espe, Al Rogotske, John Quam, Ted Thompson, Al Matzke, Dean Ostle, Jack Aamot, Jack Moors, Dick Hemstad.

1953 *(page 65)*
Front row: Noel Olson, Paul Johnson, John Pichner, Del McCoy, Jack Moors, John Gustafson, Clint Sathrum, Frank Peterson, Doug Olson, Steve Swanson, Jack Aamot.

 Second row: Ted Thompson, Ken Bergstrom, Rod Blom, Lee Simso, John Bieberstein, Roger Oie, Dick Werdahl, Chet Mathison, Don Garnett, Norm Solie.

 Third row: Erv Mikkelson, Dick Dahlager, Luther Erickson, Willie Mesna, Chuck Espe, John Edstrom, Bernie Von Wald, Dave Bolstorff, Dick Lorentzen.

 Fourth row: Burnell Olson, Bruce Halverson, Paul Quan, Mark Reinertson, Ralph Hagberg, John Gerfen, Dennis Griffin, Bill Redman, Buzz Helseth.

 Fifth row: Manager Dick Nelson, Assistant Coach Frank Wrigglesworth, Coach Ade Christenson, Chuck Lunder, Manager Marsh Pechaner.

 Not pictured: Jim Varland, Carol Brekken.

1956 *(page 69)*
Row 1: Bob Zemke, Nick Olsen, Al Lyng, Bob Kalass, Whitey Brekken, Wayne Brown, Bill Lund, Clyde Olson, Dick Norman, Dave Folkestad, Al Anderson.

 Row 2: Al Rice, Rog Stoike, Bill Yock, Warren Salveson, Tom Anderson, George Thronson, Waldo Larson, Paul Mork, Rog Strand, Larry Brynestad, Jim Stoner, Bill Rundquist.

 Row 3: Ken Dahlager, Thor Anderson, Nate Aus, Duane Swenson, Loren Rindahl, Roger Berg, Dennis Runck, Mike Simpson, Al Peterson, Don Johnson, Bob Lore.

 Row 4: Chuck Anderson, Dave Robinson, Ed Olson, Arne Nelson, Pete Pederson, Jon Wergedal, Howard Morgan, John Gunderson, Nate Schiotz.

 Row 5: Joe Edson, Jerry Sletten, Chuck Lunder, Dave Bolstorff, Ade Christenson, Jim Gabrielson, Ron Pechauer, Doug Pearson.

1960 *(page 77)*
Row 1: G. Hoven, D. Davis, W. Moir, B. Diedrich, R. Algoe, W. Greenslit, J. Rajala, K. Defor, D. Einarson, D. Jurries, W. Anderson, D. Norman.

 Row 2: Coach Bob Gelle, Coach Chuck Lunder, D. Schiotz, T. Everson, P. Hegg, H. Christensen, J. Bloedel, D. Hindermann, W. Winter, J. Bergstrom, M. Koch, S. Oppegard, V. Foss, R. Madsen, Head Trainer Arnie Anderson, Coach Tom Porter.

 Row 3: Trainer R. Swanson, P. Blom, K. Christman, D. Mohwinkel, G. Knutson, R. Ramseth, G. Ellingson, M. Aamot, N. Pratt, D. Canfield, M. Helmen, W. Mack, Trainer R. Bunt.

1961 *(page 79)*
Row 1: Student Trainer R. Wilburn, H. Christensen, B. Diedrich, J. Bergstrom, B. Anderson, Co-captain T. Everson, Co-captain B. Winter, D. Hindermann, S. Oppegard, S. Greenfield, M. Koch, J. Bloedel, Student Trainer D. Bunt.

 Row 2: Freshman Coach P. Quam, R. Madsen, D. Schiotz, P. Blom, K. McKenzie, D. Canfield, G. Knutson, D. Mohwinkel, G. Ellingson, M. Aamot, H. Fogal, T. Johnson, Line Coach C. Lunder.

 Row 3: End Coach B. Gelle, C. Peterson, J. Mostrom, T. Bogda, B. Koch, K. West, F. Meyer, D. Liesch, M. Hoven, J. Glendening, K. Throlson, J. Ruohoniemi, P. Aus, Student Trainer P. Miller, Head Coach Tom Porter.

1962 *(page 81)*
Row 1: Student Trainer Richard Bunt, Gerald Fenske, Don Mersch, John Tweeten, Tom Wieth, Wes Sime, George Anderson, Roger Stensvad, Student Trainer Gregory Nelson.

 Row 2: Coach Chuck Lunder, Ken McKenzie, Herman Fogal, Gene Knutson, Captain Don Canfield, Captain Mark Aamot, Dan Mohwinkel, Dave Schiotz, Ron Madsen, Tom Johnson, Coach Tom Porter.

 Row 3: Coach Paul Quam, Dale Liesch, Bruce Koch, John Ruohoniemi, Ted Bogda, Fred Meyer, Chuck Peterson, Jon Mostrom, Keith West, Dick Lien, Pete Aus, Coach Bob Gelle.

 Back row: Robert Heideman, James Burner, Don Struxness, Dave Hirschy, Dag Grudem, Larry Cohrt, Clark Westphal, Fred Russler, Ben Danielson, Rodney Skoge, Paul Skibsrud, Student Trainer Gerald Tripp.

1963 *(page 83)*
Row 1: Assistant Coach Chuck Lunder, Keith West, Pete Aus, Jon Mostrom, Dale Liesch, Co-captain Chuck Peterson, Co-captain Fred Meyer, Dag Grudem, John Ruohoniemi, Rod Skoge, Paul Skibsrud, Brian Kispert, Freshman Coach Deryl "Skip" Boyum.

 Row 2: Student Trainer Greg Nelson, Bob Heidemann, Jim Burner, Lenny Ackermann, Fred Russler, Larry Cohrt, Clark Westphal, Ben Danielson, Dave Hirschy, Dave Hosokawa, Roger Stensvad, Tom Nibbe, Assistant Trainer Ron Newell.

 Row 3: Head Coach Tom Porter, Don Janke, Jerry Hjelle, Wayne Mortensen, Dave Knudsen, Tom Heiberg, Howard Felber, Tom Ylvisaker, Mark Kjeldgaard, Tom Mickelson, John Schumm, Assistant Coach Bob Gelle.

 Not pictured: Neil Boyd, John Nelson, Dave Nichols.

1965 (*page 85*)

Front row: Mike Solhaug, Rod Olson, John Schumm, Harold Peterson, Tom Ylvisaker, Captain Tom Heiberg, Captain Tom Mickelson, Wayne Mortensen, Mark Kjeldgaard, Howard Felber, Doug Blanchard, Don Liesch, Manager Haven Ofstie.

Middle row: Coach Chuck Lunder, Coach Mike Stevenson, Al Wall, Gary Soderberg, Leroy Klempt, Ranier Lobitz, Erik Nilsen, Steve Refsell, Harold Mueller, Mike Wittkamper, Dave Krahn, Jim Hurd, Jim Pugh, John Anderson, Coach Paul Quam, Coach Tom Porter.

Back row: Kirk Anderson, Lee Mesna, Ward Haugen, Paul Anderson, Lee Johnson, Mike Gorton, Don Webber, Bruce Watson, unidentified, Lynn Knutson, Brice Huemoeller, Jim Kindem, Jon Hersch, Bill Forsyth, Bohdan Melnychenko.

1966 (*page 89*)

First row: Trainer Mark Lund, John Anderson, Doug Blanchard, Jim Pugh, Al Wall, Eric Nilsen, Steve Refsell, Mike Solhaug, LeRoy Klemt, Harold Mueller, Doug Williams, Rainer Lobitz, Dave Krahn, Trainer Haven Ofstie.

Second row: Coach Charles Lunder, Coach Paul Quam, James Nelson, Kirk Anderson, Ward Haugen, Bohdan Melnychenko, Lee Mesna, Paul Anderson, Conrad Braaten, Bruce Stensvad, Lynn Knutson, Jim Kindem, Gary Erickson, Jon Hersch, Coach Robert Gelle, Coach Tom Porter.

Third row: Mark Gorder, Greg Tollefson, Dan Franklin, Larry Anderson, Dennis Myers, Mike Schmiesing, Dick Blesi, Steve Fink, Dave Lundberg, Tom Goplen, Richard Omland, Dave Mueller, Jim Kemp, Dan Haertl, Don Mark, Rick Nelson.

1969 (*page 95*)

Row 1: Trainer John Adams, Tim Onnen, Arne Melby, Bob Wetterberg, Ron Hunter, Tom Saxhaug, Tim Smith, Don Krahn, Dick Hatle, Steve Wiener, Dan Johnson, Jim Gehant, Dennis Nelson, Trainer Ron Groth.

Row 2: Coach Lunder, Coach Dimick, Leon Lunder, Bill Koeckeritz, Warren Hoemann, Dick Swiggum, Tom Peinovich, Steve Ahlgren, Al Hinderaker, Greg Carlson, Gary Iverson, Scott Anderson, Douglas R. Johnson, Doug Munson, Coach Hauck.

Row 3: Rolf Paulson, Doug A. Johnson, Ralph Wasik, Charles Schweigert, Tom O'Neill, Martin Seim, Bob Matson, Mike Peterson, Mike Holmquist, Kent Johnson, Bob Freed, Steve Ashley, John Haavik, Coach Gelle.

Row 4: Ole Gunderson, Winslow Stenseng, Todd Eklund, John McBroom, Paul Olson, Bob Gustafson, Jon Johnson, Steve Schwarten, Brian Harter, Coach Porter.

1970 (*page 99*)

Row 1: Doug Johnson, Al Montgomery, Warren Hoemann, Leon Lunder, Ralph Wasik, Bob Matson, Steve Ashley, Doug Munson, Mike Holmquist, Kent Johnson, Bill Koeckeritz, Tom O'Neill, Bob Freed.

Row 2: Coach Dave Hauck, Coach Jim Dimick, Trainer John Adams, Ole Gunderson, Brian Harter, Todd Eklund, Bob Schumacher, Bob Gustafson, Paul Olson, John Johnson, Jon McBroom, Win Stenseng, Dave Schwerin, Steve Schwarten.

Row 3: Steve Sviggum, Bill Nelson, Art Hultgren, Tim Hermann, Marv Schumacher, Willard Iverson, Gary Jacobson, Mike Veldman, Jim Olson, Trainer Ron Groth.

Row 4: Coach Chuck Lunder, Trainer Steve Harmer, John Kieffer, Dave Nitz, Tom Olson, Randy Burns, Jerry Berg, Al Beal, Brock Nelson, Richard Skogrand, Coach Bob Gelle, Coach Tom Porter.

1971 (*page 101*)

Row 1: Coach Dave Hauck, Steve Sviggum, Ole Gunderson, Robert Schumacher, Stephen Schwarten, David Schwerin, Captain Paul Olson, Captain Winslow Stenseng, Brian Harter, Jon Johnson, Jon McBroom, Todd Eklund, Alan Beal.

Row 2: Coach Chuck Lunder, John Kieffer, Richard Skogrand, Thomas Olson, David Nitz, Timothy Hermann, Marvin Schumacher, Arthur Hultgren, Michael Veldman, Bill Nelson, James Hemberger, Jerry Berg, Trainer John Seitz.

Row 3: Coach Jim Dimick, Trainer Mike Scott, Robert Ferg, Robert Roeglin, Leonard Whyte, Tim Bigalke, Tim Larsen, Dave Rommereim, Brock Nelson, Arthur Arakawa, Scott Douglas, Cooper Wiggen, Larry Lindberg.

Row 4: Jeffrey Blaisdell, Gary Johnson, Charles Young, Channing Gove, Dale Hinderaker, Nick Ryder, Kim Benson, Bruce Peterson, Richard Nicoll, James Schwerin, Geoff Kaufmann, Peter Opsal, Head Coach Tom Porter, Acting Athletic Director Bob Gelle.

1972 (*page 103*)

Front row: Robert Ferg, John Kieffer, Art Arakawa, Bill Schuneman, Tim Hermann, Mike Veldman, Randy Burns, Tom Olson, Alan Beal, Bob Roeglin, Brock Nelson, Bill Nelson, Art Hultgren, Steve Sviggum, Pete Opsal, Marvin Schumacher, Kim Sigler, Jeff Blaisdell.

Second row: Head Coach Tom Porter, Coach Bob Gelle, Gary Johnson, Dave Rommereim, Ron DeBlack, Tim Larsen, Rich Nicoll, Bruce Peterson, Dale Hinderaker, Kim Benson, Jim Christianson, Lenny Whyte, Chan Gove, Dave Keller, Tim Bigalke, Warren Thunstrom, Larry Lindberg, Steve Madson, Coach Dave Hauck.

Third row: Art Yeske, Al Edward, John Wheeler, Mark Wangsness, Jim Hanson, Dale Pippin, Jim Dimick, Brad Covert, Kent Kildahl, Pat Hensel, Ross Thorfinson, Ron Beal, Maury Johnson, Scott Estervold, Brian Anderson, Coach Jim Dimick.

Fourth row: Scott Jamison, Steve Winegarden, Steve Hill, Mark Gelle, Joel Simpson, John Anderson, Ron Solyst, Greg Olson, Dale Ness, Marty Richmond, Al Delaitsch, Craig Collings, Tim Speich, Tom Monohan, Rick Peterson.

Fifth row: Dennis Miller, Rick Hultgren, Barry Kinsey, John Carlson, John Hendricks, Greg Ferguson, Steve Japs, Don Gavic.

1973 *(page 107)*
Front row: Manager Scott Douglas, Jim Hanson, Tim Carlson, Ross Thorfinnson, Len Whyte, Bob Ferg, Chan Gove, Jeff Blaisdell, Tim Larsen, Dave Rommereim, Gary Johnson, Jim Christensen, Mark Ingvoldstad, Dave Keller, Bruce Peterson, Ron Beal, Coach Chuck Lunder.

Second row: Head Coach Tom Porter, Richard Morse, Greg Olson, Steve D. Hill, Joel Simpson, Craig Collins, Mark Wangsness, Brad Covert, Jim Dimick, Dale Pippin, Al Edwards, Steve Peinovich, John Wheeler, Warren Thundstrom, Ron Solyst, Brian Anderson, Coach Dave Hauck.

Third row: Dave Tolo, Tom Bickel, Jim Wilkens, Eric Peterson, Scott Westervelt, Tom Monahan, Don Gavic, Steve J. Hill, Gregg Ferguson, Rick Hultgren, Dennis Miller, Dale Ness, Steve Winegarden, Mark Gelle, Dave Ryland, Randy Sanders, Coach Bob Gelle.

Fourth row: Coach Jim Dimick, Scott Moen, Eric Tammi, Dave Ashley, Jeff Iverson, Tim Krueger, Maury Johnson, Tom Hendricks, Peter Kindem, John Rudin, Jeff Larson, Jim Kunitz, Mark Bennett, Gary Uecke, Steve Manlove.

Back row: Roger Olson, John Kingwell, Steve Lass, Mitch Long, Tom Thorfinnson, Tim Quinlivan.

Not pictured: Charlie Mangrum, Bill Green.

1974 *(page 109)*
Row 1: Trainer Paul Christianson, Coach Jim Dimick, Maurice Johnson, Steve Madson, Brian Anderson, Craig Collins, Steve J. Hill, Al Edwards, Jim Dimick, Steve Peinovich, Jim Hanson, Mark Wangsness, Dale Hinderaker, Brad Covert, Mark Gelle, Joel Simpson, Steve D. Hill.

Row 2: Coach Dave Hauck, Coach Chuck Lunder, Eric Tammi, Dale Ness, Tom Monahan, John Kroll, Greg Olson, Rick Hultgren, Gregg Ferguson, Art Skenandore, Jim Kunitz, Mitch Long, Randy Sanders, Scott Moen, Tom Bickel, Al Tindall, Gary Uecke, Don Redix, Coach Bob Gelle, Coach Tom Porter.

Row 3: Carl Bergstrom, John Rudin, Jim Wilkens, Rick Morse, Pete Kindem, Steve Lass, Charles Mangrum, Roger Olson, Tim Kruger, Tim Carlson, Mark Bennett, Tom Thorfinnson, Dave Ryland, Bill Green, Dan Gunderson, Mark Glimmerveen, Scot Wilson, Dave Curry, Manager Jim Starks.

Row 4: Greg Sorenson, Bruce Underdahl, Mark Porter, Steve Benke, Jon Iverson, Mark Trelstad, Bruce Berglund, Dave Plummer, Joe Langfeldt, Scott Massie, Charles Cutler, Jim Case, Tom Winegarden, Mike Gass, Ed Dorsey, Brad Bergene, Steve Pentz, Bob Sullivan, Steve Pettersen, Tom Fiebiger, Greg Kolden, Mark Arvesen.

Not pictured: Steve Winegarden, Coach Rod Grubb.

1976 *(page 117)*
Front row: Steve Chiodo, Brian Larson, Mark Porter, Mark Arvesen, Jon Iverson, Andy George, Bob Benes, Dave Curry, Carl Bergstrom, Tom Fiebiger, Mike Gass, Gary Nelson.

Second row: Assistant Coach Mark Gelle, Trainer Brian Oppegaard, Jim Kunitz, Gary Uecke, Charles Mangrum, Tom Thorfinnson, Dave Ryland, Jim Wilkens, Captain Mitch Long, Captain Roger Olson, Tim Kruger, Tom Bickel, Steve Lass, Randy Sanders, John Kroll, Rick Rost, Head Coach Tom Porter.

Third row: Assistant Coach Rod Grubb, Assistant Coach Dave Hauck, Bob Ringham, Bob Strasser, Gary Mikkelson, John Ederer, Kerry Multz, Dave Mylrea, Eric Ristau, Joe Langfeldt, Steve Remes, Scott Massie, Scot Wilson, Steve VandenHeuvel, Jed Downs, McKinley Moore, Assistant Coach Jim Dimick, Assistant Coach Charles Lunder.

Fourth row: Craig Dahle, Bill Zahn, Jim Berdahl, Jim Sackrison, Charles Benson, Steve Hanson, Pete Dahlen, Steve Ostlie, Lee Chayer, Mark Simonson, Stan King, Lee Dunfee, Jeff Stevenson, John Nahorniak.

Back row: Reed Johnson, John Van Ginkel, Jeff Kier, Terry Westermann, Paul Estenson, Ed Voigt, Mark Quinnell, Tim Bates, Todd Porter, Nate Bergeland, Steve Ryland, Steve Lidke, Dave Borgwardt, Brad Klitzke, Wally Hustad, Chris Biegner, Brian Johnson, Tad Hauck, Jeff Thompson.

1977 *(page 121)*
Row 1: Line Coach T. Larsen, Manager Bruce Hatlem, J. Downs, J. Nahorniak, M. Simonson, T. Fiebiger, C. Bergstrom, M. Porter, M. Arvesen, D. Mylrea, B. Benes, D. Ryland, G. Nelson, R. Rost, Trainer D. Seefeld, Trainer Rick Wilson.

Row 2: Defensive Coach D. Hauck, S. Chiodo, S. Ostlie, G. Mikkelson, E. Ristau, J. Ederer, K. Multz, S. VandenHeuvel, C. Benson, S. King, B. Strasser, J. Van Ginkel, L. Dunfee, M. Glimmerveen, M. Jacobson, A. Hodge, Head Coach Tom Porter.

Row 3: Backfield Coach R. Grubb, T. Hauck, J. Thompson, J. Berdahl, S. Lidke, T. Bates, N. Bergeland, T. Porter, D. Borgwardt, B. Pilmer, B. Johnson, W. Hustad, T. Westermann, E. Voight, R. Johnson, M. Quinnell.

Row 4: G. Nemcek, D. Dimick, M. Jankowski, M. Chiodo, M. Schrader, F. Gelle, D. Meslow, J. Quam, D. Monke, B. Torgerson, J. Rosell, P. Lemke, G. Stading, B. Fenelon, L. Knickerbocker, Backfield Coach M. Gelle.

Row 5: S. Hoffman, J. Dougherty, B. Mathes, M. Fagerburg, T. Femrite, S. McKay, J. Anderson, G. Fiegum, B. Patterson, O. Koch, B. Pavel, D. Hird, T. VanDeinse, P. Estenson.

1978 (page 127)

Row 1: Steve Ostlie, Steve Chiodo, Gary Mikkelson, Jed Downs, Lee Dunfee, Kerry Multz, McKinley Moore, Erik Landvik, Captain Rick Rost, Captain Steve VandenHeuvel, John Nahorniak, Eric Ristau, Joe Langfeldt, Chuck Benson, John Ederer, John Van Ginkel, Mark Simonson.

Row 2: Tad Hauck, Bob Pilmer, Brian Johnson, Terry Westermann, Reed Johnson, Jim Berdahl, Ed Voigt, Tim Bates, Nate Bergeland, Dave Borgwardt, Todd Porter, Steve Lidke, Paul Estenson, Mark Quinnell, Al Hodge, Steve Hanson, Scott Nystrom.

Row 3: Jeff Olson, Gregg Fiegum, Jeff Thompson, Brian Fenelon, Eric Polson, Doug Meslow, Mike Jankowski, Steve McKay, Jeff Rosell, Fred Gelle, Bob Patterson, Dean Monke, Robert Welch, Mike Allen, Jon Anderson, Mike Schrader.

Row 4: Bob Klefsaas, Pete Kelley, Keith Tufte, Tim Logemann, Gregg Stangel, Gary Nemcek, Marc Chiodo, Dan Dimick, Todd Thorsgaard, Dan Kyllo, George Wood, Dan Backberg, Greg Johnson, Chuck Viren.

Row 5: Trainer Mark Johnson, Trainer Rick Wilson, Assistant Coach Dave Hauck, Assistant Coach Jim Dimick, Jeff Machacek, Phil Walch, Bob Blake, Brad Cleveland, Jeff Dunham, John Evanson, Manager Bruce Hatlem, Assistant Coach Carl Bergstrom, Assistant Coach Rod Grubb, Head Coach Tom Porter.

1979 (page 131)

Row 1: Trainer Rick Wilson, Trainer Mark Johnson, Brian Johnson, Terry Westermann, Bob Pilmer, Jeff Thompson, Tad Hauck, Mark Quinnell, Steve Lidke, Jim Berdahl, Mike Allen, Scott Nystrom, Bob Welch, Bob Ringham, Manager Bruce Hatlem, Manager Pete Albrecht.

Row 2: Coach Rod Grubb, Coach Tom Porter, Coach Rick Rost, Paul Estenson, Wally Hustad, Erik Landvik, Al Hodge, Dave Borgwardt, Tim Bates, Nate Bergeland, Todd Porter, Steve McKay, Fred Gelle, Bob Patterson, Brian Fenelon, Coach Joe Langfeldt, Coach Jim Dimick.

Row 3: Coach Tim Larsen, Bob Klefsaas, Chuck Viren, Keith Tufte, Dan Kyllo, Marc Chiodo, Jon Anderson, Mike Jankowski, Dan Dimick, Tim Logemann, Pat Crawford, Gregg Stangl, George Wood.

Row 4: Ray Dunfee, Mark Balstad, Steve Bohrer, Bill Hybben, Jeff Petersen, Jeff Olson, Phil Walch, Dan Backberg, Richard Kyllo, Charles Feske, Dan Wolfgram, Dave Seymour, Brad Cleveland.

Row 5: Bill Mickelson, Mark Roe, Dennis Fiedler, Robin Miller, Jon Saunders, Scott Maghan, John Ryden, Dan Downs, Jon Alberg, Dan King, Bill Schlueter, Dan Nordness, Coach Dave Hauck.

1981 (page 139)

Row 1: Trainer Mark Johnson, Tim Logemann, Pat Crawford, Dan Backberg, Chuck Viren, Dan Kyllo, Bob Klefsaas, Keith Tufte, Greg St. John, George Wood, Jeff Olson, Bill Hybben.

Row 2: Ray Dunfee, Chuck Feske, Dan Downs, Jeff Petersen, John Ryden, Jon Saunders, Dan Otterson, Rich Kyllo, Frank Kuzma, Bill Mickelson, Dennis Fiedler, Lou Woodson, Dave Caldwell, Dave Seymour.

Row 3: Brad Wolner, John Pellicci, Dana Jensen, Mike Jensen, Chris Sackrison, Jon Nydahl, Todd Nash, Tom Zima, Al Lottmann, John Fischer, Bill Nelson, Dave Christopher, Randy Peterson, Scott Olson, Coach Tom Porter.

Row 4: Coach Tim Larsen, Kevin Kinvig, Todd Melander, Kurt Johnson, Scott Olson, Paul Curtis, Kurt Hjerpe, Steve Thronson, Keith Harder, Burt Zielke, Dave Olson, Bryon Bothun, John Bennett, Coach Rod Grubb, Equipment Manager Dennis Hughes.

Row 5: Brian Jacobs, Pete Bolstorff, Paul Koehn, Tom Wahlberg, Brent Anderson, Jerome Robertson, Todd Vitols, Mike Rinke, Tom Vick, Coach Jim Dimick, Coach Dave Hauck, Coach Dennis Miller.

1985 (page 151)

Front row: Trainer Dave Maus, Tom Konat, Bill Thomas, Rusty Rogotzke, Clay Anderson, Steve Wee, Jeff Michaelson, Bruce Gutzmann, Jon Nycklemoe, Leif Syverson, Bob Bailey, Mike Zobel, Roger Forystek, Paul Koehn, Equipment Manager Ham Flory.

Row 2: Hal Norman, Mark Fredrickson, Mark Melen, Dale Evenson, Kevin Johnson, Mark York, Brian Putz, Greg VanGuilder, Tom Vick, Brad Lembke, Dave Schooler, Cory Watson, Bruce Hammond, Mike Jacobs.

Row 3: Adam Elliott, Eric Peyton, Todd Prieve, Mike Berletic, Pat Finley, Dave Tobiassen, Eric Engwall, Leif Espeland, Troy Sorensen, Jon Carlson, Kevin Taylor, Scott Elrod, Scott Anderson, Jeff Skoglund.

Row 4: Coach Tom Porter, Trainer Miriam Maakestad, Coach Ron Rasmus, Coach Kurt Johnson, Coach Jim Dimick, Erik Mikkelson, Dan Crawford, Matt Anderson, Brandt Colville, Bill Smith, Stuart Cox, Coach Bob Klefsaas, Coach Tim Larsen, Coach Dave Hauck, Doctor Greg Garnett.

Row 5: Matt McDonald, Mike Eaton, Tony Miller, Chris Reinertson, Kevin Reich, Joe Snodgrass, Eric Angell, Chris Chapman, Mike Hanson, Steve Mathre, Scott Schieber, Scott Sandstrom, Brad Hoff, Tom Birkeland.

Not pictured: John Borstad (45) and Tim Osmondson (50).

The Greatest Game: Football at St. Olaf College 1893–2003

1986–87 Norway team *(page 153)*

Front row: Scott Anderson, Erik Mikkelson, Mike Jacobs, Dave Schooler, Joe Snodgrass, Dan Crawford, Mark Thornton, Chris Reinertson, Brad Wolner.

Middle row: Cheerleader Laura Porter, Cheerleader Kirsten Janke, Hal Norman, Brian Putz, Steve Mathre, Mark Fredrickson, Adam Elliott, Brian Danielson, Stu Cox, Cory Watson, Erik Peyton, Dale Evensen, Cheerleader Ann Schultz, Cheerleader Susan Madson.

Back row: Coach Tom Porter, Coach Roy Anderson, Tony Grundhauser, Rob Warneke, Don Larson, Leif Espeland, Greg Van Guilder, Peter Tjornhom, Scott Miller, Chris Wolner, Mike Warden, Bart Halling, Coach Ron Rasmus, Coach Rod Grubb.

1988 *(page 157)*

Back row: Chris Nelson, Dean Quinnell, Kurt Friedrich, Student Trainer Lainey Brottem, Head Coach Tom Porter, Assistant Coach Tim Larsen, Dr. Gregory Garnett, Trainer Dan Hagen, Assistant Coaches Jim Dimick, Dave Hauck, Ron Rasmus, Mike Allen, Rod Grubb, Equipment Manager Percy Johnson, Brett Lillemoe, Dane Head, Steve Hoemann.

Second row: Howard Rogotzke, John Seffrood, Jim McCormick, Brian Schulte, Matt Moore, Steve A. Schmidt, Kevin Hed, Kirk Aamot, Mike Mercer, Karl Bowman, Paul Bartlett, Jon Palmen, Andy Butler, Pete Heryla, Dan Calhoun.

Third row: Dave Tetzlaff, Demitrius Simpson, Marcus Mollison, Brett Perry, Kirk Meyer, Tim Peloquin, Kent Meyer, Steve M. Johnson, Troter Bauer, Lance Newell, Jon Tostrud, Bart Rafjala, Kirk Bremer, Adam Barner, Jon Grassman.

Fourth row: Dirk McAnelly, Jon Dahl, Greg Geary, Tom Mittelstadt, Bob Ehren, Brian Danielson, Robby Warneke, Erik Haugo, Jason Halvorson, Scott Miller, Reegan Moen, Tom Miller, Dana Henriksen, Leif Mostrom, Mark Thornton.

Front row: Brent Kvittem, Dave Quam, Mike Warden, Steve Mathre, Joe Snodgrass, Erik Mikkelson, Tony Miller, Steve Shaffer, Stuart Cox, Chris Reinertson, Mark Skoog, Neil Rolland, Bart Halling, Chris Novak, Chris Wolner.

1990 *(page 161)*

Front row: Pete Heryla, Kirk Aamot, Troter Bauer, Brett Perry, Captain Kirk Meyer, Captain Jon Tostrud, Captain Kent Meyer, Jon Dahl, Steve Johnson, Tim Peloquin, Andy Butler, Matt Moore.

Row 2: Eric Bly, John Seffrood, Dan Calhoun, Howard Rogotzke, Mike Mercer, Adam Barner, Paul Bartlett, Brian Schulte, Chris Nelson, Brett Lillemoe, Steve Schmidt, Jayson Green, Dave Schmidt.

Row 3: David Keenan, Mike Fossum, Todd Organ, Jim Starr, Bjorn Larsen, Aaron Butler, Mac Early, John Harris, Tom Buslee, Brad Fuerst, Darrell Erickson, Sjur Midness.

Row 4: Trygg Wangsness, Dan Miller, Mark Nelson, Dwight Hand, John Foss, Dave Bergh, Mark Blegen, Dave Gustafson, Judd Sather, Matt Stenson, Craig Kjorlein, Keith Karpinske, Kyle Paulson.

Back row: Equipment Manager Percy Johnson, Team Doctor Greg Garnett, Coach Tom Porter, Trainer Dan Hagen, Coach Jim Dimick, Coach Ron Rasmus, Coach Mike Allen, Coach Chuck Larsen, Coach Tim Larsen, Coach Dave Hauck, Student Trainer Bob Carlson, Student Trainer Tracy Brottem.

2003 *(back cover)*

Front row: Trey Williams, Latravis Henry, Chris Ryan, Brian Hanson, Ben Deck, Bobby Andrade, Marc Olson, Anthony Rogers, Will Starr, Tony Mason, James Dawolo, Yon Olaf Boone.

Row 2: Manager Ryan Elbing, Aaron Stinar, Jeremiah Walker, Matt Erlandson, Mark Barnhart, Chris Feehan, Andre Conner, Tyler Meuleners, Craig Botnen, Mike Kuprian, Charlie Krois, Aaron Schloer, Manager Ben Hagen.

Row 3: Matt Willis, Erik Yerigan, Athletic Trainer Scott Scholl, Coach Todd Murray, Coach Gerhard Meidt, Head Coach Chris Meidt, Coach Rob McCarthy, Coach Scottie Hazelton, Coach Steve Laqua, Coach Tom Lenox, Matt Dean, David Chapman.

Row 4: Manager Jacquelyn Perreault, Zach Bunnell, Dan Klopp, Brian Collins, John Davis, Jason Wilsey, Pete Zupfer, Nick Rost, Andrew Corum, Dan O'Malley, Matt Schraan, Pete Cathcart.

Row 5: Jake Porter, Bill Germscheid, Denny Wambach, Alain Vallet-Sandre, Cory Paterson, Tony De La Hunt, Ben Veach, Nate Johnson, Thomas Warfield, Matt Bucka, Peter Grinager, Andy Kelts.

Row 6: Eli Fylling, Ben Fuller, Kristoff Hendrickson, Max Bunge, Kyle Fritze, Jeremy Lund, Evan Klefsaas, Dave Busselman, Chris O'Neill, Jason Holthus, Peter Nelson, Mike Lemmage.

Back row: Dusty Powers, Teddy Bickel, Brian Senske, Jeremy Thomas, Tilman Achberger, Nate Lund, Jared Moen, Pat Bottini, Andy Bernard, Decker Walker, Kipp Pennau.

St. Olaf Football Records

St. Olaf All-Time Coaches

CHRONOLOGICAL

Year(s)	Coach	Wins	Losses	Ties	Win Pct.
1919–28	Endre Anderson	34	25	3	0.548
1929–42, 46–48, 51–57	Ade Christenson	101	75	11	0.540
1943–45	Mark Almli	8	8	0	0.500
1949–50	Helge Pukema	7	10	0	0.412
1958–67, 69–90	Tom Porter	171	119	5	0.580
1968	Dave Hauck	5	2	1	0.625
1991–95	Don Canfield	22	27	0	0.449
1996	Rod Grubb	2	8	0	0.200
1997–2001	Paul Miller	20	30	0	0.400
2002–	Chris Meidt	9	11	0	0.450

BY TOTAL WINS

Year(s)	Coach	Wins	Losses	Ties	Win Pct.
1958–67, 69–90	Tom Porter	171	119	5	0.580
1929–42, 46–48, 51–57	Ade Christenson	101	75	11	0.540
1919–28	Endre Anderson	34	25	3	0.548
1991–95	Don Canfield	22	27	0	0.449
1997–2001	Paul Miller	20	30	0	0.400
2002–	Chris Meidt	9	11	0	0.450
1943–45	Mark Almli	8	8	0	0.500
1949–50	Helge Pukema	7	10	0	0.412
1968	Dave Hauck	5	2	1	0.625
1996	Rod Grubb	2	8	0	0.200

BY WIN PERCENTAGE

Year(s)	Coach	Wins	Losses	Ties	Win Pct.
1968	Dave Hauck	5	2	1	0.625
1958–67, 69–90	Tom Porter	171	119	5	0.580
1919–28	Endre Anderson	34	25	3	0.548
1929–42, 46–48, 51–57	Ade Christenson	101	75	11	0.540
1943–45	Mark Almli	8	8	0	0.500
2002	Chris Meidt	9	11	0	0.450
1991–95	Don Canfield	22	27	0	0.449
1949–50	Helge Pukema	7	10	0	0.412
1997–2001	Paul Miller	20	30	0	0.400
1996	Rod Grubb	2	8	0	0.200

All-Time Individual Records

Record	Player	Yards/No.	Year (Opponent)
Game Rushing	Ole Gunderson	356	1969 (Monmouth)
Season Rushing	Ole Gunderson	1,591	1969
Career Rushing	Ole Gunderson	4,060	1969–71
Game Passing	Keith Karpinske	448	1993 (Concordia)
Season Passing	Keith Karpinske	2,491	1993
Career Passing	Keith Karpinske	5,078	1990–93
Game Receptions	Frank Bass	13	2002 (Bethel)
Season Receptions	Tom Buslee	75	1993
Career Receptions	Tom Buslee	155	1990–93
Game Receiving Yards	Tom Buslee	241	1993 (Concordia)
Season Receiving Yards	Tom Buslee	1,325	1993
Career Receiving Yards	Steve Ryan	2,618	1998–2002
Game Total Points	Manuel Spriegl	36	2000 (Carleton)
Season Total Points	Ole Gunderson	132	1969
Career Total Points	Ole Gunderson	362	1969–71
Season Interceptions	Bill Thomas	10	1985
	Bob Ehren	10	1989
Career Interceptions	Steve Ashley	21	1968–70

St. Olaf Football All-Americans

All-American	Position	Year
John Gustafson	End	1953
Paul Quam	Center	1955
Duane E. Brekken	Fullback	1956
Bill Winter	Fullback	1961
Mark Aamot	Halfback	1962
John Nahorniak	Linebacker	1978
Nate Bergeland	Defensive lineman	1979
Jon Anderson	Defensive lineman	1980
Ryan Hollom	Kick returner	1997, 1999
Steve Ryan	Wide receiver	2000
Manuel Spreigl	Running back	2000

Academic All-American

Name	Year
Aaron Butler	1992–93

MIAC Conference Offensive MVP

Name	Year
Steve Ryan	2000

National Player of the Week

Name	Year
Manuel Spreigl (vs. Carleton)	2000

Single Season Rushing Leaders

Name	Year	Rush Att.	Rush Yds	Rush TD
Ole Gunderson	1969	208	1,591	19
Manuel Spreigl	2000	247	1,290	16
Ole Gunderson	1970	212	1,265	16
Manuel Spreigl	2001	231	1,045	17
Ole Gunderson	1971	188	1,043	18
Dave Krahn	1966	180	1,030	
Dave Krahn	1965	130	942	
Mike Schmeising	1968	203	921	8
Bill Winter	1961	183	892	
Mike Schmeising	1967	187	880	
Bob Wetterberg	1969	161	869	11
Steve Schwarten	1971	165	838	9
Mark Gelle	1975	172	820	10
Brian Jacobs	1984	248	791	6
Mark Aamot	1962	197	784	
Mark Gelle	1973	166	754	7
Bob Klefsaas	1980	197	752	3
Mike Schrader	1978	188	750	7
Manuel Spreigl	1999	185	724	2
Mark Quinnell	1979	187	706	3

Career Rushing Leaders

Name	Years	Rush Att.	Rush Yds	Rush TD
Ole Gunderson	1969–71	608	3,899	53
Manuel Spreigl	1998–2001	692	3,122	36
Mark Gelle	1972–75	662	2,829	24
Bob Klefsaas	1978–81	559	2,054	18
Brad Wolner	1980–83	498	1,972	9
Dave Krahn	1965–66	310	1,972	
Mike Schmeising	1967–68	390	1,801	8
Mike Berletic	1984–87	486	1,728	10
Mark Quinnell	1976–79	467	1,646	9
Eric Anderson	1993–96	383	1,572	9
Dan Kyllo	1979–81	356	1,539	12
Brian Jacobs	1981–84	500	1,434	14
Bill Winter	1960–61	292	1,318	
Tim Peloquin	1987–91	341	1,175	11
David Keenan	1990–93	253	1,043	10

(missing 1959 and 1991 statistics)

Single Season Receiving Yardage Leaders

Name	Year	Rec.	Rec. Yds	Rec. TD
Tom Buslee	1993	75	1,325	
Frank Bass	2002	73	1,109	9
Steve Ryan	2001	52	948	8
Steve Ryan	2000	53	901	7
Mike Rinke	1984	38	702	7
Mike Mercer	1990	35	669	6
Steve Ryan	1999	41	659	7
Don Larson	1987	37	650	3
Ivan Carter	1996	38	647	4
Steve Mathre	1988	35	624	3
Steve McKay	1979	36	620	4
Brian Sprout	1999	32	618	4
Brian Sprout	2001	43	596	6
John Best	1994	53	565	3
Dave Schooler	1986	36	546	2
Tait Lillemoe	1995	38	541	4
Cory Paterson	2002	31	532	4
Bryan Bass	1995	27	506	3
John Best	1993	33	474	4
Ryan Hollom	1998	34	465	2

Career Receiving Yardage Leaders

Name	Years	Rec.	Rec. Yds	Rec. TD
Steve Ryan	1998–2002	152	2,618	24
Tom Buslee	1990–93	155	2,454	

Single Season Passing Yardage Leaders

Name	Year	Pass Att.	Pass Comp.	Pass Yds	Pass TD	Int's Thrown
Keith Karpinske	1993	368	202	2,491	18	17
Brian Senske	2002	292	172	2,292	17	10
Joe Hammond	1999	243	135	2,021	12	17
Chuck Ohm	1995	275	151	1,816	12	9
Brian Senske	2000	217	124	1,706	9	8
Chuck Ohm	1996	238	117	1,548	12	8
Brian Senske	2003	228	125	1,422	10	12
Peter Schultz	1998	166	99	1,405	14	8
Chris Novak	1987	239	96	1,367	6	23
Brian Senske	2001	188	108	1,360	9	9
Keith Karpinske	1992	221	97	1,345	11	13
Leif Syverson	1985	246	112	1,315	4	16
Karl Bowman	1989	205	92	1,131	10	12

Career Passing Yardage Leaders

Name	Years	Pass Att.	Pass Comp.	Pass Yds	Pass TD	Int's Thrown
Brian Senske	2000–03	925	529	6,780	45	39
Keith Karpinske	1990–93			5,078		
Chuck Ohm	1993–96	677	345	4,069	33	22
Joe Hammond	1998–2001	407	230	3,303	22	26
Paul Anderson	1965–67	354	164	2,429	20	23
Peter Schultz	1995–98	365	186	2,299	19	21
Chris Novak	1986–89	436	172	2,293	10	34
Chris Reinerston	1985–88	320	137	1,784	11	21
Bob Klefsaas	1978–81	327	125	1,755	15	26
Karl Nienhuis	1983–84	287	125	1,681	8	21

(missing 1991 statistics)

Season Interceptions

Name	Int.	Year
Bill Thomas	10	1985
Bob Ehren	10	1989

Career Interceptions

Name	Int.	Years
Steve Ashley	21	1968–70

All-Time Summary of Scores

1919	STO	Opp.	W/L
Pillsbury Academy	25	0	W
Hamline	7	19	L
Gustavus Adolphus	27	7	W
Macalester	6	9	L
Carleton	7	15	L
Season Record	**2–3**		

1920			
Phalen Luther	54	7	W
St. Mary's	18	0	W
Hamline	6	0	W
Gustavus Adolphus	14	0	W
Macalester	14	20	L
Carleton	0	21	L
St. Thomas	6	0	W
Season Record	**4–2**		

1921			
Concordia	97	0	W
Luther	10	0	W
Macalester	7	6	W
Carleton	3	20	L
St. Thomas	2	7	L
Gustavus Adolphus	14	0	W
Season Record	**4–2**		
Conference Record	**3–2**		

1922			
Concordia	35	0	W
Macalester	14	14	L
St. John's	20	10	W
Carleton	19	0	W
Luther	35	0	W
Gustavus Adolphus	41	0	W
Season Record	**5–0–1**		

1923			
St. Mary's	31	0	W
Concordia	17	0	W
Luther	7	7	L
Macalester	21	0	W
Carleton	6	0	W
St. Thomas	14	19	L
Superior Teachers	20	12	W
Gustavus Adolphus	37	0	W
Season Record	**6–1–1**		
Conference Record	**4–1**		

1924			
St. Mary's	0	0	L
Carleton	12	16	L
Gustavus Adolphus	16	0	W
Luther	33	7	W
Concordia	16	0	W
St. John's	23	0	W
St. Thomas	14	20	L
Season Record	**4–2–1**		
Conference Record	**3–1–1**		

1925			
Phalen Luther	51	0	W
St. John's	7	0	W
Concordia	40	0	W
Luther	0	16	L
Carleton	0	13	L
Gustavus Adolphus	6	9	L
St. Mary's	11	13	L
Hamline	7	6	W
Macalester	6	28	L
Season Record	**4–5**		
Conference Record	**4–2**		

1926	STO	Opp.	W/L
Augsburg	26	0	W
Concordia	26	0	W
Carleton	0	42	L
Gustavus Adolphus	0	7	L
Luther	0	17	L
Hamline	0	19	L
Macalester	7	19	L
Season Record	**2–5**		
Conference Record	**2–3**		

1927			
Macalester	2	18	L
Augsburg	14	7	W
Concordia	12	13	L
Luther	12	7	W
Carleton	6	43	L
St. Mary's	6	20	L
Hamline	0	24	L
Season Record	**2–5**		
Conference Record	**1–4**		

1928			
Augsburg	0	13	L
St. Mary's	0	21	L
Hamline	0	0	L
Carleton	0	26	L
Concordia	0	25	L
Gustavus Adolphus	26	14	W
Luther	0	6	L
Season Record	**1–5–1**		
Conference Record	**1–3–1**		

1929			
River Falls Teachers	26	0	W
Hamline	40	19	W
St. Thomas	0	6	L
Luther	18	6	W
Carleton	25	13	W
Gustavus Adolphus	18	6	W
Concordia	12	7	W
Augsburg	51	7	W
Season Record	**7–1**		
Conference Record	**4–1**		

1930			
Hamline	52	6	W
South Dakota State	20	0	W
Macalester	26	7	W
Carleton	19	0	W
St. John's	82	0	W
Gustavus Adolphus	20	12	W
Luther	25	7	W
Augsburg	58	0	W
Season Record	**8–0**		
Conference Record	**5–0**		

1931			
North Dakota University	0	22	L
Augsburg	58	0	W
Carleton	25	6	W
St. John's	0	13	L
Gustavus Adolphus	26	0	W
St. Mary's	20	0	W
Luther	14	6	W
Concordia	21	6	W
Season Record	**6–2**		
Conference Record	**4–1**		

1932	STO	Opp.	W/L
St. Thomas	14	12	W
Concordia	7	13	L
Augsburg	26	0	W
Carleton	0	9	L
Gustavus Adolphus	0	3	L
Luther	0	7	L
St. Mary's	0	12	L
Season Record	**2–5**		
Conference Record	**2–3**		

1933			
Superior Teachers	0	6	L
Macalester	39	0	W
Augsburg	27	7	W
St. Thomas	13	20	L
Luther	14	0	W
Carleton	0	6	L
Concordia	25	13	W
Season Record	**4–3**		
Conference Record	**3–1**		

1934			
St. Thomas	2	0	W
Macalester	7	7	L
Concordia	7	19	L
Augsburg	44	8	W
Carleton	0	12	L
Luther	13	0	W
South Dakota State	6	14	L
Season Record	**3–3–1**		
Conference Record	**2–1–1**		

1935			
St. Mary's	12	0	W
Superior Teachers	0	31	L
Luther	0	7	L
Carleton	0	6	L
Concordia	20	6	W
St. Thomas	18	0	W
South Dakota State	0	34	L
Augsburg		forfeit	W
Season Record	**4–4**		
Conference Record	**4–0**		

1936			
St. Mary's	30	6	W
Macalester	33	0	W
St. John's	6	13	L
Carleton	7	26	L
Gustavus Adolphus	0	13	L
La Crosse Teachers	0	0	L
Luther	6	0	W
Season Record	**3–3–1**		
Conference Record	**2–2**		

1937			
Stout	26	0	W
Macalester	0	6	L
Concordia	7	13	L
Luther	6	19	L
Carleton	6	14	L
Hamline	6	6	L
St. Thomas	7	7	L
Season Record	**1–4–2**		
Conference Record	**0–2–2**		

1938

	STO	Opp.	W/L
Macalester	27	12	W
St. John's	14	19	L
St. Mary's	28	9	W
Carleton	6	2	W
Hamline	13	7	W
Luther	12	0	W
St. Thomas	0	7	L
Season Record	**5–2**		
Conference Record	**3–2**		

1939

	STO	Opp.	W/L
St. Thomas	0	7	L
Hamline	25	13	W
Luther	3	0	W
Macalester	6	7	L
Carleton	7	18	L
Concordia	7	7	L
Gustavus	7	21	L
Season Record	**2–4–1**		
Conference Record	**1–3–1**		

1940

	STO	Opp.	W/L
St. Mary's	6	13	L
Luther	6	12	L
Concordia	0	6	L
Carleton	6	13	L
St. John's	0	19	L
St. Thomas	20	26	L
Gustavus	6	20	L
Season Record	**0–7**		
Conference Record	**0–5**		

1941

	STO	Opp.	W/L
Concordia	0	7	L
St. Thomas	7	19	L
Luther	0	20	L
Carleton	7	7	L
Augsburg	25	0	W
Hamline	19	7	W
St. Mary's	0	24	L
Season Record	**2–4–1**		
Conference Record	**2–3**		

1942

	STO	Opp.	W/L
Augsburg	32	0	W
Concordia	6	7	L
Luther	13	13	L
Hamline	7	9	L
St. Thomas	0	28	L
Carleton	7	14	L
Macalester	6	0	W
Season Record	**2–4–1**		
Conference Record	**2–3**		

1943

	STO	Opp.	W/L
River Falls Teachers	12	20	L
River Falls Teachers	0	19	L
Luther	31	19	W
Season Record	**1–2**		

1944

	STO	Opp.	W/L
St. Thomas	0	27	L
St. Mary's	12	20	L
River Falls Teachers	20	0	W
Cornell	13	0	W
St. Mary's	21	0	W
Cornell	7	0	W
River Falls Teachers	73	6	W
Drake	13	26	L
Season Record	**5–3**		
Conference Record	**1–2**		

1945

	STO	Opp.	W/L
Gustavus Adolphus	6	8	L
St. Thomas	0	18	L
Bemidji Teachers	19	0	W
Minnesota "B"	0	12	L
St. John's	21	6	W
Season Record	**2–3**		
Conference Record	**1–2**		

1946

	STO	Opp.	W/L
River Falls	13	6	W
Macalester	19	6	W
Concordia	20	0	W
Luther	19	13	W
Carleton	14	13	W
Augsburg	7	0	W
Gustavus Adolphus	6	21	L
Minnesota "B"	6	32	L
Season Record	**6–2**		
Conference Record	**3–1**		

1947

	STO	Opp.	W/L
Pacific Lutheran	0	14	L
Hamline	0	6	L
Luther	26	7	W
Concordia	7	6	W
Augsburg	19	13	W
Carleton	14	12	W
St. John's	20	16	W
Macalester	6	14	L
Season Record	**5–3**		
Conference Record	**3–2**		

1948

	STO	Opp.	W/L
Pacific Lutheran	6	14	L
Hamline	7	7	L
Concordia	30	13	W
Luther	6	0	W
Carleton	6	13	L
Augsburg	34	7	W
Macalester	7	21	L
St. John's	13	26	L
Season Record	**3–4–1**		
Conference Record	**2–2–1**		

1949

	STO	Opp.	W/L
River Falls	34	0	W
St. Mary's	26	6	W
Hamline	0	13	L
St. Thomas	7	51	L
Carleton	13	6	W
St. John's	6	20	L
Augsburg	13	6	W
Gustavus Adolphus	0	20	L
Luther	13	6	W
Season Record	**5–4**		
Conference Record	**2–4**		

1950

	STO	Opp.	W/L
Concordia	18	12	W
University of MN-Duluth	6	19	L
St. Thomas	7	14	L
South Dakota State	14	41	L
Carleton	21	34	L
Augsburg	7	18	L
St. Mary's	27	0	W
Gustavus Adolphus	0	53	L
Season Record	**2–6**		
Conference Record	**2–4**		

1951

	STO	Opp.	W/L
Stout	13	19	L
Macalester	42	13	W
Hamline	0	7	L
St. Thomas	13	14	L
Carleton	0	13	L
St. Mary's	25	13	W
Concordia	33	27	W
Season Record	**3–4**		
Conference Record	**3–2**		

1952

	STO	Opp.	W/L
Knox	13	14	L
Simpson	41	6	W
St. John's	0	34	L
Grinnell	20	13	W
Carleton	41	12	W
Lawrence	13	26	L
Monmouth	21	18	W
Ripon	25	6	W
Season Record	**5–3**		
Conference Record	**4–2**		

1953

	STO	Opp.	W/L
Knox	28	19	W
Wartburg	35	14	W
Bethel	78	0	W
Grinnell	60	12	W
Carleton	34	0	W
Lawrence	35	13	W
Monmouth	34	0	W
Ripon	58	0	W
Season Record	**8–0**		
Conference Record	**6–0**		

1954

	STO	Opp.	W/L
Grinnell	13	13	L
Lawrence	13	6	W
Ripon	26	7	W
Carleton	13	14	L
Cornell	7	6	W
Knox	33	13	W
Monmouth	33	6	W
Coe	27	27	L
Season Record	**5–1–2**		

1955

	STO	Opp.	W/L
Grinnell	34	0	W
Northland	51	0	W
Ripon	52	12	W
Carleton	40	13	W
Cornell	20	7	W
Knox	32	6	W
Monmouth	47	0	W
Coe	14	28	L
Season Record	**7–1**		
Conference Record	**6–1**		

1956

	STO	Opp.	W/L
Lawrence	31	13	W
Ripon	32	13	W
Carleton	6	18	L
Cornell	18	35	L
Knox	40	6	W
Monmouth	34	0	W
Coe	33	13	W
Grinnell	40	13	W
Season Record	**6–2**		

1957

	STO	Opp.	W/L
Lawrence	19	13	W
Ripon	26	31	L
Carleton	6	14	L
Cornell	20	13	W
Knox	32	6	W
Monmouth	35	0	W
Coe	7	13	L
Grinnell	0	6	L
Season Record	**4–4**		

1958

	STO	Opp.	W/L
Ripon	7	40	L
Carleton	21	27	L
Cornell	13	8	W
Knox	29	21	W
Monmouth	12	20	L
Coe	14	16	L
Grinnell	29	7	W
Lawrence	24	14	W
Season Record	**4–4**		

1959

	STO	Opp.	W/L
Beloit	28	0	W
Cornell	0	19	L
Ripon	7	18	L
Knox	7	6	W
Carleton	7	0	W
Grinnell	16	6	W
Monmouth	27	14	W
Lawrence	28	8	W
Season Record	**6–2**		

1960

	STO	Opp.	W/L
Beloit	20	6	W
Cornell	21	7	W
Ripon	26	13	W
Knox	28	22	W
Carleton	13	20	L
Grinnell	21	14	W
Monmouth	36	12	W
Lawrence	16	20	L
Season Record	**6–2**		

1961

	STO	Opp.	W/L
Coe	19	8	W
Beloit	8	7	W
Cornell	7	26	L
Ripon	27	21	W
Carleton	20	27	L
Knox	34	0	W
Grinnell	22	21	W
Monmouth	35	8	W
Season Record	**6–2**		

1962

	STO	Opp.	W/L
Coe	23	8	W
Beloit	13	18	L
Cornell	15	9	W
Ripon	14	14	L
Carleton	27	13	W
Knox	10	0	W
Grinnell	7	21	L
Monmouth	27	0	W
Season Record	**5–2–1**		

1963

	STO	Opp.	W/L
Lawrence	23	8	W
Coe	17	12	W
Beloit	8	7	W
Cornell	7	35	L
Carleton	20	29	L
Ripon	19	27	L
Knox	52	8	W
Grinnell	7	26	L
Season Record	**4–4**		

1964

	STO	Opp.	W/L
Lawrence	20	0	W
Coe	6	16	L
Beloit	15	13	W
Cornell	13	28	L
Carleton	21	7	W
Ripon	0	7	L
Knox	27	6	W
Grinnell	10	28	L
Season Record	**4–4**		

1965

	STO	Opp.	W/L
Monmouth	6	7	L
Lawrence	21	27	L
Coe	34	14	W
Beloit	24	7	W
Carleton	28	20	W
Cornell	13	21	L
Ripon	22	7	W
Knox	53	0	W
Season Record	**5–3**		

1966

	STO	Opp.	W/L
Monmouth	55	14	W
Lawrence	21	24	L
Coe	19	9	W
Beloit	36	0	W
Carleton	26	7	W
Cornell	49	7	W
Ripon	47	28	W
Knox	41	0	W
Season Record	**7–1**		

1967

	STO	Opp.	W/L
Grinnell	28	20	W
Monmouth	42	32	W
Lawrence	7	28	L
Coe	34	0	W
Carleton	3	0	W
Beloit	13	14	L
Cornell	23	8	W
Ripon	21	18	W
Season Record	**6–2**		

1968

	STO	Opp.	W/L
Grinnell	28	0	W
Monmouth	21	21	L
Lawrence	21	0	W
Coe	0	19	L
Carleton	38	7	W
Beloit	44	0	W
Cornell	27	51	L
Ripon	14	10	W
Season Record	**5–2–1**		

1969

	STO	Opp.	W/L
Cornell	42	27	W
Ripon	29	13	W
Knox	49	19	W
Grinnell	55	21	W
Monmouth	38	31	W
Carleton	62	37	W
Lawrence	8	22	L
Coe	42	8	W
Beloit	82	7	W
Season Record	**8–1**		

1970

	STO	Opp.	W/L
Lawrence	14	0	W
Coe	26	10	W
Beloit	55	13	W
Cornell	28	14	W
Ripon	27	21	W
Carleton	30	13	W
Knox	56	22	W
Grinnell	35	7	W
Monmouth	41	32	W
Season Record	**9–0**		

1971

	STO	Opp.	W/L
Coe	30	6	W
Beloit	54	13	W
Cornell	37	26	W
Ripon	23	26	L
Knox	28	26	W
Carleton	35	0	W
Grinnell	51	7	W
Monmouth	33	21	W
Lawrence	30	7	W
Season Record	**8–1**		

1972

	STO	Opp.	W/L
Mayville State	30	0	W
Coe	17	7	W
Beloit	14	0	W
Ripon	14	6	W
Cornell	0	19	L
Carleton	27	14	W
Knox	6	7	L
Grinnell	56	7	W
Monmouth	7	27	L
Season Record	**6–3**		

1973

	STO	Opp.	W/L
Mayville	6	20	L
Coe	0	30	L
Beloit	35	7	W
Ripon	28	22	W
Cornell	43	12	W
Carleton	14	16	L
Knox	27	19	W
Grinnell	48	7	W
Monmouth	14	16	L
Season Record	**5–4**		
Conference Record	**5–3**		

1974

	STO	Opp.	W/L
Macalester	15	14	W
St. John's	21	51	L
Concordia	3	6	L
Augsburg	0	16	L
Hamline	14	21	L
Carleton	24	7	W
St. Thomas	6	14	L
Gustavus Adolphus	20	21	L
University of MN-Duluth	7	0	W
Season Record	**3–6**		
Conference Record	**1–6**		

1975	STO	Opp.	W/L
Macalester	35	0	W
St. John's	14	14	L
Concordia	6	9	L
Augsburg	31	6	W
Hamline	34	6	W
Carleton	48	0	W
St. Thomas	7	21	L
Gustavus	27	14	W
University of MN-Duluth	6	14	L
Season Record	**5–3–1**		
Conference Record	**3–3–1**		

1976			
Wartburg	29	7	W
Carleton	42	0	W
Augsburg	19	6	W
Hamline	3	0	W
Concordia	8	17	L
Macalester	35	0	W
Gustavus Adolphus	22	15	W
Bethel	0	20	L
St. John's	13	29	L
St. Thomas	16	0	W
Season Record	**7–3**		
Conference Record	**5–2**		

1977			
Wartburg	19	7	W
Carleton	43	0	W
Augsburg	24	13	W
Hamline	17	24	L
Concordia	6	17	L
Macalester	67	0	W
Gustavus Adolphus	15	20	L
Bethel	25	13	W
St. John's	7	21	L
St. Thomas	7	7	L
Season Record	**5–4–1**		
Conference Record	**2–4–1**		

1978			
Cornell	23	7	W
Macalester	55	13	W
Concordia	26	17	W
Hamline	27	12	W
St. Thomas	16	14	W
Gustavus Adolphus	13	21	L
St. John's	24	21	W
Carleton	22	0	W
Bethel	21	2	W
Augsburg	41	25	W
University of MN-Morris	23	10	W
Season Record	**9–2**		
Conference Record	**7–1**		

1979			
Cornell	25	37	L
Macalester	21	7	W
Concordia	13	16	L
Hamline	22	13	W
St. Thomas	31	20	W
Gustavus Adolphus	18	15	W
St. John's	9	21	L
Carleton	22	8	W
Bethel	34	7	W
Augsburg	48	14	W
Season Record	**7–3**		
Conference Record	**6–2**		

1980	STO	Opp.	W/L
Carleton	49	20	W
St. Thomas	17	0	W
St. John's	3	14	L
Augsburg	23	7	W
Michigan Tech	30	20	W
Hamline	7	25	L
Gustavus Adolphus	3	27	L
Bethel	10	9	W
Concordia	6	16	L
Macalester	21	0	W
Season Record	**6–4**		
Conference Record	**4–4**		

1981			
Carleton	12	20	L
Luther	14	2	W
St. Thomas	7	16	L
St. John's	0	23	L
Augsburg	16	38	L
Michigan Tech.	14	0	W
Hamline	10	7	W
Gustavus Adolphus	0	23	L
Bethel	21	23	L
Concordia	13	42	L
Macalester	23	20	W
Season Record	**4–7**		
Conference Record	**2–6**		

1982			
Carleton	9	0	W
Macalester	12	20	L
Concordia	11	39	L
Bethel	21	8	W
Hamline	3	21	L
St. Thomas	14	38	L
St. John's	8	38	L
Gustavus Adolphus	10	20	L
Augsburg	17	24	L
Luther	14	21	L
Season Record	**2–8**		
Conference Record	**1–6**		

1983			
Luther	0	25	L
Macalester	19	14	W
Concordia	9	14	L
Bethel	17	18	L
Hamline	9	19	L
St. Thomas	0	14	L
St. John's	12	17	L
Gustavus Adolphus	14	17	L
Augsburg	38	15	W
Carleton	24	13	W
Season Record	**3–7**		
Conference Record	**3–6**		

1984			
Luther	24	13	W
Macalester	14	28	L
Gustavus Adolphus	25	30	L
Bethel	22	7	W
St. John's	31	0	W
St. Thomas	15	35	L
Carleton	24	19	W
Concordia	10	10	L
Augsburg	26	0	W
Hamline	7	7	L
Season Record	**5–3–2**		
Conference Record	**4–3–2**		

1985	STO	Opp.	W/L
Luther	20	22	L
Macalester	10	20	L
Gustavus Adolphus	21	24	L
Bethel	9	13	L
St. John's	15	10	W
St. Thomas	0	41	L
Carleton	7	35	L
Concordia	12	2	W
Augsurg	28	16	W
Hamline	21	16	W
Season Record	**4–6**		
Conference Record	**4–5**		

1986			
Luther	6	0	W
St. Thomas	0	44	L
Hamline	16	13	W
Bethel	38	19	W
Gustavus Adolphus	15	38	L
Carleton	3	6	L
Concordia	14	39	L
Macalester	25	35	L
Augsburg	17	10	W
St. John's	16	14	W
Season Record	**5–5**		
Conference Record	**4–5**		

1987			
Luther	0	10	L
St. Thomas	0	17	L
Hamline	6	37	L
Bethel	21	13	W
Gustavus Adolphus	10	21	L
Carleton	18	37	L
Concordia	10	31	L
Macalester	28	21	W
Augsburg	28	0	W
St. John's	2	28	L
Season Record	**3–7**		
Conferene Record	**3–6**		

1988			
Luther	17	10	W
Macalester	7	14	L
Carleton	7	25	L
Bethel	17	15	W
Hamline	19	22	L
Gustavus Adolphus	30	33	L
Concordia	0	10	L
Augsburg	17	13	W
St. John's	31	34	L
St. Thomas	22	15	W
Season Record	**4–6**		
Conference Record	**3–6**		

1989			
Luther	20	13	W
Macalester	26	8	W
Carleton	27	22	W
Bethel	6	10	L
Hamline	26	5	W
Gustavus Adolphus	13	22	L
Concordia	7	24	L
Augsburg	28	0	W
St. John's	0	35	L
St. Thomas	24	21	W
Season Record	**6–4**		
Conference Record	**5–4**		

1990	STO	Opp.	W/L
Luther	22	21	W
Augsburg	34	0	W
Gustavus Adolphus	13	26	L
Macalester	43	8	W
St. Thomas	0	21	L
Bethel	24	19	W
Concordia	7	24	L
St. John's	6	45	L
Carleton	20	37	L
Hamline	6	21	L
Season Record	**4–6**		
Conference Record	**3–6**		

1991	STO	Opp.	W/L
Luther	22	21	W
Augsburg	35	13	W
Gustavus	13	28	L
Macalester	62	0	W
St. Thomas	26	25	W
Bethel	17	6	W
Concordia	24	13	W
St. John's	19	67	L
Hamline	26	23	W
Season Record	**7–2**		
Conference Record	**6–2**		

1992	STO	Opp.	W/L
Luther	13	31	L
St. Thomas	14	7	W
St. John's	7	62	L
Macalester	47	0	W
Gustavus Adolphus	9	14	L
Carleton	9	21	L
Hamline	14	17	L
Concordia	21	45	L
Bethel	27	20	W
Augsburg	20	18	W
Season Record	**4–6**		
Conference Record	**4–5**		

1993	STO	Opp.	W/L
Luther	23	14	W
St. Thomas	12	35	L
St. John's	10	71	L
Macalester	28	15	W
Gustavus Adolphus	26	23	W
Carleton	48	51	L
Hamline	13	21	L
Concordia	58	34	W
Bethel	15	17	L
Augsburg	24	26	L
Season Record	**4–6**		
Conference Record	**3–6**		

1994	STO	Opp.	W/L
Luther	15	18	L
Hamline	9	19	L
St. Thomas	20	19	W
Gustavus	12	14	L
Carleton	6	18	L
Macalester	35	25	W
Concordia	0	38	L
St. John's	15	49	L
Bethel	20	41	L
Augsburg	20	34	L
Season Record	**2–8**		
Conference Record	**2–7**		

1995	STO	Opp.	W/L
Luther	23	0	W
Hamline	21	20	W
St. Thomas	14	35	L
Gustavus Adolphus	28	22	W
Carleton	15	21	L
Macalester	35	18	W
Concordia	16	48	L
St. John's	24	21	W
Bethel	7	42	L
Augsburg	12	20	L
Season Record	**5–5**		
Conference Record	**4–5**		

1996	STO	Opp.	W/L
Luther	29	28	W
St. John's	7	36	L
Concordia	7	21	L
Augsburg	30	27	W
Macalester	17	31	L
Hamline	22	24	L
Bethel	6	30	L
Carleton	9	42	L
St. Thomas	26	49	L
Gustavus Adolphus	14	20	L
Season Record	**2–8**		
Conference Record	**1–8**		

1997	STO	Opp.	W/L
Luther	12	19	L
St. John's	7	21	L
Concordia	0	38	L
Augsburg	0	42	L
Macalester	19	3	W
Hamline	21	27	L
Bethel	10	52	L
Carleton	14	12	W
St. Thomas	3	28	L
Gustavus Adolphus	6	37	L
Season Record	**2–8**		
Conference Record	**2–7**		

1998	STO	Opp.	W/L
Carthage	0	23	L
St. Thomas	6	9	L
Augsburg	24	31	L
Bethel	28	33	L
Concordia	21	35	L
Hamline	13	14	L
Carleton	21	7	W
St. John's	0	35	L
Gustavus Adolphus	14	49	L
Macalester	33	14	W
Season Record	**2–8**		
Conference Record	**2–7**		

1999	STO	Opp.	W/L
Carthage	14	21	L
St. Thomas	3	33	L
Augsburg	27	30	L
Bethel	13	39	L
Concordia	10	17	L
Hamline	25	20	W
Carleton	27	19	W
St. John's	14	21	L
Gustavus Adolphus	17	36	L
Macalester	47	17	W
Season Record	**3–7**		
Conference Record	**3–6**		

2000	STO	Opp.	W/L
Martin Luther	21	9	W
St. John's	6	42	L
Hamline	28	18	W
Augsburg	28	6	W
Bethel	3	32	L
St. Thomas	24	15	W
Concordia	27	24	W
Macalester	34	10	W
Gustavus Adolphus	28	45	L
Carleton	42	35	W
Season Record	**7–3**		
Conference Record	**6–3**		

2001	STO	Opp.	W/L
Martin Luther	35	21	W
St. John's	31	28	W
Hamline	33	12	W
Augsburg	0	20	L
Bethel	6	38	L
St. Thomas	16	28	L
Concordia	34	33	W
Macalester	35	18	W
Carleton	28	6	W
Gustavus Adolphus	21	51	L
Season Record	**6–4**		
Conference Record	**5–4**		

2002	STO	Opp.	W/L
Carroll	57	14	W
Carleton	49	0	W
Augsburg	23	21	W
St. John's	20	59	L
St. Thomas	15	35	L
Bethel	32	36	L
Hamline	48	12	W
Macalester	34	6	W
Concordia	14	24	L
Gustavus Adolphus	23	24	L
Season Record	**5–5**		
Conference Record	**3–5**		

2003	STO	Opp.	W/L
Luther	10	23	L
Carleton	40	16	W
Augsburg	24	31	L
St. John's	6	45	L
St. Thomas	9	27	L
Bethel	7	33	L
Hamline	43	13	W
Macalester	47	14	W
Concordia	14	47	L
Gustavus Adolphus	41	27	W
Season Record	**4–6**		
Conference Record	**3–5**		

All-Time Record Versus Opponents

Opponent	Total Wins	Total Losses	Games Tied
Augsburg	34	14	
Beloit	13	2	
Bemidji Teachers	1		
Bethel	13	15	
Carleton	41	39	1
Carroll	1		
Carthage		3	
Coe	11	6	1
Concordia	21	32	2
Cornell	15	8	
Drake		1	
Grinnell	15	4	1
Gustavus Adolphus	16	34	
Hamline	22	21	4
Knox	18	2	
La Crosse Teachers			1
Lawrence	11	6	
Luther	27	16	2
Macalester	33	15	2
Martin Luther	2		
Mayville	1	1	
Michigan Tech	2		
Monmouth	15	4	1
North Dakota University		1	
Northland	1		
Pacific Luther		2	
Phalen-Luther	2		
Pillsbury Academy	1		
Ripon	15	6	1
River Falls Teachers	5	2	
Simpson	1		
South Dakota State	1	3	
St. John's	12	30	1
St. Mary's	10	7	1
St. Thomas	14	34	2
Stout	1	1	
Superior Teachers	1	2	
University of MN "B"		2	
University of MN-Duluth	1	2	
University of MN-Morris	1		
Wartburg	3		

Manning the scoreboard, 1922

Greg Van Guilder pressures the passer, 1984

Coaches, Captains, and Players

Head Coaches

Name	Seasons Coached	Name	Seasons Coached	Name	Seasons Coached
Almli, Mark	1943–45	Christenson, Ade	1929–42, 46–48, 51–57	Meidt, Chris	2002–
Anderson, Endre	1919–28			Miller, Paul	1997–2001
Canfield, Don	1991–95	Grubb, Rodd	1996	Porter, Tom	1958–67, 69–90
		Hauck, Dave	1968	Pukema, Helge	1949–50

Assistant Coaches

Name	Seasons Coached	Name	Seasons Coached	Name	Seasons Coached
Aldrich, Mike	1995-98	Grangaard, Art	1939–41	Meidt, Gerhard	2002–03
Allen, Mike	1988–90	Gross, Fred	1920	Menozzi, Craig	1997
Almli, Mark	1942, 1947–48	Gross, John	1997–2001	Miller, Dennis	1981
Anderson, Endre	1937	Grubb, Rod	1979–86, 1988	Mully, Del	1951
Bailey, Adam	2001	Hauck, Dave	1967–95	Murray, Todd	2002–03
Bentley, Aaron	1997–99	Haugen, Marshall "Mush"	1949–50	Newberry, Bob	1997–98
Bergan, Dave	1999	Hazelton, Scott	2002–03	Nygaard, Joe	1949–50
Bergstrom, Carl	1978	Hoffman, Jim	1997	Olson, R.	1931
Bolstorff, Dave	1956	Hunt, Vince "Pop"	1944–45	Persuitti, Joe	2002
Boyum, Deryl "Skip"	1959	Isaacs, Peter	1959	Pierce, LaRue	1999–2000
Browning, Keith	1997	Iverson, Carl	1935–36	Poole, Eric	2002
Bundgaard, Ax	1968	Johnson, Kurt	1985	Price, Wayne	2001
Christianson, Ade	1927–28	Johnson, Dick	1998–99	Pulkrabeck, Les	1930
Cook, Kevin	1996–97	Keenan, Dave	1994–95	Quam, Paul	1964–66
Dahl, Orville	1934	Kemming, Vic	1992–94	Ramus, Ron	1985–91
Dimick, Jim	1967–76, 78–83, 1985–91	Klefsaas, Bob	1983–86	Ross, Tom	1995–96
		Klinkhammer, Joe	1984	Soli, Dan	1933–34
Droen, Al	1932	Kluck, Darrell	1997–2001	Sand, Art	1946–47
Elliott, Adam	1992	Larsen, Tim	1975–94	Schutz, Howie	1954–55
Fassum, Pete	1924	Larsen, Chuck	1990–96	Schwartz, Chris	2001
Fassum, Mike	1994–96	Lee, Art	1920	Sorenson, Russ	1958
Fogelson, Dan	2001	Lenox, Tom	2003	Stanton, Chris	2002–03
Fremouw, Fred	1925–27	Loqua, Steve	2003	Stevenson, Mike	1965
Frykman, Malcom	1929	Lore, Bob	1958	Swanson, Carl "Cully"	1927–32
Gabrialson, Jim	1956–57	Lunder, Chuck	1952–76	Swenson, Duane	1959
Gelle, Bob	1957–74	Magrane, Scott	1989	Thompson, Dick	1946
Gelle, Mark	1976–77	Marino, Gordon	2002–03	Veldey, Selmer	1923
Gilbertson, Cliff	1937–38	McCarthy, Rob	2002–03	Walker, Dick	1997–2001
Goodwin, Chris	2001	McDonald, Matt	1991–2001	Wrigglesworth, Frank	1951–53

The 1987 staff: Trainer Dan Hagen, Dave Hauck, Mark York, Rod Grubb, Ron Rasmus, Jim Dimick, Tim Larsen, and Tom Porter

Captains

1919
Selmer Veldey

1920
Otto Glesne

1921
Arnold Flaten

1922
Ingwald Swenson

1923
Martin Cole

1924
Cully Swanson

1925
Henry Pearson

1926
Stanley Anderson

1927
Elmer Satterlie

1928
Earle Obermeyer

1929
Mark Almli

1930
Bert Larson

1931
Syl Saumer

1932
Norman Nordstrand

1933
Ralph Summers

1934
Kermit Anderson

1935
Arthur Sand

1936
John Kirkeby

1937
Norm Anderson
Erling Kloster

1938
Everett Nyman
Rudolph Ramseth

1939
Earl Thorpe

1940
Milton Nesse

1941
Andy Droen

1942
Robert Sieveke

1943
Jerry Thompson

1944
George Crenshaw
Darrell Swenson

1945
Charles Dawson

1946
Stan Tostengard

1947
Elton Lehrke

1948
Robert DeWyze
Harold Poppitz

1949
Ron Henriksen
Don Larsen

1950
Tom Porter
Russ Adamson

1951
Paul Forsberg
Harlan Hogsven

1952
Duane Hoven
Ramon Runkel

1953
John Gustafson
Clinton Sathrum

1954
Dave Bolstorff
Dick Werdahl

1955
Buzz Helseth
Paul Quam

1956
Wayne Brown
William Lund

1957
Waldo Larson
Tom Anderson

1958
Duane Swenson
Dave Robinson

1959
Ron Caple
Ron Ree

1960
Jack Rajala
Bill Greenslit

1961
Tom Everson
Bill Winter

1962
Mark Aamot
Don Canfield

1963
Chuck Peterson
Fred Meyer

1964
Brian Kispert
Clark Westphal

1965
Tom Mickelson
Tom Heiberg

1966
Mike Solhaug
Steve Refsell

1967
Lee Mesna
Kirk Anderson

1968
Dennis Myers
Mike Schmeising

1969
Tim Smith
Don Krahn

1970
Bob Matson
Steve Ashley

1971
Paul Olson
Win Stenseng

1972
Al Beal
Tom Olson

1973
Tim Larsen
Dave Rommerein

1974
Jim Dimick
Steve Peinovich

1975
Joel Simpson
Steve Madson

1976
Mitch Long
Roger Olson

1977
Mark Porter
Mark Arvesen

1978
Rick Rost
Steve VandenHeuval

1979
Steve Lidke
Mark Quinnell

1980
Jon Anderson
Bob Patterson

1981
Bob Klefsaas
Keith Tufte
Dan Kyllo

1982
Dave Seymour
John Ryden

1983
Jon Nydahl
Brad Wolner

1984
Brian Jacobs
Kurt Hjerpe
Todd Vitols

1985
Bruce Gutzmann
Jon Nycklemoe

1986
Mark Melin
Greg VanGuilder

1987
Eric Peyton
Adam Elliott

1988
Tony Miller
Steve Shaffer

1989
Tom Miller
Rob Warneke

1990
Jon Tostrud
Kirk Meyer
Kent Meyer

1991
Howard Rogotzke
Andy Butler

1992
Aaron Butler
Todd Organ
Jim Starr

1993
Judd Sather
David Keenan

1994
Jason Laukkonen
Eric Lien

1995
Craig Crosby
Trevor Olson

1996
Eric Anderson
Joshua Holmes

1997
Chad Durgin
Nicholas Johnson
Christopher Kodl
Peter Schultz

1998
Paul Minkler
Ben Dieterich
Peter Schultz
Darik Steinbach

1999
Sven Bjorklund
Ben Dieterich

2000
Jeff Flugum
Joe Hammond
Chris Nickel
Brian Sprout
Jeremy Young

2001
Joe Hammond
Zack Kent
Steve Ryan
Jeff Flugum
Marc Davies

2002
Jeff Schmidt
Neal Olson
Owen Buckmaster
Chad Thomas
Tim Baer
Reggie Fuller
Cordell Hunkins
Matt Lafferty

2003
Brian Senske
Bill Germscheid

Players

Name	Seasons
A	
Aaker, Roland	1947–49
Aamot, Cliff	1926–28
Aamot, Jack	1951–53
Aamot, Kirk	1988–90
Aamot, Mark	1960–62°
Achberger, Tilman	2000–03
Ackermann, Leonard	1963
Adams, Glenn	1932
Adams, Lawrence	1945
Adamson, Russell	1947–50°
Adan, Abdi	2000–01
Adler, Gerald	1980
Ahlgren, Steve	1968–69
Alberg, Jonathan	1979
Albrecht, Don	1946
Albrecht, Harold	1933–35
Albrecht, Timothy	1982–84
Aldrich, Michael	1991–94
Algoe, Bob	1958–60
Allen, Michael	1978–79
Almli, Mark	1927–29°
Almlie, Mark	1993–96
Alseleben, Adam	1997–2000
Altenberger, P.	1935
Amundson, Leonard	1939
Andersen, Scott	1984–87
Anderson, Allan	1940
Anderson, Allen	1956
Anderson, Anton	1937–38
Anderson, Bill	1959–61
Anderson, Brian	2002
Anderson, Brian	1972–75
Anderson, Charles	1952
Anderson, Charles	1956
Anderson, Clay	1982–85
Anderson, Don	1930
Anderson, Doug	1950
Anderson, Eric	1993–96°
Anderson, Eric	1997
Anderson, Fritz	1921
Anderson, George	1962
Anderson, Harold	1933
Anderson, Isaac	1926–27
Anderson, Joel	1982–83
Anderson, John	1964–66
Anderson, John	1972
Anderson, Jon	1977–80°
Anderson, Joshua	1993–96
Anderson, Kermit	1932–34°
Anderson, Kirk	1965–67°
Anderson, Larry	1966
Anderson, Lawrence	1946–49
Anderson, Matthew	1984–85
Anderson, Milo	1932
Anderson, Norman	1935–37°, 38
Anderson, Paul	1965–67
Anderson, Ralph	1986–87
Anderson, Scott	1968–69
Anderson, Stanley	1923–26°
Anderson, Thomas	1955–57°
Anderson, Thor	1956–57
Anderson, Vernon	1934–35
Anderson, Virgil	1923–24
Andrade, Bobby	2003
Andrews, Erik	1998
Anfinrud, Arlyn	1943
Angell, Eric	1985–87
Apland, Thorvin	1997
Appolini, Frank	1950
Arakawa, Art	1971–72
Arey, Shea	1944

Name	Seasons
Arne, John	1959
Arnett, Sean	1992–94
Arvesen, Charles	1975
Arvesen, Mark	1974–77°
Arvesen, Paul	1947
Ashley, David	1973
Ashley, Kent	1999
Ashley, Steve	1968–70°
Asleson, Ryan	1994–97
Augustson, Matthew	1992–95
Aus, Nathaniel	1956–58
Aus, Peter	1961–63
Avery, David	1982
B	
Backberg, Danny	1978–81
Baek, Sung	1997
Baer, Timothy	1999–2002°
Baglien, Brad	2001
Bailey, A. Robert	1982–85
Bailey, Ralph	1946–49
Baker, Robert	1992–95
Bakken, Joseph	1924
Baldwin, Jack	1936–37
Balstad, Mark	1979–82
Barbato, Joel	1991
Barner, Adam	1988–91
Barnes, Geo	1945
Barnhart, Mark	2002–03
Barry, Frank	1936
Barstad, Stuart	1948–50
Bartlett, Paul	1988–91
Bass, Bryan	1994–95
Bass, E.	1945
Bass, Frank	2002
Bates, Timothy	1976–79
Bauer, Troter	1987–90
Bauman, Jul	1919
Beal, Alan	1970–72°
Beal, Ronald	1972–73
Beasley, William	1996
Beck, Matthew	1987
Beckwith, Jason	1992–93
Behr, Byron	1944
Bell, Don	1947
Benes, Robert	1974–77
Bengtson, Jesse	1995–97
Benke, Steven	1974
Bennett, John	1981
Bennett, Mark	1973–75
Bennewitz, Robert	1940–41
Benrud, Vernal	1943
Benson, Charles	1975–78
Benson, Kim	1971–72
Berdahl, James	1976–79
Berg, Dave	1952
Berg, Jerry	1970–72
Berg, Oswald	1936
Berg, Walter	1940
Berg,	1931
Bergan, David	1995–98
Berge, Abraham	1999
Bergeland, Nathan	1976–79
Bergene, Bradley	1974–75
Bergeson, Hal	1948–50
Bergeson, Norman	1948–50
Bergh, David	1990–92
Berglund, Robert	1994–95
Bergstrom, Carl	1974–77
Bergstrom, John	1959–61
Bergstrom, Kenneth	1953
Berletic, Michael	1984–87

Name	Seasons
Bernard, Andy	2000–03
Bernard, Benjamin	1994–95
Berry, Christian	1995
Best, Darren	1998–2001
Best, John	1992–95
Bickel, Teddy	2003
Bickel, Thomas	1973–75
Bieberstein, John	1953–54
Biegner, Chris	1976
Bierman, Tim	1986–87
Bigalke, Timothy	1971–72
Birkeland, Thomas	1985–86
Bisbee, Mayo	1932–34
Bjerken, Maurice	1947
Bjorklund, Sven	1996–99°
Blaisdell, Garth	1937
Blaisdell, Jeffrey	1971–73
Blake, Robert	1978
Blanchard, Doug	1964–66
Blegen, Mark	1990–93
Blesi, Dick	1966
Blevins, Deward	1945
Bloedel, James	1959–61
Blom, Harold	1953
Blom, Paul	1960–62
Bloomquist, Ernest	1936–37
Bly, Eric	1990
Bly, Winifred	1926–27
Bode, Lucas	1994
Boe, Paul	1936
Boe, Rolf	1939
Bogda, Ted	1938–40
Bogda, Ted	1961
Bohrer, Stephen	1979–80
Bolstad, O.	1923
Bolstorff, Anthony	1993–96
Bolstorff, David	1953–54°, 55
Bolstorff, Peter	1981–84
Bolton, Christopher	2000
Bongsto, Oswald	1923–25
Bonniwel, Calvin	1931–33
Boone, Yon Olaf	2003
Borge,	1938
Borgwardt, Bob	1943
Borgwardt, Carl	1948–50
Borgwardt, David	1976–79
Borstad, John	1983–86
Bortolon, Ryan	1991–94
Bosaker, Peter	1994–95
Bothun, Byron	1981
Botnen, Craig	2003
Bottini, Pat	2003
Bowman, Karl	1988–89
Boyd, Neil	1963–64
Boyd, Tony	2000–01
Boyum, Allen	1955
Boyum, Deryl	1957
Braaten, Conrad	1966–67
Brackeen, Colin	1993
Brakke, Brad	1992
Bransford, Richard	1976
Brekken, Carol	1952–54
Brekken, Duane	1954–56
Bremer, Kirk	1988
Brendemuehl, Curt	1943
Brent, Matthew	1997–99
Bretheim, Eric	1999
Brevik, Roy	1935
Brinkman, Mike	2002
Brocker, Mark	1975
Brokow, Willis	1937
Brousseau, Eric	1994

Name	Seasons	Name	Seasons	Name	Seasons
Brown, Kenneth	1934	Cole, Martin	1920–23°	Downs, Daniel	1979–82
Brown, Sherman	1934–35	Collins, Brian	2002–03	Downs, John	1975–78
Brown, Vincent	1982	Collins, Craig	1972–75	Drake, Earl	1954
Brown, Wayne	1954–56°	Colville, Brandt	1984–86	Droen, Alvin	1929–31
Brunwasser, Al	1944	Comer, Walter	1936–37	Droen, Andrew	1939–41°
Brynestad, Lorens	1955–57	Conner, Andre	2002–03	Duce, Kevin	1995–98
Bucka, Matt	2001–03	Cook, Kevin	1993–95	Duckworth, Barry	2002
Buckmaster, Owen	2001–02°	Corneliussen, Steve	1937–39	Dugan, Nolan	1937–40
Bugni, Larry	1964	Covert, Bradley	1972–73	Duncanson, Scott	1977
Bunge, Leonard	1946–49	Cox, V. Stuart	1985–88	Dunfee, Lee	1975–78
Bunge, Max	2001–03	Coyle, Hal	1945	Dunfee, Raymond	1979–82
Bunnell, Zach	2003	Crawford, Daniel	1986	Dunham, Jeffrey	1978
Burner, James	1962–64	Crawford, Patrick	1978–81	Durgin, Chad	1994–97°
Burns, Joey	2001	Crenshaw, George	1944°	Dybdal, Philip	1928
Burns, Randal	1970–72	Cromling, Ted	1945		
Burns, Tim	1964	Crosby, Craig	1992–95°	**E**	
Burrell, John	1944	Crowser, Aaron	1996–99	Early, Malcolm	1989–91
Burtness, George	1928	Cruzem, Nate	1944	Eastwood, Phil	1945
Burtness, Hildahl	1922–24	Cully, Johnson	1991	Eaton, Michael	1985–87
Burtness, Jim	1945–46	Curry, David	1974–76	Ebert, Jim	1957–58
Buskirk, Ellsworth	1946–47	Curtis, Paul	1981	Eckegren, Quinten	1929
Buslee, Thomas	1990–93	Curtis, Wheeler	1946	Ederer, John	1975–78
Busselman, Dave	2001–03	Cutler, Charles	1974	Edman, Melvin	1946
Butler, Aaron	1989–92°	Cybyske, Scot	1992–95	Edstrom, John	1953
Butler, Andrew	1988–91°			Edwards, Allen	1972–74
		D		Egdahl, John	1942
C		Dahl, John	1941–42	Ehren, Robert	1987–89
Cadwallader, Gus	1944	Dahl, Jonathon	1987–90	Eickhoff, John	1998–2001
Cahoon, Richard	1994–97	Dahl, Keith	1992	Eide, Oscar	1919–21
Caldwell, David	1980–82	Dahl, Monrad	1940–41	Einarson, Dick	1958–60
Calhoun, Daniel	1988–90	Dahl, Orville	1932–33	Ekegren, G.	1930–31
Canfield, Don	1960–62°	Dahlager, Kenneth	1956–57	Eklund, Todd	1969–71
Caple, Ron	1957–59°	Dahlager, Richard	1953–55	Eletson, Chas	1944
Carlson, Ervin	1945	Dahlen, Curt	2002	Eliason, Clarence	1936
Carlson, Gregory	1968–69	Dahlen, Marlyn	1946–47	Elioff, James	1948–49
Carlson, Jason	1998–2000	Dahlen, Peter	1975–76	Ellandson, Nolan	1933–35
Carlson, John	1972	Dale, Lester	1937–39	Ellingson, Donald	1948–49
Carlson, Jonathan	1984–87	Dale, David	1982	Ellingson, Gary	1960–61
Carlson, Mark	1982	Daley, Bob	1941	Ellingson, Lloyd	1929–31
Carlson, Timothy	1973–75	Danielson, Ben	1962–64	Ellingson, Owen	1940–42
Carroll, William	1946	Danielson, Brian	1986–89	Ellingson,	1932–33
Carter, Ivan	1994–97	Davies, Marc	1998–2001°	Elliott, Adam	1984–87°
Carwell, Don	1944	Davis, Dennis	1958–60	Elrod, Scott	1984–85
Case, James	1974	Davis, John	2002–03	Elstad, Don	1943
CathCart, Peter	2002–03	Dawolo, James	2001–03	Elverum, Milford	1925
Cedar, Nathan	2002	Dawson, Charles	1945°	Embertson, Paul	1941–42
Chapman, Christopher	1985–86	Day, Robert	1942	Emerson, Gordon	1935–36
Chapman, David	2001–03	De La Hunt, Troy	2002–03	Emerson,	1930
Chayer, Lee	1975–76	Dean, Matt	2001–03	Enderson, Isaac	1928
Chiodo, Marc	1977–80	DeBlack, Ronald	1972	Enderson, Jacob	1927
Chiodo, Steven	1975–78	Decell, Grady	1945	Enersen, Peter	1997–98
Christensen, Harold	1959–61	Deck, Ben	2003	Enestvedt, C. Kristian	1992–95
Christensen, James	1972–73	DeFor, Ken	1958–60	Engebretson, Chester	1928–29
Christenson, Ade	1943	Deipenbrock, John	1943	Engelbrecht, Chad	1992–95
Christenson, Ade	1920–21	DeLaitsch, Alan	1972	Engelson, Victor	1928
Christenson, Harold	1930–32	Dennis, Brian	1982	Enger, Eli	1923–25
Christenson, Irv	1930–32	Dennis, Craig	1982	Engleson, L.	1942
Christiansen, Jacob	1920–23	Desteian, Aram	2002	Engleson, Reuben	1926–29
Christianson, Jon	1998–99	Devens, James	1950–51	Engstrom, Roger	1955
Christianson, Milt	1944	DeWyze, Robert	1942–48°	Engwall, Eric	1984–87
Christman, Ken	1960	Dibble, Lee	1944–45	Epley, Nicholas	1992–95
Christofferson, Fritz	1941–42, 46	Diedrich, Bill	1960–61	Erickson, Darrell	1989–92
Christopher, David	1980–81	Dieterich, Benjamin	1996–99°	Erickson, Gary	1966
Cirksena, Randall	1980	Dimick, Daniel	1977–80	Erickson, Luther	1952–54
Clark, Chas	1945	Dimick, James	1972–74°	Erickson, M.	1923
Clausen, Kevin	1998–2001	Dingels, Cory	1998–2001	Erickson, Thomas	1996–99
Cleff, Jack	1934	Dion, William	1942–46	Erickson,	1931
Cleve, Frank	1921–24	Doddridge, Wayne	1982	Erlandson, Matt	2003
Cleveland, Bradley	1978–79	Donhowe, Jack	1943	Espe, Charles	1952–54
Cohrt, Larry	1962–64	Dorsey, Edward	1974	Espeland, Leif	1984–87
Colberg, John	1944	Dougherty, James	1977	Estenson, Paul	1976–79
Cole, Alfred	1919	Douglas, Aaron	1997–2000	Evans, Kevin	1995–98
Cole, Bernie	1925–27	Douglas, Scott	1971	Evanson, A.	1924
Cole, Carl	1919–21	Downing, Robert	1939–40	Evanson, J.	1921

Name	Seasons
Evanson, John	1978
Evensen, Dale	1984–86
Evenson, Arnold	1925
Everson, Peter	1999
Everson, Tom	1959–61°
Excog, E.	1923
F	
Fahrni, John	1952
Fantz, Dick	1944
Feehan, Chris	2003
Feeser, Timothy	1980
Feigum, Gregg	1977–78
Felber, Howard	1963–65
Fenelon, Brian	1977–80
Fenske, Gerald	1962
Ferg, Robert	1971–73
Ferguson, Gregg	1972–75
Ferrell, Dustin	1993–96
Feske, Charles	1979–82
Fevold, Harry	1921–24
Fiebiger, Thomas	1974–77
Fiedler, Dennis	1979–82
Field, Carl	1925
Filzen, David	1983
Finch, Christian	1994–96
Finch, Michael	1992–95
Fink, Steve	1968
Finley, Patrick	1984–85
Fischer, Bob	1944
Fischer, John	1980–81
Flaten, Arnold	1919–21°
Flaten, Rudolph	1924–26
Flaten, Sigurd	1926–28
Fleming, Jay	1983–84
Fleming, Ryan	1996
Fleming, Sean	1999–2000
Flugum, Jeffrey	1998–2000°, 01°
Fogal, Herman	1961–62
Fogg, Howie	1930
Folkestad, David	1954–56
Folkins, Harry	1945
Folson, Alan	1940
Forgosh, Harold	1945
Forsberg, Paul	1950–51°
Forsell, Jim	1943
Forsyth, Bill	1965
Fortier, Clarence	1935–36
Forystek, Roger	1982–85
Foss, John	1990
Foss, Virg	1959–60
Fossen, Garth	1992–93
Fosshage, L.	1922
Fossum, Michael	1990–93
Fountaine, Charles	1995–96
Fox, Abe	1933–34
Fox, Abe	1957
Franklin, Dan	1966–68
Franks, Jules	1945
Frear, Stanton	1945
Fredrickson, Art	1942–47
Fredrickson, Mark	1983–86
Freed, Bob	1968–70
Freelove, Howard	1992
Freeman, Bryan	2002
Freid, Steven	1997–2000
Fremouw, Fred	1923–25
Friedrich, Kurt	1988
Fritsche, Victor	1927
Fritze, Kyle	2001–03
Froiland, Norman	1933–34
Frosberg, Paul	1951
Fuerst, Bradley	1989–92
Fuller, Ben	2003

Name	Seasons
Fuller, Reggie	2000–02°
Furnas, Bill	1944
Furth, Alfred	1994–97
Fylling, Eli	2003
G	
Gahnz, Jeffrey	1986
Gallicchio, Dan	1944
Garaghan, James	1937
Gardner, Joseph	1999–2001
Garnett, Donald	1952–54
Garrigan, William	1989
Gass, Michael	1974–76
Gavic, Don	1972–73
Geary, Greg	1986–89
Gee, James	1948
Gehant, James	1968–69
Gelle, Fredric	1977–80
Gelle, Mark	1972–75
George, Andrew	1976
Geraldson, Carrol	1938–39
Gerfen, John	1953–55
Germscheid, Bill	2000–03°
Geske, Jim	1948
Ghizzoni, Albert	1944
Gilbertson, Clifford	1928–30
Gilbertson, Steven	1975
Gillmer, R. Scott	1982
Gilseth, Glenn	1945
Ginsch, Darrin	1996
Glendening, James	1961
Glenn, R.	1935
Glesne, Enoch	1929–31
Glesne, Ingwald	1921–23
Glesne, Nels	1935–36
Glesne, Otto	1919–20°, 21
Glesne, Roald	1931–33
Glimmerveen, Mark	1974–77
Glisson, Bill	1964
Godsey, Sam	1941
Golberg, Johnel	1928–30
Golden, Marion	1945
Goplen, Thomas	1966–67
Gorder, Mark	1966–68
Gordon, Ralph	1946–47
Gorton, Mike	1965–66
Goss, John	1942
Gough, Kurt	1986
Gove, Channing	1971–73
Graber, Theo	1930–31
Graham, George	1992–94
Graham, William	1975
Grant, Darrion	2002
Grassman, Jon	1988
Graven, David	1947–49
Grebis, Alec	1989
Grebstad, Ernest	1928
Green, Jayson	1990–91
Green, William	1973
Greene, Charles	1940
Greene, Earl	1940–42
Greene, Richard	1974
Greenfield, Steve	1959–61
Greenslit, Bill	1958–60°
Gregor, Judd	1920–21
Gremillion, Chester	1945
Greseth, Mychal	1996–97
Griffen, Dennis	1952–54
Grigsby, Stephen	1986
Grimes, John	1944
Grinager, Peter	2002–03
Groen, Zach	2001–02
Grombacher, John	1994–97
Grose, Fred	1919

Name	Seasons
Grossman, Ray	1939
Groth, Shawn	1995–98
Grove, Ed	1931
Grover, Burton	1951
Grudem, Dag	1962–63
Gruenberg, Joe	1944
Grundhauser, Anthony	1986–87
Gunderson, Dan	1974
Gunderson, John	1955–57
Gunderson, Ole	1969–71
Guse, Leonard	1940–42
Gustafson, Bob	1969–70
Gustafson, John	1951–53°
Gutzmann, Bruce	1982–85°
H	
Haaserud, Rolf	1959
Haertl, Daniel	1966–68
Hagberg, Ralph	1953–55
Hagebak, B.	1921
Hagebak, Kenneth	1942
Hagen, Harold	1925–26
Hagen,	1928
Hagman, Kyle	1996
Haines, Philip	1932–34
Hall, Adam	1998
Hallgren, Christopher	1994–97
Halling, Barton	1986–89
Halversen, Jacob	1919
Halverson, Bruce	1953–55
Halverson, Jason	1986–89
Halverson, Juhl	1989
Halvorson, Kermit	1946–49
Halvorson, Paul	1932–34
Hammond, Bruce	1983–86
Hammond, Joseph	1998–2000°, 01°
Hand, Dwight	1990–91
Hansel, Patrick	1972
Hansen, Berkely	1946
Hansen, H.	1926
Hansen, Harris	1944
Hansen, Milton	1924
Hanson, Barshall	1950
Hanson, Brian	2000–03
Hanson, E.	1926
Hanson, H. Steven	1975–78
Hanson, Henry	1927
Hanson, Holger	1951
Hanson, James	1972–74
Hanson, John	1948–51
Hanson, Matthew	1991
Hanson, Michael	1985
Hanson, Peter	1998
Hanson, Phil	2002
Hanson, Philip	1948
Hanson, Robert	1921
Hanson,	1938
Harapat, Dick	1954–58
Harder, Keith	1981–84
Harris, Jonathan	1989–90
Harris, Jason	1992–95
Harter, Brian	1969–71
Hartwich, Corliss	1926
Hartzell, Alan	1954
Hartzell, Curtis	1957–59
Haskin, David	1997–2000
Hatle, Richard	1967–69
Hatlem, Bruce	1975
Hauck, Tad	1976–79
Haugen, Marshall	1946
Haugen, Orville	1936
Haugen, T.	1935
Haugen, Ward	1965–67
Haugland, Theodore	1920–21

Name	Seasons	Name	Seasons	Name	Seasons
Haugo, Erik	1986–89	Holland, Raymond	1947–50	Johnson, Brian	1976–79
Haugo, Joseph	1995–98	Hollom, Ryan	1996–99	Johnson, C.	1930
Hausken, Chester	1948–50	Holmes, Joshua	1993–96°	Johnson, Craig	1931–34
Havig, Harold	1919	Holmquist, Mike	1968–70	Johnson, Craig	1980
Hawley, Peter	1975	Holmstrom, Evert	1934–35	Johnson, Cully	1992
Head, Dane	1988–89	Holtan, Lestor	1925–26	Johnson, Curtis	1927
Heckel, Donald	1934	Holter, Al	1919	Johnson, Dan	1968–69
Hed, Kevin	1988	Holthus, Jason	2002–03	Johnson, Dave	1957
Hedahl, Len	1946	Horner, Mark	1987	Johnson, Dave	1957
Hedstrom, Andrew	1982	Hosokawa, Dave	1962–63	Johnson, Donald	1955–56
Hegdahl, Melvin	1929–31	Hoven, Duane	1950–52°	Johnson, Donald	1939–40
Hegg, Pete	1960	Hoven, Gary	1958–60	Johnson, Doug R.	1968–70
Heglund, Frank	1942	Hoven, Mark	1961	Johnson, Doug A.	1968–69
Heibel, Arthur	1935–36	Hoyme, Gregory	1997–2000	Johnson, Earl	1928–30
Heiberg, Mark	1991–94	Hubbard, Mark	1997–2000	Johnson, Edmund	1929–32
Heiberg, Thomas	1963–65°	Huemoeller, Bryce	1965–67	Johnson, Gary	1971–73
Heidemann, Duane	1997–2000	Huemoeller, Jon	1990	Johnson, Glenn	1945
Heidemann, Robert	1962–64	Huggenvik, Rolf	1943	Johnson, Gregory	1978
Heine, Richard	1950	Huktgren, Richard	1972	Johnson, Irv	1925
Heins, Maynard	1969	Hultgren, Arthur	1970–72	Johnson, Isaac	1997–99
Heisler, Micah	2002	Hultgren, Richard	1972–75	Johnson, Jerome	1931–32
Helgen, Olani	1927	Hunkins, Cordell	1999–2002°	Johnson, Jerry	1947–49
Hellbusch, Jon	1991	Hunt, Joel	1997–99	Johnson, Jon	1969–71
Helmen, Mike	1960	Hunter, Ronald	1967–69	Johnson, Kent	1968–70
Helseth, Buzz	1953–55°	Hurd, Jim	1965	Johnson, Kevin	1983–85
Hemberger, Jim	1971	Huseby, Jacob	2000–01	Johnson, Kurt	1981–84
Hembre, Jim	1957–59	Hussian, John	1982	Johnson, Leon	1927–29
Hemstad, Richard	1951–54	Hussian, Thomas	1980	Johnson, Lyle	1935
Hendricks, John	1972	Hustad, Wallace	1976–80	Johnson, Matt	2000–02
Hendricks, Thomas	1973	Hybben, William	1979–81	Johnson, Maurice	1972–73
Hendrickson, Andrew	1994–96			Johnson, Max	1933–34
Hendrickson, Kristoff	2000–03	**I**		Johnson, Nate	2001–03
Hendrickson, Paden	1998–2001	Indall, Floyd	1926–27	Johnson, Nicholas	1995–97°
Henningson, David	1984	Ingbritsen, Keith	1950–52	Johnson, Paul	1925–27
Henricks, Kevin	1991	Ingvalstad, Carsten	1924–25	Johnson, Paul D.	1951–53
Henricks, Mike	1992	Ingvalstad, Kenneth	1928–30	Johnson, Reed	1976–78
Henriksen, Veryle	1949–50	Ingvalstad, Lestor	1926–27	Johnson, Richard	1968
Henriksen, Ronald	1946–49°	Ingvalstad, Orlando	1932	Johnson, Steven	1987–90
Henriksen, Dana	1987–89	Irrthum, Jeremy	1993–96	Johnson, Tom	1961–62
Henry, Latravis	2003	Isaacs, Pete	1957–58	Johnson, Van	1932–34
Herfindal, Donald	1936–38	Isvik, Elmer	1922	Johnson, William	1922–26
Hermann, Timothy	1970–72	Iverson, Carl	1930–32	Johnston, Roger	1955
Herrlinger, Roger	1952	Iverson, Gary	1967–69	Jones, Kenneth	1974
Hersch, Jon	1965–67	Iverson, Jeffrey	1973	Jorgenson, Bob	1940
Heryla, Pete	1988–91	Iverson, Jon	1974–76	Juel, Leslie	1936–37
Hessert, Robert	1945	Iverson, Joshua	1997–99	Juel, Martin	1936
Heyer, Kipp	1986	Iverson, Willard	1970	Julson, Nate	2001–02
Hildebrandt, Daniel	1997–98			Jurries, Don	1957–60
Hildebrandt, Lin	1929–30	**J**		Juull, Laurie	1950
Hildenbrand, Michael	1992	Jacobs, Brian	1981–84°	Juveland, Omar	1946
Hill, Steve D.	1972–75	Jacobs, Michael	1983–86		
Hill, Steven J.	1973–75	Jacobsen, Christopher	1998–99	**K**	
Hinderaker, Al	1968–69	Jacobsen, Ken	1944	Kaiser, Chris	1992–93
Hinderaker, Dale	1971–74	Jacobson, Abe	1932	Kalass, Robert	1955–56
Hindermann, Dave	1959–61	Jacobson, C.	1921	Kallander, Lawrence	1950–51
Hinds, Ray	1935–36	Jacobson, Chris	2000	Kallas, James	1946–49
Hirschy, Dave	1962–64	Jacobson, Gary	1970	Karpinske, Keith	1990–93
Hjany, Bob	1964	Jacobson, Mark	1976–77	Kaufmann, Geoffrey	1971–72
Hjelle, Jerry	1963	Jacobson, Morris	1924–26	Kavaney, Brendon	1993–94
Hjerpe, Kevin	1982–84	Jacobson, Robert	1949–51	Keenan, David	1990–93°
Hjerpe, Kurt	1981–84°	Jaglin, Christopher	1983	Keller, David	1972–73
Hoagberg, Michael	1998–2001	Jameson, Scott	1972	Keller, Matthew	2000–01
Hodge, Alan	1976–79	Janke, Donald	1963	Keller, Matthew	1997
Hoemann, Steven	1988–91	Jankowski, Michael	1977–80	Kelley, Peter	1978
Hoemann, Warren	1968–70	Jeffords, James	1949	Kellgren, Tim	1964
Hoff, Bradley	1985–87	Jensen, Dana	1980–81	Kelly, William	1991–92
Hoffman, Stephen	1977	Jensen, Michael	1980–82	Kelsey, Kenneth	1933
Hofkens, Matt	2001	Jensen, Otto	1921–23	Kelts, Greg	2000
Hogsven, Harlan	1949–51°	Jenson, Edwin	1930–32	Keltz, Andy	2002–03
Hohag, David	1967	Jirik, Scott	1986–87	Kent, Zachary	1998–01°
Hoidahl, Ted	1919–21	Johannessen, Gordon	1955	Kern, Dustin	1995–96
Hokeness, Ken	1959	Johnson, Albert	1948	Kieffer, John	1970–72
Holdener, Ben	1944	Johnson, Art	1950–52	Kier, Jeffrey	1976
Holger, Jonathan	1996	Johnson, Bill	1950	Kildahl, Kent	1972

Name	Seasons
Kindem, Arnie	1936–37
Kindem, James	1965–67
Kindem, Peter	1973–74
Kindem, Roald	1948
Kindling, Al	1944
King, Geo	1944
King, Daniel	1979
King, Stanley	1975–77
Kinsey, Barry	1972
Kinvig, Kevin	1980–81
Kirkeby, John	1933–36°
Kispert, Brian	1962–64°
Kittelson, Troy	1987
Kjeldgaard, Mark	1963–65
Kjelgaard, Daniel	1929
Kjorlien, Craig	1990–93
Klefsaas, Evan	2003
Klefsaas, Robert	1978–81°
Klein, Paul	1984
Klemp, Norman	1936
Klemt, LeRoy	1964–66
Klenk, Bob	1944
Kleven, Stan	1959
Klitzke, Bradley	1976
Kloeckl, Dean	1995
Klopp, Dan	2002–03
Kloster, Erling	1935–37°
Knox, Martin	1920–21
Knudsen, David	1963–64
Knutson, Floyd	1939–41
Knutson, Gene	1960–62
Knutson, Kenneth	1948
Knutson, Lynn	1965–67
Knutson, Wade	1993–96
Koch, Bruce	1961
Koch, Mel	1959–61
Koch, Ordell	1977
Kodl, Christopher	1994–97°
Koeckeritz, Bill	1969–70
Koehn, Paul	1981–85
Kolden, Gregory	1974–75
Konat, Thomas	1984–85
Koolmo, Graham	1992–93
Koomen, Sean	2000–02
Korynta, Kyle	1999
Kosmo, O.	1923
Krahn, Dave	1965–66
Krahn, Donald	1967–69°
Krahn, Nathan	1993–96
Krause, Stuart	1980
Krois, Charlie	2001–03
Kroll, John	1974–76
Kruger, Timothy	1973–76
Kuehnast, Todd	1992
Kukkonen, John	1996–99
Kunitz, James	1973–76
Kuntze, Lowell	1940–41
Kuprian, Mike	2003
Kuzma, Frank	1980–82
Kvittem, Brent	1986–89
Kyllo, Daniel	1978–81°
Kyllo, Richard	1979–82

L

Name	Seasons
LaBeau, Wilbur	1937–38
LaBlanc, Mahlon	1941–47
Lace, Vern	1946
Lafferty, Matthew	1999–02°
Landsteiner, Jacob	1998–2001
Landvik, Erik	1975–79
Landvik, Evan	1982–84
Langfeldt, Joey	1974–78
Langie, Paul	1995–97

Name	Seasons
Larsen, Bjorn	1989–91
Larsen, Donald	1946–49°
Larsen, Jay	1998, 2000–01
Larsen, Marvin	1949–51
Larsen, Paul	1946–48
Larsen, Timothy	1971–73°
Larson, Brian	1975–76
Larson, Burt	1928–30°
Larson, Carl	1946–48
Larson, Donald	1984–87
Larson, Garrick	1987–89
Larson, Jeffrey	1973
Larson, Lloyd	1952
Larson, Ted	1928
Larson, Waldo	1955–57°
Larson,	1931
Larson,	1931
Lass, Steven	1973–76
Last, Thomas	1980, 82–83
Latisch, Jim	1950
Laukkonen, Jason	1991–94°
Lawson, John	1994
Lecy, Henry	1930–32
Lee, Victor	1955
Lee,	1938
Lee, Arthur	1919
Legrid, Bernie	1925–27
Lehrke, Elton	1942, 46–47°
Leirfallon, Jarle	1932–35
Leitch, Cecil	1956–57
Lembke, Bradley	1982–85
Lemmage, Mike	2003
Lepse, James	1976
Libby, James	1944
Lidke, Steven	1976–79°
Lien, Dick	1962
Lien, Eric	1991–94°
Liesch, Dale	1961–63
Liesch, Don	1964–66
Lillemoe, Brett	1988, 89–91
Lillemoe, Tait	1992–95
Lindberg, Larry	1971–72
Lindstrom, Stuart	1948
Linman, Dean	1943–44
Linz, Bill	1944
Lipira, Dominic	1945
Lium, Ade	1923–25
Lobitz, Ranier	1964–66
Loftness, Theodore	1975
Logemann, Timothy	1978–81
Long, Mitchell	1973–76°
Long, Brian	1975
Longie, Christopher	1992–94
Lore, Robert	1956–57
Lorentson, Don	1940
Lorentson, Richard	1953
Lottmann, Alan	1980–83
Love, Fred	1936
Loving, David	1989, 92
Lueck, Dan	1968
Lund, Andrew Si	1994
Lund, Elwood	1937–39
Lund, Jeremy	2003
Lund, Jonathan	1992–95
Lund, Lucius	1929–31
Lund, Nathan	2000–03
Lund, Russell	1931–33
Lund, William	1954–56°
Lunde, Robert	1920–22
Lunder, Leon	1968–70
Lundgren, Stanley	1928
Lutzke, Paul	1944
Lyng, Alan	1954–56

Name	Seasons
M	
MacGuffie, Andrew	1992–95
Machacek, Jeffrey	1978
Mack, Wes	1960
Madden, James	1945
Madsen, Ron	1960–62
Madson, Dennis	1957
Madson, John	1957–58
Madson, Richard	1941–42
Madson, Stephen	1972–75°
Maes, Aaron	1995–96
Maghan, Scott	1979–80, 82
Magrane, Joel	1989, 91–92
Malamen, Paul	1968
Maland, Donald	1949–51
Manary, David	1995–96
Manary, Matthew	1995–98
Mandell, Chas	1946
Mangrum, Charles, Jr.	1973–76
Marfia, Tony	1944
Maring, Arnold	1930
Mark, Don	1966
Marks, Christopher	1996
Marsden, Jonathan	1995–97
Martin, Harold	1944
Martin, William	1945
Martinson, Marvin	1924–25
Marvick, Otis	1919–21
Masis, Andres	1997–99
Mason, Brian	1975
Mason, Leslie	1925
Mason, Lowell	1949, 52
Mason, Luther	1942
Mason, Tony	2003
Massie, C. Scott	1974
Mathison, Chester	1950, 53
Mathre, Steven	1985–88
Matson, Bob	1968–70°
Mattson, Krister	1997
Matzke, Alan	1951
Mauer, Russell	1949–51
Maurer, Bob	1944
McBroom, Jon	1969–71
McCallum, Peter	1975
McCleur, John	1944
McClung, Peter	1989
McCormick, James	1988
McCoy, Delbert	1951–53
McCullough, C.	1945
McCullough, Charles	1948
McDonald, Matthew	1985–87
McGrath, Ken	1936
McKay, Steven	1977–80
McKenzie, Ken	1961–62
McKenzie, Kenneth	1927–28
McKenzie, Loren	1928–29
McNamara, John	1944
McNamara, John	2000–01
McPherson, Gavin	1989
Medeck, Gregory	1999–2000
Melander, Todd	1981–83
Melby, Arne	1967–69
Melby, M.	1922–23
Melin, M. Mark	1983–86°
Melnychenko, Bohdan	1965–67
Mennes, Harold	1924–26
Mercer, Michael	1988–91
Merkner, Christopher	1993–96
Mersch, Don	1962, 64
Meslow, Douglas	1977–78
Mesna, Lee	1965–67°
Mesna, Willard	1951–54
Meuleners, Tyler	2003
Meyer, Brian	1991

Name	Seasons
Meyer, Fredric	1961–63°
Meyer, Kent	1987–90°
Meyer, Kirk	1987–90°
Meyers, Daniel	1999–2002°
Meyners, Theodore	1927–29
Michaelson, Jeffrey	1982–85
Michelson, Bob	1944
Mickelson, Harold	1928–30
Mickelson, John	1932–33
Mickelson, Thomas	1963–65°
Mickelson, William	1952
Mickelson, William T.	1979–82
Midness, Bill	1942
Midness, Sjur	1990–93
Mielke, Milo	1924–25
Mikkelson, Erik	1985–88
Mikkelson, Ervin	1953–55
Mikkelson, Gary	1975–78
Miller, Aaron	1991–92
Miller, Anthony	1985–88°
Miller, Daniel	1990
Miller, Dennis	1972–73
Miller, Ray	1944
Miller, Scott	1986–89
Miller, Thomas	1986–89°
Miller, Wendell	1952
Miller, Robin	1979
Minkler, Paul	1995–98°
Misterek,	1932
Mittelstadt, Thomas	1986–89
Modory, Grant	1993–96
Moeller, Carl	1945
Moen, David	1987
Moen, Jared	2001–03
Moen, Reegan	1987–88
Moen, Scott	1973–74
Moen, Sig	1954
Moeser, Lyle	1940
Mohns, Carl	2000–01
Mohwinkel, Dan	1960–62
Moir, West	1958–60
Mollison, Marcus	1987
Monke, Dean	1977–78, 80
Monohan, Thomas	1972–75
Monson, Gordon	1950
Monson, Kenneth	1943
Monson, Rueben	1940–41
Montgomery, Al	1970
Moore, Jason	2002
Moore, Matthew	1988–90
Moore, McKinley	1975–78
Moors, Jack	1951–53
Morehead, Ed	1946–47
Morgan, Howard	1956–58
Morgenson, Jack	1950
Moris, Walter	1943
Mork, Paul	1956–57
Morris, John	1980
Morse, Richard	1973–74
Mortensen, Wayne	1963–65
Moseman, Courtney	1998–2001
Moseman, Jamey	1995–98
Mostrom, Jon	1961–63
Mostrom, Leif	1986–89
Mueller, Dave	1966–68
Mueller, Harold	1964–66
Muesing, William	1941
Multz, Kerry	1975–78
Munson, Berton	1925–26
Munson, Doug	1968–70
Muus, Paul	1968
Mydland,	1939
Myers, Dennis	1966–68°
Mylrea, David R.	1975–77

Name	Seasons
N	
Nadelhoffer, Chas.	1934
Naeb, Hal	1945
Nahorniak, John	1976–78
Nanzer, William	1935–36
Narbo, Martin	1940
Nasby, David	1952
Nasby, Oliver	1948
Nash, Todd	1980–81
Neff, F.	1924
Nelson, Arnold	1957–58
Nelson, Arnold T.	1946–47
Nelson, Arnold W.	1946–48
Nelson, Bill	1970–72
Nelson, Brock	1970–72
Nelson, Christian	1988–91
Nelson, Dennis	1968–69
Nelson, Gary	1975–77
Nelson, Gene	1955
Nelson, Glen	1939
Nelson, Glenn	1937
Nelson, Haakon	1996–99
Nelson, James	1935–36
Nelson, Jerry	1951
Nelson, Jim	1966
Nelson, John	1963–64
Nelson, Jon	1992–94
Nelson, Mark	1990
Nelson, Newell	1919
Nelson, Peter	2003
Nelson, Richard	1968
Nelson, Rick	1966
Nelson, Roger	1952–54
Nelson, S. Arnold	1956
Nelson, Stan	1946
Nelson, W.	1942
Nelson, Walt	1946
Nelson, Warren	1946
Nelson, William	1939
Nelson, William F.	1980–83
Nelson,	1938
Nemcek, Gary	1977–78
Ness, Dale	1972–75
Ness, Al	1930–32
Nesse, Milton	1938–40°
Nesse, James	1937–40
Nesset,	1929
Netland, William	1928
Neubauer, Steven	1986
Newby, Harry	1930–32
Newell, Lance	1987–88
Nibbe, Thomas	1962–64
Nichols, David	1963
Nickel, Christopher	1997–2000°
Nickerson, Lynn	1968
Nicklassen, Henry	1934–35
Nicoll, Richard	1971–72
Niebeling, Troy	1983
Nienhuis, Karl	1983–84
Nilsen, Erik	1965–66
Nilson, Eugene	1943
Nitz, Dave	1970–71
Noble, Douglas	1983
Nordness, Daniel	1979
Nordstrand, Norman	1930–32°
Norman, Dave	1958–60
Norman, Hal	1983–86
Norman, Richard	1954–56
North, Ovid	1944
Novak, Christopher	1986–89
Novotney, Austin	1992
Nycklemoe, John	1982–85°
Nydahl, Jonathan	1980–83°

Name	Seasons
Nyman, Everett	1935, 36–38°
Nystrom, Scott	1975, 78–79
O	
Oberg, Chad	1987
Obermeyer, Earl	1927–28°
Obermeyer, Pete	1957–59
O'Donnell, Dick	1945
Ofstehage, Orville	1925
Ohm, Charles	1993–96
Oie, Roger	1951, 53–54
Olsen, Nicholas	1954–56
Olsen, Rodney	1964–65
Olson, Bert	1922
Olson, Bradley	1981–84
Olson, Burnell	1952–54
Olson, Clarence	1938–40
Olson, Clyde	1954–56
Olson, David	1981–84
Olson, Douglas	1951–53
Olson, Edwin	1956–57
Olson, Gregory	1972–75
Olson, Jeffrey	1978–81
Olson, Jerome	1938–39
Olson, Jim	1970
Olson, John	1950
Olson, Marc	2003
Olson, Matthew	1996–98
Olson, Merle	1925–26
Olson, Neal	1999–2002°
Olson, Noel	1952–53
Olson, Paul	1969–71°
Olson, Ralph	1923–24
Olson, Roger	1973–76°
Olson, Rufus	1927–30
Olson, Scott	1980–81
Olson, Sven	2000
Olson, Sven C.	1996–97
Olson, Thomas	1970–72°
Olson, Trevor	1992–95°
Olson,	1937
O'Malley, Dan	2003
Omann, Ronald, Jr.	1993–96
Omland, Richard	1966–68
O'Neill, Chris	2002–03
O'Neill, Patrick	1982–84
O'Neill, Thomas	1968–70
Onnen, Tim	1968–69
Oppegard, Stan	1959–61
Opperud, Erling	1929
Opsal, Peter	1971–72
Orchard, Welland	1944
Organ, Todd	1989–92°
Orstad, David	1998–99
Ose, Alvin	1937–39
Osmondson, Timothy	1982–85
Ostlie, Dean	1950–52
Ostlie, Steven	1975–78
Otterson, Daniel	1979–81
Overby, Luverne	1943
Ovington, Richard	1949–51
P	
Palmen, Jon	1988
Paperniak, Adam	1998
Parker, David	1997–98
Parker, Steven	1992
Passolt, James	1931
Paterson, Cory	2002–03
Patnode, Daniel	1998–99
Patterson, Robert, Jr.	1977–80°
Paulson, Kyle	1990–93
Paulson, Rolf	1968–69
Paulson, William	1996

Name	Seasons
Paulsrud, J.	1921
Pavel, Walter, Jr.	1977
Pearson, Henry	1922–25°
Pederson, Bill	1939
Peinovich, Steven	1972–74°
Peinovich, Thomas	1967–69
Pekarna, Timothy	1996–98
Pellicci, John	1980–82
Peloquin, Timothy	1987–90
Pemberton, John	1979
Pennau, Kipp	2000–03
Pentz, Stephen	1974
Perry, Brett	1987–90
Peters, Dan	1991
Petersen, Jeffrey	1979–82
Petersen, Randall	1980–83
Peterson, Alvin	1956
Peterson, Austin	1920–21
Peterson, Bob	1943
Peterson, Bruce	1971–73
Peterson, Charles	1961–63°
Peterson, Dick	1955
Peterson, Eric	1972
Peterson, Frank	1951–53
Peterson, Gerhard	1936–38
Peterson, Gordon	1942, 46
Peterson, Harold	1964–65
Peterson, Jim	1957
Peterson, Mike	1968–69
Peterson, Richard	1954
Peterson, Royal	1942, 46–47
Peterson, Terence	1930–32
Peterson, William	1937–38
Peterson,	1932
Petit, Colin	1993
Petterson, Steven	1974
Peyton, Eric	1984–87°
Phillips, Franklin	1939
Picchietti, Matthew	1999
Pichner, John	1951–53
Pilmer, Robert	1976–79
Pilon, Jeremiah	1996
Pippin, Dale	1972–73
Pitts, Gaylord	1935–36
Plummer, David	1974
Podojil, Frank	1945
Polson, Eric	1978
Poppitz, Kelley	1941–42, 47–48°
Porter, Jake	2002–03
Porter, Todd	1976–79
Porter, Tom	1948–50°
Porter, Mark	1974–77°
Pouelson, John	1945
Poupore, Bob	1943
Powers, Dusty	2000–03
Praetorius, John	1974
Pratt, Neal	1960
Premo, Ozro	1921–22
Presthus, R.	1939
Prieve, Todd	1984–85
Pugh, Jim	1965–66
Putz, Brian	1984–87
Putzier, Fred	1920–22

Q

Name	Seasons
Quale, Leroy	1940–41
Qualsett, Richard	1968
Quam, Conrad	1927–30
Quam, David	1986–89
Quam, Jeffrey	1982
Quam, Joel	1977
Quam, John	1950–52
Quam, Nels	1921
Quam, Paul	1953–55°

Name	Seasons
Quie, Al	1946
Quinlivan, Timothy	1973
Quinnell, Dean	1988
Quinnell, Mark	1976–79°

R

Name	Seasons
Radke, Leigh	1985
Rajala, Barton	1987–89
Rajala, Jack	1958–60°
Ramseth, Bob	1960
Ramseth, George	1928
Ramseth, Rudolph	1936–38°
Randolph, Kyle	1992–94
Rasmussen, Christopher	1991–94
Rath, Jacob	1999–2001
Redman, William	1952–54
Redstone, Clint	1940–42
Ree, Ronald	1957–59°
Rees, Brian	1977
Refling, Harold	1938–40
Refsell, Steve	1964–66°
Reich, Kevin	1992
Reich, Kevin A.	1985–86
Reichel, Glenn	1946–48
Reinertson, Elbert	1922–23
Reinertson, John	1948–49
Reinertson, M. Christian	1985–88
Reinertson, Mark	1953–55
Reinger, Bruce	1957
Reischl, Thomas	1975
Remes, Stephen	1975–76
Rice, Allen	1955–57
Richert, Bill	1959
Richmond, Martin	1972
Rife, Joshua	1996–2000
Riley, Charles	1937–38
Rindal, Loren	1955–57
Ringham, Robert	1975–76, 79
Rinke, O. Michael	1981–84
Ristau, Corey	1996–99
Ristau, Eric	1975–78
Ritland, Gay	1937–39
Robertson, Jerome	1981–82
Robertson, Tyrome	1981–82
Robinson, David	1956–58°
Robinson, Frank	1945
Roe, Mark	1979
Roeglin, Robert	1971–72
Rogers, Anthony	2002–03
Rognstad, Joe	1926
Rogotzke, Albert	1951
Rogotzke, Albert E.	1982–85
Rogotzke, Howard	1988–91°
Rolland, Neil	1986–89
Rolvaag,	1938
Rommereim, David	1971–73°
Rorstad, Alf	1928–29
Rose, Howie	1942, 46
Rosell, Jeffrey	1977–78
Rosendahl, John	1936–38
Rost, Nick	2003
Rost, Rick	1975–78°
Rotramel, James	1949–51
Rudin, John	1973–74
Rudy, Jack	1944–45
Runck, Dennis	1956–58
Rundquist, William	1956
Runkel, Ramon	1950–52°
Ruoheniemi, John	1961–63
Ruska, Anton	1945
Russler, Fred	1962
Ryan, Chris	2003
Ryan, Steven	1998–2001°
Ryden, John	1979–82°

Name	Seasons
Ryland, David	1974–77
Rysdal, Alton	1948

S

Name	Seasons
Sabean, Jesse	2001
Sackrison, Chris	1980–82
Sahni, Neel	1997–98
Salveson, Warren	1955–57
Sampson, Marcus	1922
Sanborn, Jon	1984
Sand, Arthur	1933–35°
Sand, Nathan	1992–94
Sanders, Randy	1973–76
Sandstrom, Scott	1985
Sandvold, Norris	1948–49
Santelman, Lyle	1949–50
Santleman, Larrie	1931–33
Sather, Judd	1990–93°
Sathrum, Clinton	1951–53°
Satterlie, Elmer	1925–27°
Saumer, Syl	1929–31°, 33
Saunders, Jon	1979–82
Sauvage, Norman	1957
Saxhaug, Thomas	1967–69
Schacht, Ryan	1998
Schaffler, Scott	1997, 99
Schatz, D.	1941
Schendel, Steve	1966
Schiager, P.	1921
Schieber, Scott	1985–87
Schink, Donald	1945
Schiotz, Dave	1960–62
Schiotz, Eiler	1929–31
Schiotz, Nathan	1956–58
Schlanbusch, Ernie	1940–42
Schloer, Aaron	2003
Schlueter, William	1979
Schmidt, Christopher	1991–92
Schmidt, David	1989–92
Schmidt, Herbert	1924–25
Schmidt, Jeffrey	1999–2002°
Schmidt, Kurt	1980
Schmidt, Steven	1988–91
Schmiesing, Michael	1966–68°
Schmiesing, Steven	1980
Schmitz, David	1979
Schoeb, David	1995–96
Schoenecker, Jerod	1997
Schoewe, Greg	1941
Schoitz, Nathan	1957
Schooler, David	1983–86
Schraan, Matt	2000–03
Schrader, Michael S.	1982–84
Schrader, Michael W.	1977–78, 80
Schroeder, Harvey	1957–59
Schulte, Brian	1988–91
Schultz, Peter	1995–97°, 98°
Schumacher, Bob	1970–71
Schumacher, Marvin	1970–72
Schumm, John	1963–65
Schunemann, Bill	1972
Schutz, Sam	2000–01
Schwake, Melvin	1937–39
Schwarten, Steven	1969–71
Schweigert, Charles	1968–69
Schwerin, Dave	1970–71
Schwerin, Jim	1971
Schwietz, Jeremy	1999–2000
Scrimgeour, Bill	1944–46
Seffrood, John	1988–91
Seig, Mavlin	1931
Seilset, L.	1921
Seim, Martin	1968–69
Selness, David	1968

Name	Seasons
Senske, Brian	2000–03°
Sethre, Art	1943
Severseike, Otis	1925
Seymour, David	1979–82°
Shaffer, Steven	1987–88°, 89
Shaft, Marc	1978
Sharbo, Paul	1964
Sharp, John	1945
Sheffert, Christopher	1995
Sherry, Nicholas	1995
Sherve, Karl	1992
Shirley, Leo	1934
Shwake, Melvin	1936
Sibole, John	1946–48
Siemers, Maynard	1929
Sieveke, Robert	1940–42°
Silcox, Dave	1960
Silva, Josh	2000
Sime, Wes	1962
Simonson, Mark	1976–78
Simonson, Ray	1937
Simpson, Demetrius	1988
Simpson, Joel	1972–75°
Simpson, Wayne	1956–58
Simso, Lee	1952–54
Simundson, Melvin	1922–23
Sindelar, Scott	1975
Skelbred, Peter	1943
Skenandore, Artley	1973–74
Skibsrud, Paul	1962–64
Skoge, Rodney	1962–64
Skogland, Howell	1924
Skoglund, Dorvan	1936–37
Skoglund, Jeffrey	1984–86
Skogrand, Rick	1970–71
Skoog, Mark	1987–89
Smedstad, Ovid	1933–35
Smith, Erik	1993–95
Smith, Jim	1941
Smith, Tim	1967–69°
Smith, William	1984–87
Snodgrass, T. Joe	1985–88
Sobieski, Adam	1997
Soderberg, Gary	1964–65
Solberg, Art	1927
Solberg, Clarence	1935
Solhaug, Mike	1964–66°
Soli, Dan	1930–32
Sollie, Norman	1953–55
Solyet, Ronald	1972
Sorem, Ernest	1931
Sorensen, Troy	1984–86
Sorenson, Everett	1957
Sorrenson, Russell	1946–47
Sorteberg,	1924
Speich, Timothy	1972
Spille, R.	1933–35
Spreigl, Manuel	1998–2001
Sprout, Brian	1998–2000°, 01
St. Clair, John	1944
St. John, Gregory	1978–82
Stageberg, Rolf	1926–28
Stahlecker, Derek	2002
Stai, Richard	1957–59
Stangl, Gregg	1978–80
Stangler, Joseph	1987
Stanton, Douglas	1993–94
Stark, Andrew	1995–96
Stark, Danny	1992
Starkweather, Scott	1993–94
Starr, James	1989–92°
Starr, Will	2003
Stauffer, Joseph	1989
Stefanisin, Al	1944

Name	Seasons
Steffens, Howard	1939–40
Steinbach, Darik	1995–98°
Stelflug, Bradley	1986
Stenseng, Winslow	1969–71°
Stenson, Matthew	1990–93
Stensvad, Bruce	1966–67
Stensvad, Roger	1962–64
Stevenson, Eric	1997–99
Stevenson, Jeffrey	1975–76
Stieg, Joshua	1993–94
Stinaff, Eric	1989
Stinar, Aaron	2002–03
Stinespring, Donald	1991–92
Stockman, John	1997–2000
Stoike, Roger	1955–57
Stokes, Arthur	1928
Stokka, Maynard	1943
Stoltenberg, Thomas	1967–68
Stoner, James	1956–57
Stoops, Tom	1945
Storaasli, Olaf	1935–36
Storlie, Curtis	1993–96
Strand, Bob	1946
Strand, Halvor	1920–21
Strand, Roger	1955–56
Strasser, Robert, Jr.	1975–76
Streefland, Mark	1994
Streefland, Michael	1993–94
Stromner, Gus	1946–47
Struble, James	1998–2001
Struve, Gregory	1997–2000
Struxness, Don	1962
Sucher, Melvin	1943
Sullivan, Bob	1945
Sullivan, Robert	1974
Summers, Ralph	1931–33°
Sundahl, Sidney	1936
Sviggum, Steven	1970–72
Swanson, Carl	1921–24°
Swanson, Howard	1931–32
Swanson, Jeremy	1996
Swanson, L.	1942
Swanson, Lester	1929–32
Swanson, Richard	1948
Swanson, Steve	1951–53
Swartz, Ira	1946
Swenby, Paul	1944
Swennumson,	1926
Swenson, Darrell	1944°
Swenson, Duane	1956–58°
Swenson, Glenn	1946–49
Swenson, Ingwald	1919–22°
Swenson, Ryan	2001
Swenson, Ryan	2002
Swiggum, Richard	1967–69
Syverson, Leif	1982–85
Syverson, Scott	1996–99
Syverud, Knut	1922–24

T

Name	Seasons
Tammi, Eric	1973–74
Tandberg, Elmer	1920–21
Tang, Warren	1962
Tapager, Alonzo	1922
Taylor, Kevin	1984–85
Tellekson, Cecil	1929–31
Tengdin, Robert	1948–51
Teppo, Noel	1992
Terrizi, Rudy	1945
Tetzlaff, David	1988–89
Thielbar, Rodney	1992
Thieschafer, Charles	1993–94
Thomas, Chad	2000–02°
Thomas, Chad	1986

Name	Seasons
Thomas, Jeremy	2003
Thomas, William	1982–85
Thomas, Ryan	1997
Thompson, Ardell	1946–47
Thompson, Edward	1946–49
Thompson, Harvey	1919
Thompson, Jeffrey	1976–79
Thompson, Jerry	1942–43°
Thompson, John	1948–49
Thompson, Lloyd	1948
Thompson, Mark	1968
Thompson, Paul	1941
Thompson, Ray	1925–27
Thompson, Richard	1938–40
Thompson, Ted	1951–53
Thorfinnson, Ross	1972–73
Thorfinnson, Thomas	1973–76
Thornberg, G.	1922
Thornton, Mark	1986–89
Thorp, Richard	1948
Thorpe, Dick	1945–47
Thorpe, Don	1944
Thorpe, Earl	1937–39°
Thorsgaard, Todd	1977–78
Thorson, Orin	1920–22
Thorson, Roy	1935–37
Thowsen, Arnold	1948–51
Throlson, Ken	1961
Thronson, George	1955–57
Thronson, Stephen	1981–84
Thune, Elgar	1919
Thunstrom, Warren	1972–73
Tiede, Daniel	1983–84
Tindall, Alphonso	1974–75
Tjomsland, Scott	1987
Tjornhom, Peter	1986–87
Tobiassen, David	1984–87
Tollefson, Daniel	1997
Tollefson, Gregory	1966–67
Tollefson, Matthew	1995–98
Tolo, David	1973
Tonolli, Dave	1964
Torgerson, Aurele	1936–38
Torgerson, Robert	1977
Torgerson, Theodore	1926
Tostengard, Stan	1941–42, 46°
Tostrud, Jon	1987–90°
Trebbin, James	1938–40
Trelstad, A. Mark	1974
Tretsven, Shane	1998–2001
Tronnes, Hans	1929
Trout, George	1949–51
Tucker, Chester	1944
Tucker, Tom	1937–41
Tufte, Keith	1978–81°
Tunem, A.	1923
Turner, Fred	1945
Turner, Jeffrey	1995
Turnquist, John	1958–59
Tweeten, John	1962
Twite, Martin	1947
Tzitzon, Paul	1945

U

Name	Seasons
Uecke, Gary	1973–76
Underdahl, Laurentius	1927–29
Urban, Chas	1945
Urstad, Herman	1926
Utter, Steven	1995

V

Name	Seasons
Vallet-Sandre, Alain	2001–03
Van Ginkel, John	1976–78
Van Guilder, Gregory	1983–86°

Name	Seasons
VandenHeuvel, Steven	1975–78°
Varland, James	1951–53
Vatland, Shane	1998–2001
Veach, Ben	2003
Vegoe, Eric	1997–2000
Veldey, Harmon	1928–30
Veldey, Selmer	1919°
Veldman, Jacob	1994
Veldman, Michael	1970–72
Viall, Robert	1940–41
Vibre, Harold	1930
Vick, Thomas	1981–85
Viezbicke, Walt	1941
Vig, E.	1923
Vikre, Harold	1932–34
Viren, Charles	1978–81
Viren, Thomas	1982
Vitols, Todd	1981–84°
Voigt, Edwin	1976–78
Voigt, Paul	1980
Voldahl, Nels	1919
Von Wald, Bernard	1953–55
Vorhes, Art	1943
Voxland, Willis	1949

W

Name	Seasons
Wahlberg, Thomas	1981
Walch, Philip	1978–79
Walker, Decker	2000–03
Walker, Jeremiah	2003
Wall, Alan	1964–66
Walter, Lloyd	1943
Walters, Jacob	1995–98
Wambach, Dennis	2000–03
Wangsness, Mark	1972–75
Wangsness, Robert	1928–29
Ward, Robert	1998–2001
Warden, Michael	1986–88
Warfield, Thomas	2003
Warneke, Rob	1986–89°
Wasik, Ralph	1968–70
Watson, Bruce	1965

Name	Seasons
Watson, Cory	1983–86
Watson, Donnie	1974–75
Webber, Don	1965
Wee, Stephen	1983–86
Wee,	1930
Weeks, Elmer	1945
Weith, Tom	1962
Welch, Robert	1976–80
Welle, Jason	1997–2000
Wenaas, John	1952
Weng, Armin	1950
Wensman, Scott	1993–96
Werdahl, Richard	1951–54°
Wergedahl, Jon	1955–57
West, Bill	1964
West, Keith	1961–63
Westerfelt, Scott	1973
Westermann, Terry	1976–79
Westover, Darrell	1939–40
Westphal, Clark	1962–64°
Weswig, Paul	1932
Wetterberg, Robert	1967–69
Wheeler, John	1972–73
Whyte, Leonard	1971–73
Wiberg, James	1991–94
Wicklund, Wilbur	1940
Wiener, Steven	1967–69
Wigley, Thomas	1983
Wigstrom, Dean	1964
Wilgus, Bill	1945
Wilke, Paul	1937–39
Wilken, Robert	1951–52
Wilkens, James	1973–76
Willett, Bryce	1967
Williams, Doug	1964, 66
Williams, Trey	2002–03
Williams, Matthew	1991–92
Williamson, Gehrig	1997–98, 2000
Willis, Matt	2000–03
Wilsey, Jason	2002–03
Wilson, Eric	1982–84
Wilson, Scot	1974–76

Name	Seasons
Wilson, Stan	1943
Wilson, Troy	1993–96
Winegarden, Steven	1972–75
Winegarden, Thomas	1974
Winter, Bill	1959–61°
Wittkamper, Mike	1965
Wojnicz, Andrew	1995
Wold, Allen	1947–48
Wolfgram, Danny	1979
Wolgamot, Douglas	1998–2001
Wolner, Bradlee	1980–83°
Wolner, Christopher	1986–89
Wood, George	1978–81
Woodson, Lewis	1981–82
Wright, Larry	1940–42
Wulff, Robert	1948–50
Wylde, Michael	1992–95

Y

Name	Seasons
Yates, Jack	1992–93
Yerigan, Eric	2003
Yeske, Arthur	1972
Ylvisaker, Thomas	1963–65
Yock, William	1956
York, Mark	1983–85
Young, Bert	1944
Young, Chuck	1971
Young, Jeremy	1997–2000°

Z

Name	Seasons
Zahn, Vernon	1939–41
Zarling, Layard	1939
Zemke, Robert	1954–56
Zielke, Burton	1981–82
Zima, Thomas	1980–81
Zimmerman, David	1989–90
Zimmerman, Ken	2002
Zimmerman, Robert	1946–49
Zobel, Mike	1982–85
Zorn, Travis	1993–95
Zupfer, Pete	2000–03

° Captain

The 2003 team runs onto the field (photo courtesy of Ann Germscheid)

215